Whispers in the Cedars:

Port Gibson, Mississippi's Wintergreen Cemetery

by

William L. Sanders

1875 Porters Chapel Rd.
Vicksburg, Ms. 39180

DORRANCE
PUBLISHING CO
EST. 1920
PITTSBURGH, PENNSYLVANIA 15238

Dorrance Publishing Co
585 Alpha Drive
Pittsburgh, PA 15238
Visit our website at www.dorrancebookstore.com

ISBN: 978-1-4809-2513-7
eISBN: 978-1-4809-2283-9

Annual tours of beautiful Wintergreen Cemetery, appropriately named the "Whispers in the Cedars" tours, were begun in 2013, the sesquicentennial year of the Battle of Port Gibson. This book's title is used with the kind permission of the friends of the "Whispers" group.

This book is dedicated to the memory of my mother,
Martha Frances *Lewis* Sanders [February 4, 1931 – January 25, 2004]

Contents

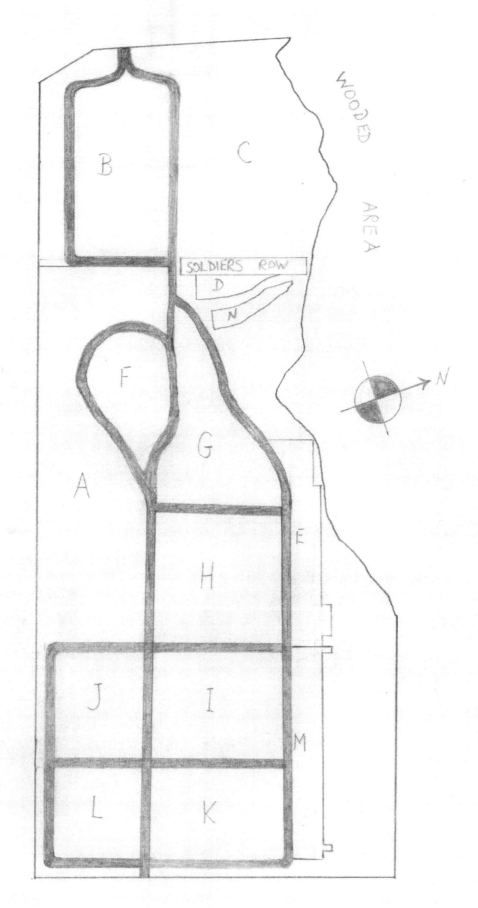

Wintergreen Cemetery

About the Cemetery…

What is now Wintergreen Cemetery started as the family burial ground for the family of Samuel Gibson, founder of the Town of Port Gibson, and was taken from a corner of their field that they had used for agricultural purposes. Section C is the location bearing the Gibson family graves, and as such, is the oldest part of this cemetery. Being initially a family plot, and then growing from there, the first families could not have envisioned the beautiful creation that they started, to become one of Claiborne County's many cherished treasures. They had no reason to think about things like surveying the plots and lots, much less labeling each individual plot for future reference. Because of all this, those buried in this section, at least at first, appear to be placed in a rather haphazard fashion, and unless enclosed in fences, not really assigned to any particular lot at all.

This place of rest has, through the early years, been referred to by many names, such as the Port Gibson burying ground, Port Gibson Grave Yard and Port Gibson Cemetery, as found in numerous last will and testament records.

The name WINTERGREEN, as we know it today, was used as early as 1866, found in the deed records for the sale of a plot of land by Alexander H. Peck to Lemuel O. Bridewell.

According to a Minute Book entry, dated February 13, 1907, a group organized to oversee and maintain Wintergreen Cemetery was known as the Protestant Cemetery Association, whose purpose seems to be that of raising and maintaining funds for upkeep and enhancement of this hallowed ground. When the association was organized, the cemetery was in a poor state of upkeep, with its fences falling down. As one of the first orders of business, discussions of poor fencing prompted the Association to adopt a plan to erect iron fencing across the front of the Cemetery, stabilized by a brick base and supports. The final accepted plan was to order fence design #15 from Nelson Iron Works of Knoxville, Tennessee, mounted on a brick foundation with brick posts at the ends of the fence and at the gate. Fence installation appears to have been completed around July of 1907. With later erection of additional fencing around the perimeter, a 1910 entry indicated that "the cemetery is now enclosed in a woven wire fence, & I am happy to say that we have had no complaints from hogs or cattle."

An entry in the minutes, dated March 16, 1909, shows some unique and interesting instructions for the grave keepers, requesting the following:

"that the undertaker be requested to have a tarpaulin to put the dirt on that is taken out of new graves, so that it will not be scattered on the square. That he also be requested to have new graves swiftly molded, & not packed, and grey moss thrown on them, and that the grave diggers be provided with white suits while filling the graves." This was adopted and the undertaker notified.

Later business included the formation of drainage ditches to drain water away from the roads, and the installation of water lines for irrigation.

Another valuable enhancement was made to the cemetery, in the form of a donation, as described in this resolution: "Whereas the old iron and wooden bridge near the front entrance to Greenwood (sic) Cemetery after a long and useful service of many years, had fallen into a state of disrepair; and whereas, the heirs and surviving children of the late lamented Mr. and Mrs. Stephen Schillig, as a memorial to their deceased parents, have replaced, at their own expense, said iron and wooden structure with a concrete bridge, beautiful in design and strong in material..." This bridge, with its separate pedestrian lane, is still in use today and bears a bronze plaque which reads: "IN MEMORY OF OUR PARENTS, JOSEPHINE JAUCH AND STEPHEN SCHILLIG, 1923."

The solicitation of funds had always been a priority and a challenge of the Association, and many plans were discussed and put to use, seeking funds from such sources as families of the deceased and the Odd Fellows Fraternal organization, for maintaining their respective squares inside the cemetery. Funds were also sought on a few occasions from the City of Port Gibson itself.

Another nice addition to the cemetery is explained in this resolution:

"Whereas, the Port Gibson Protestant Cemetery has for years been without a speaker's and guest's stand accommodations, and whereas in 1936 the United Daughters of the Confederacy of Claiborne County and others did erect in said cemetery and present to said Cemetery Association a speaker and guest stand, thereby adding to the comfort and convenience of all attending Decoration Day and other exercises there, now therefore:

Be it resolved, that the grateful thanks of said association be, and hereby are tendered."

(Author's comment: Although the exact location of this speaker's stand was not given, it would be fitting to imagine that it was set up just south of Soldiers Row, and in fact may consist of the wrought iron seating on the raised concrete structure, an appropriate vantage point for giving eulogies to the Confederate dead.)

Until around the year 1946, the cemetery's eastern boundary extended only to a line at approximately the eastern boundaries of Sections A, H and E. Around that time the Protestant Cemetery Association bought the expanse of land extending further eastward to Bridewell Lane. This addition was organized into sections and lots, with appropriate roadways, to complete the cemetery that we use and treasure today.

Besides those graves listed throughout the fifteen sections of this cemetery, Mississippi Confederate Grave Registration records indicate the following soldiers are also buried here. These men, along with the information from their cards, are:

- James B. Allen [September 21, 1831 – July 9, 1864]. Mr. Allen was a Private in CO. G, 28TH MISS CAV, and his next of kin was Mrs. Nancy C. Allen, his wife. He died in service.
- C. L. Barrett [April 9, 1837 – May 1, 1863]. C. L. Barrett was a 2nd Lieutenant in CO. A, 16TH MISS INF and CO A, 24TH BATT MISS CAV. He died of wounds received in service.
- C. H. "Paul" Barrot [March 18, 1835 – May 1, 1863]. C. H. Barrot was a private (and Lieutenant?) in CO. A, 4TH MISS REGT CAV / OWEN'S SCOUTS SIGNAL CORPS. He died from wounds received in action. (This may be Claude Hipolitus Barrot, husband of Mary T. *Morrison* Barrot.)
- John Bird [March 12, 1841 – May 8, 1923]. John was a Private/4th Sergeant in CO. B, 9TH MISS CAV, transferred to 1ST LOUISIANA ART. His next of kin was Catherine Bird, his wife.
- Ben F. Booth [May 18, 1837 – May 1, 1863]. Ben was a Private, then Sergeant in CO. A, 24TH MISS CAV / CO. K, MISS INF. He died in service. (According to marriage records, a Ben F. Booth was married to Anna G. Harrington. Anna is buried in plot B-20, the same plot containing an unidentified C. S. A. stone. It is possible that this C. S. A. stone belongs to Mr. Booth.)
- Walter A. Broughton [May 11, 1843 – July 2, 1908]. Walter was a Private in CO. A, 4TH MISS CAV. His next of kin was Sarah J. Broughton, his wife.
- Zibu B. Butler [September 6, 1839 – May 1, 1863]. Zibu served as Private, then Sergeant, then Lieu-

tenant in CO. K, 12TH MISS IN / ABBY BATT ART. He died in service.

- N. A. Hancock [November 21, 1839 – March 9, 1904]. N. A. Hancock was a Private in CO. G, 16TH MISS INF.
- W. H. B. Healy [November 14, 1838 – March 9, 1904]. W. H. B. Healy was a Private in CO. G, 16TH MISS INF and CO. C, 4TH MISS CAV.
- John Lischer [September 16, 1841 – May 4, 1863]. John was a Private in CO. A, 24TH MISS BATT CAV. He was killed in battle.
- J. V. McPherson [September 14, 1839 – March 8, 1904]. J. V. McPherson was a Private in CO. K, 12TH MISS INF.
- E. H. Moore [November 18, 1832 – March 9, 1904]. E. H. Moore was a Private in CO. C, 4TH MISS BATT CAV.
- J. T. Moore [August 23, 1828 – March 8, 1904]. J. T. Moore was a Captain in CO. G, 16TH MISS INF.
- James H. Myers [August 14, 1841 – May 3, 1863]. James was a Private in CO. B, 6TH MISSOURI INF. He was killed in battle.
- Dr. E. H. Polland [May 14, 1835 – March 8, 1904]. Dr. Polland was a Private in CO. G, 16TH MISS INF.
- Edward J. Ross [March 9, 1845 – January 10, 1929]. Edward was a Private in CO. K, 3RD MISS INF. His next of kin was G. J. Ross, his son, and he died of old age.
- John Smith [September 19, 1832 – March 6, 1904]. John was a Private, then Sergeant, in CO. C, 10TH MISS INF.
- Henry Staub [September 14, 1833 – March 8, 1904]. Henry was a Private in CO. F, 10TH MISS CAV. He died of "stomach trouble."
- Robert Watt [March 17, 1839 – December 8, 1911]. Robert was a Private in MOODY'S BATTERY, LA ART, ATTACHED TO 36 REGT INF.
- Leonard H. Wilkinson [1846 – after September 6, 920]. Leonard was a Private in CO. A, 24TH MISS BATT CAV, MOORMAN'S.

THE CEMETERY, by Irwin Russell
I stand within this solemn place
and think of days gone by;
I think of many an old time face:
Here's where those faces lie.
But when I leave this life-have left
my every present care,
I'll find a home of care bereft;
My friends are living there.

—words found on memorial plaque,
located south of Soldiers Row, facing metal benches

About this Book...

The purpose of this book is not only to list those laid to rest in this beautiful, historic burial ground, but also to provide an easy and accurate way to locate specific graves, by using the maps and locations referenced within. In the process of cataloging all of these burials, it has become necessary, at times, to deviate from location information used in previous surveys. Sometimes a grave location referenced in this book may vary slightly from the location used in other references. However, it is my humble opinion that the use of the information provided here, along with this book's maps, will accurately lead visitors to the graves of interest with very little difficulty.

At least a couple of surveys of Wintergreen Cemetery have been conducted at different times in the past. When dealing with the large volume of burials and stones, having the surveys to match exactly would have been an impossibility. And, with this book, it can be assured that this survey will also reveal stones previously unknown, and reflect the fact that some stones found in earlier years were somehow removed, for reasons unknown. This particular survey will reveal only what I have personally discovered, and will not attempt to make comparisons with previous surveys.

If at all possible, I have tried to let the stones speak! In other words, if any wording or symbols that would reveal any biographical information, organization affiliation, relationship, character or military service could be found on a particular stone, I have let that stone speak for itself.

The listing of every source of documentation for every burial listing would be a near-impossible task, so that will not be attempted. However, I found that there were a number of resources that I was led to return to time after time, and these, listed below, are my most trusted references:

- Personal records of every grave visited. Every stone that represents a person buried in Wintergreen Cemetery and found in this book has been personally visited by me, and information has been copied from the stones as accurately as possible. If a stone is so eroded or cracked that accurate information is impossible to read, I have tried to make that note.
- Claiborne County marriage records. The source of almost all marriage years, from Claiborne County, was from that court house's many volumes of marriage records, personally copied by me and put to use here.
- *The Port Gibson Reveille's* "Looking Back" column. This source contains a wealth of information on births, deaths, marriages and relationships for reference and verification purposes.
- Mississippi Confederate Grave Registration Cards, preserved on microfilm at Mississippi Department of Archives and History in Jackson, Mississippi (microfilm reels numbered starting with #17806). Unfortunately, these cards are only as accurate as the information given to the recording personnel. It is

said that many young men wanted to participate in the cause of defending their southern homeland, but being too young to serve, lied about their years of birth, so as to be accepted for duty. And, in comparing card information with that on stones, almost all death dates seem to be different. So, this particular reference may be of more use, if only for the purpose of determining the soldier's name, war record and burial location.

- Old references listing yellow fever victims. A main source is a listing from the book, *St. Joseph Parish: Claiborne-Jefferson Counties, MS*, pp. 65-68, compiled and transcribed by Ann Beckerson Brown and Walter Lee Salassi. Other listings compiled from old newspaper entries were also utilized. Please note that there probably exist many more victims of this dreaded disease who were probably not recognized in this book, due to lack of specific reference. Anyone dying in the fall of 1853 or 1878 is always suspect, especially if he or she was one of multiple family members dying during the same time period.

- Protestant Cemetery Association Minute Book. This great reference source, kindly loaned by Mr. Hank Drake, documents the Association's start in 1907, and includes all milestones and challenges experienced in the development of Wintergreen Cemetery until the year 1963.

- *Genealogy from Glenwood Funeral Home Records, Port Gibson, MS,* 28 January 1951 through December 2002, by Grady and Martha *Price* Leese. It appears that a large majority of those buried in Wintergreen Cemetery after 1951 were handled by Glenwood Funeral Home, and those are all referenced in this book. The information provided in a typical entry will include combinations of information, to include name of deceased, date of birth, date of death, father, mother, where born, where died, military status, marital status, name of spouse, names of siblings, and names of children. May it suffice to say that this particular reference was a major contributor in the sorting of information that went into this book, and that information has been proven to be very accurate.

It is my sincere wish that the reader will find this book not only valuable as a genealogical reference tool, but may find it entertaining as well. I hope you enjoy it!

Wintergreen Cemetery

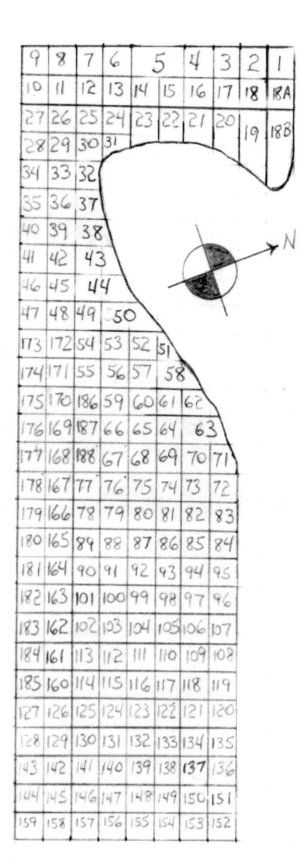

Section A

Section A

[A-1: Blake, Claiborne, Patterson, Stanford]
- Mary (Jane) *Patterson* Stanford [1812 – 1901], "widow of Osmun Claiborne and of Richard Clement Stanford, mother of Captain F. O. Claiborne." Mary married Osmun Claiborne in 1832.
- F. O. Claiborne [died June 24, 1863, aged 29 years], "...of Mississippi, and Capt. of 3rd Maryland Art'y. Died at his guns, Vicksburg...erected by his comrades." This is not a military stone.
- Thomas Blake [died Feb. 28, 1851, in the 37th year of his age]

"Farewell dear Ferd! The turf will grow
green above thee, for it will be
watered by a mother's tears."
—on stone of F. O. Claiborne

[A-2: Bolander, Creighton, Price, Shunk]
- Joseph Bolander [died Nov. 1876], "a native of Germany."
- Fletcher Creighton [died April 2, 1871, aged 78 years], "a native of Ireland." Fletcher married Mrs. Caroline M. McCaleb in 1828.
- Jessie Price [Aug. 19, 1869 – May 20, 1870], "daughter of Rev. Robt. & Mary R. Price."
- Maria Shunk [died Oct. 14, 1852*, in the 46 ??? (rest unreadable)], "wife of Isaac Shunk." *Year of death is unreadable; year given was found in a funeral notice.

[A-3: Dochterman, Patton, Phillips, Simms, Wheeler]
- Benjamin Dochterman [July 27, 1809 – Nov. 14, 1875], "born in Lancaster Co. Penn...died in Claiborne Co. Miss." A biographical tribute reads: "a fond husband, loving father and faithful friend."
- Martha A. *Phillips* Dochterman [Dec. 23, 1821 – May 7, 1890], "wife of Benjamin Dochterman, born in Adams Co., Miss...died in Claiborne Co., Miss." Martha married Benjamin Dochterman in 1843. A son, Isadora S. Dochterman, is buried in Grand Gulf Cemetery.
- Alice W. *(Wheeler)* Simms [July 18, 1852 – June 14, 1925]. Alice married J. B. Patton in 1869 and Ludolphus A. Simms in 1875.
- Infant Son Patton [born & died Aug. 14, 1872], "infant son of J. B. & Alice W. Patton."

"A lovely being, scarcely found or moulded,
A rose with all its sweetest leaves yet folded."
—on stone of Infant Son Patton

[A-4: Brown, McIntosh, Wilson]
- John T. Brown [Dec. 28, 1802 – Mar. 7, 1850], "a native of Virginia."
- John Curtis McIntosh [Aug. 3, 1908 – Feb. 11, 1910]
- Maunsel G. Wilson [Dec. 5, 1810 – Nov. 3, 1884], a Mason, "born Spartenburg (sic), S. C....died Port Gibson, Miss." Mr. Wilson's information is etched on one half of a double stone. The other half is blank.

[A-5: Redish, Varnado]
- George W. Redish [May 25, 1870 – Mar. 15, 1909]
- Bessie May Redish [June 10, 1893 – Jan. 6, 1907]
- James F. Redish [Mar. 30, 1908 – May 5, 1908]
- Katherine "Kate" Varnado [Aug. 14, 1879 – Mar. 14, 1907], "wife of W. S. Varnado" and "a devoted wife and loving mother."

[A-6: Parr, Scott]
- William L. Parr [died July 10, 1845, aged 31 years], "a native of Virginia, and adopted son of South Carolina, a citisen (sic) of Mississippi for the last 10 years."
- Clarence Scott [Jan. 27, 1905 – Mar. 6, 1906], "son of L. E. and L. B. Scott."

[A-7: Arnette, Devine, Reeding]
- Albert M. Arnette [Aug. 25, 1843 – Oct. 12, 1920]. Albert is a Civil War veteran and, according to Mississippi Confederate Grave Registration records, he was a Private in Co. A, 2nd Kentucky Regt. Cavalry, and he died of old age.
- Sarah J. Arnette [Jan. 20, 1849 – Aug. 2, 1897]. Sarah J. and Albert M. Arnette share a common stone.
- Frank Lee Arnette [Mar. 18, 1901 – Dec. 31, 1901], "son of J. D. & Lola L. Arnette."
- Edward Reeding [died Jan. 9, 1845, aged 23 years]
- Henry Devine [died November 7, 1844, aged 32 years]. This very interesting stone gives Mr. Devine's final wishes in its biographical epitaph. It reads, in its entirety: "Sacred to the memory of Henry Devine, a native of Ireland who died in Port Gibson November 7th, 1844, aged 32 years. During the prolonged illness that preceded his death, he...expressed a wish only to live long enough to vote for HENRY CLAY for the PRESIDENCY. His wish was granted. The last act of his life was to vote the WHIG TICKET, having done which he declared that he died satisfied. His remains were followed to the grave by his fellow members of the Port Gibson Clay Club and by them this stone is erected."

[A-8: Andrews, Fortson, Marshall, Traylor, Williams]
- W. P. Traylor [Feb. 11, 1838 – Sept. 4, 1899], a Mason and member Woodmen of the World, Port Gibson Camp No. 5.
- Fannie B. *Fortson* Williams [Sept. 11, 1868 – Aug. 18, 1906], "wife of J. C. Williams."
- Infant Son Williams [no dates], "infant son of J. C. & F. B. Williams."
- Infant Daughter Williams [no dates], "infant daughter of J. C. & F. B. Williams."
- William E. Andrews [died Feb'y 9, 1843, in his 31st year], "son of John & Catharine Andrews, of Rowan Co., North Corolina (sic)."
- J. A. Marshall [died April 12, 1840, aged 24 years], member Independent Order of Odd Fellows.

[A-9: Humphreys, Pruett]
- J. A. Humphreys [Dec. 16, 1863 – Nov. 14, 1910], member Woodmen of the World. Mr. Humphreys married Mrs. Nettie Israel in 1900. Nettie is buried in combined plot E-29/30, with the last name of TAYLOR. A daughter, Alma *Humphreys* Taylor Jones, is also buried with her mother.

- H. M. Pruett [died Sept. 16, 1841, in his 28th year]

[A-10/27/28: Carraway, Davis, Holder, Hudson] This whole area of three plots is lined with brick, designed to be a single family burial ground.

- Henry Harrison Hudson [Nov. 12, 1869 – Jan. 12, 1939]
- Melvina *Carraway* Hudson [July 19, 1867 – June 15, 1932]. Melvina married Henry Hudson in 1888, and they share a common grave location. Besides their son William, listed below, they have sons, Herbert B. and Edward Hudson, buried in combined plot A-39/40.
- William Henry "Paw Paw" Hudson, Sr. [Oct. 14, 1892 – May 9, 1963]. William is the son of Henry Harrison and Melvina *Carraway* Hudson. Besides his first two wives, listed below, he also married Bertha Foster in 1931.
- Daisy Belle *(Davis)* Hudson [July 26, 1897 – June 15, 1916], "wife of W. H. Hudson." Daisy married William Henry Hudson, Sr. in 1912.
- Jerrell C. Hudson [June 2, 1916 – March 12, 2000], "MSGT, US ARMY, WORLD WAR II." This is a military stone. Jerrell is the son of William Henry and Daisy Belle *Davis* Hudson. He married Frances Stubbs in 1945, and married Burma Faye Scarborough in 1949.
- Bertha *Holder* Hudson [March 30, 1887 – April 30, 1930], "wife of W. H. Hudson." Bertha married William Henry Hudson, Sr. in 1918. They have children, Sarah *Hudson* Riley, buried in plot I-58, and William Henry Hudson, Jr. in plot M-93.
- James Francis Hudson [August 20, 1925 – July 8, 2007], "Brother & Uncle." James is the son of William Henry and Bertha *Holder* Hudson.

[A-11: Faulk, Foreman, Hullum, Johnson]

- Alfred Faulk [Nov. 5, 1856 – Sept. 22, 1935]
- Clara *Johnson* Faulk [July 31, 1855 – Dec. 27, 1907], "wife of A. Faulk, born Grand Gulf, Miss…died Warrenton, Miss." Clara is the daughter of Charles and Elizabeth W. Johnson, buried in Grand Gulf Cemetery. She married Alfred Faulk in 1877. Her epitaph reads: "In memory of my darling wife, a pure hearted woman, the greatest gift of God to man."
- Alfred William Faulk [May 14, 1881 – Feb. 26, 1910], "Husband." Alfred is the son of Alfred and Clara *Johnson* Faulk. He married Julia A. Foster in 1905.
- Charles Johnson Faulk [May 31, 1885 – August 14, 1963], "Daddy."
- Alice *Hullum* Faulk [August 27, 1893 – June 21, 1980], "Mother." Alice is the wife of Charles Johnson Faulk.
- Bessie *Faulk* Foreman [Aug, 8, 1881 – Jan. 27, 1944], "Mother" and "wife of D. H. Foreman." Bessie married D. H. Foreman in 1908.

[A-12: Allred, Callender, Watson]

- J. A. Watson [Dec. 9, 1836 – July 10, 1907]
- Mary E. *(Allred)* Watson [Dec. 27, 1841 – May 29, 1900]. Mary married John A. Watson in 1863.
- Matthew B. Watson [Mar. 18, 1866 – July 19, 1950], "Father" and "husband of Eva C. Watson." Matthew is the son of John A. and Mary E. *Allred* Watson.
- Eva J. *Callender* Watson [Aug. 10, 1869 – Nov. 30, 1939], "Mother" and "wife of M. B. Watson." Eva married Matthew B. Watson in 1889.
- Evon Alpheus Watson [Feb. 29, 1892 – May 27, 1923]. Evon is the son of Matthew B. and Eva *Callender* Watson. He married Myrtie Horton in 1913. Myrtie is buried in plot A-106, with the last name of SMITH.
- Sarah Candis Watson [Feb. 12, 1870 – July 23, 1889]
- Margaret J. Watson [Feb. 16, 1874 – Dec. 20, 1888]. Sarah Candis and Margaret Watson share a common stone with the inscription: "daughters of M. E. & J. Watson."

- Infants Watson [died Sept. 15, 1908], "infants of M. B. & E. J. Watson." These two unnamed infants share a common stone.

[A-13: Beggs, Ellis, Foote]

- Julian L. Foote [Aug. 30, 1812 – Jan. 21, 1891]
- Eliza F. *(Ellis)* Foote [Mar. 4, 1817 – Apr. 2, 1876]. Eliza married Julian L. Foote in 1837.
- Thomas L. Foote [Jan. 10, 1854 – June 26, 1876]. Thomas shares a common obelisk with Julian L. and Eliza F. Foote.
- Catharine Foote [July 7, 1841 – July 3, 1842]
- Anna E. Foote [July 10, 1849 – Nov. 12, 1850]
- George K. Foote [June 17, 1856 – July 3, 1858]. Catherine, Anna and George share a common stone with the inscription: "children of J. L. & E. Foote."
- George F. Beggs [Dec. 11, 1861 – Jan. 21, 1862], "Brother" and "son of John & M. A. Beggs."
- John Beggs [aged 3 mo. & 19 ds.], "son of John & M. A. Beggs."
- William W. Beggs [July 12, 1864 – Dec. 14, 1881], "Brother" and "son of John & M. A. Beggs."

Note: the parents of the three Beggs children were John and Mary A. *Foote* Beggs.

[A-14: Briscoe, Parks, Reed]

- Thomas Parks [July 13, 1779 – June 30, 1831]
- Elizabeth *Reed* Parks [July 26, 1779 – Aug. 21, 1864], "consort of Thomas Parks."
- Thomas Parks, Jr. [Oct. 26, 1809 – June 6, 1861]
- John C. Parks [May 8, 1802 – Nov. 25, 1865]. Thomas, Jr. and John Parks share a common obelisk with Thomas and Elizabeth Parks.
- Sarah Ann *Parks* Briscoe [died Dec. 9, 1836, aged 25 years, 10 mo's], "wife of Eli C. Briscoe, & daughter of Thomas & Elizabeth Parks." Sarah married Eli C. Briscoe in 1830. A daughter, Margaret E. *Briscoe* Jelks, is buried in plot B-57.

[A-15: Jackson, Simonson, Thaler, Ungerer, Wield]. It is noted that all stones in this lot, with the exception of those of Robert M. Jackson and Joseph P. Ungerer, have no dates on them, and judging by appearance, <u>all</u> were installed very long after the actual deaths. Separate sources tell us that a number of residents by the name of Simonson, Thaler and Ungerer were victims of the dreaded yellow fever epidemic of 1878. Those buried here whose dates of death cannot be confirmed may well be victims of this epidemic.

- Fredrick Ungerer, Sr. [no dates]
- Magdalene Ungerer [no dates]. Magdalene married Fredrick Ungerer, Sr. in 1868. Separate sources tell us that she was previously married to a Mr. Wield and that she died in 1918.
- Maurice Thaler [no dates]. A separate source tells us that Maurice died in January, 1939.
- Caroline *(Wield)* Thaler [no dates]. Caroline is the daughter of Magdalene Ungerer, by her first marriage to Mr. Wield. She married Maurice Thaler in 1879. Separate sources tell us that she died in 1897. Maurice and Caroline also have a son, George W. Thaler, buried in plot I-37, and a daughter, Caroline *Thaler* Moore, buried in Warren County.
- Maurice Thaler, Jr. [no dates]. Maurice is believed to be the son of Maurice and Caroline *Wield* Thaler.
- Katie Lee Thaler [no dates]
- Maria Wield [no dates]. Maria is the daughter of Magdalene Ungerer, by her first marriage to Mr. Wield. Separate sources tell us that she died in 1883.
- Joseph P. Ungerer [Oct. 27, 1901 – Aug. 22, 1908]. Joseph has two stones, both with the same information.
- Rosina Ungerer [no dates]
- August Simonson [no dates]. Other sources tell us that Mr. Simonson was the first local victim of the dreaded yellow fever epidemic of 1878, and that he died on August 8th of that year.

- Robert M. Jackson [Oct. 30, 1930 – Oct. 31, 1930]

[A-16: Griffiing, Nance]

- James J. Nance [Jan. 21, 1821 – May 14, 1873]. James married Mary E. Ritchey in 1856.
- Elvie Griffing [Feb. 2, 1881 – April 9, 1962]. Elvie is the daughter of Carlton P. and Jennie E. *Nance* Griffing.
- Harvey Griffing [Feb. 9, 1888 – Oct. 20, 1900], "son of J. E. & C. P. Griffing."
- Dalton P. Griffing [May 24, 1890 – September 5, 1954], "SGT, CO B, 1 INF MISS NG, WORLD WAR I." This is a military stone. Dalton is the son of Carlton P. and Jennie E. *Nance* Griffing.

[A-17: no stones]

[A-18: Bomer, Hart, Humphreys, Smith]. This lot has a memorial stone bearing the words: "Lawrence A. SMITH, Sr. Family."

- Lawrence A. Smith, Sr. [Aug. 25, 1857 – Feb. 27, 1939]
- Lelia A. Smith [June 16, 1860 – Feb. 20, 1933]. Lelia is the wife of Lawrence A. Smith, Jr. Besides those listed here, they have a son, Arthur Neil Smith, buried in plot A-136.
- Lawrence A. Smith [died July 28, 1939, age 58 years]. Lawrence is the son of Lawrence A. and Lelia A. Smith.
- Ethel *Smith* Humphreys [Aug. 16, 1883 – April 8, 1912]. Ethel is the daughter of Lawrence A. and Lelia A. Smith. She married Charles D. Humphreys in 1911. Charles is buried in plot B-39.
- Infant Son Humphreys [no dates]. This infant is buried with his mother, Ethel *Smith* Humphreys, and they share a common stone.
- Harry Barton Smith [Nov. 26, 1885 – Dec. 9, 1933]. Harry is the son of Lawrence A. and Lelia A. Smith.
- Ellie *(Hart)* Smith Bomer [1890 – 1958]. Ellie married Harry Barton Smith in 1911. After his death she married a Mr. Bomer.
- Gertrude A. Smith [died September 17, 1950, age 76 years]

[A-18a: Crisler, Pearson, Wood]

- L. S. Pearson [Aug. 10, 1866 – Dec. 5, 1936]. Lawrence S. is the son of Charles A. Pearson, buried in Pearson cemetery in Grand Gulf Military State Park, and Clara *Warren* Pearson, buried in plot F-18.
- Sarah Jane *Wood* Pearson [Feb. 1, 1867 – Feb. 10, 1936], member Daughters of the American Revolution, and "wife of Lawrence S. Pearson." Sarah is the daughter of James D. and Mary *Lacy* Wood, buried in plot C-38. She married Lawrence S. Pearson in 1892. Besides those listed below, they also have a son, George B. Pearson, buried in plot J-41.
- Charles W. Pearson [November 9, 1892 – January 18, 1961], "MISSISSIPPI, PFC, CO C, 113 AMMO TN, 38 DIVISION, WORLD WAR I." This is a military stone. Charles is the son of L. S. and Sarah Jane *Wood* Pearson.
- Lawrence S. Pearson, Jr. [January 4, 1894 – September 1938]. Lawrence is the son of L. S. and Sarah Jane *Wood* Pearson.
- Joseph H. Pearson [June 18, 1900 – August 8, 1981]. Joseph is the son of L. S. and Sarah Jane *Wood* Pearson.
- Edgar T. Crisler [March 9, 1905 – February 5, 1975]. Edgar is the son of Henry Herbert and Eugenia *Morris* Crisler, buried in plot H-42.
- Sarah *P(earson)*. Crisler [May 29, 1906 – May 3, 1993], member Daughters of the American Revolution. Sarah is the daughter of L. S. and Sarah Jane *Wood* Pearson. She married Edgar T. Crisler in 1930. They have a son, Edgar Theodore Crisler, Jr., buried in plot K-21.

[A-18b: no stones]

[A-19: Daniell, Hughes, Magruder, McCaa, Person]

- William Thomas Magruder [Jan. 16, 1825 – Dec. 8, 1889]. William is the son of Thomas B. and Elizabeth *Harrington* Magruder, buried in plot C-19.

- Maria Jane *Hughes* Magruder [June 24, 1832 – Apr. 25, 1871], "his wife." Maria married William Thomas Magruder in 1851, and they share a common stone. Besides those offspring listed below, they have a daughter, Elizabeth *Magruder* Disharoon, buried in plot A-61.
- William Hughes Magruder [Dec. 22, 1852 – Sept. 13, 1853]. William is the son of William Thomas and Maria Jane *Hughes* Magruder.
- Infant Daughter Magruder [Dec. 22, 1852 (only date)], "infant daughter of Wm. T. & Maria Magruder." She and her brother, William Hughes Magruder, listed above, were twins.
- Henry Hughes Magruder [Jan. 26, 1854 – May 15, 1876]. Henry is the son of William Thomas and Maria Jane *Hughes* Magruder.
- Joseph Moore Magruder [May 29, 1856 – Mar. 21, 1904]. Joseph is the son of William Thomas and Maria Jane *Hughes* Magruder.
- Priscilla *Daniell* Magruder [April 3, 1851 – Jan. 5, 1932]. Priscilla is the daughter of Smith Coffee Daniell II and Catharine S. *Freeland* Daniell, buried in Freeland Cemetery. She married Joseph Moore Magruder in 1888.
- Robert Harper Magruder [June 17, 1858 – Jan. 16, 1925]. Robert is the son of William Thomas and Maria Jane *Hughes* Magruder.
- Benjamin Hughes Magruder [Sept. 10, 1859 – Dec. 16, 1925]. Benjamin is the son of William Thomas and Maria Jane *Hughes* Magruder.
- Thomas Baldwin Magruder [Jan. 28, 1863 – Feb. 12, 1924]. Thomas is the son of William Thomas and Maria Jane *Hughes* Magruder.
- William Lindsay Magruder [June 14, 1864 – Jan. 17, 1866]
- Mary H. *Magruder* McCaa [Feb. 21, 1866 – Feb. 14, 1947], "wife of R. L. McCaa." Mary is the daughter of William Thomas and Maria Jane *Hughes* Magruder. She married Robert Lee McCaa in 1937.
- Nannie Hughes Magruder [June 9, 1867 – July 19, 1931]. Nannie is the daughter of William Thomas and Maria Jane *Hughes* Magruder.
- James Person Magruder [Apr. 22, 1871 – June 8, 1906]. James is the son of William Thomas and Maria Jane *Hughes* Magruder.
- Katesie *Person* Magruder [Sept. 27, 1879 – Mar. 31, 1969]. Katesie is the daughter of James Wells and Isabella *Myles* Person, buried in plot B-27. She married James Person Magruder in 1902. They have a son, James Person Magruder, buried in plot M-48.

[A-20: Bertron, Calhoun, Daniell, Hughes, Maddox]

- William Hughes [Jan. 12, 1825 – Sept. 22, 1893], "died at Greenwood (Plantation)." William is a Civil War veteran and, according to Mississippi Confederate Grave Registration records, he was an Ordnance Sergeant in Co. C, 4th Miss. Batt. Cavalry.
- Mary *Bertron* Hughes [April 16, 1837 – June 1, 1929], "Mother" and "wife of William Hughes." Mary is the daughter of Samuel Reading Bertron, buried in plot F-4, and Caroline *Christie* Bertron, buried in Waterman Crane Cemetery. She married William Hughes in 1856. Besides their children listed below, others include Louise *Hughes* Berger, buried in plot A-110, Henry H. and James B. Hughes in plot B-52 and Clarissa *Hughes* Watkins in plot A-112.
- William Young Hughes [Jan. 17, 1857 – Dec. 31, 1946]. William is the son of William and Mary *Bertron* Hughes.
- Sarah *Calhoun* Hughes [died Mar. 10, 1928, age 76 yrs.], "wife of Wm. Y. Hughes." Sarah married William Young Hughes in 1888.
- John Chambliss Hughes [Feb. 18, 1892 – Oct. 14, 1948]. John is the son of William Young and Sarah *Calhoun* Hughes. John married Vivian Kathryne Allen in 1913. Vivian is buried in plot H-11, with the

last name of FARR. They have daughters, Florence Kathryne *Hughes* McBride, buried in plot I-17, and Dolores *Hughes* Grafton in plot J-110.

- Thomas Freeland Daniell [November 18, 1852 – October 16, 1933]. Thomas is the son of Smith Coffee Daniell II and Catharine S. *Freeland* Daniell, buried in Freeland Cemetery. He married Catharine M. Crane in 1878, and they have a daughter, Katherine *Daniell* Magruder, buried in plot G-31.
- Caroline Christie *Hughes* Daniell [March 31, 1859 – February 6, 1924], "wife of Thomas Freeland." Caroline is the daughter of William and Mary *Bertron* Hughes. She married Thomas Freeland Daniell in 1888.
- Little Nancy Daniell [Nov. 9, 1890 – Sept. 15, 1902], "daughter of Thomas Freeland and Caroline Hughes Daniell."
- Nannie *Hughes* Daniell [Nov. 17, 1865 – Sept. 30, 1887], "wife of Smith Coffee Daniell." Nannie is the daughter of William and Mary *Bertron* Hughes. She married Smith Coffee Daniell III in 1884. Smith Coffee Daniell is buried in Freeland Cemetery. Their offspring are Smith Coffee Daniell IV, buried in plot A-112 and Mary *Daniell* Bagnell in plot G-23.
- Mary Bertron Hughes [Sept. 23, 1873 – June 21, 1934]. Mary is the daughter of William and Mary *Bertron* Hughes.
- Ashby A. Maddox (originally named Turner Ashby Maddox) [Apr. 2, 1875 – Dec. 14, 1942]. Ashby is the son of Dr. Adderton and Jennie L. *O'Steen* Maddox, buried in plot F-22.
- Emily *Hughes* Maddox [1876 – 1929], "wife of A. A. Maddox." Emily is the daughter of William and Mary *Bertron* Hughes. She married Ashby A. Maddox in 1903, and their names appear on opposite sides of a common stone.

[A-21: Bland, Rollins, Whitney]
- Lucian Bland [Feb. 15, 1842 – Aug. 13, 1910], "beloved husband of Rose Rollins." Lucian is the son of Maxwell W. Bland, buried in Copiah County, and Emeline *Evans* Bland, buried in Douglass Cemetery.
- Rose *Rollins* Bland [Dec. 5, 1847 – Nov. 14, 1926], "his wife." Rose and Lucian Bland share a common stone.
- Lizzie Bland Whitney [no dates]
- Lucie Russell Bland [Dec. 23, 1861 – June 9, 1884], "daughter of Lucian & Rose R. Bland."
- Rose Ella Bland [Feb. 9, 1875 – Sep. 16, 1881], "daughter of Lucian & Rose R. Bland."
- Infant Son Bland [June 15, 1880 – June 19, 1880], "infant son of Lucian & Rose Bland."
- Russell Bland [Feb. 26, 1890 – March 23, 1890], "son of Lucian and Rose Bland."
- Rose Russell Bland [Dec. 10, 1892 – Aug. 10, 1972], member Daughters of the American Revolution.
- Lucian Bland [Oct. 6, 1898 – Mar. 7, 1902], "son of M. W. & S. W. Bland."

"There in the Shepherd's bosom,
white as the drifted snow,
is the little Rose we missed one morn,
from the household flock below."
—on obelisk of Rose Ella Bland

[A-22: Douglass, Rollins]

- George Douglass [March 24, 1832 – Aug. 29, 1873]
- James Stuart Douglass [March 3, 1838 – April 16, 1890]
- Mary B. *Rollins* Douglass [Mar. 7, 1836 – Mar. 7, 1903], "Mama" and "wife of Jas. S. Douglass…erected by oldest daughter, Captain Blanche D. Leathers 1860 – 1940." Mary married James Stuart Douglass in 1857. (As a note, Mary's daughter, Blanche *Douglass* Leathers, and son-in-law were rather famous as

steamboat captains on the Mississippi River. Blanche and her husband are buried in one of the old Masonic cemeteries in New Orleans.)

- Archie Douglass [July 6, 1863 – Sept. 28, 1895]
- Bowling L. Douglass [died Jan. 17, 1896, aged 1 month]. Bowling and Archie Douglass share a common obelisk.
- Infant Daughter Douglass [born Sept. 18, 1858], "infant daughter of James S. & Mary B. Douglass."
- James S. Douglass [Aug. 18, 1867 – Oct. 10, 1882], "son of James S. & M. B. Douglass."
- James M. Gillespie Douglass [Mar. 15, 1872 – Apr. 25, 1878], "son of James S. & M. B. Douglass."
- Infant Son Douglass [April 15, 1879], "infant son of J. S. & M. B. Douglass."

[A-23: no stones]

[A-24: Benton, Noble]. This lot is enclosed by a wrought iron fence.

- W. H. Benton [Aug. 16, 1842 – May 3, 1920], C. S. A. stone. W. H. has a son, Dr. John Burnett Benton, buried in plot G-4. According to Mississippi Confederate Grave Registration records, he was a Private in Co. H, 10th Miss. Regt. Infantry, and he died of old age.
- Emma Benton [Dec. 30, 1847 – July 19, 1915], "his wife." Emma married W. H. Benton in 1884, and they share a common stone. Their infant child, Dudley Benton, is buried in Rocky Springs Cemetery.
- E. F. Noble [died Feb. 10, 1886, aged 72 years]. E. Fenwick Noble married Mrs. Martha M. Hull in 1879. She is buried in Sarepta Cemetery. Mr. Noble later married Mrs. Maddie Carden in 1883.

[A-25: Douglass, Muir, Skinner, Vaughan, Wheatley, Wright]

- Sallie D(ouglass). Skinner [Oct. 24, 1829 – Oct. 4, 1903], "wife of A. A. Skinner." Sallie married Thomas N. Muir in 1846. She married George S. Wright in 1854. She married A. A. Skinner in 1881.
- J. H. Vaughan [June 27, 1834 – May 10, 1884], C. S. A. stone. According to Mississippi Confederate Grave Registration records, J. H. was a Private in Owen's Scouts, Powers Regt. Cavalry.
- Emma Muir Vaughan [Apr. 16, 1849 – Dec. 19, 1930], "Mother."
- Thomas Muir Vaughan [Nov. 28, 1871 – Nov. 13, 1909]
- Freddie H. Vaughan [June 28, 1875 – March 27, 1888]
- Sallie Vaughan Wheatley [Jan. 25, 1877 – Jan. 15, 1940]

"And when the reaper Death passed by,
He read the words and smiled,
Then folded in his icy arms,
The lovely little child.
The mother wept; she will not weep
When all her days are run,
And at the gates of Paradise
She meets her little one."
—on stone of Freddie H. Vaughan

"Husband, darling, are you waiting,
For me on the Golden Strand?
Are you yearning to enfold me,
Or to grasp my outstretched hand?
Ah, the meeting is not distant,
For I feel life's day grow late;
Soon in Heaven we'll be united
When I, too, have reached the Gate."

—on stone of J. H. Vaughan

[A-26: Andrews, Austin, Brock, Burch, Chaffin, Clark, Hedrick, Venables]
- J. W. Andrews [Sept. 2, 1822 – Sept. 17, 1900], C. S. A. stone, a Mason. J. W. is a Civil War veteran and, according to Mississippi Confederate Grave Registration records, he was a Private in Co. D, 24th Miss. Regt. Cavalry.
- Letitia A. *(Venables)* Andrews [Dec. 25, 1826 – Jan. 16, 1908], "Mother." Letitia married John W. Andrews in 1853. She had previously married William Clark in 1849.
- John Allison Hedrick [June 1, 1851 – Oct. 16, 1918], "Father." John married Fannie Chaffin in 1871, and they share a common stone. After her death he married Myra A. Johnson in 1913.
- Fannie *Chaffin* Hedrick [May 7, 1850 – Sept. 24, 1910], "Mother." Besides the daughter listed below, they have an infant son, John Walter Hedrick, buried in Hedrick Cemetery, and a daughter, Mary *Hedrick* Moore, buried in plot A-86.
- Cameron William Burch [Feb. 25, 1859 – Feb. 7, 1917]
- Mary E. *(Clark)* Burch [Jan. 23, 1850 – Dec. 2, 1907], "Wife." Mary is the daughter of William and Letitia A. *Venables* Clark, now Andrews. She married Cameron William Burch in 1887. Her epitaph reads: "She was a loyal friend, a noble daughter, and a devoted wife." She had previously been married to a Mr. Brock.
- Ruth *Hedrick* Burch [July 31, 1876 – March 26, 1945]. Ruth is the daughter of John Allison and Fannie *Chaffin* Hedrick. She married Cameron William Burch in 1908, after the death of his first wife.
- Ruth *Burch* Austin [March 6, 1913 – October 23, 2007], "wife of James W. Austin, Jr." Ruth is the daughter of Cameron William and Ruth *Hedrick* Burch.

[A-29: Barnes, Hullum, Nailer]
- George Barnes [Sept. 14, 1829 – July 21, 1875], C. S. A. stone. This stone is engraved with the word, MEMORIAL, and he shares this stone with his wife Louisa. He has a military stone in Asbury Cemetery in Warren County.
- Louisa *Nailer* Barnes [Mar. 9, 1830 – Oct. 25, 1906], "wife of George Barnes." Note that her maiden name is often spelled as NAILOR.
- Elise *Barnes* Hullum [1852 – 1925], "Mother."

[A-30: McDougall, Shreve, Wickliffe]
- John Alexander Shreve [1854 – 1930]. John is the son of Charles and Margaret B. *Hackley* Shreve, buried in plot F-9.
- Sue Willie *Wickliffe* Shreve [1852 – 1909], "wife of J. A. Shreve." Besides those listed below, other children include Infant Daughter Shreve, buried in plot F-9, and John A. Shreve, buried in plot E-40.
- Margaret *Shreve* McDougall [1879 – 1946]. Margaret is the daughter of John and Sue Willie *Wickliffe* Shreve. She married Duncan McDougall in 1912. He is buried in plot A-107.
- Charles Shreve [1881 – 1898]. Charles is the son of John and Sue Willie *Wickliffe* Shreve.

[A-31: Davenport, Hastings]
- John G. Hastings [Nov. 19, 1840 – Mar. 12, 1893], C. S. A. stone, member Woodmen of the World, Camp No. 5. John is the son of John Granbery and Rebecca Ann *Chambliss* Hastings. His father is buried in plot C-30. He married Ann Maria Davenport in 1866. She is also buried plot C-30. After Ann's death he married Olivia A. Valentine in 1877. According to Mississippi Confederate Grave Registration records, he served as Sergeant and Lieutenant in Co. H, 12th Miss. Regt. Infantry, Army of Northern Virginia, and he died of heart trouble.
- F. Abbey Davenport [Feb. 2, 1855 – Dec. 26, 1873], "son of Ephriam (sic) & F. A. Davenport."

[A-32: Dochterman, Foster]

- Charles W. Foster [Jan. 12, 1847 – Apr. 8, 1928], C. S. A. stone. According to Mississippi Confederate Grave Registration records, Charles was a Private in Companies A and C, 4th Miss. Regt. Cavalry, and he died of old age.
- Emma F. *(Dochterman)* Foster [Sept. 18, 1845 – June 6, 1914], "wife of Chas. W. Foster." Emma married Charles W. Foster in 1868.
- C. B. Dochterman [Mar. 7, 1848 – Dec. 23, 1916], "Father."
- Ida Joyce *Foster* Dochterman [Aug. 12, 1865 – Dec. 18, 1944], "Mother…wife of C. B. Dochterman." Ida married C. Benjamin Dochterman in 1896.
- Infant Daughter Dochterman [Feb. 8, 1899], "infant daughter of C. B. & I. J. Dochterman."
- Alice Louise Dochterman [July 4, 1904 – Aug. 7, 1908]

[A-33/34: Drake, Mathews, Myers, Sullivan, Turpin]

- Elijah Steele Drake [Oct. 14, 1841 – Jan. 4, 1914], C. S. A. stone. Elijah is the son of Benjamin M. and Susan P. H. *Magruder* Drake, buried in Jefferson County.
- Ellen Davis *Turpin* Drake [Jan. 12, 1848 – Aug. 21, 1930], "wife of Elijah Steele Drake." Ellen married Elijah Steele Drake in 1869, and they share a common obelisk. They also each have separate stones with identical information. Besides their children listed below, others are: Joseph Turpin Drake, buried in plot H-51, and Laura Stevenson *Drake* Satterfield, buried in plot D-5.
- Infant Daughter Drake [November 21, 1914], "infant daughter of Mary Person and Joseph Turpin Drake." Her parents are buried in combined plot H-51/52.
- Rebekah Hutton Turpin [June 22, 1846 – Sept. 20, 1915]. Rebekah is a sister to Ellen Davis *Turpin* Drake.
- Jane Ruth Drake [Dec. 25, 1871 – Feb. 19, 1948]. Jane is the daughter of Elijah Steele and Ellen *Turpin* Drake.
- Kate Archer Drake [Apr. 21, 1874 – Aug. 16, 1949]. Kate is the daughter of Elijah Steele and Ellen *Turpin* Drake.
- Ellen Davis Drake [Sept. 29, 1875 – Jan. 11, 1951], member Daughters of the American Revolution, "a missionary to China for twenty-six years." Ellen is the daughter of Elijah Steele and Ellen *Turpin* Drake.
- H. Winbourne Magruder Drake [Apr. 20, 1877 – Nov. 17, 1943]. H. Winbourne is the son of Elijah Steele and Ellen *Turpin* Drake.
- Mildred R. *Myers* Drake [Feb. 21, 1878 – May 21, 1959], "wife of H. W. M. Drake." Mildred married H. Winbourne Drake in 1902.
- Mary Nelson Drake [Jan. 31, 1905 – Apr.11, 1905]
- Harrison Ingalls Sullivan [September 28, 1902 – March 1, 1946], "MISSISSIPPI, PHARMACIST MATE 3 CL, U. S. N. R." This is a military stone. He also has a civilian stone.
- Evelyn N. *Drake* Sullivan [August 31, 1907 – September 8, 1978], "wife of Harrison Ingalls Sullivan." Evelyn is the daughter of H. Winbourne and Mildred *Myers* Drake. She married Harrison Sullivan in 1934.
- Henry Myers Drake [March 9, 1913 – February 8, 1984]. Henry is the son of H. Winbourne and Mildred *Myers* Drake.
- Johnnie *Mathews* Drake [July 14, 1916 – March 5, 1985]. Johnnie is the wife of Henry Myers Drake.

[A-35: Hudson, Latham, Nabers]

- Edward Earl Latham [July 16, 1920 – Sept. 26, 1972]. Edward married Bertha Henry Hudson in 1944.
- Helen Beatrice Hudson [Dec. 16, 1922 – Sept. 30, 1929]
- Arthur D. Nabers [September 9, 1935 – July 14, 1993]. Arthur shares a common grave location with Norine *Hudson* Nabers, whom he married in 1962. Norine's stone gives only her birth date of July 24, 1932.

[A-36/37: Barber, Simrall]
- John W. Barber, M. D. [January 17, 1850 – November 2, 1940]
- Hattie M. Barber [Jan. 15, 1862 – Apr. 26, 1904], "wife of J. W. Barber."
- Leonard Ross Barber [Jan. 20, 1895 – Sept. 22, 1896], "son of J. W. & H. M. Barber."
- Kate *Simrall* Barber [October 6, 1870 – January 8, 1959]. Kate married John W. Barber in 1908, after the death of his first wife. They have a daughter, Katharin *Barber* Showman, buried in plot M-99.

[A-38: Cochran, Martin, Murdoch]
Sometime before the year 1995, the following three stones were brought to this lot. They are much older and harder to read than the ones already established, although it is believed that all represented by stones were related. The actual bodies are probably not here, but are believed to be buried in the Westside, or Cochrandale Community of Claiborne County. The three older stones are those of:
- George Cochran Murdoch [died Nov. 1, 1812, aged 2 months], "infant child of John Murdoch."
- Hugh Cochran [1748 – 1806], "born in Leek in the Kingdom of Ireland…and died in Claiborn (sic) C'y…aged 58 years." This is the oldest known gravestone yet found in Claiborne County.
- John Martin [Oct. 11, 1807 – Oct. 20, 1843], "born in the Parish of (unreadable location) Perthshire Scotland…He died overseer of his plantation…, respected by this community and his employer as a faithful…& honest man." It is believed that his foot stone, with the initials J.M., remains at the original grave site.

The graves original to this plot are those of:
- William Bristol Murdoch [June 17, 1843 – April 23, 1903], C. S. A. stone. According to Mississippi Confederate Grave Registration records, William served as Captain in Gen Herbert Staff, Louisiana Commissary.
- Annie Amis Murdoch [July 12, 1844 – Jan. 16, 1910]. Annie is the wife of William Bristol Murdoch, and they share a common obelisk.

[A-39/40: Abbott, Clark, Holder, Hudson, St. Claire]
- Herbert B. Hudson [Dec. 24, 1894 – Feb. 4, 1966]. Herbert and his brother Edward, below, are sons of Henry Harrison and Melvina *Carraway* Hudson, buried in combined plot A-10/27/28.
- Ottie *Holder* Hudson [Sept. 5, 1895 – July 6, 1921]. Ottie is the daughter of William Holder, buried in Jefferson County, and Sarah Jane *Price* Holder, buried in Herlong Cemetery. She married Herbert B. Hudson in 1917. They have a daughter, Willie Ruth *Hudson* Scott, buried in plot I-68.
- Vivian G. *(Abbott)* Hudson [Sept. 5, 1895 – July 3, 1992]. Vivian was the second wife of Herbert B. Hudson, and the two of them share a common grave location. Besides Herbert, listed below, they also have a son, James Edward Hudson, buried in combined plot K-3/20.
- Herbert B. Hudson, Jr. [Oct. 10, 1924 – Mar. 8, 1985]. Herbert is the son of Herbert and Vivian G. *Abbott* Hudson.
- Edward Hudson [February 18, 1900 – February 26, 1924]. Edward's grave has two stones, both with the same information.
- Marie *A(bbott)*. St. Claire Hudson [May 22, 1901 – October 27, 1989]. This stone is very confusing and misleading. First, Marie is a sister to Vivian G. *Abbott* Hudson, listed above. She first married Edward Hudson, and they share a common grave site. She and Mr. Hudson have a daughter, Alice *Hudson* Prouty, buried in plot K-19a. She later married a Mr. St. Claire, and even later married John T. Clark in 1950. Mr. Clark is buried in plot E-35.

[A-41/42: Dungan, Hudson]
- "Katy" Hudson [Nov. 27, 1992], "baby daughter of Angie & George Hudson, Jr."
- Phyllis *Dungan* Hudson [1939 – 2014]. Phyllis is the daughter of James O. and Clara *Pace* Dungan, buried in Copiah County. She married George Acker Hudson in 1962.

- Infant Daughter Hudson [March 26, 1966], "infant daughter of George A. and Phyllis Hudson."

[A-43: Bertron, Harding]

- Samuel Reading Bertron [February 26, 1865 – June 30, 1938], "born in Port Gibson." Samuel is the son of Samuel Reading and Ottilie *Mueller* Bertron, buried in plot F-4.
- Caroline *Harding* Bertron [October 24, 1865 – August 1, 1933], "wife of Samuel Reading Bertron, born in Port Gibson." Caroline is the daughter of James N. and Elizabeth *Maury* Harding, buried in plot B-31. She married Samuel Reading Bertron in 1888.

[A-44: Blomquist, Wheeless]

- George W. Wheeless [Sept. 18, 1846 – May 13, 1928], C. S. A. stone. George and his sister, Sarah Ann *Wheeless* Blomquist, listed below, are children of Green B. and Elizabeth Davis Wheeless, buried in plot F-13. According to Mississippi Confederate Grave Registration records, he was a Private in Co. D, Miss, Batt. Cavalry, and he died of old age.
- Sanfred Blomquest (sic) [died Oct. 1, 1905]
- Sarah Ann *(Wheeless)* Blomquist [died March 20, 1939]. Sarah married Sanfred Blomquist in 1890. They have a son, Carl Wheeless Blomquist, buried in plot A-145.

[A-45/46: Barr, Disharoon, McCay]

- George Lindsay Disharoon, Jr. [Oct. 18, 1919 – Jan. 11, 2002], "LT COL, US ARMY, WORLD WAR II, KOREA, BRONZE STAR MEDAL & 2 OLC, PURPLE HEART." This is a bronze military plaque. George and his brother Benjamin Magruder Disharoon, listed below, are sons of George Lindsay and Florine *Levy* Disharoon, buried in plot A-61. George married Sarah Yvonne Schooler in 1945. Sarah is buried in plot I-13, with the last name of McNEIL. George also has a civilian stone.
- Elizabeth Linda Disharoon [Dec. 17, 1947 – Oct. 16, 2005]. Elizabeth is the daughter of George Lindsay and Sarah Yvonne *Schooler* Disharoon.
- Joyce *McCay* Disharoon [Jan. 1, 1923 – Jan. 23, 1997]. Joyce is the daughter of Robert Bernard and Ida *Fulton* McCay, buried in combined plot H-12/13. She is George Lindsay Disharoon's second wife, marrying in 1978, and they share a common grave location. She had previously been married to a Mr. Barr.
- Benjamin Magruder Disharoon [May 13, 1927 – November 7, 2002]. Benjamin shares a common stone with Susan *Clay* Disharoon, whom he married in 1959. Susan's side has only her birth date of January 3, 1935.

[A-47/48: Barland, Disharoon, Young]

- Charles Edward Barland [Nov. 20, 1921 – Feb. 3, 2001], "TEC 4, US ARMY, WORLD WAR II." This is a military stone. Charles also has a civilian stone. He is the son of Charles H. and Ruth *Segrest* Barland, buried in combined plot A-133/134/137. He married Nancy Rie Disharoon in 1949.
- Sylvia *Disharoon* Young [April 1, 1921 – May 31, 1977], member Daughters of the American Revolution. Sylvia is the daughter of George Lindsay and Florine *Levy* Disharoon, buried in plot A-61. She married James Ernest Young in 1947. Sylvia has a son, James. E. Young III, buried in plot E-33.

[A-49: Hall, Nott]

- Harry M. Hall [1863 – 1943]
- A. M. Hall [1873 – 1922]
- Anna Jane *Hall* Nott [July 3, 1870 – May 5, 1952]

[A-50: Goepel, Mangel, Polle]. This lot has a memorial obelisk bearing the name GOEPEL.

- Herman Goepel [Mar. 20, 1847 – May 23, 1915], "Father."
- Sallie *P(olle)*. Goepel [Mar. 10, 1855 – Sept. 28, 1929], "Mother." Sallie married Herman Goepel in 1875. Besides those offspring buried in this plot, they have a daughter, Minnie *Goepel* Manns, buried in plot F-33.
- Carl August Goepel [Apr. 27, 1878 – July 26, 1921], "Husband." Carl is the son of Herman and Sallie

Polle Goepel.

- Herman Lamar Goepel [Jan. 19, 1882 – Aug. 14, 1904]. Herman is the son of Herman and Sallie *Polle* Goepel.
- William Frederick Goepel [July 11, 1886 – May 11, 1908]
- Sallie *G(oepel)*. Mangel [Nov. 19, 1888 – May 2, 1936]. Sallie is the daughter of Herman and Sallie *Polle* Goepel. She married James Mangel in 1913.
- Frank L. Goepel [Feb. 28, 1893 – May 6, 1933]. Frank is the son of Herman and Sallie *Polle* Goepel.
- Annie Lydia Goepel [May 13, 1882 – Jan. 10, 1939]. Annie is the daughter of Herman and Sallie *Polle* Goepel.

[A-51/52: Keep, Roberts]

- George Keep [1851 – 1902]. George Married Minnie Roberts in 1899.
- Benjamin Roberts [Feb. 11, 1845 – Dec. 23, 1901]

> "An amiable father here lies at rest.
> As ever God with His image blest;
> The friend of man, the friend of truth,
> The friend of age, the guide of youth."
> — on stone of Benjamin Roberts

[A-53: Cronin, Middleton, Reed, Synnott]

- Joseph B. Cronin [Oct. 6, 1849 – Oct. 8, 1908], "a native of England."
- Catherine P. Cronin [Nov. 11, 1852 – Oct. 13, 1949], "Mother." Catherine is the wife of Joseph B. Cronin.
- E. E. Cronin [Nov. 23, 1880 – July 15, 1938]
- Lillie *M(iddleton)*. Cronin [Apr. 15, 1883 – Oct. 27, 1959]. Lillie married Ernest E. Cronin in 1903.
- Jesse Overton Reed [Nov. 7, 1892 – Jan. 27, 1973], "PFC, US ARMY, WORLD WAR I." This is a military stone.
- Vivian *Cronin* Reed [Sept. 4, 1904 – May 31, 1995]. Vivian is the wife of Jessie Overton Reed.
- Robert Ernest Reed [Oct. 11, 1927 – Dec. 27, 1993]. Robert is the son of Jesse and Vivian *Cronin* Reed.
- Lorena "Lolo" *Synnott* Reed [Dec. 1, 1927 – Dec. 4, 1995]. Lorena is the wife of Robert Ernest Reed.
- William John Cronin [Aug. 9, 1888 – July 12, 1913]
- Myrtle Cronin [Sept. 26, 1907 – June 5, 1908]
- Joseph B. Cronin [June 13, 1910 – June 17, 1912]

[A-54: Brantley]

- Florence V. Brantley [June 11, 1866 – July 21, 1915]

[A-55: Bearden]

- Norman Shelby "Dank" Bearden [August 1, 1911 – August 15, 1990]. Norman and his brother Robert, listed below, are sons of Norman Cooper and Martha *Utz* Bearden, buried in plot A-57. Norman married Ruth Merle Twiner in 1955, and they share a common stone. Ruth's side has only her birth date of March 22, 1935.
- Robert Mosley Bearden [Feb. 18, 1914 – July 4, 1999], "CPL, US ARMY, WORLD WAR II." This is a bronze military plaque. He also has a civilian stone. Robert married Vivian Lanell Hynum in 1938. Vivian is buried in plot K-17.

[A-56: Valentine, Wilkinson] Also located in this lot is a single C. S. A. stone, whose owner cannot be identified.

- Samuel R. Wilkinson [1882 – 1947]
- Franklin Hunt Valentine [Sept. 15, 1886 – Aug. 4, 1914]. Franklin married Lillian Wilkinson in 1909.

She is buried in the Natchez City Cemetery, with the last name of CORDES.

[A-57: Bearden, Cooper, Godbold, Lusk, Smith, Utz]

- Mathew G. Bearden [Jan. 12, 1850 – Dec. 8, 1898]
- Flora A. *(Cooper)* Bearden [Dec. 5, 1852 – June 13, 1938]. Flora married Mathew G. Bearden in 1871, and they share a common stone.
- Richard R. Bearden [Aug. 22, 1872 – Mar. 30, 1954]. Richard is the son of Mathew G. and Flora *Cooper* Bearden. He married Mattie Nesmith in 1913. She is buried in plot I-72, with the last name of FRY.
- Norman Cooper Bearden [Feb. 26, 1875 – July 26, 1952]. Norman is the son of Mathew G. and Flora *Cooper* Bearden.
- Martha *Utz* Bearden [Nov. 14, 1884 – March 28, 1920]. Martha is the daughter of Priscilla S. *Jefferies* Utz, buried in plot A-70. She married Norman Cooper Bearden in 1902. Besides their son listed below, other children include Flora *Bearden* Trevilion and Martha *Bearden* Gates, buried in plot A-174, Norman Shelby and Robert Mosley Bearden in plot A-55 and Jeanne *Bearden* Spencer in plot B-42.
- John Cooper Bearden [Apr. 1, 1904 – Apr. 10, 1961]. John is the son of Norman Cooper and Martha *Utz* Bearden.
- Lauriellen *L(usk)*. Bearden [Dec. 24, 1909 – Jan. 31, 1969]. Lauriellen is the daughter of Adolph Lusk, buried in Copiah County, and Sadie *Goza* Lusk, buried in plot A-151, with the last name of CUPER. She first married a Mr. Godbold before marrying Albert Lee Smith, Jr. in 1934. She married John Cooper Bearden in 1943. She has a daughter, Sara Frances *Godbold* Fife, buried in plot I-70.

[A-58: Craig, Stead]

- Joseph Alexander Craig [February 1842 – May 1907]
- Katie E. *Stead Craig* [November 1848 – April 1928], "wife of Joseph A. Craig."

[A-59: Archer, Hill, Percy, Rogers]

- James Rowan Percy, M. D. [Sept. 16, 1837 – June 5, 1877], C. S. A. stone, "Father."
- Lizzie Barnes *Archer* Percy [Aug. 19, 1843 – July 29, 1909], "Mother…wife of James Rowan Percy." Lizzie is the daughter of Richard Thompson and Ann *Barnes* Archer, buried in Archer Cemetery. She married James Rowan Percy in 1870, and they share a common stone.
- Daniel Jackson Hill [July 20, 1869 – Oct. 2, 1923], "Husband."
- Elizabeth *Percy* Hill [Dec. 14, 1872 – July 26, 1925], "Wife." Elizabeth married Daniel Jackson Hill in 1916, and they share a common stone.
- Joel Cooper Rogers [Sept. 29, 1861 – July 19, 1930], "Father."
- James B. Rogers [Sept. 25, 1895 – July 19, 1930], United State Marine Corps, "Brother." James is the son of Joel Cooper Rogers, and they share a common stone.

[A-60: Anderson, Person, Plantz]

- Dr. Lomax Strudwick Anderson [Aug. 5, 1871 – Jan. 25, 1909]
- Louise *Person* Anderson [June 28, 1872 – Sept. 23, 1949]. Louise and her sisters, Belle and Frances, are daughters of James Wells and Isabella *Myles* Person, buried in plot B-27. Louise married Lomax Anderson in 1898.
- Belle *Person* Plantz [June 20, 1870 – Dec. 25, 1945], member Daughters of the American Revolution. Belle married Samuel Plantz in 1916.
- Frances W. Person [Jan. 28, 1874 – Mar. 23, 1948], member Daughters of the American Revolution.

[A-61: Disharoon, Frydinger, Hartley, Levy, Magruder]

- Levin Disharoon [May 1, 1787 – Nov. 25, 1852], a Mason.
- Elizabeth *(Hartley)* Disharoon [Feb. 20, 1792 – Sept. 27, 1853], "wife of Levin Disharoon." Elizabeth married Levin Disharoon in 1817, and they share a common obelisk with the inscription: "My Mother and Father."

- Levin William Disharoon [December (crack through date), 1833 – February 6, 1868], C. S. A. stone. According to Mississippi Confederate Grave Registration records, Levin served as Sergeant and Lieutenant in Co. A, 24th Batt. Miss. Cavalry and Owen's Scouts, and he died from "wounds."
- Sylvia *Frydinger* Disharoon [Sept. 20, 1834 – Nov. 28, 1927], "wife of Levin W. Disharoon." Sylvia married Levin W. Disharoon in 1853.
- William Levin Disharoon [Feb. 23, 1855 – Oct. 2, 1878]. William was a yellow fever victim.
- John Buckingham Disharoon [May 12, 1858 – Aug. 6, 1865]
- Alice May Disharoon [May 18, 1864 – Oct. 1, 1878], "daughter of Levin & Sylvia Disharoon." Alice was a yellow fever victim. William Levin, John Buckingham and Alice May Disharoon are children of Levin William and Sylvia *Frydinger* Disharoon, and they share a common obelisk with the inscription: "Our Children."
- George Frydinger Disharoon [Apr. 30, 1856 – July 27, 1908]. George is also a son of Levin William and Sylvia *Frydinger* Disharoon.
- Elizabeth *Magruder* Disharoon [Sept. 5, 1861 – Sept. 12, 1951], "wife of George F. Disharoon." Elizabeth is the daughter of William Thomas and Maria Jane *Hughes* Magruder, buried in plot A-19. She married George Disharoon in 1882.
- Infant Son Disharoon [Mar. 6, 1891], "infant son of Geo. F. & Lizzie M. Disharoon."
- George Lindsay Disharoon [Feb. 7, 1892 – Oct. 6, 1952], "Father." George is the son of George Frydinger and Elizabeth *Magruder* Disharoon.
- Florine *Levy* Disharoon [May 1, 1893 – Sept. 10, 1979], "Mother." Florine is the daughter of Byron H. and Julia *Goodman* Levy, buried in Port Gibson Jewish Cemetery. She is the wife of George Lindsay Disharoon. They have sons, George Lindsay, Jr. and Benjamin Magruder Disharoon, buried in combined plot A-45/46, and a daughter, Sylvia *Disharoon* Young, buried in combined plot A-47/48.

[A-62: Humphreys, Madden, Whitfield]
- Eugene Wimberly Whitfield [July 10, 1863 – Aug. 12, 1925]
- Shelby *Humphreys* Whitfield [Oct. 3, 1860 – Jan. 2, 1943]. Shelby married Eugene Wimberly Whitfield in 1892.
- Hervey Eugene Whitfield [Feb. 14, 1896 – May 12, 1912]. Hervey is the son of Eugene Wimberly and Shelby *Humphreys* Whitfield, and the three of them share a common obelisk.
- Ray Vernon Madden [August 10, 1892 – December 17, 1954]
- Mary *Whitfield* Madden [September 1, 1897 – August 31, 1987]. Mary is the daughter of Eugene Wimberly and Shelby *Humphreys* Whitfield. She married Ray Vernon Madden in 1919, and they share a common stone.

[A-63: Downing, Humphreys, Jefferies, Taliaferro]
- Daniel Burnet Humphreys [Jan. 14, 1838 – July 1886], C. S. A. stone, "in memory of my husband." Daniel is the son of David G. and Mary *Cobun* Humphreys, buried in plot H-10.
- Katherine Watson Shelby *Jefferies* Humphreys [Apr. 5, 1841 – Oct. 21, 1878], "wife of Daniel B. Humphreys." Katherine married Daniel Humphreys in 1860. She was a yellow fever victim.
- Katharine Flynn Humphreys [Aug. 27, 1861 – Jan. 22, 1864]
- Nathaniel Jefferies Humphreys [Aug. 6, 1865 – Oct. 16, 1921]
- Fay *Taliaferro* Humphreys [Oct. 10, 1875 – Feb. 12, 1964]. Fay is the daughter of Charles Adams and Elizabeth *Rice* Taliaferro, buried in plot A-75. She married Nathaniel Humphreys in 1897.
- George Wilson Humphreys [May 19, 1872 – March 31, 1947]
- Merle *Downing* Humphreys [January 2, 1880 – March 24, 1948]
- Evana Jefferies Humphreys [Sept. 28, 1874 – Oct. 4, 1878]. Evana was a yellow fever victim.

[A-64: Clarke, Ikerd, Tanner]

- Thomas Ray Ikerd [Oct. 6, 1875 – Nov. 30, 1940]
- Cinderella *T(anner)*. Ikerd [died Feb. 14, 1969]. Cinderella is the wife of Thomas Ray Ikerd.
- Lula May Ikerd [Sept. 25, 1907 – July 18, 1909]
- William L. Clarke [March 21, 1909 – November 9, 1975], "Husband."
- Tommie Lee *Ikerd* Clarke [July 13, 1909 – March 14, 1992], "Wife." Tommie is the daughter of Thomas Ray and Cinderella *Tanner* Ikerd. She is the wife of William L. Clarke, and they share a common grave location.

[A-65: Drexler, Hamilton, Jefferies, Mann]. This lot has a memorial stone bearing the names DREXLER on one side and MANN on the other.

- James J. Mann [1863 – 1933]
- Sarah *Jefferies* Mann [Sept. 3, 1871 – Aug. 15, 1948], member Daughters of the American Revolution. Sarah is the daughter of F. S. and Kate *Ellett* Jefferies, buried in plot B-25. She married James Jett Mann in 1898.
- E. Barton Drexler [Apr. 21, 1890 – Oct. 16, 1973]. Edwin Barton is the son of Henry Clay and Alice H. *Banks* Drexler, buried in Owens Cemetery.
- Georgia *M(ann)*. Drexler [Oct. 3, 1900 – Feb. 15, 1979]. Georgia is the daughter of James J. and Sarah *Jefferies* Mann. She married Edwin Barton Drexler in 1926.
- Shelby Jefferies Mann [Feb. 2, 1903 – May 26, 1990]. Shelby is the son of James J. and Sarah *Jefferies* Mann.
- Eleanor *H(amilton)*. Mann [Nov. 12, 1907 – Dec. 7, 1981]. Eleanor is the wife of Shelby Jefferies Mann.

[A-66: Archer, Marye]

- Abram Barnes Archer [Sept. 29, 1836 – July 24, 1913], C. S. A. stone. Abram is the son of Richard Thompson and Ann *Barnes* Archer, buried in Archer Cemetery.
- Anna *Marye* Archer [Oct. 9, 1843 – Nov. 26, 1912], "wife of Abram B. Archer." Anna is the daughter of James T. and Mary P. *Hoopes* Marye, buried in plot B-36.

[A-67/76/77/167/178/188: Bertron, Gage, Magill, Massie, McConaughy, Nicholson, Person, Prichard, Sandifer, Van Horn] These lots are situated within large stone boundary markers and have a memorial stone bearing the names PERSON on one side and GAGE-BERTRON on the other.

- Robert Douglass Gage [Oct. 16, 1860 – Dec. 12, 1953]. Robert is the son of James A. and Rose *Russell* Gage, buried in plot B-34.
- Lena *Van Horn* Gage [Nov. 8, 1865 – April 30, 1920], "wife of Robert D. Gage."
- Roberta *Person* Gage [Jan. 25, 1878 – April 28, 1962], member Daughters of the American Revolution, "wife of Robert D. Gage." Roberta and James Wells, below, are children of James Wells and Isabella *Myles* Person, buried in plot B-27. Roberta married Robert Gage in 1922, after the death of his first wife.
- James Wells Person [May 2, 1881 – Apr. 11, 1952]
- Mary Anna *Gage* Person [Mar. 29, 1887 – Aug. 15, 1970]. Mary is the daughter of Robert Douglass and Lena *Van Horn* Gage. She married James Wells Person in 1912, and they share a common stone.
- Adele LaNoue *Prichard* Person [Dec. 23, 1923 – Dec. 20, 1950], "wife of James W. Person." Adele married James Wells Person, Jr. in 1946.
- James Vertner Gage [Mar. 21, 1889 – Nov. 16, 1960]. James is the son of Robert Douglass and Lena *Van Horn* Gage.
- Leah *Nicholson* Gage [Dec. 15, 1890 – Jan. 25, 1926], "wife of James Vertner Gage." Two sons, John Rollins and Howell Nicholson Gage, are buried in combined plot A-168/177.
- Gladys *Sandifer* Gage [Jan. 24, 1908 – Dec. 9, 1999], "wife of James Vertner Gage."
- John Bothwell McConaughy [Mar. 1, 1912 – May 30, 1972]

- Mary Anna Gage *Person* McConaughy [June 25, 1913 – Feb. 8, 1983]. Mary is the daughter of James Wells and Mary Anna *Gage* Person. She married John Bothwell McConaughy in 1936.
- Lena Lucile Person [Sept. 23, 1914 – Sept. 22, 1968]. Lena is the daughter of James Wells and Mary Anna *Gage* Person.
- Lena Lucile *Gage* Bertron [Dec. 19, 1890 – Aug. 22, 1914], "wife of Samuel R. Bertron, Jr." Lena is the daughter of Robert Douglass and Lena *Van Horn* Gage. She married Samuel Bertron, Jr. in 1914.
- Robert Douglass Gage, Jr. [Oct. 13, 1896 – Aug. 9, 1970]. Robert is the son of Robert Douglass and Lena *Van Horn* Gage.
- Elizabeth *Massie* Gage [Aug. 27, 1898 – Apr. 14, 1989]. Elizabeth is the wife of Robert Douglass Gage, Jr. A son, Robert D. Gage, III is buried in combined plot A-169/176.
- Isabella Myles Person [Jan. 29, 1916 – Mar. 14, 2009]. Isabella is the daughter of James Wells and Anna *Gage* Person.
- Malvina *Person* Magill [March 11, 1921 – June 25, 1979]. Malvina is the daughter of James Wells and Anna *Gage* Person. She married Thomas J. Magill, Jr. in 1941.

[A-68: Spragins]
- Lennie Thomas Spragins [Nov. 17, 1876 – Mar. 1, 1914], "beloved husband of Carrie S. Spragins." Lennie married Carrie A. Shaifer in 1904.
- Infant Son Spragins [May 17, 1907 – May 18, 1907], "infant son of Lennie T. & Carrie S. Spragins."

[A-69: Gage, Hartwell, Spencer]. This lot has a memorial obelisk bearing the name SPENCER.
- Samuel Marshall Spencer [Dec. 19, 1837 – Dec. 30, 1910]
- Carrie T. (*Gage*) Spencer [Nov. 10, 1839 – Nov. 11, 1913]. Carrie is the daughter of James A. and Rose *Russell* Gage, buried in plot B-34, and wife of Samuel Marshall Spencer.
- Rose Spencer [Aug. 13, 1868 – Dec. 15, 1881]
- Horatio N. Spencer [1871 – 1951]. Horatio is the son of James G. and Lucy *Jones* Spencer, buried in plot B-46.
- Ellie May *H(artwell)* Spencer [1876 – 1948]. Ellie married Horatio Spencer in 1900, and they share a common stone. They have sons, William Hartwell Spencer buried in plot A-162, Horatio Nelson Spencer, Jr. in plot I-57, and James Grafton Spencer in plot M-57.

"Transplanted now by angel hands,
To yon bright world on high;
The tender plant that budded here,
Will blossom in the sky."
—on stone of Rose Spencer

[A-70: Brady, Jefferies, Thrasher, Utz]. This lot has a memorial stone bearing the names THRASHER on one side, and JEFFERIES on the other.
- Stephen Thrasher [1831 – 1913]. Stephen was married three times. He married his second wife, Mrs. Elizabeth *Belknap* Hamilton, in 1875. She is buried in plot F-19.
- Martha *J(efferies)* Thrasher [1849 – 1928]. Martha first married Joseph Brady in 1873. Later she became the third wife of Stephen Thrasher.
- Priscilla S. Brady [Oct. 12, 1878 – April 12, 1955], member Daughters of the American Revolution. Priscilla is the daughter of Joseph and Martha *Jefferies* Brady.
- Joseph Brady [1880 – 1884]
- Eliza P. Brady [1884 – 1942]. Eliza is the daughter of Joseph and Martha *Jefferies* Brady.
- Albert Neville Brady [1886 – 1959]. Albert is the son of Joseph and Martha *Jefferies* Brady.

- Henrietta A. Brady [July 6, 1903 – Dec. 4, 1972], member United Daughters of the Confederacy. Henrietta is the wife of Albert Neville Brady. They have a son, James O. Brady, buried in plot H-99, and a daughter, Martha *Brady* Lum, in combined plot M-87/88.
- Priscilla S. *(Jefferies)* Utz [1855 – 1928]. Priscilla married Willard Humphrey Utz in 1881. Willard is buried in Warren County. They have a daughter, Martha *Utz* Bearden, buried in plot A-57.

[A-71: Barth, Lutz]
- Sarah Lutz [Dec. 26, 1850 – Aug. 21, 1936], "Grandmother."
- Allen Lutz [Sept. 29, 1870 – Sept. 25, 1960], "Father." Allen is the son of Sarah Lutz.
- Carrie *(Barth)* Lutz [Apr. 1, 1877 – Apr. 6, 1970], "Mother." Carrie is the wife of Allen Lutz. They have daughters Coral *Lutz* Storment, Iva *Lutz* Kelly and Alice *Lutz* Taylor buried in plot J-71. Sarah, Allen and Carrie share a common stone.

[A-72: Nusom]
- J. J. Nusom [Apr. 20, 1860 – Sept. 12, 1896], member Woodmen of the World, Camp No. 5. J. J. married Mrs. E. Horn Kelly in 1881.

[A-73: Ker, Terry, Watson]
- Louis Wantland Watson [Sept. 2, 1843 – Oct. 27, 1918]. Louis married Olivia Rowan in 1865. She is buried in plot C-22.
- Martha *(Ker)* Terry [no dates]. Martha married William Terry in 1818.
- Mary Terry [no dates]
- David Ker Terry [no dates]. Mary and David are the children of Mary *Ker* Terry, and they share a common stone.

[A-74: Allen, Howard, Morehead, O'Connor, Palfrey, Rayner]
- Richard Sessions Morehead [June 24, 1871 – Jan. 30, 1951]
- Mildred *O'Connor* Morehead [July 17, 1882 – Oct. 6, 1969], "wife of Sessions Morehead." Mildred was previously married to a Mr. Palfrey. She married Richard Sessions Morehead in 1920. They have a daughter, Mary Sessions *Morehead* Goodwin, buried in combined plot A-172/173.
- Benjamin Hughes Morehead [Nov. 1, 1873 – Oct. 5, 1942]. Benjamin and his brother, Richard Sessions Morehead, listed above, are sons of Benjamin and Mary *Sessions* Morehead, buried in plot B-15.
- Emma Eugenia *Allen* Morehead [Apr. 2, 1871 – Aug. 25, 1937], "wife of Benjamin H. Morehead." Emma married Benjamin Hughes Morehead in 1895.
- Mary Thelma *Morehead* Rayner [Mar. 24, 1896 – Sept. 8, 1953], "wife of Ira C. Rayner." Mary is the daughter of Benjamin Hughes and Emma Eugenia *Allen* Morehead. She married Ira Rayner in 1920.
- Benjamin Morehead Rayner [Jan. 19, 1923 – Jan. 10, 1925], "Our Baby." Benjamin is the son of Ira and Mary *Morehead* Rayner.
- Charles Allen Morehead [Aug. 8, 1901 – Aug. 26, 1957]. Charles is the son of Benjamin Hughes and Emma Eugenia *Allen* Morehead.
- Mildred Pratt Howard [June 24, 1915 – Jan. 1, 1995]. Mildred is the wife of Douglas Turner Howard, buried in plot I-88.

[A-75/80: Gordon, Murff, Rice, Taliaferro, Van Hook, Webers]. This combined plot has a memorial stone bearing the name TALIAFERRO.
- Charles Adams Taliaferro [1844 – 1915], C. S. A. stone, member Woodmen of the World.
- Elizabeth *Rice* Taliaferro [1845 – 1931]. Elizabeth is the wife of Charles Adams Taliaferro. Besides those offspring listed below, they have a daughter, Faye *Taliaferro* Humphreys, buried in plot A-63.
- James Van Hook [1857 – 1918], member Woodmen of the World.
- Mariella *Taliaferro* Van Hook [1866 – 1941]. Mariella is the daughter of Charles and Elizabeth *Rice* Taliaferro and wife of James Van Hook.

- Harvey Johnson Murff [March 31, 1876 – March 29, 1947]
- Bessie Taliaferro *Van Hook* Murff [Aug. 5, 1886 – Jan. 16, 1974]. Bessie is the daughter of James and Mariella *Taliaferro* Van Hook. She married Harvey Johnson Murff in 1907.
- Julia Fay Murff [May 1, 1917 – July 2, 1918]
- Julia Fay Van Hook [Jan. 21, 1890 – Aug. 20, 1974]. Julia is the daughter of James and Mariella *Taliaferro* Van Hook.
- Balmayne M. Van Hook [June 7, 1893 – Dec. 29, 1983]. Balmayne is the daughter of James and Mariella *Taliaferro* Van Hook.
- Bessie Pearl Taliaferro [1870 – 1945]. Bessie is the daughter of Charles and Elizabeth *Rice* Taliaferro.
- Balmayne Taliaferro [1872 – 1935]. Balmayne is the daughter of Charles and Elizabeth *Rice* Taliaferro.
- Charles A. Taliaferro [Feb. 26, 1878 – Sep. 18, 1882], "only son of C.A. & E. M. Taliaferro."
- Edwynne Rice Taliaferro [1881 – 1967]. Edwynne is the daughter of Charles and Elizabeth *Rice* Taliaferro.
- Josie B. *Taliaferro* Gordon [Sept. 23, 1883 – Nov. 26, 1964]. Josie is the daughter of Charles and Elizabeth *Rice* Taliaferro. She married William Preston Gordon in 1905. William is buried in plot F-12. They have a son, William P. Gordon, buried in plot A-141.
- Paul Hermann Webers [May 11, 1866 – Mar. 14, 1928]

[A-78/166/179: no stones]

[A-79: Gradick]
- Griffin Christopher Gradick [1873 – 1953]. Griffin married Lizzie Johnson in 1894.
- Griffin C. Gradick, Jr. [1903 – 1918]

[A-81: McFatter, Williams]
- William A. McFatter [died April 9, 1930], "MISSISSIPPI, PVT., 10 FIELD ARTY., 3 DIV." This is a military stone. William married Margaret J. Hudson in 1848. Margaret is buried in Jefferson County. Besides Jeff, listed below, they have a son, John Adams McFatter, buried in plot I-4.
- Jeff McFatter [1850 – 1921]. Jeff is the son of William and Margaret *Hudson* McFatter.
- Kate *(Williams)* McFatter [1861 – 1953]. Kate married Jeff McFatter in 1881, and they share a common stone. Besides Dan, listed below, other children are: Mary *McFatter* Kling, buried in combined plot I-48/49, and Arissa *McFatter* Jordan, buried in plot E-20.
- Dan. S. McFatter [1890 – 1963]. Dan is the son of Jeff and Kate *Williams* McFatter.

[A-82: Cason]
- Omar Augustus Cason [Aug. 22, 1865 – Feb. 10, 1921]. Omar married Mrs. Jessie May Watson in 1920.

[A-83: Fife, Hudson]
- Farris A. Fife [Aug. 15, 1845 – Jan. 17, 1922]. Farris married Dewildia Porter in 1867. Dewildia is buried in Sarepta Cemetery.
- Isaac M. Fife [1884 – 1951]. Isaac is the son of Farris and Dewildia *Porter* Fife.
- Emmie M. *(Hudson)* Fife [May 8, 1892 – April 1, 1918], member of Woodmen Circle. Emmie married Isaac M. Fife in 1909.
- Gladys Fife [June 25, 1913 – June 30, 1913], "infant of I. M. and E. M. Fife."

[A-84: Barber, Tabor, Walne]
- Richard Eugene Walne [Apr. 24, 1845 – Aug. 14, 1925], C. S. A. stone.
- Margaret *Tabor* Walne [Dec. 2, 1848 – Aug. 3, 1930]. Margaret married Richard Walne in 1871, and they share a common stone. Besides offspring listed below, a daughter, Flora *Walne* Brownlee, is buried in plot G-35.
- James Hunt Walne [June 27, 1875 – June 16, 1954]. James is the son of Richard and Margaret *Tabor* Walne. He married Miss Annie G. Walker in 1905.

- George Tabor Walne [Dec. 17, 1880 – Sept. 6, 1939]. George is the son of Richard and Margaret *Tabor* Walne.
- Lucie *Barber* Walne [Jan. 14, 1883 – Nov. 1, 1967]. Lucie married George Tabor Walne in 1903.
- George Tabor Walne, Jr. [April 16, 1903 – January 1, 1951]
- Richard Legrande Walne [Mar. 12, 1890 – Feb. 8, 1928]

[A-85: Brashear, Taylor]
- Joseph Newton Brashear [Aug. 1, 1863 – Nov. 2, 1922]
- Cornelia *Taylor* Brashear [Feb. 6, 1875 – March 14, 1948]. Cornelia is the daughter of John P. and V. E. Taylor, buried in plot F-27. She married Joseph Newton Brashear in 1897.

[A-86: Callender, Hedrick, Moore, Torrey, Trim]
- John Basil Moore [1865 – 1953]
- Kate *C(allender)*. Moore [July 24, 1867 – August 28, 1925]. Kate married John Basil Moore in 1890.
- Sallie C. *(Trim)* Moore [Sept. 7, 1878 – July 5, 1951]. Sallie is the second wife of John Basil Moore.
- Edward Bernard Moore [December 21, 1890 – May 25, 1964], "MISSISSIPPI, S2, US NAVY, WORLD WAR I." This is a military stone. Edward is the son of John Basil and Kate *Callender* Moore.
- Mary *Hedrick* Moore [1886 – 1959]. Mary is the daughter of John Allison and Fannie *Chaffin* Hedrick, buried in plot A-26. She was first married to a William H. Torrey, and they have a daughter, Frances *Torrey* Segrest, buried in plot A-97. She later married Edward Bernard Moore in 1917.
- James Evon Moore [March 8, 1895 – Oct. 19, 1922], a Mason. James is the son of John and Kate *Callender* Moore.

[A-87: Chandler, Clark, Twomey]
- Marcus D. Twomey [1879 – 1922]
- Olive A. *(Chandler)* Twomey [1878 – 1959]. Olive is the wife of Marcus D. Twomey, and they share a common stone.
- Clyde Clark [May 5, 1907 – Oct. 14, 1986], "Husband."
- Beatrice *T(womey)*. Clark [Dec. 1, 1904 – Apr. 24, 1989], "Wife." Beatrice is the daughter of Marcus and Olive *Chandler* Twomey.
- Charles P. Twomey [Aug. 29, 1907* – Feb. 1, 1941]. Charles is the son of Marcus and Olive *Chandler* Twomey. *Year of birth could be 1927, as a "2" is superimposed over the "0."

[A-88: Cutrer, Holt]. This lot has a memorial stone bearing the name HOLT.
- Alfred Holt, M. D. [May 29, 1861 – Dec. 21, 1936]
- Julia O. Holt [Dec. 5, 1865 – Sept. 16, 1936]
- Barnard S. Holt [Jan. 3, 1887 – Sept. 7, 1923]
- Horatio O. Holt [Oct. 2, 1891 – June 13, 1948]. Horatio is the son of Alfred Holt.
- Mae *Cutrer* Holt [Dec. 30, 1901 – Aug. 22, 1989]

[A-89: Bobo, Pahnka]
- Charlie B. Bobo [1875 – 1950], "Father."
- Christine *Pahnka* Bobo [Dec. 4, 1877 – July 31, 1964]. Christine is the daughter of Herman and Lottie *Thaler* Pahnka, buried in Jefferson County. She married Charlie B. Bobo in 1896.
- Ruby Lee Bobo [1911 – 1931]

[A-90/164: Cossar, Freeland, McCarthy, Pittman, Winters]
- Thomas Henry Freeland [Aug. 16, 1863 – Feb. 12, 1931]. Thomas Henry and Priscilla Covington Freeland, listed below, are children of Thomas Augustin and Mary Cecilia *Beall* Freeland. Mary is buried in Freeland Cemetery.
- Hannah *Winters* Freeland [Sept. 19, 1872 – Nov. 10, 1959]. Hannah is the daughter of Hiram and Elizabeth *Schofield* Winters, buried in Jefferson County. She married Thomas Henry Freeland in 1899.

- Priscilla Covington Freeland [Oct. 30, 1875 – Oct. 23, 1956]
- Thomas Henry Freeland, Jr. [Jan. 24, 1902 – Aug. 13, 1979]. Thomas is the son of Thomas and Hannah *Winters* Freeland.
- Rosa *Pittman* Freeland [Aug. 13, 1904 – July 12, 1995]. Rosa is the daughter of Frank and May *Bedon* Pittman, buried in plot C-23. She is the wife of Thomas Henry Freeland, Jr.
- Frances *Freeland* McCarthy [July 9, 1932 – Sept. 17, 1972]. Frances is the daughter of Thomas Henry and Rosa *Pittman* Freeland.
- Mary Cecilia Freeland [May 31, 1900 – Aug. 3, 1964]. Mary is the daughter of Thomas and Hannah *Winters* Freeland.
- Charles G. Cossar [June 8, 1902 – July 21, 1955]
- Elizabeth *Freeland* Cossar [April 16, 1908 – February 23, 1971]. Elizabeth is the daughter of Thomas and Hannah *Winters* Freeland. She married Charles Gordon Cossar in 1938.

[A-91: Callender, Herring]
- J. A. Callender [Sept. 2, 1862 – Jan. 2, 1938]
- Ida W. *(Herring)* Callender [Dec. 24, 1866 – Aug. 3, 1955]. Ida married J. A. Callender in 1885. A daughter, Beatrice Louise *Callender* Minnis, is buried in plot H-47, and a son, Hugh Marion Callender, is buried in plot I-46.
- John M. Callender [Dec. 28, 1900 – Feb. 28, 1927]

"The golden gates were opened wide,
A gentle voice said 'Come,'
And angels from the other side,
Welcomed our loved one home."
—on stone of John M. Callender

[A-92: Eggen, Harrell, Russum, Storment, Thomas]
- W. H. Russum [May 30, 1876 – Oct. 14, 1928]. Walter H. married Allie O. Jones, his first wife, in 1900. She and their infant daughter are buried in Herlong Cemetery. He married his third wife, Nellie *Humphreys* Russum, in 1911. Nellie is buried in plot I-50, along with three sons, William H. and Dewitt Russum.
- Nonnie E. *Harrell* Storment [May 28, 1887 – Oct. 8, 1951], "Mother…nee-Nonnie E. Harrell, wife of W. H. Russum." Nonnie is the second wife of Walter H. Russum, marrying in 1904. They have a son, William H. Russum, buried in Herlong Cemetery. She later married Elmer H. Storment in 1934.
- Charlie G. Thomas [Apr. 21, 1900 – June 2, 1970], a Mason, "Daddy."
- Thelma *Russum* Thomas [June 13, 1905 – Nov. 19, 1964], "Mother." Thelma is the daughter of Walter H. and Nonnie E. *Harrell* Russum. She is the wife of Charlie Gage Thomas, and they share a common grave location.
- Lucille *Russum* Eggen [May 26, 1913 – Oct. 31, 1989]

[A-93: Brown, Clark, Jones, Seals, Young]
- C. L. Young [Sept. 12, 1854 – Nov. 26, 1926], a Mason, "Father."
- Nannie M. *(Seals)* Young [June 14, 1859 – Aug. 17, 1941], "Mother…wife of C. L. Young." Nannie married Cornelius L. Young in 1876.
- Robert B. Jones [Nov. 20, 1870 – May 17, 1935]
- Sallie V. *(Young)* Jones [Nov. 15, 1876 – Mar. 14, 1958]. Sallie is the daughter of Cornelius and Nannie *Seals* Young. She married Robert B. Jones in 1890. Their son, J. Mack Jones, is buried in plot A-98.
- David W. Clark [1886 – 1959]. David, and Addie Clark listed below, are children of Horace W. Clark,

buried in plot A-104, and Fannie *Andrews* Clark, buried in Herlong Cemetery.
- Mamie *B(rown)*. Clark [Oct. 6, 1893 – Feb. 5, 1980]. Mamie is the daughter of Marshall E. and Ida *Clark* Brown, buried in plot G-49. She married David Wesley Clark in 1913.
- Miss Addie Clark [1888 – 1934]

[A-94/95: Davis, Havis, Herring, Middleton]. This combined plot has a memorial stone bearing the name DAVIS.
- John W. Davis [April 23, 1848 – July 19, 1929]
- Julia A. *(Havis)* Davis [July 20, 1851 – Dec. 20, 1935], "Mother…" Julia is the wife of John W. Davis. Besides their son listed below, other children are Carrie E. and Edward Davis, buried in plot J-33.
- E. W. Davis [Mar. 25, 1874 – Jan. 28, 1947], "Father." E. W. is the son of John W. and Julia *Havis* Davis.
- Rhodie Belle *(Middleton)* Davis [Aug. 9, 1879 – Nov. 6, 1953], "Mother." Rhodie married E. W. Davis in 1899.
- James Wilbur Davis [Apr. 26, 1931 – Apr. 26, 1932], "son of P. E. & Grace Davis." James Wilbur is the grandson of E. W. and Rhodie Belle *Middleton* Davis.
- John G. Herring [1866 – 1929]
- Frederick Edwin Herring [1870 – 1953], a Mason.
- Julia Iva *(Davis)* Herring [1879 – 1946]. Julia married Frederick Edwin Herring in 1898, and they share a common stone.
- Charles Howard Herring [Sept. 25, 1941 – Sept. 26, 1941]

[A-96: Black, Hay, Warren]
- Martin Syms Warren [Apr. 7, 1843 – Nov. 3, 1937]
- Mary Susan *Black* Warren [Jan. 7, 1843 – Mar. 18, 1931]. Mary married Martin Syms Warren in 1868, and they share a large square vault with the inscription: "A happy union for 62 years." They have a child, Lillian *Warren* Hay, buried in combined plot A-148/155.
- Charles Lee Hay [June 10, 1939], "Baby…infant son of Mr. & Mrs. Chas. F. Hay."

[A-97: Enochs, Fox, Scott, Segrest, Torrey]. This lot has a memorial stone bearing the name SEGREST.
- R. A. Segrest, M. D. [1880 – 1931], a Mason, "Father."
- Ibbye *Scott* Segrest [Oct. 3, 1883 – Oct. 31, 1971], "Mother." Ibbye is the daughter of Robert M. and Mattie B. *Shelby* Scott, buried in Hermanville Cemetery. She married R. A. Segrest in 1904.
- Robert A. Segrest [Aug. 29, 1905 – Mar. 27, 1982]. Robert is the son of R. A. and Ibbye *Scott* Segrest.
- Annie Lou "Polly" *Enochs* Segrest [Nov. 1, 1909 – Sept. 24, 2005]. Annie married Robert A. Segrest in 1933.
- David M. Segrest, M. D. [Sept. 27, 1906 – July 16, 2000], "dedicated physician, son of Ibbye Scott and R. A. Segrest, Sr., M. D."
- Oren R. Segrest [July 10, 1908 – April 18, 2003], "a loving husband and daddy." Oren is the son of R. A. and Ibbye *Scott* Segrest.
- Frances *T(orrey)*. Segrest [Oct. 2, 1910 – Nov. 10, 1999], "a precious mother and wife." Frances is the daughter of William H. and Mary *Hedrick* Torrey. Mary is buried in plot A-86 with the last name of MOORE. Frances is the wife of Oren R. Segrest.
- Marjorie *Fox* Segrest [Aug. 28, 1931 – May 22, 1994], "Grammy." Marjorie is the wife of Oren R. Segrest, Jr.

[A-98: Crawford, Jones, McGhee, Rush, Selden]
- Edwin Lee McGhee [Mar. 15, 1874 – Nov. 8, 1959]
- J. Mack Jones [August 9, 1894 – March 14, 1982], a Mason. J. Mack is the son Robert B. and Sallie *Young* Jones, buried in plot A-93.
- Emma *Rush* Jones [November 15, 1896 – May 31, 1975], member Daughters of the American Revolution. Emma is the daughter of Thomas L. and Mary Adelia *Kelly* Rush, buried in plot H-93. She and J.

Mack Jones share a common grave location, a vase with the words, "Married Jan. 21, 1917."

- Harper M. Jones [November 2, 1917 – March 7, 1994], a Mason. Harper is the son of J. Mack and Emma *Rush* Jones.
- Margaret Alice *(Selden)* Jones [April 20, 1921 – Aug. 2, 1949], "beloved wife of John Martin Jones." Margaret married John, son of J. Mack and Emma *Rush* Jones, in 1943. John is buried in plot H-100.
- Mark H. Crawford [May 22, 1918 – January 13, 1988], a Mason, "2ND LT, US ARMY AIR CORPS, WORLD WAR II." This is a military stone. He also has a civilian stone. Mark married Mary Frances Jones, daughter of J. Mack and Emma *Rush* Jones, in 1945.

[A-99: Compton, Houston, Millsaps, Walters]
- Franklin P. Millsaps [Oct. 18, 1877 – June 1, 1941]. Franklin is the son of F. P. and Martha *Valentine* Millsaps. Martha is buried in Rembert Cemetery.
- Ada Bell *Compton* Millsaps [June 20, 1880 – Sept. 27, 1971]. Ada is the wife of Franklin P. Millsaps.
- Edgar L. Houston [July 3, 1897 – Dec. 19, 1930]
- Ella Mae *Millsaps* Walters [November 15, 1910 – November 22, 1961], "Mother." Ella is the daughter of Franklin P. and Ada Bell *Compton* Millsaps. She married Edgar L. Houston in 1928. After Edgar's death she married a Mr. Walters.
- Edgar Leon Houston, Jr. [1929 – 2013]
- Alex Compton Millsaps [Jan. 28, 1923 – Sept. 19, 1976]. Alex is the son of Franklin P. and Ada Bell *Compton* Millsaps.

[A-100: Buchignani, Ross, Salee]
- Sidney J. Ross [May 14, 1872 – Sept. 15, 1931]
- Mary M. *(Salee)* Ross [Nov. 6, 1874 – July 5, 1954]. Mary is the wife of Sidney J. Ross, and they share a common stone.
- Samuel Robert Ross [October 28, 1906 – November 27, 1963]. Samuel is the son of Sidney J. and Mary *Salee* Ross.
- Edward Raphael Buchignani, Jr. [April 12, 1908 – December 14, 1976]
- Alice Camille *Ross* Buchignani [June 30, 1909 – October 11, 2003]. Alice is the daughter of Sidney J. and Mary *Salee* Ross. She married Edward Raphael Buchignani in 1933, and they share a common stone.

[A-101: Groves, Neal, Thomas]
- William P. Groves [Mar. 5, 1866 – Jan. 8, 1943], "Father."
- Mary Bell *(Neal)* Groves [Feb. 28, 1879 – June 17, 1969], "Mother." Mary is the wife of William P. Groves.
- Asbury B. Thomas [July 22, 1885 – March 9, 1945], "Husband." Asbury married Vaude Groves in 1943.

[A-102: Bolls, Humphreys, Israel, Jackson, Trim]
- Ola *Humphreys* Jackson [March 6, 1879 – January 22, 1946], "Our Mom." Ola married Ernest Israel in 1896. She later married J. A. Bolls in 1910, and later married a Mr. Jackson.
- David R. Israel [Jun. 21, 1897 – Dec. 12, 1966], "US ARMY, WORLD WAR I, SILVER STAR." This is a military stone. David is the son of Ernest and Ola *Humphreys* Israel. He married Josie Williams in 1957.
- Maggie *Humphreys* Trim [Dec. 30, 1884 – Dec. 13, 1951], "Mother." Maggie married B. F. Trim in 1909.

[A-103: Davis, Rousseau]
- Josie Louise Rousseau [November 23, 1859 – January 3, 1940]
- Mary Eliza Davis [October 27, 1871 – January 21, 1960]. Mary Eliza and her brother James, listed below, are children of Joseph G. and Mattie *McDonald* Davis, buried in plot G-37.
- James Chalmers Davis [May 18, 1880 – March 16, 1966]
- Edna Rousseau Davis [November 11, 1881 – November 26, 1936]

- Edna Ruth Davis [1912 – 2002]

[A-104: Allred, Clark, Howard, McCain]. This lot has a memorial stone bearing the name CLARK.

- Horace W. Clark [Oct. 9, 1863 – Apr. 22, 1935], "Father." Horace married Fannie Andrews, his first wife, in 1885. She is buried in Herlong Cemetery. Their children, David W. and Miss Addie Clark, are buried in plot A-93.
- Lela *Allred* Clark [Jan. 8, 1876 – Oct. 8, 1953], "Mother." Lela is the daughter of Sylvester and Mary Jane *McClure* Allred, buried in Jefferson County. She is the second wife of Horace W. Clark.
- Clythus S. Clark [Nov. 11, 1908 – Mar. 4, 1990], "Husband." Clythus is the son of Horace W. and Lela *Allred* Clark.
- Mildred *Howard* Clark [Oct. 19, 1907 – Mar. 15, 1982], "Wife." Mildred is the daughter of Jasper Douglas and Kate *Turner* Howard, buried in Howard Cemetery. She married Clythus S. Clark in 1938.
- Horace L. Clark, Sr. [May 12, 1911 – Oct. 22, 1947], "MISSISSIPPI, PFC, 309 INF, 78 DIV, WORLD WAR II." This is a military stone.
- Ree *McCain* Clark [October 19, 1912 – October 10, 1993]. Ree is the wife of Horace L. Clark, Sr.

[A-105: Cannada, Lewis]

- Leon Eugene Lewis [May 7, 1898 – March 25, 1969]
- Irene *Cannada* Lewis [January 18, 1899 – February 11, 1973]. Irene is the wife of Leon Eugene Lewis.
- Carmen Lewis [Dec. 6, 1926 – April 14, 1935]. Carmen is the daughter of Leon Eugene and Irene *Cannada* Lewis.

[A-106: Carmichael, Horton, Loviza, Smith, Watson]

- Robert L. Horton, D.D.S. [April 17, 1864 – June 15, 1932]. Other sources tell us that Dr. Horton was first married to a woman named Mary.
- Emma *Carmichael* Horton [unreadable dates]. This stone is badly eroded or chipped, and is practically unreadable. The size and inscriptions tell us that this is Robert L. Horton's second wife, Emma. They married in 1904. Other sources tell us that she was born on Jan. 11, 1875, and died on May 15, 1961.
- Robert L. Horton, Jr. [December 19, 1894 – January 22, 1970]. Robert is the son of Robert L. Horton, Sr. and his first wife, Mary.
- Maria *Loviza* Horton [March 19, 1890 – December 20, 1980]. Maria is the wife of Robert L. Horton, Jr.
- Myrtie May Horton [July 29, 1924 – November 12, 2005]. Myrtie is the daughter of Robert L. and Maria *Loviza* Horton.
- James Henry Smith [February 29, 1896 – July 1, 1969]
- Myrtie *Horton* Smith [November 1, 1896 – February 13, 1992]. Myrtie is the daughter of Robert L. Horton, Sr. and his first wife, Mary. She first married Evon Alpheus Watson in 1913. He is buried in plot A-12. After Evon's death she married James Henry Smith in 1926.

[A-107: Magruder, McDougall, Selden]

- Nickolas McDougal (sic) [Dec. 22, 1847 – Jan. 14, 1935]. Nickolas is the son of Duncan McDougall, buried in plot B-16.
- Alice *Magruder* McDougall [Nov. 22, 1852 – Dec. 24, 1932]. Alice married Nickolas McDougall in 1876. Besides those listed below, a daughter, Ann *McDougall* Freeman, is buried in plot B-16.
- Thomas M. McDougall [June 21, 1878 – Oct. 6, 1945], "Son." Thomas is the son of Nickolas and Alice *Magruder* McDougall.
- Duncan McDougall [March 14, 1880 – April 9, 1944], "ARKANSAS, PVT, CO K, 1 REGT INFANTRY." This is a military stone. Duncan is the son of Nickolas and Alice *Magruder* McDougall. Duncan married Margaret Shreve in 1912. She is buried in plot A-30.
- Jerry R. McDougall [Feb. 27, 1888 – Mar. 26, 1969]. Jerry is the son of Nickolas and Alice *Magruder* McDougall.

- Nicholas D. McDougall [Mar. 7, 1891 – April 17, 1942], "Son." Nicholas is the son of Nickolas and Alice *Magruder* McDougall.
- Margaret *M(cDougall)* Selden [Dec. 10, 1894 – Nov. 10, 1981], "US ARMY, WORLD WAR I." This is a military stone. She also has a civilian stone. Margaret is the daughter of Nickolas and Alice *Magruder* McDougall. She married John A. Selden in 1920. They have a daughter, Maria *Selden* Warren, buried in plot I-53.

[A-108: Bennett, Cleveland, Goodrum, McCaa, Trevilion]
- David E. McCaa [Oct. 2, 1862 – June 9, 1937]
- Jessie A. *(Trevilion)* McCaa [Apr. 24, 1866 – Aug. 21, 1939]. Jessie married David E. McCaa in 1882. Besides those listed below, they have a daughter, Josie *McCaa* Nelson, buried in combined plot I-7/8.
- Pearla *McCaa* Cleveland [Nov. 23, 1892 – Oct. 28, 1979]. Pearla is the daughter of David E. and Jessie A. *Trevilion* McCaa. She married Earl Cleveland in 1939.
- David Ernest McCaa, Sr. [Mar. 8, 1895 – Nov. 22, 1968]. David is the son of David E. and Jessie A. *Trevilion* McCaa. After the death of his first wife, Myrtle, he married Mrs. Anna Catherine *Norwood* Tohill in 1954.
- Myrtle *G(oodrum)*. McCaa [Sept. 1, 1904 – Jan. 14, 1954]. Myrtle married David Ernest McCaa in 1920. They have a son, David Ernest McCaa, buried in combined plot K-33/34, an infant son, James, buried in Hutchinson Cemetery, and daughters, Jessie Mae *McCaa* Ellis and Hazel *McCaa* Headley, buried in Headley Cemetery.
- Lee Roy McCaa [Aug. 13, 1902 – July 29, 1969].]. Lee Roy is the son of David E. and Jessie A. *Trevilion* McCaa.
- Barbara Hazel *(Bennett)* McCaa [Sept. 8, 1905 – Mar. 5, 1976]

[A-109: Shaifer, Washburn, Weiler]
- John Charles Weiler [1877 – 1937]
- Margaret *Shaifer* Weiler [1890 – 1950]
- Montfort Washburn [August 7, 1883 – December 27, 1963]. Montfort is the husband of Gladys *Fly* Washburn, buried in combined plot H-71/72/89/90.

[A-110: Berger, Hughes]
- Auguste Berger [Feb. 7, 1867 – Sept. 20, 1937]
- Louise *Hughes* Berger [Sept. 12, 1879 – Aug. 2, 1962]. Louise is the daughter of William and Mary *Bertron* Hughes, buried in plot A-20. She married Auguste Berger in 1911, and they share a common grave location.
- Frederick Charles Berger [Nov. 7, 1914 – Aug. 1, 1978]. Frederick is the son of Auguste and Louise *Hughes* Berger.

[A-111: Addison, Loeb, McGilvary, Richmond]. This lot has a memorial stone bearing the name RICHMOND.
- Mary *McG(ilvary)*. Richmond [Dec. 12, 1852 – Aug. 14, 1946], "wife of T. Y. Richmond…Mama." Mary is the daughter of William M. and Mary F. McGilvary, buried in combined plot D-13/14. She married Thomas Y. Richmond in 1870. He is buried in Pattona Cemetery, along with their sons, Warren McGilvary and Thomas Jackson Richmond. Besides these and the ones listed below, they have a daughter, Mary *Richmond* Ellis, buried in Jefferson County.
- William Mandeville Richmond [July 0, 1877 – Aug. 28, 1952]. William is the son of T. Y. and Mary *McGilvary* Richmond.
- Ernestine Richmond [Oct. 24, 1879 – Sept. 19, 1945], "daughter of Mary M. and Thomas Y. Richmond."
- Enid Richmond [June 18, 1883 – Oct. 4, 1942], "daughter of Mary M. & Thomas Y. Richmond."
- Hattie *Richmond* Loeb [Apr. 14, 1885 – Sept. 10, 1960]

- Leslie R. Addison [July 10, 1891 – Sept. 1, 1962], "born Lawrence, Kansas."
- Vera *Richmond* Addison [Jan. 2, 1890 – May 28, 1983], "born Hermanville, MS." Vera is the daughter of T. Y. and Mary *McGilvary* Richmond and wife of Leslie R. Addison.

[A-112: Daniell, Hughes, Morse, Rucker, Watkins, Wollfarth]

- Smith C. Daniell IV [March 11, 1885 – Nov. 6, 1970], "MISSISSIPPI, MAJOR, ENGINEER CORPS, WORLD WAR I & II." This is a military stone. Smith is the son of Smith Coffee Daniell III, buried in Freeland Cemetery, and Nancy *Hughes* Daniell, buried in plot A-20.
- Clarissa *Hughes* Watkins [Dec. 24, 1870 – Jan. 6, 1960]. Clarissa is the daughter of William and Mary *Bertron* Hughes, buried in plot A-20. She married Marcellus M. Watkins in 1894. Besides those listed below, they have a daughter, Louise *Watkins* Davenport, buried in combined plot A-125/126.
- Margaret Williams *Watkins* Rucker [Apr. 28, 1899 – Oct. 6, 1991]. Margaret is the daughter of Marcellus and Clarissa *Hughes* Watkins.
- Oscar Wollfarth [Jan. 4, 1895 – Mar. 25, 1979], "PVT, US ARMY, WORLD WAR I." This is a military stone.
- Mary Kate *Watkins* Morse Wollfarth [Sept. 30, 1901 – Mar. 27, 1983]. Mary is the daughter of Marcellus and Clarissa *Hughes* Watkins, and the wife of Oscar Wollfarth. Her connection with the name MORSE is unknown.

[A-113: Brandon, Crocker]

- Roscoe M. Brandon [May 5, 1905 – November 28, 1968]
- Gladys *C(rocker)*. Brandon [July 1, 1907 – February 24, 1989]. Gladys is the wife of Roscoe Brandon, and they share a common grave location.
- Joann Marie Brandon [Sept 21, 1937 – Dec. 18, 1937], "Our Darling Baby."

[A-114: Harrell, Hicks, Powers, Russell, Seawright, Ungerer]

- Frederick C. Ungerer [June 22, 1870 – October 29, 1943]
- Dannie M. *Hicks* Ungerer [August 22, 1876 – March 29, 1969]. Dannie is the daughter of W. T. and Margaret J. *Dunbar* Hicks. Margaret is buried in plot G-38. Dannie married Frederick Ungerer in 1896, and they share a common stone. Besides their son listed below, they have a daughter, Katie *Ungerer* Powers, buried in plot I-37.
- John L. Ungerer [Dec. 12, 1903 – Sept. 22, 1949], "MISSISSIPPI, AS, US NAVY, WORLD WAR I." This is a military stone. He also has a civilian stone. John is the son of Frederick C. and Dannie M. *Hicks* Ungerer.
- Pauline *R(ussell)*. Ungerer [Apr. 25, 1907 – Sept. 2, 1964]. Pauline married John Ungerer in 1929, and they share a common grave location.
- Patricia *Ungerer* Seawright [July 30, 1936 – July 29, 1986]. Patricia is the daughter of John and Pauline *Russell* Ungerer. She married Kenneth Seawright in 1960.
- Maggie Bernard *(Ungerer)* Harrell [Sept. 26, 1906 – April 18, 1965], "loved and known by all as Peggy." Maggie is the daughter of Frederick C. and Dannie *Hicks* Ungerer.
- James L. Powers [1909 – 1963], a Mason. James married J. Lucille Ungerer in 1933.

[A-115: Ives, Mitchell, Standrod, Valentine]

- John W. Standrod [July 22, 1871 – Feb. 3, 1938], member Woodmen of the World, "beloved husband of Bessie Valentine Standrod."
- Bessie *V(alentine)*. Standrod [Jan. 22, 1882 – Jan. 29, 1944]. Bessie and her siblings Richard and Henrietta, below, are children of Richard and Ellen *Dohan* Valentine, buried in Rembert Cemetery.
- Richard Valentine [1883 – 1945]
- Everette F. Mitchell [Dec. 10, 1884 – Mar. 2, 1976]
- Henrietta *Valentine* Mitchell [November 15, 1892 – June 8, 1985]. Henrietta married Everette F. Mitchell in 1915.

- Elizabeth *Mitchell* Ives [May 1, 1919 – August 5, 1985]. Elizabeth is the daughter of Everette and Henrietta *Valentine* Mitchell.
- Charles G. Mitchell [Jul. 14, 1941 – Apr. 11, 2009], "US MARINE CORPS" and "loving son and brother." This is a military stone.

[A-116/117: Beesley, Lingle, Lum, Nelson, Sutton, Wheeless]. This double lot has a memorial stone bearing the name WHEELESS.

- Green Berry Wheeless [Feb. 27, 1857 – Dec. 18, 1942]. Green is the son of Green B. and Elizabeth *Davis* Wheeless, buried in plot F-13.
- Daisy *Lum* Wheeless [Sept. 23, 1881 – April 2, 1960]. Daisy is the daughter of Erastus and Mary Emma *Powell* Lum, buried in Lum Cemetery. She married Green Berry Wheeless in 1904. Besides those listed below, they have a daughter, Eunice *Wheeless* Hay, buried in combined plot A-148/155.
- Virgil Berry Wheeless [June 6, 1907 – May 27, 1985]. Virgil is the son of Green and Daisy *Lum* Wheeless.
- Elizabeth *Sutton* Wheeless [August 1, 1908 – November 4, 1986]. Elizabeth married Virgil Berry Wheeless in 1932.
- Sam Leslie Roberts, Jr. [August 27, 1937 – July 14, 2007].
- Susan *Wheeless* Roberts [December 17, 1936 – October 16, 2004]. Susan is the daughter of Virgil Berry and Elizabeth *Sutton* Wheeless. She is the wife of Sam Leslie Roberts, Jr., and they share a common stone.
- John C. Wheeless [January 2, 1909 – September 21, 1996]. John is the son of Green and Daisy *Lum* Wheeless.
- Linnie *Lingle* Wheeless [February 20, 1910 – June 18, 1987]. Linnie is the wife of John C. Wheeless.
- James A. Beesley [July 6, 1922 – April 19, 2008]. James is the son of Henry and Jennie *McCall* Beesley, buried in Jefferson County.
- Joan *Wheeless* Beesley [September 14, 1935 – May 1, 2008]. Joan is the daughter of John C. and Linnie *Lingle* Wheeless. Joan first married Clyde Luther Nelson, Jr. in 1955. They have a daughter, Stephanie Lynn Nelson, buried in combined plot I-7/8. Clyde is buried in plot C-76. Joan then married James A. Beesley, and they share a common grave location.
- Sarah Catherine Wheeless [September 14, 1945 – May 16, 2012]. Sarah is the daughter of John C. and Linnie *Lingle* Wheeless.

[A-118/119/120/121: French, Miller]. This four-lot area is enclosed in ornamental railing and has a large boulder memorial in its center, bearing the name FRENCH.

- Chauncy French [Sept. 25, 1876 – Apr. 30, 1938]
- Grace Elizabeth *Miller* French [Apr. 1, 1877 – July 11, 1960], "wife of Chauncy French."

[A-122: Anderson, Dale, Billingslea]

- Robert B. Billingslea [June 7, 1860 – February 6, 1942]
- William Cyrus Billingslea [Dec. 29, 1889 – Aug. 9, 1972]. William is the son of Robert B. Billingslea.
- Genevieve *A(nderson)*. Billingslea [January 23, 1888 – May 20, 1954]. Genevieve is the daughter of G. W. and Mary E. *Luster* Anderson, buried in Hinds County. She is the wife of William Cyrus Billingslea. She had previously married John J. Dale, buried in Louisiana. A son, John Jarvis Dale, Sr., is buried in plot H-74.
- William Cyrus Billingslea, Jr. [Apr. 6, 1928 – Dec. 31, 1990], "S2, US NAVY, WORLD WAR II." This is a military stone. William is the son of William and Genevieve *Anderson* Billingslea. He married Blanche St. John in 1949.

[A-123: Abraham, Brooks, Hamilton, McCaa]

- Jacob L. Abraham [1889 – 1943]. Jacob is the son of Louis and Julia *Levy* Abraham, buried in the Port

Gibson Jewish Cemetery.

- Phoebe *Hamilton* Abraham [1895 – 1982], member Daughters of the American Revolution. Phoebe is the daughter of Robert Lee and Nellie *Allen* Hamilton, buried in plot F-19. A twin brother, Stephen Thrasher Hamilton, is buried in plot H-34. Phoebe married Jacob Abraham in 1915, and they share a common grave location. Besides Jake Abraham, listed below, other offspring include: Phoebe Cleve *Abraham* Spencer, buried in plot B-42, Stephen Thrasher Abraham in plot I-73 and Lee H. Abraham in plot J-106.
- Jake Louis Abraham [Sept. 20, 1916 – Oct. 14, 1987]. Jake is the son of Jacob L. and Phoebe *Hamilton* Abraham.
- Jane *Brooks* McCaa Abraham [Mar. 28, 1917 – Apr. 19, 1999]. Jane is the wife of Jake Louis Abraham, and they share a common stone. She was previously married to Nelson McCaa.

[A-124: Cooper, Meadows, Strickland]
- Mary K. Strickland [1866 – 1947]
- Lenard S. Strickland [Sept. 26, 1889 – April 5, 1954], "Father." Lenard is the son of Mary K. Strickland. His first two wives are listed below. After the death of his second wife he married a third time, to Mrs. Minnie Louise Chesnut, in 1944.
- Maud E. *(Meadows)* Strickland [1891 – 1923]. Maud is the first wife of Lenard S. Strickland. They have daughters, Ola *Strickland* Dodson, buried in plot E-31 and Ruby *Strickland* Hartley, in combined plot M-70/75.
- Gladys *(Cooper)* Strickland [Aug. 31, 1900 – Oct. 17, 1943], "Mother…wife of L. S. Strickland." They have a daughter, Martha Dale *Strickland* Brock, buried in plot H-86.

[A-125/126: Davenport, Sayre, Seale, Watkins]
- Joseph Davenport [July 31, 1872 – Dec. 8, 1964]. Joseph and his sister, Eva *Davenport* Seale, listed below, are children of E. J. and Drucilla *Darden* Davenport, buried in plot F-20.
- Louise *Watkins* Davenport [June 8, 1897 – Mar. 12, 1980]. Louise is the daughter of Marcellus and Clarissa *Hughes* Watkins. Clarissa is buried in plot A-112. Louise married Joseph Davenport in 1918.
- Joseph Davenport, Jr. [Oct. 27, 1919 – Apr. 18, 2000], "SK1, US NAVY, WORLD WAR II." This is a military stone. Joseph is the son of Joseph and Louise *Watkins* Davenport.
- Mary Kathryn *Sayre* Davenport [June 28, 1925 – Feb. 10, 2007], "wife of Joseph Davenport Jr., mother of Joseph Davenport III., Tom Sayre and Sim Sayre."
- W. L. Seale [May 25, 1875 – Dec. 17, 1944]
- Eva *Davenport* Seale [Jan. 3, 1882 – Mar. 4, 1960]. Eva married William L. Seale in 1908.

[A-127: Barnes, Goshorn, Proffitt, Russell]
- C. B. Russell [Oct. 2, 1884 – Sept. 12, 1945]
- Jennie *G(oshorn)*. Russell [Aug. 20, 1877 – Apr. 10, 1956], "Mother." Jennie married a Mr. Barnes before marrying Mr. Russell. Her name can be found spelled as GOSHORN or GOOSHORN.
- Mae Ella Barnes [Feb. 24, 1894 – Nov. 5, 1966], "a dear faithful aunt." Mae is the daughter of Jennie *Goshorn* Russell.
- Frederick A. Barnes [Jan. 13, 1896 – Jan. 6, 1965], "LOUISIANA, PVT, CO L, 53 PIONEER INF, WORLD WAR I." This is a military stone. Frederick is the son of Jennie *Goshorn* Russell.
- George R. Barnes [April 10, 1934 – April 28, 1999], "beloved brother and son." George is the son of Frederick A. Barnes.
- William D. Barnes [1901 – 1981]. William is the son of Jennie *Goshorn* Russell.
- Mary J. Barnes [1910 – 1949]. Mary shares a common stone with William D. Barnes, and is assumed to be his first wife.
- Mary G. *Proffitt* Barnes [Oct. 25, 1922 – June 28, 1980]. Mary is a wife of William D. Barnes.

[A-128/142/143: Brown, Huff, McLendon, Meadows, Richardson, Sudduth, Thomas]
- Walter Hulon Brown [1880 – 1959]
- Dora *McLendon* Brown [1883 – 1954]. Dora is the wife of Walter Hulon Brown, and they share a common stone. Besides those listed below, other children are Anse J. Brown, buried in plot I-10, and Beatrice *Brown* Hay in combined plot A-148/155.
- W. F. (Bill) Brown [May 17, 1905 – Feb. 25, 1969]. Bill is the son of Walter Hulon and Dora *McLendon* Brown. His four infants listed below were born to a later wife.
- Virgie Mae *(Meadows)* Brown [May 7, 1911 – January 9, 1935], "wife of W. F. Brown."
- Billie Jean *Brown* Huff [July 3, 1927 – May 12, 1999]. Billie is the daughter of W. F. and Virgie Mae *Meadows* Brown, and wife of Charles Lambert Huff, buried in Jefferson County. Billie shares a common stone with her father.
- Infant Son Brown [Sept. 28, 1945], "infant son of Mr. & Mrs. W. F. Brown."
- Infant Son Brown [Nov. 12, 1946], "infant son of Mr. & Mrs. W. F. Brown."
- Infant Son Brown [Oct. 29, 1949], "infant son of Mr. & Mrs. W. F. Brown."
- Infant Son Brown [June 24, 1951], "infant son of Mr. & Mrs. W. F. Brown."
- Ella *Brown* Thomas [December 10, 1901 – June 13, 1986]. Ella is the daughter of Walter Hulon and Dora *McLendon* Brown.
- Charles Zack Richardson [Jan. 18, 1903 – Jan. 30, 1961]
- Gertrude *B(rown)* Richardson [Feb. 3, 1907 – Mar. 8, 1988]. Gertrude is the daughter of Walter Hulon and Dora *McLendon* Brown. She is the wife of Charles Zack Richardson, and they share a common stone.
- George Huff Brown, Sr. [November 30, 1911 – January 13, 1988], a Mason. George is the son of Walter Hulon and Dora *McLendon* Brown.
- Joe Meek Sudduth, Jr. [Feb. 1, 1906 – Sept. 3, 1949]
- Odie Lee *(Brown)* Sudduth [Dec. 1, 1912 – Jan. 3, 1998]. Odie is the daughter of Walter Hulon and Dora *McLendon* Brown. She is the wife of Joe Meek Sudduth, and they share a common stone.

[A-129: Baker, Barnett, Irby, King]
- William Dean Irby [May 16, 1876 – Apr. 4, 1964]
- Gertrude *Baker* Irby [Sept. 8, 1874 – Jan. 14, 1948]. Gertrude married William Dean Irby in 1902, and they share a common stone. Besides their daughter listed below, they have daughters Ora Delle *Irby* Westrope and Ona *Irby* Sanders, and a foster-son, Robert R. Worsham, buried in plot J-39.
- Walter C. Barnett [Jan. 2, 1889 – Feb. 3, 1965], a Mason.
- Otis Dean *Irby* Barnett [Jan. 18, 1903 – Feb. 24, 1995], member Order of the Eastern Star. Otis is the daughter of William Dean and Gertrude *Baker* Irby. She is the wife of Walter C. Barnett, and they share a common stone. She had previously married S. G. King in 1920.
- Julia Merle King [Feb. 6, 1928 – Sept. 29, 1944]

[A-130: Adams, Dow, Harrell]
- Henry Lot Harrell [Feb. 11, 1868 – June 10, 1919], member Woodmen of the World.
- Nima Jane *(Dow)* Harrell [1871 – 1954], "Mother." Nima married Henry Harrell in 1890.
- James J. Harrell [1870 – 1955]. James married Lou Keenan in 1891.
- B. F. Dow [1885 – 1950], "Father."
- Stella *(Harrell)* Dow [1883 – 1962], "Mother." Stella married B. F. Dow in 1903, and they share a common stone.
- Hewlin F. Dow [July 25, 1904 – Oct. 10, 1906], "son of B. F. & S. Dow."
- Mamie Harrell [1893 – 1909]
- Madie Harrell Adams [1900 – 1920]. Madie and Mamie Harrell share a common stone.

[A-131: Harvey, Sprott]

- Charles Elder Sprott [July 13, 1883 – Sept. 2, 1944]. James is the son of James T. and Nancy *Wilson* Sprott, buried in plot B-2.
- Kate Lee *Harvey* Sprott [Nov. 4, 1877 – May 26, 1968]. Kate married Charles Elder Sprott in 1909.

[A-132: Chamberlain, Cogan, Ellis, Piazza]

- Clyde Stuart Cogan [1875 – 1947]
- Irene *C(hamberlain)*. Cogan [Jan. 14, 1881 – May 8, 1956]. Irene is the daughter of John Darden and Ellen *Spence* Chamberlain, buried in Jefferson County, and wife of Clyde Stuart Cogan.
- Eli George Ellis [August 1, 1907 – December 6, 1985], "born El Munsif, Lebanon." Eli is the son of George and Thomenie *Oudy* Ellis, buried in combined plot G-42/43.
- Kathryn *Cogan* Ellis [November 21, 1914 – June 28, 1998], "born Lorman, MS." Kathryn is the daughter of Clyde and Irene *Chamberlain* Cogan, and wife of Eli George Ellis.
- Preston Dante Piazza [August 16, 1949 – March 17, 2013]. Preston is the son-in-law of Eli George and Kathryn *Cogan* Ellis.

[A-133/134/137: Barland, Hamilton, Martin, McGuffee, Segrest]. This lot has a memorial stone bearing the name BARLAND.

- Charles H. Barland [1872 – 1946]. Charles and his brother Edward B. Barland, listed below, are sons of Charles Henderson and Mittie *Houston* Barland, buried in Sarepta Cemetery, Mittie with the last name of SMITH.
- Ruth *Segrest* Barland [1884 – 1970]. Ruth is the daughter of Thomas J. and Lavinia *Rives* Segrest. Thomas is buried in Segrest Cemetery. Ruth married Charles H. Barland in 1921. Their children include: Charles Edward Barland, buried in combined plot A-47/48, and Harold Segrest Barland, buried in Hermanville Cemetery.
- Edward B. Barland [1876 – 1945]
- Jimmie *Martin* Barland [1878 – 1965]. Jimmie is the daughter of J. P. and Mary Frances Martin, buried in Sarepta Cemetery. She married Edward B. Barland in 1900.
- John G. Hamilton [May 10, 1910 – Sept. 18, 1981]
- Mae *B(arland)*. Hamilton [Sept. 17, 1904 – June 28, 1990]. Mae is the daughter of Edward B. and Jimmie *Martin* Barland, and the wife of John G. Hamilton.
- Henry Edward Barland [Nov. 21, 1907 – Oct. 14, 1962]. Henry is the son of Edward B. and Jimmie *Martin* Barland.
- Florine *McGuffee* Barland [Nov. 17, 1916 – Dec. 12, 2004]. Florine married Henry Edward Barland in 1936, and they share a common grave location.

[A-135: Batton, Jenkins, Ledbetter]

- William Nathan Jenkins, M. D. [Sept. 9, 1895 – June 2, 1977]. William is the son of William Nathan and Pearl *Redus* Jenkins, buried in Copiah County.
- Helen *Ledbetter* Jenkins [Aug. 20, 1895 – Nov. 26, 1981]. Helen is the wife of William Nathan Jenkins, and they share a common stone.
- Alexander Alford Batton, Jr. [August 17, 1945 – June 3, 2006]. Alexander is the son of Alexander Alford and Isabella *Drake* Batton, buried in combined plot H-51/52.

[A-136: Barnes, Bomer, Smith]. This lot has a memorial stone bearing the name SMITH.

- Arthur Neil Smith [June 2, 1888 – June 12, 1968]. Arthur is the son of Lawrence A. and Lelia A. Smith, buried in plot A-18.
- Lottie *(Barnes)* Bomer Smith [Aug. 13, 1889 – March 3, 1981]. Lottie married Arthur Neil Smith in 1914. It is unclear where the name BOMER comes from.
- Edwin B. Smith [Oct. 2, 1919 – April 30, 1943], "LOUISIANA, 2D LIEUTENANT, 90 AAF BOMB GP, WORLD WAR II." This is a bronze military plaque.

- Louise Miles Smith [June 21, 1914 – April 16, 1989]

[A-138: Cleveland, Housley, Slayton]

- Lizzie *S(layton)*. Housley [Nov. 29, 1891 – May 14, 1985], "Mother." Lizzie is the daughter of Rowan C. and Mary A. *Ikerd* Slayton, buried in plot G-46. She married W. A. Housley in 1915.
- Rowan Housley [Sept. 4, 1918 – July 29, 1948], "Son." Rowan and his mother, Lizzie, share a common grave location.
- David L. Cleveland [May 31, 1910 – Mar. 29, 1999]. David is the son of Samuel L. and Minnie *McFerrin* Cleveland, buried in plot H-100.
- Eula L. *(Housley)* Cleveland [Jan. 4, 1917 – Apr. 15, 2008]. Eula is the daughter of Lizzie *Slayton* Housley. She married David L. Cleveland in 1933.

[A-139: McAmis, Preskitt, Scruggs, Todd]

- W. R. Preskitt [1859 – 1938], "Father." The children of W. R. Preskitt include Effie *Preskitt* Manis, buried in plot E-24, and John W. Preskitt, buried in combined plot M-70/75.
- Nancy J. Preskitt [1888 – 1911], "beloved wife and mother."
- Charles A. McAmis [1886 – 1950], "Father."
- Edna *P(reskitt)*. McAmis [1894 – 1974], "Mother." Edna is the daughter of W. R. Preskitt. She is the wife of Charles A. McAmis, and they share a common grave location.
- Elton Lee McAmis, Sr. [Mar. 1, 1916 – Mar. 3, 1997], "CAPT, US ARMY, WORLD WAR II, MEDICAL DOCTOR." This is a bronze military plaque. Elton is the son of Charles A. and Edna *Preskitt* McAmis. He married Mrs. Mary *Brown* Boyte in 1974. Another stone that he shares with his wife has "Elton Lee McAmis, Sr., M. D…Retired Surgeon, Captain U. S. Army Medical Corp." Mary's side has only her birth date of February 24, 1931.
- Rev. Hollis B. Todd, PhD [August 28, 1917 – February 19, 2002]
- Julia *McAmis* Todd, PhD [August 5, 1918 – September 13, 2006]. Julia is the daughter of Charles A. and Edna *Preskitt* McAmis. She married Rev. Hollis B. Todd in 1940.
- Billie Rowe Scruggs [Nov. 14, 1929 – Aug. 26, 2004]. Billie shares a common stone with Judith Myers Scruggs. Judith's side has only her birth date of April 23, 1945.

[A-140: Boyd, Jordan, Stuckey, Wynn]

- Earl Jordan [1897 – 1955], "Dad." Earl is the son of James J. and Laura *Covington* Jordan, buried in Herlong Cemetery.
- Annie Mae *(Boyd)* Jordan [1900 – 1973], "Mom." Annie is the wife of Earl Jordan, and they share a common stone. Besides their son listed below, they have sons Harry M. Jordan, buried in plot M-118, and Earl Barron Jordan in plot K-31.
- Jesse Hugh Jordan [Mar. 3, 1921 – Oct. 17, 1989], "SGT, US ARMY, WORLD WAR II." This is a bronze military plaque. Jesse is the son of Earl and Annie Mae *Boyd* Jordan. He also has a stone that shows him as a Mason, with the nickname, "Pete."
- Mary K. *(Wynn)* Jordan [Feb. 14, 1927 – Nov. 23, 1950]. Mary married Jesse Hugh Jordan in 1944. This is Jesse's first wife.
- Bobbie J. *Stuckey* Jordan [Mar. 11, 1931 – July 25, 2012], member Order of the Eastern Star. Bobbie married Jesse Hugh Jordan in 1954, after the death of his first wife, and they share a common grave location.

[A-141: Gordon, Woodall]

- William P. Gordon [July 16, 1907 – Jan. 31, 1985]. William is the son of William P. Gordon, buried in plot F-12, and Josie B. *Taliaferro* Gordon, buried in combined plot A-75/80.
- Dorothy *W(oodall)*. Gordon [Oct. 5, 1919 – Dec. 29, 2010]. Dorothy is the wife if William P. Gordon, and they share a common grave location.

[A-144: no stones]

[A-145: Blomquist, Cannada, Watson]

- Carl Wheeless Blomquist [December 9, 1891 – April 15, 1969]. Carl is the son of Sanfred and Sara Ann *Wheeless* Blomquist, buried in plot A-44.
- Bessie *Cannada* Blomquist [September 11, 1905 – July 2, 1990]. Bessie married Carl Blomquist in 1924, and they share a common grave location.
- Roy Foote Watson [November 18, 1923 – June 17, 1950]. Roy married Joyce Blomquist in 1946.

[A-146: Greer, Hynum, Jones, Raines]

- C. C. Greer [1881 – 1966]
- Willie R. *(Jones)* Greer [1882 – 1950]. Willie married Christopher Columbus Greer in 1905, and they share a common grave location. Besides their daughter listed below, they have a daughter, Olis *Greer* Baker, buried in plot J-12.
- William Joseph Hynum [August 11, 1908 – July 4, 1975]. William married Marie Pierce in 1945.
- Robert Alec Hynum [Aug. 26, 1902 – May 18, 1972]. Robert and his brother William, listed above, are sons of Luther Lee and Edna Pearl Hynum, buried in Hedrick Cemetery.
- Jewell Mae *(Greer)* Hynum [June 29, 1907 – Aug. 3, 2000]. Jewell is the daughter of Christopher Columbus and Willie R. *Jones* Greer. She married Robert Alec Hynum in 1923.
- Bertie Mildred Hynum [Dec. 9, 1924 – May 6, 2012]. Bertie is the daughter of Robert Alec and Jewell Mae *Greer* Hynum, and the three of them share a common stone.
- Urbon Thomas Raines [April 22, 1927 – January 23, 2008], "Father."

[A-147: Freeman, Greer, Mason]

- Samuel Levy Mason [August 18, 1882 – September 22, 1958]
- Lula Lee *(Freeman)* Mason [March 2, 1884 – March 15, 1963]. Lula is the wife of Samuel Levy Mason.
- Edgar Lamar Mason [June 23, 1905 – Dec. 5, 1976]
- Thelma *Greer* Mason [Oct. 3, 1916 – May 7, 1949]. Thelma married Edgar Lamar Mason in 1934.

[A-148/155: Brown, Hay, Warren, Wheeless]. These combined lots have a memorial stone bearing the name HAY.

- George William Hay [1882 – 1952]
- Lillian *Warren* Hay [1882 – 1978]. Lillian is the daughter of Martin Syms and Mary Susan *Black* Warren, buried in plot A-96, and wife of George William Hay.
- K. Warren Hay [September 10, 1905 – December 11, 1993], "Loving Father." Kenneth Warren is the son of George William and Lillian *Warren* Hay.
- Beatrice *B(rown)*. Hay [December 3, 1909 – January 22, 1988]. Beatrice is the daughter of Walter Hulon and Dora *McLendon* Brown, buried in combined plot A-128/142/143. She married Kenneth Hay in 1934.
- William Henry Hay [Feb. 18, 1910 – Mar. 7, 2002]. William is the son of George William and Lillian *Warren* Hay.
- Eunice *Wheeless* Hay [Oct. 6, 1911 – Sept. 22, 2005]. Eunice is the daughter of Green Berry and Daisy *Lum* Wheeless, buried in combined plot A-116/117. She married William Henry Hay in 1934, and they share a common grave location.

[A-149: Buckley, Newman, Sumrall]

- Robert G. Sumrall [July 23, 1907 – Nov. 11, 1964], a Mason.
- Florence *B(uckley)*. Sumrall [Feb. 10, 1904 – June 14, 1988]. Florence is the wife of Robert G. Sumrall, and they share a common grave location. A son, James E. Sumrall, died in 1982 and was cremated. Although not marked, his cremains may have been buried in this plot. Another son, Billy Ray Sumrall, is buried in plot K-11.
- Jack B. Newman [Sept. 11, 1906 – Sept. 7, 1949], a Mason, "Father."

- Annie *(Buckley)* Newman [Oct. 6, 1906 – May 12, 1999], member Order of the Eastern Star, "Mother." Annie is the sister of Florence *Buckley* Sumrall and wife of Jack B. Newman.

[A-150: Foster, Humphreys]
- Samuel Cobun Humphreys [July 30, 1908 – March 17, 1963]. Samuel is the son of Benjamin Grubb and Bessie Lee *Williams* Humphreys, buried in Warren County.
- Gus B. Foster [July 26, 1899 – Sept. 21, 1948]. Gus is believed to be the husband of Katherine *Humphreys* Foster, sister of Samuel Cobun Humphreys, listed above.

[A-151: Cuper, Goza, Lusk]. This lot has a memorial stone bearing the name CUPER-LUSK.
- Joseph E. Cuper [Oct. 23, 1879 – Aug, 20, 1951], "MISSISSIPPI, ASST BAND LDR, 140 FA, 39 DIV, WORLD WAR I." This is a military stone.
- Sadie *Goza* Cuper [Sept. 7, 1890 – Apr. 15, 1972]. Sadie is the daughter of Joseph B. and Mary Ellen *Lord* Goza, buried in Copiah County, and the wife of Joseph E. Cuper. She was previously married to Adolph Lusk, also buried in Copiah County. Besides Joseph, below, she has a daughter by her first marriage, Lauriellen *Lusk* Bearden, buried in plot A-57.
- Joseph B. Lusk [Sept. 30, 1911 – May 17, 1945], "MISSISSIPPI, 1ST LIEUT, 307 INF, 77 DIV, WORLD WAR II." This is a bronze military plaque. Joseph is the son of Adolph and Sadie *Goza* Lusk.

From Port Gibson Reveille's "Looking Back" column (week of January 22, 1949): "The body of young Joseph B. Lusk…has been brought back from the Pacific area where he lost his life in defense of his country."

[A-152: Coen, Hartley, Smith]
- Albert L. Smith, Sr. [Jan. 0, 1883 – Nov. 9, 1975]
- Sarah Ada *(Coen)* Smith [Feb. 11, 1874 – Oct. 11, 1948]. Sarah and Albert L. Smith share a common stone with the inscription "Married Oct. 14, 1910." She had been previously married to a Mr. Hartley.
- William Smith [Sep. 7, 1890 – Dec. 28, 1979], "F3, US NAVY, WORLD WAR I." This is a bronze military plaque. He also has a civilian stone whose grave location he shares with Mittie L. *Hartley* Smith.
- Mittie L. *Hartley* Smith [May 10, 1901 – Dec. 4, 1989], "Our Beloved Mother." Mittie is the daughter of Sarah Ada *Coen* Hartley, listed above with the last name of SMITH. She is the wife of William Smith.

[A-153/154: Brown, Deal, Hill, McCurley, Ritter]
- Samuel H. Hill [1894 – 1977], "Our Father." Samuel is the son of William J. and Lou Ann *Mullinix* Hill, buried in Hill Cemetery.
- Estille *R(itter)*. Hill [1895 – 1948], "Our Mother." Estille is the wife of Samuel H. Hill. Besides those listed below, they have a son, Clyde A. Hill, buried in plot J-86.
- John Lowe Brown [Sept. 7, 1914 – Aug. 24, 1979]. John is the son of Washington G. and Alice M. *Adair* Brown, buried in plot E-32.
- Jessie Lee *(Hill)* Brown [Apr. 19, 1915 – Nov. 24, 1988]. Jessie is the daughter of Samuel H. and Estille *Ritter* Brown. She married John Lowe Brown in 1935.
- Blanche Eleanor *Hill* Deal [Aug. 10, 1917 – Dec. 26, 1996], "Beloved Mother." Blanche is the daughter of Samuel H. and Estille *Ritter* Hill.
- Claude H. Hill [Dec. 8, 1922 – Oct. 7, 2005]. Claude is the son of Samuel H. and Estille *Ritter* Hill.
- Mary Ann *(McCurley)* Hill [Jan. 26, 1931 – Oct. 26, 1996]. Mary Ann married Claude H. Hill in 1948, and they share a common grave location.

[A-156: Hays, Ingram, Jones]
- Henry R. Jones [June 22, 1893 – Nov. 25, 1953]. After the death of his first wife, he married Mrs. Alma Taylor in 1950, or possibly 1952 (they have two different marriage licenses, the weddings being performed by two different ministers). Alma is buried in combined plot E-29/30.
- Mary E. *(Ingram)* Jones [Feb. 18, 1886 – April 3, 1949]. Mary is the wife of Henry R. Jones.
- Helen Marie *(Jones)* Hays [May 13, 1919 – May 9, 1990]. Helen is the daughter of Henry R. and Mary

Ingram Jones. Her husband, Owen Clyde Hays, Jr., is buried in combined plot H-91/92.

[A-157: Clark, Segrest]

- Bridger D. Segrest [Aug. 30, 1886 – Nov. 20, 1970], a Mason. Bridger is the son of John D. and Nettie C. *Bridger* Segrest, buried in plot H-50.
- Lucy *C(lark)*. Segrest [Oct. 24, 1888 – Mar. 7, 1982], member Order of the Eastern Star. Lucy is the daughter of George W. and Addie L. *Evans* Clark, buried in Sarepta Cemetery. She married Bridger D. Segrest in 1904, and they share a common grave location.

[A-158: Alford]

- Alcus E. Alford [1901 – 1951]. According to the <u>Town of Port Gibson, Minute Book L</u>, Mr. Alford was a marshal of the Town of Port Gibson for six years and was killed in the line of duty.

[A-159: Adams, Brown, Davis

- Isaac N. Brown [March 13, 1886 – October 18, 1957]. Isaac is the son of Isaac P. and Ellen J. *Wells* Brown. Isaac, his dad, is buried in Clarke Cemetery. He first married Mary Ella Barnes in 1907.
- Mattie Josephine *(Davis)* Brown [February 27, 1905 – February 24, 1952].Mattie married Isaac Brown in 1925, and they share a common stone. Mattie is Isaac's second wife.
- Frances Louise Adams [Oct. 25, 1947 – Sept. 4, 1983]

[A-160: Bryant, Morgan, Neal, Nelson, Smith]

- Gus Morgan [Aug. 25, 1889 – Dec. 28, 1969], "Father."
- Nettie *N(eal)*. Morgan [Nov. 28, 1894 – Nov. 11, 1973], "Mother." Nettie is the wife of Gus Morgan, and they share a common grave location.
- Juanita *Morgan* Smith [Nov. 14, 1924 – Sept. 27, 2005], "Our loving mother." Juanita is the daughter of Gus and Nettie *Neal* Morgan. She married George Smith in 1940.
- Rev. Clyde W. Nelson [Dec. 24, 1902 – Dec. 28, 1956]
- Ruthie Mae Nelson [June 23, 1913 – Jan. 30, 1945], "Mother."
- Baby Girl Bryant [no dates]

[A-161: Emrick, Gaines, Gary, Valentine]

- Daniel Joseph Valentine [March 8, 1874 – April 11, 1945], "beloved husband of Virginia Gary." Daniel and his sister Cora, below, are children of Richard and Ellen *Dohan* Valentine, buried in Rembert Cemetery.
- Virginia *Gary* Valentine [January 15, 1876 – March 5, 1965], "beloved wife of Daniel J. Valentine."
- Gary J. Valentine [Aug. 16, 1916 – Oct. 13, 1944], "MISSISSIPPI, PFC, 337 INF, WORLD WAR II." This is a military stone.
- Arthur C. Emrick [June 26, 1887 – March 13, 1958], "MISSISSIPPI, PFC, CO F, 317 INFANTRY, WORLD WAR I." This is a military stone. Arthur is the son of William J. and Lottie *Campbell* Emrick, buried in Taylor-Emrick Cemetery.
- Edna *Gary* Emrick [Nov. 14, 1897 – Aug. 14, 1988]. Edna is the wife of Arthur C. Emrick.
- James Leslie Gaines, Sr. [January 22, 1884 – March 11, 1950], "Father."
- Cora *Valentine* Gaines [July 22, 1884 – March 4, 1976], "Mother." Cora is the wife of James Leslie Gaines, Sr.
- James Leslie Gaines, Jr. [November 20, 1908 – July 16, 1965], "Son." James is the son of James Leslie and Cora *Valentine* Gaines, and the three of them share a common grave location. He married Elizabeth Gunn in 1930.

[A-162: Spencer, Starnes]

- William Hartwell Spencer [June 22, 1906 – Aug. 5, 1982]. William is the son of Horatio N. and Ellie May *Hartwell* Spencer, buried in plot A-69.
- Madalyn *Starnes* Spencer [Feb. 19, 1906 – Dec. 12, 1989]. Madalyn is the daughter of M. B. and Lillian

Davis Starnes, buried in plot H-27. She married William Hartwell Spencer in 1927, and they share a common grave location.

[A-163: no stones]

[A-165: Frost, King, Norton, Thornhill, Wactor, Wroten]

- Eva *Wactor* King [June 3, 1892 – March 4, 1956], "Mother." After marrying Mr. King, Eva married G. W. Norton in 1931.
- Jess J. Frost [Feb. 14, 1911 – Oct. 10, 1946]
- Edward A. Frost [May 7, 1930 – Jun. 25, 1992], "CPL, US ARMY, KOREA." This is a military stone.
- George Warren Wroten [June 2, 1900 – Nov. 18, 1986]. George is the son of Eugene W. and Misouria E. *Walters* Wroten, buried in plot H-5. His first wife, Maude *Shannon* Wroten, is buried in plot H-5.
- Amy Dell *(King)* Wroten [Feb. 27, 1915 – Jan. 30, 1992], "Mother." Amy is the daughter of Eva *Wactor* King. She married George Warren Wroten in 1956. She had previously been married to a Mr. Frost.
- Charles L. Thornhill [Feb. 25, 1931 – Sept. 2, 1995]

[A-168/177: Foulks, Gage]

- John Rollins Gage [January 2, 1916 – May 18, 1993]. John and his brother Howell Nicholson Gage, listed below, are sons of James Vertner and Leah *Nicholson* Gage, buried in combined plot A-67/76/77/167/178/188.
- Alice *Foulks* Gage [March 30, 1918 – July 12, 2002]. Alice is the wife of John Rollins Gage, and they share a common stone.
- Howell Nicholson Gage [June 17, 1917 – May 11, 1974]. Besides his son listed below, Howell has a daughter, Leah *Gage* Hynum Torrey, buried in plot A-187.
- Richard Vertner Gage [August 12, 1961 – June 3, 1979]. Richard is the son of Howell Nicholson Gage.

[A-169/176: Gage]

- Robert Douglass Gage, III [Jan. 29, 1921 – July 21, 1991]. Robert is the son of Robert Douglass and Elizabeth *Massie* Gage, buried in combined plot A-67/76/77/167/178/188.

[A-170/175: Luebbers, Spencer, Truluck]

- Hazel Richard Truluck [Oct. 24, 1904 – April 7, 1961]
- Ann *Spencer* Truluck [Aug. 11, 1914 – Dec. 31, 1993]. Ann and her sister, Margaret *Spencer* Luebbers, listed below, are daughters of Meredith Jones and Lillie *Mason* Spencer, buried in plot B-42. Ann married Hazel Richard Truluck in 1935.
- Margaret *Spencer* Luebbers [Feb. 2, 1916 – May 23, 1968]. Margaret married Lawrence Francis Luebbers in 1944.

[A-171: no stones]

[A-172/173: Goodwin, Morehead]

- Grover Salter Goodwin [April 19, 1916 – November 11, 1996]
- Mary Sessions *Morehead* Goodwin [November 9, 1922 – June 5, 2010]. Mary is the daughter of Richard Sessions and Mildred *O'Connor* Morehead, buried in plot A-74. She married Grover Goodwin in 1943, and they share a common stone.

[A-174: Bearden, Gates, Trevilion]

- Henry Howell Gates [Jan. 25, 1905 – Aug. 3, 1968]
- Martha *Bearden* Gates [Apr. 14, 1908 – Apr. 5, 1994]. Martha and her sister, Flora *Bearden* Trevilion, listed below, are daughters of Norman Cooper and Martha *Utz* Bearden, buried in plot A-57. Martha married Henry Howell Gates in 1927.
- Thomas H. Trevilion [1907 – 1965]. Thomas is the son of John T. and Laura C. *Emrick* Trevilion, buried in plot H-29.
- Flora *B(earden)*. Trevilion [1906 – 1992]. Flora married Thomas H. Trevilion in 1931.

- John B. Trevilion [July 24, 1934 – May 13, 2013]. John is the son of Thomas H. and Flora *Bearden* Trevilion.
- Thomas H. Trevilion, III [1964 – 1965]

[A-178: no stones]

[A-180: Bryant, Cochran, Cressman, Fife, Hustind, Porterpan, Simms, Van, Williams]

- Esther *(Fife)* Cochran [January 1, 1885 – April 9, 1951]. Esther married Eddie Bryant in 1903, James D. Simms in 1912 and Joseph Porterpan in 1914. She later married Mr. Cochran.
- James D. Williams [May 16, 1874 – Oct. 25, 1946]
- Lula *(Fife)* Van Williams [Dec. 4, 1890 – Mar. 22, 1977]. This stone is rather misleading, because neither Lula's maiden name nor her final last name are found on the stone. Her maiden name is FIFE, and she is a sister to Esther *Fife* Cochran, listed above. Lula married L. Cressman in 1908, and they have a son, Louis Cressman, buried in Hermanville Cemetery. She later married James D. Williams, and they share a common stone. She later married Tom Hustind in 1956, and HUSTIND is her final last name. At one point she was married to a Mr. Van.

[A-181: no stones]

[A-182: no stones]

[A-183: no stones]

[A-184: Stampley, Walton]

- Walter C. Stampley [August 5, 1883 – July 7, 1955], a Mason.
- Allah Eloise *(Walton)* Stampley [January 18, 1894 – November 21, 1952], member Order of the Eastern Star. Allah is the daughter of James Thomas and Lena Ann *Norwood* Walton, buried in Shiloh Baptist Church Cemetery. She married Walter C. Stampley in 1915, and they share a common stone.
- Walter J. Stampley [April 21, 1916 – June 7, 1945], a Mason, "Husband." Walter is the son of Walter C. and Allah Eloise *Walton* Stampley. He married Q. B. Anderson in 1935. Q. B. is buried in combined plot M-44/45, with the last name of TANNER.

[A-185: Ayo, Berner, Rogers, Sink, Zerlin]

- Forrest Sink [1863 – 1952]. Forrest married Ada Wood in 1888.
- Lottie *Rogers* Sink [1896 – 1971]. Lottie is the daughter of George C. and Martha *Harrell* Rogers, buried in Hedrick Cemetery.
- Cora *Sink* Berner [1915 – 2006]. Cora and her sister, Rubye, listed below, are daughters of Lottie *Rogers* Sink.
- Rubye *S(ink)*. Ayo [April 5, 1921 – December 24, 2011]
- Betty Twomey Zerlin [1932 – 1996]

[A-186: no stones]

[A-187: Gage, Hynum, Torrey]

- Marvin Winfred "Skeeter" Hynum [Nov. 25, 1947 – Sept. 3, 2007]. Marvin is the son of Julius W. and Ada *Fife* Hynum. Julius is buried in Hynum Cemetery.
- Leah "Libba" *Gage* Hynum Torrey [Jan. 27, 1949 – Apr. 22, 2013]. Leah is the daughter of Howell Nicholson Gage, buried in combined plot A-168/177. She married Marvin Hynum in 1970. After his death she married a Mr. Torrey.

[A-188: not used]

Section B

[B 1: Cockbaine, Gray, Reid]
- Henry Cockbaine [died Aug. 26, 1868, aged 67 years]
- John S. Gray [died July 1, 1854, aged 40 years], "a native of Butler Co. Ohio."
- Andrew W. Reid [May 22, 1800 – Sept. 24, 1853], "died of yellow fever."
- Samuel D. Reid [Nov. 4, 183? – Sept. 8, 1853], "son of A. W. & Rhody Reid...died of yellow fever."

[B-2: Sprott, Thompson, Wilson]
- Charles W. Wilson, M. D. [Aug. 8, 1810 – Sept. 23, 1852], a Mason, "born in Hickman Co. Tenn...and died in Port Gibson."
- Elizabeth *(Thompson)* Wilson [Aug. 14, 1811 – Sept. 29, 1852], "wife of Charles W. Wilson, who was born in Claiborne Co. Miss...and died in Port Gibson." Elizabeth married Charles W. Wilson in 1833, and they share a common obelisk.
- John Wilson [March 26, 1836 – December 7, 1854]
- Lucy Wilson [August 29, 1848 – July 26, 1854]
- Charles Wilson [no dates], "Our little Charlie has left us." This short inscription is the only information on the stone. An old funeral notice tells us that Charlie's middle initial was "W," that he was the infant son of Dr. C. W. and Elizabeth Wilson, and that his funeral was on the afternoon of August 15, 1848.
- James T. Sprott [Mar. 22, 1852 – Nov. 28, 1915]
- Nancy *W(ilson)*. Sprott [Sept. 28, 1852 – Aug. 25, 1924]. Nancy married James T. Sprott in 1875, and they share a common stone. Besides Frederick, listed below, other children are Charles Elder Sprott, buried in plot A-131, and Bernard Sprott in Port Gibson Catholic Cemetery.
- Frederick M. Sprott [Oct. 7, 1892 – Feb. 9, 1945]. Frederick is the son of James T. and Nancy *Wilson* Sprott. He married Mrs. Jeanette Butler in 1915.
- James Malcolm Sprott [Nov. 6, 1920 – March 21, 1921], "son of F. M. and J. R. Sprott."

"Thou art gone to the grave, but we will not deplore thee;
Though sorrows and darkness encompass the tomb,
The Saviour has passed through it portals before thee.
And the lamp of His love is thy guide through the gloom."
—on obelisk of Charles W. Wilson

Section B

6	5	4	3	2	1
7	8	9	10	11	12
18	17	16	15	14	13
19	20	21	22	23	24
30	29	28	27	26	25
31	32	33	34	35	36
42	41	40	39	38	37
43	44	45	46	47	48
54	53	52	51	50	49
55	56	57	58	59	60

N

[B-3: Acree, Foster, Saunders, Sillers, Stuart]
- Josiah Foster [April 13, 1808 – March 31, 1852], "Brother...born at Pittsgrove N. J...died in Port Gibson Miss."
- William Sillers [May 31, 1816 – Mar. 30, 1891]
- Ann Caroline *Stuart* Sillers [Feb. 17, 1823 – Nov. 9, 1875], "wife of William Sillers."
- The following four SILLERS names share a common obelisk with William and Caroline *Stuart* Sillers.
- James Sillers [June 4, 1843 – Oct. 8, 1870]
- William Sillers, Jr. [Aug. 9, 1846 – Nov. 10, 1884]
- Jeannie C. Sillers [Sept 18, 1858 – Dec. 27, 1866]
- Beauregard Sillers [July 24, 1861 – Oct. 10, 1861]
- Webster J. Saunders [1844 – 1915]
- Fannie *Sillers* Saunders [1850 – 1906]. Fannie and Webster share a common stone.
- F. M. Acree [May 13, 1850 – Jan. 7, 1895]
- Mary B. Acree [Feb. 6, 1849 – Dec. 5, 1895], "wife of F. M. Acree." F. M. and Mary B. Acree share a common obelisk.

"The church yard hath an added stone,
and heaven one spirit more."
—on obelisk of William Sillers

[B-4: Sayer] This lot contains a lone C. S. A. stone, whose owner cannot be identified.
- William D. Sayer [Sep. 21, 1817 – Jan. 21, 1853], "born in Newport R. I." William married Harriet B. Watson in 1847.
- William Watson Sayer [Dec. 10, 1848 – Sep. 4, 1850], "eldest child of W. D. & H. B. Sayer."
- Percy G. Sayer [died Feb. 27, 1853, aged 7 mos. & 10 days], "son of W. D. & H. B. Sayer."

[B-5: Hedrick, Long, Miller, Wade]
- Thomas H. Wade [Feb. 5, 1806 – Sept. 13, 1853]. Thomas was a victim of the yellow fever epidemic.
- Rachel *(Hedrick)* Wade [Aug. 9, 1812 – Aug. 23, 1853], "wife of Thomas H. Wade." Rachel married Thomas H. Wade in 1829, and they share a common stone.
- Albert M. Miller [died July 8, 1910]
- Alice *L(ong)*. Miller [died Jan. 8, 1913]. Alice married Albert Miller in 1871.

[B-6: Bridgers, English, Hall, Hilliard, Humphreys, Johnson, McNeil, Megrew, Miller]
- C. R. Megrew [Feb. 6, 1825 – May 1, 1888], member Independent Order of Odd Fellows, "an honest man" and "Erected by his sister."
- M. Rebecca Megrew [1819 – June 7, 1901]. M. Rebecca is the sister of C. R. Megrew. She specified in her last will and testament: "it is my will that my body be buried decently in the Port Gibson Cemetery and that a neat stone be erected over my last resting place, similar to the one that marks my brother's grave." Her will was carried out.
- Rev. George Hall [June 4, 1804 – Sept. 4, 1878], "born in Keene N. H. of English ancestry...died of yellow fever at Port Gibson Miss."
- Kate *(McNeil)* Humphreys Hilliard [Sept. 3, 1847 – June 8, 1904]. Kate's relationship status can best be described by a "Looking Back" column from <u>The Port Gibson Reveille</u>: THIS WEEK, 1904, "Mrs. Kate H. Hilliard, 57, nee McNeil, died on June 8th at the home of her son, Mr. E. A. Humphreys. Widow of the late Sampson B. Humphreys, she is survived by her second husband, Mr. H. B. Hilliard..."
- Sampson Bridgers [June 19, 1838 – Apr. 5, 1914], "Father." Sampson is the son of Margaret *Humphreys*

Bridgers, buried in Alfred Barnes Cemetery. He is a Civil War veteran and, according to Mississippi Confederate Grave Registration records, was a private in Co. A, 4th Miss. Regt. Cavalry, and he died of old age.

- Nellie *English* Bridgers [Nov. 25, 1842 – May 30, 1914], "Mother" and "wife of Sampson Bridgers." Nellie is the daughter of William D. and Ann *Patton* English, buried in plot B-24. She married Sampson Bridgers in 1859, and they share a common stone. Besides Benjamin H. Bridgers, listed below, a daughter, Mary Ophelia *Bridgers* Bridgers is buried in plot G-45.
- Eugene Erthy Johnson, Sr. [Dec. 16, 1896 – Mar. 25, 1966]
- Nellie *Bridgers* Johnson [Sept. 20, 1896 – Dec. 28, 1974]. Nellie is the daughter of D. I. and Mary Ophelia *Bridgers* Bridgers, buried in plot G-45. She is the wife of Eugene Erthy Johnson, and they share a common stone.
- Benjamin H. Bridgers [1860 – 1907], "son of Sampson & Nellie Bridgers."
- Margaret Harrison Miller [1865 – 1937]

[B-7/18: Bertron, Green, Humphreys, Maury, Owen, Smith]

- Col. Ralph Humphreys [1735 – 1789]. This is a memorial stone. The entire inscription reads: "In memory of Col. Ralph Humphreys, Revolutionary Soldier, died in Claiborne Co. Erected by Ralph Humphreys Chapter National Society Daughters of the American Revolution, 1905." Col. Humphreys' actual burial spot is believed to be in or around Grindstone Ford Cemetery, just off the Natchez Trace Parkway in Claiborne County.
- James H. Maury [Sep. 18, 1796 – June 1, 1874]
- Lucinda *(Smith)* Maury [May 6, 1804 – April 11, 1876]. According to Bible records, Lucinda married James H. Maury in 1822. They share a common obelisk with the inscription: "To our beloved parents." Besides those listed below, a daughter, Elizabeth *Maury* Harding, is buried in plot B-31.
- Benjamin G. Humphreys [1808 – 1882]. Benjamin Grubb Humphreys is the son of George Wilson and Sarah *Smith* Humphreys, buried in Humphreys Cemetery. He first married Mary McLaughlin in 1832, and she, too, is buried in Humphreys Cemetery, along with their son, Thomas McLaughlin Humphreys. Mr. Humphreys is noteworthy, in that he served as a Confederate officer in the Civil War, and served the State of Mississippi as governor during the Reconstruction Era. When northern control of government was established, Mr. Humphreys was forcibly removed from office, refusing to voluntarily leave the office he was elected to serve. He also has a military stone, located in Soldiers Row of this cemetery. According to Mississippi Confederate Grave Registration records, he rose from Captain, to Colonel, to Brigadier General in Co. I, 21st Miss. Regt., attached to the Army of Virginia.
- Mildred *Maury* Humphreys [1823 – 1899]. Mildred is the daughter of James H. and Lucinda *Smith* Maury. She married Benjamin Grubb Humphreys in 1839, and they share a common stone.
- Julian Maury Humphreys [Oct. 18, 1840 – July 12, 1849]
- Sarah Smith Humphreys [Feb. 10, 1843 – Sep. 25, 1845]. Julian and Sarah Humphreys share a common stone with the inscription: "Children of B. G. & M. H. Humphreys."
- James Maury Humphreys [Oct. 28, 1845 – Sept. 3, 1851]
- Benjamin George Humphreys [Jun. 15, 1848 – July 26, 1852]. James and Benjamin Humphreys share a common stone with the inscription: "Children of B. G. & M. H. Humphreys."
- Elizabeth Fontaine *Humphreys* Bertron [June 25, 1856 – Oct. 22, 1878]. Elizabeth is the daughter of Benjamin Grubb and Mildred *Maury* Humphreys. According to Humphreys Genealogy and Bible records, she married James Crane Bertron, buried in plot F-4, in 1878. She was a victim of the yellow fever epidemic.
- Anne Maury [no dates]
- Julian Maury [no dates]

- Lucy Maury [no dates]. Anne, Julian and Lucy Maury share a common stone with the inscription: "Children of J. H. & L. Maury, 1850."
- William Maury [no dates]
- Philip Maury [no dates]. William and Philip Maury share a common stone with the inscription: "Children of James H. & L. Maury."
- James Fontaine Maury [July 21, 1842 – April 22, 1875]. James is the son of James H. and Lucinda *Smith* Maury. He is a Civil War veteran and, according to Mississippi Confederate Grave Registration records, he served as Captain in 21st Miss. Regt. Infantry Army of Northern Virginia, and died of heart trouble.
- Elizabeth *Owen* Maury [Feb. 2, 1847 – Feb. 15, 1920]. Elizabeth is the wife of James Fontaine Maury.
- Franklin Hervey Maury [Jan. 27, 1875 – Dec. 17, 1892]. Franklin is the son of James Fontaine Maury. The name of Franklin's mother is unclear.
- Mildred Green [Dec. 1, 1861 – Oct. 23, 1864], "daughter of A. A. & C. Green." Mildred's parents are Abram A. and Caroline *Maury* Green.

[B-8: Baldwin, McDougall, McEvers, Moore]
- Parene *McEvers* McDougall [Oct. 17, 1840 – Sept. 5, 1876], "wife of John McDougall of New Orleans."
- Lemuel N. Baldwin [died July 24, 1893]
- Mary J. *(McDougall)* Baldwin [died May 13, 1899], "His wife." Mary is the daughter of Nicholas and Elizabeth McDougall, buried in plot B-16. She married Judge Lemuel N. Baldwin in 1842, and they share a common stone.
- William H. Moore [1838 – 1878], C. S. A. stone. According to Mississippi Confederate Grave Registration records, William was a Private in Co. K, 12th Miss. Infantry and Co. I, 21st Miss. Infantry, and he died of yellow fever.
- Ada *McDougall* Moore [July 21, 1844 – Nov. 25, 1925]. Ada is the daughter of Duncan McDougall, buried in plot B-16. She married William H. Moore in 1865. From the book, *Claiborne County, Mississippi, The Promised Land*, by Katy McCaleb Headley, a footnote tells of these rather gruesome yellow fever casualties: "…William Moore, and his little children died in this epidemic in Port Gibson and…the wife, Ada McDougall Moore, dug the graves and buried her dead alone."
- Ella Moore [Apr. 1866 – Sept. 1878]. Ella is the daughter of William H. and Ada *McDougall* Moore.
- Duncan Moore [1871 – 1878]. Duncan is the son of William H. and Ada *McDougall* Moore.

[B-9: Johnston, Jones, Meug, Tilden, West]
- Benjamin F. West [March 13, 1805 – August 22, 1845]
- Mrs. Paulina *Meug* West [died November 1, 1833, aged 25 years 8 mo's & 13 days], "wife of Benjamin F. West, and youngest daughter of George and Mary Meug of Louisville Kentucky." A biographical epitaph reads: "She lived believing in Christ, and died full of hope, having numerous relatives and friends to mourn her early loss." Paulina married Benjamin F. West in 1828.
- Thomas Franklin West [died August 27, 1834, aged 15 mo's and 4 days]
- M. D. Tilden [died Jan. 15, 1855]
- Gabriella *Johnston* Tilden [Aug. 3, 1816 – Jan. 26, 1908], "Mother." Gabriella was second the wife of Benjamin F. West. After his death she married Marmaduke D. Tilden in 1849.
- Benjamin F. West, M. D. [Feb. 27, 1843 – Feb. 17, 1872], C. S. A. stone.
- Ely Ross Jones [1840 – 1916], C. S. A. stone, "Father."
- Mary *West* Jones [1844 – 1926], "Mother." Mary married Ely Jones in 1868, and they share a common stone.
- Walter Cato West [died Nov. 25, 1839, aged 2 years, 4 months & 23 days], "son of Benjamin F. & Gabriela (sic) I. West."
- Emily McIntyre Tilden [died Oct. 18, 1853, aged 3 yrs, 5 months], "daughter of M. D. & G. J. Tilden."

- Marmaduke Tilden [July 23, 1851 – Apr. 19, 1852], "son of M. D. & G. J. Tilden."
- Belle Tevis Tilden [died Feb. 11, 1942]

"The God of love will sure indulge,
The flowing tear, the heaving sigh;
When righteous persons all around
When tender friends and kindred die."
—on stone of Mrs. Paulina *Meug* West

[B-10: Maxwell, Turpin]. Besides the stones listed below, there exists another tall stone with the words: "To My Children."
- Dr. James Maxwell [Sept. 25, 1779 – Dec. 9, 1823]
- Emma S. *(Maxwell)* Turpin [May 8, 1821 – Oct. 16, 1853]. Emma married David H. Turpin in 1837. A son, Pike Maxwell Turpin, is buried in Grand Gulf Cemetery.
- L. P. Maxwell [Sept. 20, 1814 – July 13, 1855]

[B-11: Brewer, Eisely, Hartge, Manion, Nourse, Randolph, Westcott]. This lot was established as Wintergreen Cemetery's Fraternity Section. Though none of these men appear to be related to each other, they all seem to be of high profession and/or members of fraternal organizations.
- George J. Westcott, M. D. [Nov. 7, 1812 – Sept. 22, 1846], "born at Milford, Otsego Co. New York… died at Port Gibson."
- Hon. William M. Randolph [died Feb. 20, 1850, aged 37 years], member Independent Order of Odd Fellows, "…of Virginia, for 16 years a citizen of Miss. and at his death Probate Judge of Claiborne Co." A biographical epitaph reads: "He was honest, amiable, charitable, an upright and incorruptible judge, a useful and honored citizen."
- William F. Eisely [July 11, 1814 – May 6, 1856], a Mason and member Independent Order of Odd Fellows, "born…in Sunbury, Pa."
- Emilius Brewer [May 6, 1823 – April 5, 1855], a Mason and member Independent Order of Odd Fellows, "born in Wilbraham, Mass…died at Port Gibson, Miss."
- Levine G. Hartge [died Dec. 30, 1851, in the 28th year of his age], "professor of music in the Port Gibson Female Academy." A biographical epitaph reads: "This monument is erected as a tribute of respect to Professor Hartge, by his pupils, friends, and members of Franklin Lodge No. 5, I. O. O. F."
- Willard A. Nourse [April 4, 1825 – Sep. 6, 1853], member Independent Order of Odd Fellows. A biographical epitaph reads: "He was an honest man and sincere friend." Willard was a victim of the yellow fever epidemic.
- Valentine Manion [died Oct. 30, 1860, aged 25 years], member Independent Order of Odd Fellows.

[B-12: Fulkerson, McBryde, Starkey]
- Horace S. Fulkerson [April 28, 1818 – April 5, 1891]
- Charlotte E. *(McBryde)* Fulkerson [Oct. 8, 1825 – May 6, 1914]. Charlotte married Horace Fulkerson in 1845.
- A. C. Fulkerson [Oct. 21, 1852 – May 19, 1939]
- Graeme Fulkerson [died July 13, 1856, aged 3 years 20 days], "son of H. S. & C. E. Fulkerson." This small stone has a little bit of significance in that a photograph of its likeness was chosen, either by the famous Mississippi author Eudora Welty herself or an editor/publisher, to grace the cover of her book, *Country Churchyards*, a photographic collection of her visits to old burial grounds in the area.
- Miss Jennie Fulkerson [July 6, 1861 – Dec. 14, 1943]
- Joseph Starkey [May 10, 1811 – Dec. 28, 1849], "a native of Castlemorton, Worcestershire, England."

[B-13: Bolls, Chambliss, Richardson, Sharbrough, Wilkinson]. This lot has one lone C. S. A. stone whose owner cannot be identified.

- Col. Leonard Covington Wilkinson [died March 18, 1848, in the 34th year of his age]. A biographical epitaph reads: "He was a highly respected citizen, an indulgent master, a kind father, and an affectionate husband. He has left a widow, and only son, to deplore their irreparable loss."
- Mrs. Mary D. *(Chambliss)* Richardson [Oct. 8, 1825 – June 26, 1882], "daughter of Gen. P. C. & Drusilla Chambliss, wife of the late Dr. R. E. Richardson." Mary married Col. Leonard Wilkinson in 1846. After his death she married Dr. Robert E. Richardson in 1854.
- Elizziebeth N. *Bolls* Chambliss [June 24, 1829 – Dec. 13, 1901], "Our Mother" and "wife of Cortez Chambliss." Elizziebeth married Cortez Chambliss in 1847.
- Ella Susan Chambliss [Jan. 26, 1850 – July 9, 1853], "daughter of Cortez & E. N. Chambliss."
- Elizabeth *C(hambliss).* Sharbrough [July 9, 1857 – June 5, 1920], "wife of F. W. Sharbrough." Elizabeth is the daughter of Cortez and Elizziebeth *Bolls* Chambliss. She married F. W. Sharbrough in 1888.
- Bessie May Chambliss [Feb. 7, 1888 – June 1, 1890], "daughter of Q. W. & M. L. Chambliss."
- Lillie Elizziebeth Chambliss [July 19, 1891 – Sept. 11, 1901], "first dau. of A. P. & I. A. Chambliss."

[B-14: Harper, Lyles, Maxwell]

- Sarah M. *Lyles* Harper [died April 17, 1839], "wife of R. W. Harper and daughter of Col. Wm. & Sarah Lyles."
- James Harper [died June 2, 1840, at 17 years]. James' stone has the inscription: "Erected by his sisters."
- James Maxwell [born & died May 1, 1841]
- John Maxwell [Feb. 23, 1845 – Aug. 22, 1845]. James and John share a common stone with the inscription, "Children of Jas. A. & Sarah M. Maxwell."

[B-15: Anderson, Brashear, Harper, Hughes, McAlpine, Morehead, Sessions]

- B. Hughes [died July 7, 1842, in the 54th year of his age]
- Nancy *Brashear* Hughes [Jan. 7, 1797 – Dec. 29, 1875], "wife of Benjamin Hughes."
- Henry Hughes [Apr. 17, 1829 – Oct. 3, 1862], C. S. A. stone. According to Mississippi Confederate Grave Registration records, Henry served as Captain and Colonel in Co. H, 12th Miss. Infantry and Co. D, 4th Miss. Cavalry, and was killed in battle.
- B. W. Morehead [died April 23, 1844, aged 33 years]
- Robert W. Harper, M. D. [1792 – 1867]. Robert married his first wife, Catherine C. Archer, in 1841.
- Mary Ann *Hughes* Morehead-Harper [1821 – 1876]. Mary's first husband was B. W. Morehead. After his death she married Dr. Robert W. Harper in 1859.
- Daniel Vertner McAlpine [July 21, 1837 – Dec. 5, 1907], C. S. A. stone.
- Julia T. *Morehead* McAlpine [Mar. 27, 1840 – Jan 24, 1905], "wife of D. Vertner McAlpin (sic)." Julia is the daughter of B. W. and Mary Ann *Hughes* Morehead. She married Daniel Vertner McAlpine in 1861. They have four children, Edward Kirby McAlpine, Benjamin Morehead McAlpine, Charles Morehead McAlpine and Mary *McAlpine* Bagnell, all buried in plot C-29.
- Benjamin H. Morehead [July 31, 1841 – Nov. 28, 1892]. Benjamin is the son of B. W. and Mary Ann *Hughes* Morehead.
- Mary *Sessions* Morehead [Oct. 23, 1845 – April 15, 1918], "wife of Benj. H. Morehead." Mary married Benjamin Hughes Morehead in 1869. Besides their sons listed below, other offspring include Richard Sessions Morehead and Benjamin Hughes Morehead, buried in plot A-74, and Maria *Morehead* Anderson, buried in plot F-28.
- Ben Morehead Anderson [June 23, 1901 – March 21, 1905]. Ben is the son of Robert Buckner Anderson, buried in plot I-38, and Maria *Morehead* Anderson in plot F-28.
- Robert Harper Morehead [Dec. 18, 1869 – Aug. 27, 1903]. Robert is the son of Benjamin H. and Mary

Sessions Morehead.

- W. H. Morehead [Dec. 17, 1880 – Nov. 28, 1927]. William Hughes Morehead is the son of Benjamin H. and Mary Sessions Morehead. He married Mrs. Eliza B. Floweree in 1915.
- Henry Walton Morehead [died June 7, 1844, aged 13 months], "infant son of Mary A. & the late B. W. Morehead."

[B-16: Baldwin, Freeman, McDougall]

- Hon. Nicholas McDougall [March 4, 1781 – Nov. 5, 1851], "born at Schenectady N. Y...died at Port Gibson."
- Elizabeth McDougall [Oct. 17, 1785 – July 22, 1850], "wife of Hon. N. McDougall, born at Hillsdale N. Y...died at Port Gibson." Nicholas and Elizabeth share a common obelisk. Besides those listed below, they have a daughter, Mary Jane *McDougall* Baldwin, buried in plot B-8.
- Duncan McDougall [died March 13, 1850, aged 39 years 6 mo. & 15 days]. Duncan is the son of Nicholas and Elizabeth McDougall. His children include a daughter, Ada *McDougall* Moore, buried in plot B-8, and Nickolas McDougall in plot A-107.
- Kate Aubrey McDougall [Oct. 5, 1840 – Dec. 1, 1925]. Kate is the daughter of Duncan McDougall.
- Crovolin McDougall [died Sept. 15, 1830, aged 13 years 9 months and 15 days], "daughter of N. and E. McDougall, born in Duanesburg, State of New York."
- Ann *McDougall* Freeman [Sept. 1, 1885 – Dec. 11, 1965]. Ann is the daughter of Nickolas and Alice *Magruder* McDougall, buried in plot A-107. She married Guy C. Freeman in 1908.
- Charles H. Baldwin [July 31, 1834 – May 14, 1854], "eldest son of Orrin & Sarah Baldwin, of Atwater Ohio...died in New Orleans." A memorial epitaph reads: "Erected by his uncle who loved him when living, and mourned him when dead."

[B-17: Dakin, Foote, Heath, McVoy, Perkins, Roberts, Watson]

- Joseph McVoy [Oct. 24, 1796 – Jan. 18, 1845], a Mason, "born in Lexington District South Carolina." His memorial reads: "A memorial by an affectionate wife."
- Thomas Jenkins Dakin [March 1, 1817 – April 10, 1883], "born in Hudson, N. Y."
- Martha *McVoy* Dakin [February 12, 1827 – April 23, 1864], "wife of T. J. Dakin, born in Lexington District, S. C." Martha is the first wife of Thomas Dakin. They married in 1845, and they share a common obelisk.
- Socrates Dakin [Sept. 15, 1846 – July 8, 1849], "eldest son of Thomas J. & Martha Dakin."
- Robert Dakin [July 12, 1851 – Sept. 12, 1851], "infant son of Thomas J. & Martha Dakin." Socrates and Robert Dakin share a common stone.
- Eliza Eugenia *Watson* Dakin [June 19, 1830 – Mar. 10, 1917]. This stone is inscribed with the words: "To My Wife." Eliza is Thomas Dakin's second wife, marrying in 1867.
- Adolph Heath [died Oct. 14, 1853, aged 82 years 7 m's & 13 d's], "a native of Penn., died in Claiborne Co. Miss."
- Julia Ann Heath [died Oct. 4, 1853, aged 73 years 11 m's & 19 d's], "wife of Adolph Heath, a native of Penn., died in Claiborne Co. Miss." Julia and Adolph share a common stone with the inscriptions: "Our Father and Mother" and "Erected by their children." She was a victim of the yellow fever epidemic.
- Joel Perkins [Apr. 6,1806 – June 6, 1884]
- Elizabeth Roberts *(Heath)* Perkins [Mar. 15, 1806 – Dec. 24, 1893], "wife of Joel Perkins." Elizabeth Heath married Joel Perkins in 1838. It is unclear if the name ROBERTS is her middle name or a previous married name.
- Pinkard M. Perkins [Dec. 27, 1835 – Nov 10, 1886], C. S. A. stone, "son of Joel & Elizabeth Perkins." Pinkard, along with his father and mother, share a common obelisk. According to Mississippi Confederate Grave Registration records, he was a Private in Co. F, 48th Miss. Infantry and Co. F, 2nd Miss. In-

fantry.

- Virginia *F(oote)*. Perkins [1847 – 1916]. Virginia married Pinkard M. Perkins in 1867.
- J. D. McVoy [March 8, 1858 – Oct. 10, 1861]
- W. J. McVoy [June 27, 1850 – Oct. 16, 1861]
- J. McVoy [Jan. 25, 1852 – Oct. 21, 1861]. J. D., W. J. and J. McVoy all share a common stone with inscription: "Children of W. J. & S. A. McVoy." (W. J. McVoy married Sarah A. Heath in 1849.)

[B-19: Dorsey, Duval, Light, Montgomery, Rotrock, Stampley]

- Julia L. Montgomery [died April 28, 1850, aged 33 years], "wife of Rev. H. H. Montgomery. A native of Greensborough, N. C. She died in Port Gibson, Miss." Her memorial reads: "Erected by her husband."
- Gertrude Caroline Rotrock [died Sept. 20, 1851, in the 32 year of her age], "consort of D. S. Rotrock, a native of Greene Co. N. Y."
- William Henry Rotrock [July 31, 1840 – Nov. 25, 1851], "son of D. S. & G. C. Rotrock: born in Natchez...died in Port Gibson."
- Gabriel Duval [died Oct 3, 1855, aged 45 years]
- Henrietta Duval [died June 4, 1853, aged 44 years]. Gabriel and Henrietta share a common stone.
- Margaret M. *(Duval)* Light [Mar. 15, 1838 – June 20, 1912], "Mother." Margaret married Edward B. Dorsey in 1855, William Stampley in 1862 and J. R. Light in 1879. She and William Stampley have a daughter, Elizabeth *Stampley* Watson, buried in plot H-1.

"Rest thee loved one, we have laid thee,
In the cold and silent grave,
Tears perfume the bed we made thee,
Soon thy abode we'll have to brave.
With sad hearts we must leave thee,
Lonely do all things appear,
But hope tells us we shall meet thee,
In Paradise to us, most dear."
—on stone of Gertrude Caroline Rotrock

[B-20: Booth, Ewing, Harrington, Rhodes]. This lot contains one C. S. A. stone whose owner cannot be identified.

- Sarah Rhodes [died Oct. 8, 1853, in the 65th year of her age], "wife of Thomas Rhodes, died of yellow fever."
- Sally Ann Ewing [died July 27, 1844, in her 9th year], "daughter of John & Sarah Ewing."
- Matilda Elizabeth Ewing [died March 15, 1846, in her 8th year], "daughter of John & Sarah Ewing."
- John Thomas Ewing [died March 15, 1848, aged 7 days], "son of John & Sarah Ewing."
- Joseph Benjamin Ewing [died Sept. 6, 1852, aged 3 years 5 m. & 16 d.], "son of John & Sarah Ewing."
- Anna E. *(Harrington)* Booth [Feb. 28, 1828 – April 14, 1852], "wife of Benj. F. Booth." Anna married Benjamin F. Booth in 1847.

[B-21: Donald, Dunbar, Harris, Jefferies, Sager, Sevier]. This family name of SEVIER is rich in history, in that James Thomas Sevier is the grandson of John Sevier, an American soldier, frontiersman and politician, and the first governor of Tennessee. This lot also contains two C. S. A. stones whose owners cannot be identified.

- James Thomas Sevier [Mar. 11, 1814 – Sept. 9, 1836], "son of George W. & Catharine H. Sevier, of Tennessee."
- Eliza *Sevier* Jefferies [Dec. 21, 1848 – Nov. 29, 1919]. Eliza married William T. Jefferies in 1868.
- John Sevier Donald [died March 13, 1850, aged 20 mo's & 21 days], "son of John T. & Eliza M. Don-

ald."
- Sarah Knox Sevier [Aug. 25, 1868 – May 26, 1890]
- Isaac Dunbar [July 17, 1861 – May 13, 1863], "son of R. J. S. & Mary K. Dunbar"
- Sadie K. *(Harris)* Sager [1880 – 1969]. Sadie married George H. Sager in 1908.

"There is no fireside however defended,
But hath one vacant chair;
There is no fold, however tended,
But one dead lamb is there."
—on stone of Isaac Dunbar

[B-22: Atchison, Estes, Girault, Lobdell, Parkinson, Stowers]. This plot contains one C. S. A. stone whose owner cannot be identified.

This plot contains, among the others graves, a large raised slab whose wording as to its contents is best quoted, rather than listed. The words inscribed on this slab are: "Beneath this slab in one grave lie the remains of:
- John Lobdell. Born May 16, 1782: died Sept. 10, 1827, also
- Mary, Born March 3, 1792. She was married to John Lobdell, Sept. 15, 1808. Married a second time to William Estes, in 1828, and died Jan. 6, 1835. And four of their children whose remains were removed from Warren Co., Miss. to this place in 1846.
- Joshua Lobdell. Born July 3, 1815, died Dec. 15, 1816.
- Isaac Elum Lobdell. Born April 8, 1817, died May 23, 1831.
- Martha Margaret Lobdell. Born Oct. 8, 1820, died Oct. 30, 1836.
- Eliza Mary Lobdell. Born March 20, 1822, died Sept. 2, 1822.
Erected by their surviving children as a tribute of respect to the Best of Parents."

Other stones in this lot are:
- Jonathan Conger Lobdell [Apr. 16, 1813 – Aug. 19, 1852]
- Col. George R. Girault [Apr. 13, 1815 – Dec. 13, 1857]. Col. Girault first married Henrietta McCaleb in 1833. They have a daughter, Elizabeth *Girault* Shaifer, buried in plot C-61.
- Richard Parkinson [no dates]
- Emily J. *(Stowers)* Parkinson [no dates], "His Wife" and "Erected by John R. Parkinson." Emily married three times: first to Jonathan Conger Lobdell, then to Col. George R. Girault in 1854, and finally to Richard Parkinson in 1861, with whom she shares a common monument. A son, John Richard Parkinson, is buried in plot B-29.
- Infant Son Lobdell [1843], "infant son of J. C. & E. J. Lobdell."
- Louie E. Lobdell [May 15, 1848 – Oct. 12, 1854], "son of J. C. & E. J. Lobdell."
- James Noble Lobdell [March 1, 1850 – Aug. 5, 1855]. James is the son of Jonathan Conger and Emily J. *Stowers* Lobdell. Besides these listed, Jonathan and Emily have a daughter, Juliet C. *Lobdell* Stowers, buried in plot B-26.
- George Elvyne Girault [July 4, 1855 – Aug. 4, 1856]. George is the son of Col. George R. and Emily J. *Stowers* Girault.
- Richard Parkinson, Jr. [Nov. 1, 1861 – April 20, 1862]. Richard is the son of Richard and Emily J. *Stowers* Parkinson. An interesting note is that James Noble Lobdell, George Elvyne Girault and Richard Parkinson, Jr., as children of one mother and three different fathers, share a common monument with the words: "Our Children."
- Martha Cordelia *Girault* Atchison [died May 20, 1858, in the 49th year of her age], "consort of Dr. Matthew Atchison and daughter of Col. John Girault, late of Natchez Miss."

[B-23: Brown, Hopkins, Johnston, Meek, Olcott, Petty, Small, Wharton]
- Mary *Petty* Hopkins [stone cracked, dates missing], "only daughter of Capt. J. Petty of Ky. and wife of Richard Hopkins."
- M. O. Hopkins [June 7, 1815 – July 21, 1870], "Father."
- Enfield *Johnston* Hopkins [Oct. 2, 1820 – Feb. 20, 1905], "Mother" and "wife of M. O. Hopkins."
- Infant Son Hopkins [died July 28, 1845]
- Anna Ruby Hopkins [Aug. 13, 1851 – Sept. 20, 1852]. Anna Ruby and the infant son Hopkins share a small common obelisk with the inscription: "Children of M. O. & E. J. Hopkins."
- Mary *Hopkins* Meek [Sept, 28, 1846 – Mar. 3, 1915], "daughter of M. O. & E. J. Hopkins." Mary married William C. Meek in 1889.
- Charles Dabney Wharton [July 11, 1846 – Oct. 1, 1890], C. S. A. stone. Charles is the son of Dr. Richard Goode and Mary Catharine *Cronly* Wharton, buried in plot B-47.
- Sue *Hopkins* Wharton [Feb. 12, 1849 – July 27, 1917], "daughter of M. O. & E. J. Hopkins and wife of C. D. Wharton." Sue married Charles Wharton in 1874.
- Charles Richard Wharton [May 3, 1875 – Sept. 24, 1945], "son of Charles D. Wharton and Sue H. Wharton."
- Enfield Wharton [Sept. 14, 1881 – Sept. 2, 1941], "daughter of Charles D. Wharton and Sue H. Wharton."
- Paul Hopkins Wharton [Jan. 29, 1887 – Jan. 22, 1973]. Paul is the son of Charles D. and Sue *Hopkins* Wharton. He first married Nannie Cobun Humphreys in 1914. Nannie is buried in plot H-10.
- Elizabeth *Brown* Wharton [Oct. 30, 1892 – Sept. 5, 1973]. Elizabeth is Paul Hopkins' second wife. They married in 1953 and share a common stone. Elizabeth was previously married to a Mr. Small.
- Mary Wharton [March 1, 1889 – April 23, 1977]. Mary is the daughter of Charles D. and Sue Hopkins Wharton.
- Deana J. Olcott [April 26, 1894 – May 15, 1963]

[B-24: English, Mason, Patton]. This plot contains one C. S. A. stone whose owner cannot be identified, located beside Emily Virginia Mason.
- William D. English [Feb. 8, 1808 – Sept. 21, 1853], "born in Loudon County Va....died in Port Gibson Miss." His biographical epitaph reads: "He was kind and affectionate to all, and highly esteemed for his many virtues." William was a victim of the yellow fever epidemic.
- Ann *Patton* English [Nov. 27, 1817 – May 15, 1882], "Mother" and "wife of Wm. D. English." Ann is the daughter of James and Ellenor Patton. Ellenor is buried in plot C-57, with the last name of WATKINS. Ann married William D. English in 1840. Besides their son listed below, their daughter, Nellie *English* Bridgers, is buried in plot B-6.
- William D. English [died Jan 25, 1848, aged 3 years 2 mo. & 10 days], "son of W. D. & Ann English."
- Emily Virginia Mason [died July 24, 1865], "wife of Jas. S. Mason."
- Alice Douglass Mason [died July 23, 1861, aged 18 yrs. 11 mos.], "dau. of J. S. & E. V. Mason."
- Milford Delaware Mason [March 7, 1854 – March 12, 1855], "infant son of James S. & Emily V. Mason."
- Jennie E. Mason [died Sep. 3, 1878, aged 18 years], "daugh. of Jas. S. & E. V. Mason, died of yellow fever in Port Gibson, Miss."
- Lilly T. Mason [no dates]. According to a "Looking Back" column in the *Port Gibson Reveille*, Miss Lilly Mason was the daughter of J. S. Mason, and she died Dec. 28, 1910, at 55 years of age.

"In a dreamless sleep are thine eyelids closed,
And pale that sunny brow,
And thy dimpled hand on thy bosom fair,

Lie folded and quiet now."
—on stone of William D. English

[B-25: Ellett, Howell, Jefferies, McInnis, Turner]
- James Turner [Dec. 5, 1816 – Sept. 5, 1852], "a native of Grafton Gloucestershire, England"
- Rebecca Ellett [died Aug. 20, 1860], "wife of H. T. Ellett."
- E. S. Jefferies [August 21, 1842 – July 10, 1919], C. S. A. stone, Southern Cross of Honor and member Woodmen of the World.
- Kate *Ellett* Jefferies [June 18, 1845 – Dec. 20, 1915], "wife of E. S. Jefferies." Kate is the daughter of H. T. and Rebecca Ellett. Besides those listed below, other children are William Terry Jefferies, James Earl Jefferies and Nathaniel Jefferies, buried in plot G-52, Sarah *Jefferies* Mann in plot A-65, and Berry *Jefferies* Byrnes in plot H-17.
- Henry Ellet (sic) Jefferies [Nov. 4, 1864 – June 15, 1907]
- Evan Shelby Jefferies, Jr. [Sept. 19, 1869 – May 5, 1905]
- Jennie *Jefferies* McInnis [1874 – 1954]. Jennie is the daughter of Evan Shelby and Kate *Ellett* Jefferies. She married John McInnis in 1911.
- Joseph Ellett Jefferies [1883 – 1959]. Joseph is the son of Evan Shelby and Kate *Ellett* Jefferies.
- Serana A. Howell [July 7, 1850 – Feb. 8, 1851], "daughter of S. & A. Howell."

[B-26: Lobdell, Stamps, Stowers]. This plot is enclosed in a wrought iron fence, with the words: "STOWERS/1859" on its gate.
- Lewis Stowers [died July 12, 1848, in the 60th year of his age], "died at Harrodsburg Ky."
- Margaret Stowers [May 20, 1797 – Jan. 30, 1849], "wife of Lewis Stowers." Lewis and Margaret Stowers share a common obelisk with the inscription: "REMEMBRANCER: Born in Mississippi and united in the faith of Christ; in the hope of heaven they died."
- Samuel Stowers [October 26, 1818 – December 26, 1856]
- John W. Stowers [April 14, 1821 – Dec. 26, 1844], "son of Lewis & Margaret Stowers."
- James Marshall Stowers [died Aug. 28, 1839, in his 17th year], "son of Lewis & Margaret Stowers."
- B. Franklin Stowers [July 4, 1831 – June 13, 1858]. Benjamin Franklin Stowers married Kate E. Coleman in 1854.
- William Stowers [Dec. 5, 1833 – Jan. 16, 1860]. William married Mary E. Coleman in 1856.
- Kate F. Stowers [March 17, 1858 – Oct. 25, 1858], "daughter of W. & M. Stowers."
- Lewis Edward Stowers [Aug. 31, 1836 – Dec. 19, 1872], C. S. A. stone.
- Juliet C. *Lobdell* Stowers [1844 – 1904], "wife of Lewis E. Stowers." Juliet is the daughter of Jonathan Conger and Emily J. *Stowers* Lobdell, buried in plot B-22. She married Lewis Edward Stowers in 1865. Three children, Benjamin F., Lewis Edward and Margaret Marshall Stowers, are buried in plot B-29.
- Volney Stamps [Mar. 18, 1803 – Apr. 27, 1879], "born…near Gallatin Sumner Co, Tenn. Died…Bowling Green Plantation, Port Gibson Miss."
- Jane *Stowers* Stamps [no dates], "wife of Volney Stamps." Jane married Volney Stamps in 1832, and they share a common obelisk. According to a funeral notice, Jane died in October, 1885.
- Gabriel Stowers [Apr. 15, 1827 – Sep. 8, 1859], "born…Port Gibson, Miss., died at Sweet Springs Va." Gabriel married Josephine Irish in 1849.

[B-27: Braman, Clark, Myles, Person, Wells] This plot is enclosed in a wrought iron fence.
- James J. Person [July 1812 – Feb. 19, 1877], "native of No. Carolina."
- Harriette *Wells* Person [Sept. 29, 1809 – June 27, 1888], "wife of James J. Person."
- Louise A. Person [June 2, 1840 – Jan. 19, 1855], "daughter of James J. & Harriette W." Louise and her parents all share a common stone with the inscription: "THERE IS NO PARTING IN HEAVEN."

Their names also appear with other family members on a large obelisk.

- James Wells Person [Jan. 7, 1844 – April 8, 1906], C. S. A. stone. James is the son of James J. and Harriette *Wells* Person.
- Isabella *Myles* Person [March 12, 1849 – May 3, 1908]. Isabella is the daughter of Dr. William and Amanda M. *McCall* Myles, buried in plot F-17. She married James Wells Person in 1867, and they share a common stone. Their names also appear on the large obelisk noted above. Besides their daughter Harriette, listed below, other children include Belle *Person* Plantz, Louise *Person* Anderson and Frances W. Person, buried in plot A-60, Roberta *Person* Gage and James Wells Person, in combined plots A-67/76/77/167/178/188, Mary *Person* Drake in combined plot H-51/52, Katesie *Person* Magruder in plot A-19 and Myles Person in plot G-53.
- Harriette Amanda Person [June 20, 1868 – October 18, 1937], member Daughters of the American Revolution. Harriette is the daughter of James Wells and Isabella *Myles* Person.
- John Wells [died January 15, 1840, aged 37 years], "of Northampton, Mass."
- William E. Wells [Feb. 6, 1806 – May 18, 1841], "born at Greenfield, Mass…died at Port Gibson."
- Nancy Allen *(Clark)* Wells [Jan. 5, 1807 – Aug. 16, 1843], "wife of Wm. E. Wells, born at Northampton, Mass…died at Port Gibson."
- Moses Clark Wells [June 26, 1841 – July 2, 1841], "son of Wm. E. & Nancy A. Wells."
- Otis Braman [died Nov. 13, 1855, in the 39th year of his age], "a native of Massachusetts, died of yellow fever."
- Louise Electa *Wells* Braman [July 7, 1807 – Jan. 23, 1892], "wife of Otis Braman." Louise married Otis Braman in 1842, and they share a common obelisk.
- Amelia *Wells* Clark [died May 15, 1845, aged 29 years, 1 month, and 15 days], "wife of Moses Clark." Amelia married Moses Clark in 1842.
- Infant Son Clark [died Sept. 15, 1843, aged 30 days], "infant son of Moses & Amelia W. Clark."
- Ella Amelia Clark [died Aug. 21, 1845, aged 10 months and 9 days], "daughter of Moses & Amelia W. Clark." Ella and the infant son share a common stone.

"Earth hath her dust,
Friends her memory
and the Redeemer her spirit."
—on stone of Amelia *Wells* Clark

[B-28: Loring]
- Israel Loring [February 2, 1768 – June 18, 1843], C. S. A. stone, a Mason, "born at Sudbury, Massachusetts…died at Port Gibson, Miss." and "A Memorial by His Nephews." This obelisk is the only stone in this plot, but it shows, in beautiful art work and symbolism, Mr. Loring's involvement in and offices held in the Masonic fraternity.

[B-29: Applegate, Irish, Parkinson, Stowers]. This lot contains a memorial stone bearing the name STOWERS.
- George Irish [died Sept. 17, 1836, aged 37 years], "Husband" and "born near Newport Rhode Island, and died in Port Gibson."
- Ann E. *(Applegate)* Irish [died Jan. 17, 1837, aged 22 years], "Wife" and "born in Louisville Kentucky, and died at Grand Gulf." Ann married George Irish in 1831, and they share a common stone.
- John Richard Parkinson [Aug. 15, 1863 – Jan. 6, 1942], a Mason. John is the son of Richard and Emily J. *Stowers* Parkinson, buried in plot B-22.
- Margaret Marshall Stowers [July 5, 1866 – Dec. 2, 1937], member Daughters of the American Revolution. Margaret, along with her brothers, Benjamin F. and Lewis Edward Stowers, listed below, are chil-

dren of Lewis Edward and Juliet C. *Lobdell* Stowers, buried in plot B-26.

- Benjamin F. Stowers [Aug. 16, 1867 – June 16, 1913], member Woodmen of the World.
- Lewis Edward Stowers [Feb. 5, 1872 – June 20, 1947]

[B-30: Ross, Taylor, Wade]

- Walter Wade, M. D. [March 9, 1810 – July 15, 1862], "born Richland Dist, S. C…died at his residence, Rosswood, Jefferson County." After the death of Martha *Taylor* Wade, listed below, he married Mrs. Mabella J. Chamberlain in 1859.
- Martha *T(aylor)*. Wade [Nov. 14, 1813 – June 27, 1848], "wife of Walter Wade M. D. Born near Columbia S. C., by her side an…"
- Infant Son Wade [no dates]. An infant son of Walter and Martha *Taylor* Wade, mother and son likely died together in childbirth.
- James Taylor Wade [Jan. 30, 1843 – Nov. 2, 1921]
- Martha Rives *Wade* Wade [Nov. 24, 1844 – Oct. 7, 1928], "wife of Dunbar Bisland Wade, daughter of Dr. Walter Wade & Martha Taylor Wade." Martha married Dunbar Bisland Wade in 1863. Dunbar is buried in Jefferson County.
- Charlotte Pricilla Wade [Aug. 5, 1873 – Jan 6, 1938], "Sister."
- Battaille Dunbar Wade [Jan. 27, 1876 – Sept. 15, 1906], "son of D. B. & M. R. Wade."
- Sallie Marshall Wade [Feb. 27, 1878 – May 4, 1948]
- Richard Ross Wade [1880 – 1959]. Richard is the son of Dunbar and Martha *Wade* Wade.
- Wilson W. Ross [died March 27, 1941], "MISSISSIPPI, PVT, US ARMY." This is a military stone.
- Catherine *Wade* Ross [Feb. 27, 1883 – Aug. 23, 1953]. Catherine is the daughter of Dunbar and Martha *Wade* Wade. She married Wilson Ross in 1908.
- Jack Ross Wade [Jan. 9, 1886 – Sept. 30, 1926], member Woodmen of the World.

[B-31: Harding, Maury, Wilkinson]

- James N. Harding [Dec. 18, 1813 – June 11, 1872]
- Elizabeth *M(aury)*. Harding [July 6, 1825 – Mar. 23, 1891]. Elizabeth is the daughter of James H. and Lucinda *Smith* Maury, buried in combined plot B-7/18. She married James N. Harding in 1844, and they share a common obelisk with the inscription: "In Memory of Our Parents." Besides those listed below, they have a daughter, Caroline *Harding* Bertron, buried in plot A-43.
- Richard Harding [died August 5, 1848, aged 2 years 11 months and 22 days], "son of J. N. & E. M. Harding."
- James Maury Harding [September 20, 1849 – January 1, 1929]. James is the son of James N. and Elizabeth *Maury* Harding.
- Lucinda Smith Harding [died January 23, 1852], "infant daughter of J. N. & E. M. Harding."
- Andrews Wilkinson [June 3, 1849 – May 16, 1921]
- Elizabeth *Harding* Wilkinson [July 17, 1854 – June 25, 1918], "wife of Andrews Wilkinson." Elizabeth is the daughter of James N. and Elizabeth *Maury* Harding.
- Herbert Wilkinson [Nov. 17, 1874 – March 3, 1895]. Herbert is the son of Andrews and Elizabeth *Harding* Wilkinson.
- Elizabeth Maury Wilkinson [Jan. 17, 1877 – July 4, 1957]. Elizabeth is the daughter of Andrews and Elizabeth *Harding* Wilkinson.
- Philip Harding Wilkinson [December 13, 1881 – February 4, 1922]. Philip is the son of Andrews and Elizabeth *Harding* Wilkinson.
- Andrews Wilkinson, Jr. [June 25, 1886 – Dec. 3, 1911]
- Ann Faulkner Wilkinson [Oct. 21, 1895 – Oct. 4, 1922]
- Anna Boursiquot Harding [died Aug. 30, 1859], "infant daughter of J. N. & E. M. Harding."

[B-32: Coleman, Lape, Yorke]. This plot is enclosed in a wrought iron fence.
- William Lape [died June 8, 1847, aged 39 years]
- William Lape [died Jan'y 22, 1848, aged 3 mos], "infant son of William Lape."
- Laura F. Coleman [Nov. 12, 1842 – July 12, 1844], "youngest daughter of John B. & Catharine Coleman."
- Louise B. Coleman [born Dec. 23, 1848], "infant daughter of J. B. & Catharine Coleman." This stone is broken with date of death missing.
- Rebecca E. (Coleman) Yorke [Jan. 9, 1846 – Sept. 16, 1870], "wife of Col. P. Jones Yorke." Rebecca married Col. Patton Jones Yorke, an officer in the Union Army, in 1865.
- Louis S. Yorke, Jr. [Feb. 14, 1870 – Aug. 4, 1870], "son of P. Jones and Rebecca E. Yorke." Louis and his mother share a common obelisk.

[B-33: Anketell, Butler, Murdoch]. This plot contains a lone C. S. A. stone, facing north-south, whose owner cannot be identified.
- Rev. Zebulon Butler, D. D. [Sept. 27, 1803 – Dec. 23, 1860]. Rev. Butler's biographical epitaph reads: "He was the founder of the Presbyterian Church of this town, and for 33 years its pastor."
- Mary Anne Butler [Feb. 8, 1811 – Oct. 6, 1863], "His Wife." Mary is the wife of Rev. Zebulon Butler. Besides those listed below, they have a son, Lord John Butler, buried in plot F-6.
- Chester Pierce Butler [June 17, 1840 – Feb. 19, 1860]
- William Chaplain Butler [Aug. 17, 1844 – Dec. 24, 1863]
- Henrietta Maria Butler [Dec. 25, 1846 – Sept. 6, 1867]
- Ruth Conyngham Butler [May 17, 1852 – March 18, 1876], "buried in Wilkesbarre Pa."
- Ellen Murdoch Butler [Nov. 9, 1830 – March 4, 1877]. The preceding five names share a common obelisk with Rev. Zebulon and Mary Anne Butler, with the inscription: "Their Children."
- Anne Jane Butler [May 15, 1836 – July 11, 1859], "daughter of Z. & M. A. Butler, born in Port Gibson."
- Mary Esther Butler [(died) aged 20 years & 7 mos.], "second daughter of Rev. Zebulon and Mary Butler."
- Sarah Sylvina Butler [(died) in her 15th year], "third daughter of Rev. Z. & M. A. Butler."
- Esther (Anketell) Murdoch [died Apr. 23, 1843, aged 58 yrs.], "wife of John Murdoch, born in Ireland & died in Port Gibson."
- Ellen Anktelle (sic) Murdoch [died Nov. 5, 1855]
- Ziba Butler Murdoch [died Oct. 6, 1863]. Ellen and Ziba Murdoch share a common obelisk with Esther Murdoch, with the inscription: "A Memorial by Her Children."
- John Murdoch [Nov. 29, 1844 – Oct. 9, 1915], C. S. A. stone.
- John Murdoch [died Dec. 24, 1842, at 14 mo's], "infant son of John & Frances L. Murdoch."

[B-34: Fulkerson, Gage, Hogg, McCaleb, Rollins, Russell]
- Amariah Rollins [March 21, 1808 – Dec. 9, 1889]. Amariah's biographical epitaph reads: "A devoted husband, an indulgent father and a true friend. The memory of a good man is the heritage of his people – the pride and comfort of his children. This tribute erected by his affectionate wife and loving children."
- Lucinda R(ussell). Rollins [Sept. 13, 1818 – Nov. 6, 1897], "wife of A. Rollins." Lucinda married Amariah Rollins in 1834, and they share a common obelisk. They also have individual stones bearing the words "Father" and "Mother," along with their birth and death dates.
- Rose Emeline Rollins [July 24, 1840 – Aug. 14, 1840]
- John Russell Rollins [Apr. 24, 1838 – Sep. 9, 1844]
- Harry Percy Rollins [Jan. 14, 1862 – July 8, 1865]
- Annie Maria Rollins [Mar. 8, 1844 – July 29, 1844]. The four children listed above share a common

obelisk with the words: "Children of Amariah Rollins & Lucinda Russell."

- Thomas T. Hogg, M. D. [died Oct. 25, 1840, aged 26 years], a Mason, "a native of Tennessee." A memorial inscription reads: "This memento is erected by an affectionate wife."
- J. A. Gage [Oct. 9, 1812 – Nov. 1, 1891]
- Rose *Russell* Gage [1821 – Oct. 24, 1863], "wife of J. A. Gage." Rose first married Dr. Thomas T. Hogg, listed above, in 1837. After his death she married James A. Gage in 1845. She is James Gage's first wife. Besides those listed below, they have a daughter, Carrie T. *Gage* Spencer, buried in plot A-69, and Robert Douglass Gage, buried in the combined plot A-67/76/77/167/178/188.
- James R. Gage [1846 – 1906], C. S. A. stone. James is the son of James A. and Rose *Russell* Gage.
- John Rollins Gage [July 24, 1848 – July 17, 1918]. John is the son of James A. and Rose *Russell* Gage.
- Lucie E. Gage [July 18, 1850 – June 7, 1852], "daughter of James A. & Rosanna Gage."
- Louis M. Gage [June 27, 1855 – Oct. 2, 1899]. Louis is the son of James A. and Rose *Russell* Gage.
- Mary E. Gage [Apr. 27, 1857 – Nov. 9, 1874]
- Sallie *F(ulkerson)*. Gage [Aug. 14, 1835 – Sept. 12, 1913], "wife of James A. Gage." Sallie is James Gage's second wife, marrying in 1866.
- Johnnie B. McCaleb [June 30, 1877 – Jan. 1, 1900], "son of J. B. & A. M. McCaleb." Johnnie's mother, Annie *Rollins* McCaleb, is buried in plot F-7.

[B-35: Grafton, Marshal, Marshall, Mount, Sittler, Spencer]

- Mrs. Catharine Sittler [died Dec. 24, 1858, aged 73 years], "a native of Winchester Va....died in Port Gibson, Miss...A Mother in Israel."
- Samuel Marshall [died July 17, 1843, aged 79 years], "a native of Pa. After a residence of 60 years in Mississippi he died in Port Gibson." A biographical epitaph reads: "For 30 years he was a ruling elder of the Presbyterian Church on Pine Ridge. He lived the life of the righteous and his end was peace."
- James Grafton [December 15, 1785 – February 4, 1851], "born in Adams Co. Mississippi." A biographical epitaph reads: "In early life he united himself to the people of God & for many years was a ruling elder of the Presbyterian Church." James first married Mrs. Maria *Spencer* Goddard in 1834. She is buried in plot C-50.
- Elizabeth *S(pencer)*. Grafton [April 23, 1789 – Nov. 11, 1855], "a native of Lyme, Ct." Her biographical epitaph reads: "A member of the Presbyterian Church." Elizabeth is the second wife of James Grafton. They married in 1841 and share a common obelisk.
- H. N. Spencer [Nov. 22, 1798 – April 18, 1876], "born in Lyme Ct...died near Port Gibson." Horatio N. Spencer was first married to Theresa Goddard, who is buried in plot C-50, along with their two children, Maria Elizabeth and Horatio G. Spencer.
- Sarah Ann Spencer [Nov. 20, 1809 – Mar. 20, 1854], "wife of H. N. Spencer." Sarah is Horatio N. Spencer's second wife, and they share a common obelisk. Besides the sons listed below, they have sons Horatio M., Samuel M. and William Catlin Spencer, buried in plot C-50, and James G. Spencer in plot B-46.
- John Brockway Spencer [April 22, 1847 – June 30, 1847]
- William Butler Spencer [March 4, 1849 – Sept. 28, 1850]. John Brockway and William Butler Spencer share a common stone with the inscription: "children of H. N. & S. A. Spencer."
- Roena S. Marshal [died Apr. 16, 1867, aged 23 yrs. 7 mo.], "adopted daughter of H. N. & Sarah Spencer."
- Priscilla Spencer [Mar. 4, 1820 – Nov. 3, 1876]
- Samuel Spencer [aged 13 months], and...
- Infant Son Mount #1[no dates]
- Infant Son Mount #2 [no dates], "two infant sons of E. & E. E. Mount." The Mount sons are children of Elijah and Emeline E. *Spencer* Mount, and they share a common stone with Samuel Spencer.

- Aseneth Maria Spencer [Sept. 8, 1815 – July 18, 1844], "daughter of William Spencer of Lyme, Ct… died at Port Gibson," Her biographical epitaph reads: "She was a member of the Presbyterian Church; and died in the full assureance (sic) of hope."

[B-36: Archer, Hoopes, Jeffries, Marye, Railey]

- Passmore Hoopes [Oct. 17, 1794 – May 19, 1865], "born at West Chester Pa."
- Eliza T. Hoopes [July 2, 1796 – March 22, 1848], "wife of Passmore Hoopes, born in West Chester Pa."
- Edward Barnes Hoopes [Jan. 26, 1828 – July 10, 1875], C. S. A. stone, "only son of Eliza T. & Passmore Hoopes." Edward married Elizabeth T. Murphy in 1851. She is buried in plot C-14a, along with a daughter, Elizabeth M. Hoopes. They also have a daughter, Helen Kate *Hoopes* Mason, buried in plot B-42.
- James T. Marye [Dec. 19, 1814 – Aug. 10, 1867]
- Mary P. *(Hoopes)* Marye [July 25, 1820 – Oct. 1, 1868]. Mary married James T. Marye in 1839. They have a daughter, Anna *Marye* Archer, buried in plot A-66.
- James Marye Archer [Feb. 13, 1879 – May 16, 1897]
- Henry Wyles Marye [November 1, 1840 – June 20, 1841]
- William Downing Marye [June 24, 1845 – April 27, 1851]
- Mary Connor Marye [June 15, 1861 – Sept. 18, 1868]
- James Green Railey [Sept. 30, 1826 – Feb. 27, 1853], "son of J. & M. S. Railey." James married Ann Elizabeth Hoopes in 1850.
- Ernest Hoopes Railey [Jan. 31, 1852 – Sept. 15, 1869]
- Thomas S. Jeffries [died August 1839, aged 13 years], "son of James & Sarah Ann Jeffries."

[B 37: Broughton, Merrifield]. This plot has a lone C. S. A. stone whose owner cannot be identified.

- Samuel Preston Merrifield [died Oct. 18, 1848, aged 8 days], "infant son of Henry P. & Marion E. Merrifield."
- Clara Elizabeth Broughton [Sept. 20, 1851 – Aug. 3, 1858], "daughter of T. W. & M. L. Broughton."

> "When her heart knew naught of sorrow
> And her soul was free from sin
> Was she in her beauty gathered
> Underneath Jehovah's wing."
> —on stone of Clara Elizabeth Broughton

[B-38: Emerson, Forbes, Hodge]

- Ann Maria *Forbes* Hodge [June 10, 1814 – Oct. 26, 1851], "wife of A. W. Hodge: a native of Vt. Third daughter of Gen'l A. & Sarah Forbes, of Windsor." Ann married Alexander W. Hodge in 1836. She had previously been married to a Mr. Emerson.
- Henry Ashton Hodge [died Aug. 14, 1848, aged 2 years 2 mo's & 23 days], "4th son of A. W. & A. M. Hodge."
- Ida Forbes [Dec. 27, 1848 – Oct. 14, 1922]

[B-39: Barron, Jefferies, Humphreys, Lawson, Myles, Prince]

- Priscilla Shelby Jefferies [Apr. 6, 1784 – Feb. 1860], "Our Grand Mother."
- Mrs. Catharine Shelby *(Jefferies)* Prince [June 6, 1800 – July 8, 1860]
- George Wilson Humphreys [Sept. 16, 1819 – Dec. 26, 1907]. George is the son of David G. and Mary *Cobun* Humphreys, buried in plot H-10.
- Catharine Baylissa *Prince* Humphreys [Aug. 24, 1825 – Nov. 24, 1870], "wife of G. W. Humphreys." Catharine is the daughter of Catharine Shelby *Jefferies* Prince. She married George Wilson Humphreys in 1844. Besides those listed below, other children include David George and Samuel Cobun Humphreys,

buried in plot H-10, and Baylis Earl Humphreys in plot G-51.

- Charles D. Humphreys [June 20, 1885 – May 5, 1937]. Charles is the son of Samuel Cobun and Nannie *Hamilton* Humphreys, buried in plot H-10. Charles was married three times, first to Ethel Smith in 1911. She is buried in plot A-18, along with their infant son. After the death of Bonnibelle *Barron* Humphreys, his second wife, he married Fannie Magruder in 1919. She is buried in plot G-31, with the last name of EATON.
- Bonnibelle *Barron* Humphreys [July 26, 1890 – Feb. 20, 1918], "second wife of C. D. Humphreys." Bonnibelle is the daughter of Dr. Edmund D. and Nannie *Slay* Barron, buried in plot E-15. She married Charles D. Humphreys in 1914, after the death of his first wife.
- George Wilson Humphreys [June 20, 1884 – Jan. 6, 1919], "Husband." George is the son of Baylis Earl and Elizabeth *Hamilton* Humphreys, buried in plot G-51.
- Loretta Elizabeth *(Lawson)* Humphreys [died Jan. 25, 1921], "wife of Geo. Wilson Humphreys." Loretta married George Wilson Humphreys in 1912.
- William Prince Humphreys [Nov. 19, 1845 – Nov. 6, 1864], C. S. A. stone, "son of G. W. & C. B. Humphreys…C. S. A." According to Mississippi Confederate Grave Registration records, William was a Private in Co. C, 4th Miss. Cavalry, and was "accidentally killed."
- Frederick F. Myles [April 25, 1851 – July 1, 1915]. Frederick is the son of Dr. William and Amanda M. *McCall* Myles, buried in plot F-17.
- Katesie Prince *Humphreys* Myles [Dec. 29, 1853 – Sep. 11, 1879], "wife of Gen. F. F. Myles." Katesie is the daughter of George Wilson and Catharine *Prince* Humphreys. She married Frederick F. Myles in 1876. They have a daughter, Baylissa *Myles* Liebman, buried in plot F-17.
- Benjamin Humphreys [Feb. 12, 1857 – Oct. 7, 1878], "son of G. W. & C. B. Humphreys…a victim of yellow fever."
- Mary Coburn Humphreys [Aug. 7, 1860 – July 10, 1864], "daughter of G. W. & C. B. Humphreys." It is possible that Mary's middle named should be spelled COBUN.

[B-40: Burnet, Duncan, Milliken, Parker]. This plot is enclosed in a wrought iron fence.
- John Milliken [died Aug. 23, 1845, aged 73 years], "a native of North Carolina."
- A. W. P. Parker [died Nov. 22, 1837, aged 37 years], "a native of Kentucky."
- James Porter Parker [January 20, 1793 – June 14, 1860], "a native of Lexington, Ky."
- Mary Jane *(Milliken)* Parker [June 26, 1812 – Nov. 29, 1887]. Jane is the daughter of John Milliken. She married James Porter Parker in 1828.
- Martha R. *(Parker)* Duncan [July 20, 1832 – June 19, 1859], "wife of S. P. Duncan." Martha married Samuel P. Duncan in 1854.
- W. E. Parker [1835 – 1908]. William is the son of James Porter and Mary Jane *Milliken* Parker. (Whole name: William St. J. E. Parker).
- Elizabeth *Burnet* Parker [July 24, 1846 – May 10, 1930], "wife of W. E. Parker." Elizabeth is the daughter of John and Elizabeth K. *Shaifer* Burnet, buried in plot C-36a. She married William E. Parker in 1874.
- Mary D. Parker [died Dec'r 12, 1863, aged 23 years]
- Mary D. Parker [March 28, 1874 – Oct. 8, 1876]
- Mary M. Parker [Oct. 10, 1876 – Oct. 18, 1878]. Mary D. and Mary M. Parker share a common monument with the inscription: "Children of John M. and Roberta Parker." These are grandchildren of James Porter and Mary Jane *Milliken* Parker.

[B-41: Frazer, Strong, Walker, Wilson]
- Samuel Walker [died Sept. 22, 1853, aged 49 years & 6 mos.], "a native of New-Jersey, and a citizen of Port Gibson, for 20 years." His memorial reads: "By his affectionate sons." Samuel was a victim of the yellow fever epidemic.

- Margaretta Walker [died July 11, 1860, aged 60 years], "Our Loss is Her Gain." A memorial epitaph reads: "Erected by her affectionate nephews as a grateful tribute to her Christian fortitude and maternal attentions."
- William E. Walker [died Sept. 13, 1861, aged 31 years & 6 mos.]. William married Elizabeth J. King in 1854.
- James S. Frazer [died Dec. 2, 1884, aged 63 y's. 10 ds.]
- Lizzie Frazer [died Sep. 4, 1853, aged 23 years]. James S. and Lizzie Frazer share a common obelisk. Elizabeth also has an individual stone. She was a victim of the yellow fever epidemic.
- Sarah Clark Strong [died March 31, 1845, aged 15 days], "daughter of Geo. P. & M. P. Strong."
- Smith Gordon Wilson [Jan. 2, 1843 – Aug. 17, 1896]. Smith married Carrie G. Bush in 1869.

[B-42: Abraham, Bearden, Downing, Hoopes, Mason, McLendon, Morris, Spencer]. This plot is enclosed in a wrought iron fence and holds a lone C. S. A. stone, whose owner cannot be identified.

- Helen Kate *Hoopes* Mason [Sept. 7, 1856 – Oct. 14, 1894], "wife of Chas. S. Mason, daughter of E. B. & E. T. Hoopes." Helen's father, Edward Barnes Hoopes, is buried in plot B-36, and her mother, Elizabeth T. *Murphy* Hoopes, is buried in plot C-14a. Helen married Charles S. Mason in 1879. Besides those listed below, they have a daughter, Kate Hoopes Mason, also buried in plot C-14a.
- Meredith Jones Spencer [July 9, 1876 – Sept. 18, 1948]
- Lillie *Mason* Spencer [July 7, 1883 – Nov. 13, 1962]. Lillie is the daughter of Charles S. and Helen Kate *Hoopes* Mason. She married Meredith Jones Spencer in 1909. Besides those listed below, two daughters, Ann *Spencer* Truluck and Margaret *Spencer* Luebbers, are buried in combined plot A-170/175.
- Elizabeth *Spencer* McLendon [Oct. 15, 1911 – Nov. 26, 1993], member Daughters of the American Revolution. Elizabeth is the daughter of Meredith Jones and Lillie *Mason* Spencer. She married Douglas Franklin McLendon in 1937.
- Meredith Jones Spencer, Jr. [Nov. 15, 1917 – Feb. 19, 1943]. Meredith is the son of Meredith Jones and Lillie *Mason* Spencer.

From *Port Gibson Reveille's* "Looking Back" column (week of February 21, 1943): "Corp. Meredith Jones Spencer, Jr. was fatally burned on February 19th when his hut at Camp Shelby was destroyed by fire."

- Jeanne *Bearden* Spencer [July 16, 1917 – June 16, 1998], member Daughters of the American Revolution. Jeanne is the daughter of Norman Cooper and Martha *Utz* Bearden, buried in plot A-57. She married Meredith Jones Spencer, Jr. in 1940.
- Elvyn Passmore Hoopes Spencer [Jan. 5, 1920 – July 20, 2003]. Elvyn is the son of Meredith Jones and Lillie *Mason* Spencer.
- Phoebe Cleve *Abraham* Spencer [Aug. 16, 1921 – Feb. 1, 1999]. Phoebe is the daughter of Jacob L. and Phoebe *Hamilton* Abraham, buried in plot A-123. Phoebe and Elvyn Spencer share a common grave location, a vase with the words, "Married Oct. 12, 1940."
- James S. Mason [Aug. 29, 1887 – May 7, 1891], "son of C. S. and H. K. Mason."
- Perla V. *Morris* Mason [Mar. 23, 1863 – Oct. 24, 1915], "wife of C. S. Mason." Perla is the daughter of William T. and May *McCaleb* Morris, buried in plot C-13, and is Charles S. Mason's second wife. They married in 1896.
- James Campbell Downing [Sept. 25, 1845 – Aug. 5, 1853], "second son of Wm. P. V. & N. B. Downing", and
- Mary Esther Downing [Dec. 20, 1848 – Aug. 6, 1853], "only daughter of the same parents." James Campbell and Mary Esther Downing share a common obelisk.
- Single stone with the word "Infant" [no dates]

[B-43: Kavanaugh, Kelledy, Watt]

- Eliza Watt [died July 8, 1855, aged 42 years], "wife of Robert Watt."

Unfortunately, these KELLEDY stones have been heavily damaged in years past, possibly by a fallen tree, and are now, sadly, a pile of rubble. It is believed that Patrick and Katherine are both buried here, based on initials on their foot stones.

- Patrick Kelledy [ ], based on foot stone with the initials, P.K.
- Katherine *Kavanaugh* Kelledy [unreadable dates], "beloved wife of Patrick Kelledy." This information was pieced together from many parts, and is all that is available. According to a *Port Gibson Reveille* "Looking Back" column, Katherine died January 15, 1895, at the age of 62. She married Patrick Kelledy in 1866.

"Weep not for her who dieth,
For she sleeps and is at rest;
And the couch whereon she lieth,
Is the green earth's quiet breast."
—on obelisk of Eliza Watt

[B-44: McGill]
- Ann Jennette McGill [Dec. 11, 1818 – May 31, 1851], "consort of A. J. McGill: born in Philad'a, Pa... died in Port Gibson."
- William R. McGill [died June 1, 1840, aged 4 mo. & 16 days], "son of A. J. & Ann Jennette McGill."
- Charles Clifton McGill [Oct. 19, 1843 – Feb. 3, 1852], "2nd son of A. J. & Ann Jennette McGill."
- Benjamin Franklin McGill [March 29, 1846 – Nov. 3, 1848], "3rd son of A. J. & Ann Jennette McGill."
- Louis Stanley McGill [Jan. 4, 1849 – Sept. 26, 1852], "son of A. J. & A. J. McGill."

[B-45: Darnall, Heslep, McCorkle, Reeves]. This nice family plot is enclosed in a wrought iron fence.
- Isaac B. McCorkle [Feb. 18, 1801 – Oct. 11, 1875], "born in South Carolina."
- Susan A. *(Darnall)* McCorkle [died Dec. 7, 1839, in her 25th year], "wife of Isaac B. McCorkle, a native of S. Carolina." Susan married Isaac B. McCorkle in 1833.
- Elizabeth A. McCorkle [July 14, 1837 – Dec. 22, 1851], "daughter of I. B. & S. A. McCorkle." Elizabeth and her parents share a common obelisk.
- Joseph McCorkle [no dates]
- Almoth B. Heslep [Dec. 23, 1838 – Jan. 17, 1879], C. S. A. stone, "a native of Georgia." His biographical epitaph reads: "A dutiful son: an affectionate brother: a faithful friend." A portion of Mr. Heslep's last will and testament reads: "I desire my mortal remains to be interred by the side of my late uncle Isaac B. McCorkle, in the Port Gibson Cemetery. And I direct that a suitable monument be erected to my memory and that the square or lot...be enclosed with a good and substantial iron fence and that the costs thereof be paid out of my estate."
- Hiram Reeves [July 25, 1819 – Sept. 17, 1871]

[B-46: Gilkey, Jones, Montgomery, Spencer, Smyth]
- Israel Spencer [Apr. 15, 1791 – Sep. 11, 1870]
- Mary Spencer [Feb. 18, 1793 – Apr. 10, 1872]. Israel and Mary Spencer share a common stone with the inscription: "Husband and Wife." Besides their son Horatio, listed below, they have a son, Israel Selden Spencer, buried in plot C-50.
- Horatio Samuel Spencer [Aug. 30, 1826 – Dec. 22, 1857], "son of Israel & Mary N. Spencer."
- Selden Spencer [Mar. 23, 1837 – June 3, 1878], C. S. A. stone.
- James G. Spencer [1844 – 1926], "COWAN'S B'TRY., 1 MISS. LT. ARTY., C.S.A." This is a military stone. James is the son of H. N. and Sarah Ann Spencer, buried in plot B-35. He served as United States Representative from Mississippi in the 54th Congress. According to Mississippi Confederate Grave Reg-

istration records, he was a Private, and he died of old age.

- Lucy *J(ones)*. Spencer [Oct. 27, 1846 – Aug. 19, 1913], "Mother, Home, Heaven." Lucy is the daughter of Joseph E. and Martha A. *Green* Jones, buried in Jones Cemetery. She married James G. Spencer in 1866. Besides their two daughters listed below, they have a son, Horatio N. Spencer, buried in plot A-69.
- Sarah Marshall Spencer [July 3, 1869 – Nov. 9, 1914], "Sister" and "daughter of James G. & Lucy J. Spencer."
- Elizabeth Grafton Spencer [July 28, 1873 – Dec. 25, 1962], "Sister" and "daughter of James G. & Lucy J. Spencer."
- Henry S. Montgomery [Nov. 13, 1843 – Apr. 27, 1872], "son of Rev. Samuel Montgomery & grandson of Israel Spencer." A biographical epitaph reads: "A member of the Presbyterian Church."
- Virginia Josephine *(Smyth)* Gilkey [died Dec. 11, 1845, aged 19 years, ? months & 2 days], "wife of A. Gilkey." Virginia married Abner Gilkey in 1843. (This stone is cracked, making some parts unreadable.)
- Virginia Frances Gilkey [died August 7, 1846, aged 9 months and 28 days], "daughter of A. & V. J. Gilkey."

[B-47: Cronly, Grafton, Hastings, Meyerkort, Schneider, Wharton, White]

- Mrs. Louisa *(White)* Cronly [died Sept. 5, 1887, aged 83 y'rs, 18 d'ys]. Louisa is the daughter of Larkin and Mary *McCaleb* White. A stone with the simple inscription, "Dear Mary," located at McCaleb-Hermitage Cemetery, is believed to mark the grave of Louisa's mother. Louisa married Louis Cronly in 1824. Louis is buried in Grand Gulf Cemetery, along with four of their young children.
- Richard Goode Wharton, M. D. [Jan. 11, 1815 – July 23, 1896], "born at Cartersville, Va....died as physician beloved." An inscription on his obelisk reads: "Richard Goode Wharton and Mary Catherine Cronly were married Oct. 9, 1845."
- Mary Catharine *(Cronly)* Wharton [July 15, 1827 – Jan. 28, 1867]. Catharine is the daughter of Louis and Louisa *White* Cronly and wife of Richard Goode Wharton. Besides those listed below, they have a son, Charles Dabney Wharton, buried in plot B-23.
- Robert M. Hastings [Nov. 30, 1842 – May 23, 1879], C. S. A. stone, a Mason, member Independent Order of Odd Fellows. Robert's first wife was Julia Caroline Hastings. She is buried in plot C-30, along with an infant daughter.
- Harriet Louisa *(Wharton)* Hastings [July 12, 1848 – Sept. 26, 1922], "wife of Robert M. Hastings." Harriet is the daughter of Richard Goode and Mary Catharine *Cronly* Wharton, and second wife of Robert M. Hastings. They married in 1873. Besides those listed below, they have a son, Richard Granbery Hastings, buried in plot G-23.
- Infant Son Hastings [no dates], "infant son of R. M. & H. L. Hastings."
- Roberta Kate *Hastings* Meyerkort [May 28, 1878 – October 3, 1965], "wife of Edmund Alexander Meyerkort." Roberta is the daughter of Robert M. and Harriet Louisa *Wharton* Hastings. She married Edmund Meyerkort in 1903.
- Roberta Louisa Meyerkort [March 26, 1904 – September 3, 1988]. Roberta is the daughter of Edmund Alexander and Roberta Kate *Hastings* Meyerkort.
- Austin Cronly Wharton [June 22, 1850 – Aug. 3, 1917]
- Charlotte Wharton [Nov. 23, 1852 – Feb. 21, 1929]
- Louis Wharton [died Oct. 9, 1856, aged 2 years & 6 d's], "son of R. G. & M. C. Wharton."
- Kate *Wharton* Grafton [Mar. 10, 1858 – Apr. 16, 1940], "wife of Dr. C. W. Grafton of Union Church, Miss., daughter of R. G. & M. C. Wharton." Kate married Dr. Grafton in 1891. He is buried in Union Church Cemetery in Jefferson County.
- Lucy Wharton [died Aug. 10, 1885]. Lucy is the daughter of Dr. Richard Goode and Mary Catharine

Cronly Wharton.

- John Schneider [died Sept 17, 1853, in the 22 year of his age], "a native of Germany." John was a victim of the yellow fever epidemic.

[B-48: Jordan, Lee, Parks, Thompson, Wilson]. This plot is enclosed in a wrought iron fence.

- Francis B. Lee [March 22, 1786 – Nov. 9, 1851], "a native of France…a resident of Port Gibson nearly 30 years."
- Clarissa *(Parks)* Lee [July 2, 1805 – July 22, 1872], "wife of Francis B. Lee." Clarissa married Francis B. Lee in 1828, and they share a common obelisk.
- Francis P. Lee [March 29, 1830 – May 7, 1833]
- William T. Lee [birth date unreadable – May 4, 1833]
- George W. Lee [Dec. 2, 1843 – (partly unreadable), 1844]. Francis, William and George Lee share a common stone with the inscription: "(partly unreadable) infant sons, Children of ???? & Clarissa Lee."
- Ellen Olivia *(Lee)* Jordan [Aug. 27, 1840 – April 26, 1870], "wife of James B. Jordan." Ellen married James B. Jordan in 1861. James is buried in plot C-58.
- Matilda Elizabeth *Parks* Wilson [May 18, 1815 – Sep. 19, 1857], "wife of John P. Wilson." Matilda married Thomas W. Thompson in 1839 and John P. Wilson in 1853.

[B-49: Dawson, Harmon, Hoel, Magruder, Neal, Sims, Venables]

- Mrs. E H. *(Sims)* Hoel [Oct. 27, 1803 – Oct. 3, 1865]. Eliza married Joseph Harmon in 1820, and later married James Hoel in 1837.
- Frances N. P. *(Harmon)* Venables [Sept. 6, 1828 – June 2, 1852], "wife of John F. Venables." Frances married Mr. Venables in 1850.
- Joseph R. Neal [Feb. 27, 1816 – Sept. 14, 1853], a Mason and member Independent Order of Odd Fellows. Joseph was a victim of the yellow fever epidemic.
- William McD. Sims [May 19, 1810 – Feb. 7, 1882], a Mason. On William's obelisk are the letters, HTWSSTKS, arranged in a circle, indicating a higher office in the Masonic organization. (Incidentally, the letters stand for "Hiram The Widow's Son, Sent To King Solomon.")
- Rebecca J. *(Harmon)* Sims [June 9, 1826 – Jan. 14, 1900]. Rebecca married Joseph R. Neal, listed above, in 1843. After his death she married William McD. Sims in 1856, and they share a common obelisk.
- Frances E. Neal [Mar. 5, 1846 – Aug. 21, 1900]. Francis is the daughter of Joseph R. and Rebecca Jane *Harmon* Neal.
- Ida Agnes Neal [Nov. 28, 1848 – Mar. 11, 1924]. Ida is the daughter of Joseph R. and Rebecca Jane *Harmon* Neal. She has a twin sister, Martha L. *Neal* Magruder, buried in plot G-57.
- Louisiana E. Sims [Sept. 25, 1857 – Oct. 24, 1865], "daughter of Wm. & Rebecca J. Sims."
- Carrie *Sims* Magruder [July 7, 1860 – Dec. 10, 1880], "wife of R. W. Magruder, and daughter of Wm. McD. & R. J. Sims." Carrie married Robert Walter Magruder in 1880. Robert is buried in plot G-31.
- Sarah O. Magruder [October 30, 1874 – Oct. 6, 1876], "daughter of I. D. & M. L. Magruder." Sarah's parents are buried in plot G-57. Sarah's final resting place is marked by one of those metal grave "stones."
- Carrie *M(agruder)*. Dawson [1890 – 1956]. Carrie is the also the daughter of Isaac Dunbar and Martha L. *Neal* Magruder.

[B-50: Thomson]

- Benjamin W. Thomson [March 8, 1817 – Sept. 14, 1852], a Mason. A biographical inscription reads: "This stone is placed here as a memorial of affection for one, who was a kind husband, an indulgent parent, and a good citizen." Benjamin married Caroline M. Robertson in 1842.
- Benjamin Franklin Thomson [died Sept. 25, 1856, aged 9 yrs. 9 ms. 4 ds.], "son of B. W. & C. M. Thompson (sic)."
- Albert Gallatin Thomson [Nov. 28, 1850 – May 5, 1852], "son of B. W. & C. M. Thomson."

[B-51: Cotton, Garrison, Harris, Jones, Ross]

- Elizabeth Hunter *Harris* Cotton [Aug. 28, 1798 – Apr. 14, 1871], "Mother Cotton" and "born in North Carolina…married Joseph Cotton Oct. 19, 1813, died in Port Gibson, Miss."

- Rev. John Griffing Jones. His entire obelisk inscription reads as follows: "Rev. John Griffing Jones, born in Jefferson Co., Miss. Aug. 23, 1804. An itinerant Methodist preacher 64 years. By his ministry 'much people was added unto the Lord.' Not a single day of 71 years given to sin. Died Oct. 1, 1888. He lived and died 'in full assurance of faith'." Rev. Jones' place in history will be forever secure, due to the following resolution, unanimously adopted by the Mississippi Conference of the Methodist Episcopal Church South: "Resolved, that the Mississippi Annual Conference do hereby request Rev. John G. Jones to prepare for publication a complete History of Methodism as connected with the Mississippi Conference." Having answered this request, Rev. Jones has become the pioneer Methodist historian in Mississippi.

- Jane Oliphant *Ross* Jones. Jane's interesting biographical inscription reads: "Jane Oliphant Ross, born in Jefferson Co., Miss., Feb. 15, 1808, married Rev. John G. Jones of the Miss. Annual Conference Aug. 31, 1828. For nearly 55 years the faithful and inspiring wife of an itinerant preacher. Died July 14, 1883." Jane and Rev. John Griffing Jones share a common stone.

- Rev. John A. B. Jones [Dec. 9, 1830 – Jan. 13, 1910], "son of Rev. John G. Jones." Rev. Jones' biographical inscription reads: "An itinerant minister 57 years."

- Lucy M. *Cotton* Jones [Mar. 31, 1829 – Aug. 24, 1894], "wife of Rev. J. A. B. Jones…married Mar. 31, 1829." Lucy's biographical inscription reads: "A self-sacrificing, earnest consistent Christian from childhood. Fulfilling every obligation, performing every duty. Strong in faith, abundant in good works."

- Infant Son Jones [died May 20, 1856, aged 12 hours], "infant son of Rev. John A. B. and Lucy M. Jones."

- Miss Mary E. Ross [died August 19, 1856, aged 19 years & 9 mo.], "died in Christian confidence." Mary's biographical inscription reads: "She was beautiful in person, of high intellectual endowments, elegant in her manners and from her childhood a worthy member of the Methodist Church."

- Howard Jones [died in 1872, aged 2 mo's], "son of F. A. & F. O. Jones."

- Albert E. Garrison [died Oct. 6, 1853, aged 16 mos. & 16 days], "son of T. & M. M. Garrison."

[B-52: Buck, Christie, Crane, Hughes, Richards, Watson, Young]. This plot is enclosed in a wrought iron fence, with its gate bearing the name WILLIAM YOUNG.

- William Young [April 16, 1786 – March 10, 1863], "born in Stevenston, Ayrshire, Scotland…and died at his residence in Claiborne Co. Miss." A memorial inscription reads: "Erected by Clarissa Young, Feb. 9, 1866."

- Clarissa *Crane* Young [January 1, 1798 – February 5, 1877], "daughter of Waterman Crane and Catharine Brashear." Clarissa's parents, along with her first husband, William Christie, and daughter, Caroline *Christie* Bertron, are buried in Waterman Crane Cemetery. Clarissa married William Young in 1821.

- James W. Watson [Feb. 11, 1824 – Jan. 28, 1899]

- Miriam *Buck* Watson [1825 – 1903], "wife of J. W. Watson." Miriam is the daughter of William R. and Maria Buck, buried in plot C-26. Besides those listed below, other children, Maria Flower *Watson* Briscoe, James Waterman Watson and William Young Watson, are all buried in plot G-53.

- William Young Watson [July 20, 1849 – Feb. 19, 1863], "son of James W. & Miriam Watson, born in Claiborne County, Miss." A memorial inscription reads: "Erected by Clarissa Young."

- Miriam Watson [Jan. 31, 1857 – Feb. 21, 1857], "daughter of James W. & Miriam Watson."

- James B. Hughes [May 21, 1868 – Sept. 20, 1869]

- Henry H. Hughes [Oct. 28, 1862 – Nov. 14, 1862]. James and Henry Hughes share a common stone with the inscription: "Sons of Wm. & Mary Hughes." Their parents are buried in plot A-20.

- Elizabeth Cowles Richards [Oct. 1, 1832 – Mar. 1, 1863]

[B-53: Kirkbride, Lynch, Massey, Thrasher]. This plot is enclosed in a wrought iron fence.

- John B. Thrasher [Oct. 9, 1800 – Sept. 13, 1878], "born in Pendleton County Ky." A biographical epitaph reads: "He was an able lawyer and for fifty-two years a member of the Port Gibson bar." Besides the obelisk he shares with his wife, he also has his own stone. John was a victim of the yellow fever epidemic.
- Eliza Thrasher [died July 1, 1857], "wife of J. B. Thrasher, died in Port Gibson." A memorial inscription reads: "Erected by her husband." Eliza and her husband share a common obelisk.
- Mary Brown *Massey* Lynch [1849 – 1878]. Mary married Joseph E. Lynch in 1866. She was a victim of the yellow fever epidemic.
- Marie Louise Lynch [died Dec. 7, 1871, aged 3 years, 11 mos. & 7 d's], "daughter of J. E. & Mary M. Lynch."
- Sarah B. *Massey* Kirkbride [1851 – 1878]. Sarah married J. J. Kirkbride in 1873. She was a victim of the yellow fever epidemic.

[B-54: Hall, Ikerd, McCall, Mullin, Norman]

- L. F. B. Hall [dates unreadable], "born in Lincoln (rest unreadable)."
- Elizabeth *(Norman)* Hall [Nov. 28, 1799 – July 6, 1862], "wife of L. F. B. Hall, a native of Georgia." Elizabeth married L. F. B. Hall in 1824.
- Virginia A. *(Hall)* McCall [1826 – Aug. 7, 1845]. Virginia married John P. McCall in 1844.
- Clara B. *Hall* Ikerd [Jan. 2, 1864 – Mar. 9, 1900], "wife of E. H. Ikerd." Clara married E. H. Ikerd in 1892.
- Robert Emmet Hall [April 17, 1868 – Sept. 6, 1870], "infant son of F. C. & E. Hall." Robert is the grandson of L. F. B. and Elizabeth *Norman* Hall.
- Nettie J. Mullin [July 31, 1872 – June 11, 1893], "wife of John J. Mullin, born in Port Gibson."

[B-55: Hannum, McComb]

- Belle *McComb* Hannum [no dates]. Belle's obelisk contains only the following words: "A TRIBUTE to her memory and her faith, by her affectionate husband, ARNOLD HANNUM." She married Arnold Hannum in 1846.

[B-56: Richey]

- George W. Richey [died Oct. 3, 1867, aged 68 years]. This stone is broken up into many pieces. George's last name and year of death were obtained from a separate source. George married Mary Pate in 1835.

[B-57: Briscoe, Ellis, Jelks]

- David C. Ellis [Nov. 22, 1810 – Apr. 28, 1868], a Mason. David married Cynthia Ann Parks in 1844.
- John Hunter Ellis [June 27, 1846? – Feb. 6, 1853], "son of D. C. & C. A. Ellis." A crack through the stone makes the birth year uncertain.
- David C. Ellis, Jr. [Mar. 17, 1848 – Apr. 14, 1869]
- Willie C. Ellis [Jan. 28, 1858 – Mar. 20, 1877]
- Fred T. Ellis [1884 – 1922]
- Margaret E. *(Briscoe)* Jelks [Dec. 11, 1832 – May 5, 1856], "consort of J. W. Jelks." A memorial inscription reads: "Erected by her affectionate husband, J. W. Jelks." Margaret is the daughter of Eli C. and Sarah Ann *Parks* Briscoe. Sarah is buried in plot A-14. Margaret married James W. Jelks in 1853.
- Infant Jelks [no dates]. This infant of James W. and Margaret E. *Briscoe* Jelks is buried with its mother, and they share a common stone.

[B-58: Burns, Davis, Kelley, Naasson, Wylie]

- Harvey Davis [died Oct. 9, 1845, in the 47th year of his age]
- Mary Davis [died June 2, 1850, in the 38th year of her age], "wife of Harvey Davis."
- Charlotte E. *(Davis)* Wylie [Apr. 7, 1833 – Sept. 20, 1859], "wife of James Wylie." Charlotte married James Wylie in 1859.

- James Davis [Dec. 10, 1836 – Nov. 11, 1837]
- Sarah J. Davis [Dec. 5, 1838 – Feb. 4, 1853]. James and Sarah share a common stone bearing the words: "Children of Harvey & Mary Davis."
- Joshua Kelley [Sep. 20, 1813 – Sep. 2(?), 1861], a Mason and member Independent Order of Odd Fellows.
- Isabella E. *(Burns)* Kelley [Sept. 13, 1820 – Dec. 20, 1897]. Isabella married Joshua Kelley in 1837.
- Mary Elizabeth Kelley [April 27, 1840 – Sept. 18, 1844]
- Mary Jane Kelley [Nov. 18, 1847 – June 26, 1852]. Mary Elizabeth and Mary Jane share a common stone bearing the words: "Children of Joshua & Isabella E. Kelly (sic)."
- Ann Eliza Kelley [Feb. 18, 1843 – (date of death buried in concrete)], "daugh. of J. & I. E. Kelley."
- Sarah P. Burns [March 7, 1836 – Sep. 21, 1855]
- John J. Naasson [July 8, 1880 – Mar. 10, 1903]. John married Nettie Griffing in 1902.

[B-59: Briggs]
- Susan L. Briggs [Dec. 24, 1847 – July 24, 1851], "daughter of W. F. & E. L. Briggs."
- Infant Daughter Briggs [born Jan. 7, 1852], "infant daughter of W. F. & E. L. Briggs."

[B-60: Killikelly, McArn, Moore]
- John B. McArn [Jan. 23, 1814 – Feb. 2, 1853], "a native of Richmond Co. N. C."
- Robert Brown Killikelly [died July 29, 1843, aged 14 mos., 9 days], "son of B. B. & M. M. Killikelly." Robert is the son of Rev. Bryan Bernard Killikelly, an Episcopal minister who served Port Gibson in the 1840s.
- Charles Wilson Moore [June 5, 1850 – Aug. 1, 1851], "son of R. M. & P. M. Moore."

Section C

WOODED AREA

8	7	6	5	4	3	2	1
9	10	11	12	13	14a	14b	15	16
24	23	22	21	20	19	18	17
25	26	27	28	29	30	31	32	33
40	39	38	37	36b	36a	35	34
41	42	43	44	45	46	47
55	54	53	52	51	50	49	48
56	57	58	59	60	61	62	63
71	70	69	68	67	66	65	64
72	73	74
75	76	77	78	79	80	81	82
89	88	87	86	85	84	83

N

Section C

Section C is the location bearing the graves of the Samuel Gibson family, and as such, the oldest part of what eventually came to be known as Wintergreen Cemetery. Being initially a family plot, and then growing from there, the first families could not have envisioned the beautiful creation that they started. They had no reason to think about things like surveying the plots and lots, much less labeling each individual plot for future reference. Because of all this, those buried here, at least at first, appear to be placed in a rather haphazard fashion, and not really assigned to any particular lot at all. These initial listings represent lone graves, and are not assigned to any particular lot.

[C-1/2: Berry, Bland, Goslin, Taylor] This lot has a lone C. S. A. stone whose owner cannot be identified.
- Col. R. J. Bland [died Sept'r 14, 1840, in his 29 year]
- Albert Henry Goslin [Aug. 26, 1837 – Aug. 13, 1856]. According to a funeral notice, Albert is the son of Henry L. and Susan C. *Robertson* Goslin.
- Betty *Berry* Taylor [November 22, 1856 – November 16, 1933]. Betty married James Madison Taylor in 1893. James is buried in plot D-9.

[C-3: Schuetze]
- William Schuetze [Feb. 21, 1854 – Sept. 12, 1894]

[C-4: Arnold]
- Jessie W. Arnold [Nov. 10, 1889 – Jan. 17, 1892], "daughter of J. V. & F. R. Arnold."
- Johnnie Arnold [Dec. 23, 1897 – May 1, 1899], "son of J. V. & F. R. Arnold." Jessie and Johnnie Arnold are children of John V. and Florence *Smith* Arnold, buried in Jefferson County.

[C-5: Hall]
- Elvira Hall [died May 29, 1864, aged 26 years 8 mos. & 3 days], "daughter of A. J & C. Hall."

[C-6: Meek]
- Fannie Meek [Apr. 8, 1853 – Aug. 26, 1856], "daughter of Wm. F. & Martha Ann Meek."

[C-7: Barrot, Brashear, Cole, Colson, Foote, Harris, Singleton]. All of these graves are enclosed in a wrought iron fence, except for that of Mary Bradford *Harris* Colson and her infant daughter.
- James Edward Cole [July 3, 1812 – Sept. 20, 1864]
- Frank H. Foote [Jan. 27, 1843 – May 18, 1920], C. S. A. stone, "Father", and "Claiborne Volunteer Infantry, Company F, 48 Miss. Regiment, Army of Northern Virginia." This is not a military stone. From

a condensed obituary we can see that Mr. Foote was associated with work on the Vicksburg National Military Park, was a veteran of the Civil War, and was deeply interested in matters pertaining thereto. He was a gallant soldier and spent much time since the war in gathering data relative to the soldiers who went from this county. He probably had the only history of this kind ever preserved.

- Bettie A. *(Cole)* Foote [Jan. 29, 1841 – May 12, 1906], "Mother." Bettie married Frank H. Foote in 1865.
- Enola Frances Foote [Aug. 25, 1867 – Sept. 30, 1868], "daughter of F. H. & B. A. Foote."
- Janie Foote [Nov. 18, 1870 – Nov. 14, 1875]. "Our Darling Janie" is the only name on the stone. The last name of FOOTE is found on her foot stone. Janie is the daughter of Frank H. and Bettie A. *Cole* Foote.
- Anon K. Brashear [Feb. 26, 1869 – June 12, 1932]
- Nora *Foote* Brashear [July 29, 1873 – Sept. 21, 1950]. Nora is the daughter of Frank H. and Bettie A. *Cole* Foote. She married Anon K. Brashear in 1896.
- Mildred Elizabeth Brashear [Mar. 21, 1901 – Mar. 22, 1991]. Mildred is the daughter of Anon K. and Nora *Foote* Brashear.
- Anona V. Brashear [Feb. 1, 1904 – Feb. 15, 1977]. Anona is the daughter of Anon K. and Nora *Foote* Brashear.
- Elinor Wood Brashear [Apr. 5, 1906 – Feb. 7, 1909]. Elinor is the daughter of Anon K. and Nora *Foote* Brashear.
- Joseph E. Barrot [April 6, 1837 – Feb. 24, 1872], C. S. A. stone. Joseph was married twice, first to Sarah R. Perkins in 1860. Joseph's middle initial has been removed from the stone. His footstone shows the initials, J. E. B.
- Rebecca James *(Cole)* Colson [Aug. 16, 1843 – Nov. 26, 1907], "Mother." Rebecca married Joseph E. Barrot in 1869. After his death she married Henry Melville Colson in 1875.
- Marion Alma Singleton [Mar. 2, 1880 – Oct., 1880], "daughter of Rev. H. R. & Mrs. I. A. Singleton." Marion's father, Rev. Hiram Rivers Singleton, was a minister at the local Methodist Church during the latter 1800s.
- Mary Bradford *(Harris)* Colson [May 16, 1843 – Oct. 16, 1873], "wife of H. M. Colson." Mary married Henry Melville Colson in 1870.
- Infant Daughter Colson [no dates]. This unnamed infant shares a common stone with Mary Colson.

[C-8: Summers]
- J. H. Summers [died Nov. 6, ????]. This stone is broken into many pieces with much missing information.

[C-9: Haug, Hulburt]
- Dr. G. W. Haug [March 1, 1826 – Aug. 31, 1875], "born in Freudenstadt Wurtemberg Germany." Hermon C. Hulburt [Jan. 20, 1848 – Aug. 8, 1852], "son of Martin N. & Sinai Hulburt." Hermon's mother, Sinai, is buried at the Hulburt grave site in Claiborne County.

"His eyes are closed, his lips are still,
Convulsed he feels no more.
He has left a world of sorrow here,
And now in pleasure dwell.
Those flowers I trained of many a hue
Along thy path to bloom,
And little thought that I must strew
Their tears upon thy tomb."
—on stone of Hermon C. Hulburt

[C-10: Bethea, Buchanan]
- Philip Bethea [April 7, 1817 – Aug. 2, 1871], a Mason.
- Missouri Catherine *(Buchanan)* Bethea [Feb. 15, 1822 – April 8, 1863], "wife of Philip Bethea." Missouri married Philip Bethea in 1839.
- Richard Wharton Bethea [July 28, 1845 – May 6, 1865], C. S. A. stone, "son of Philip & Missouri C. Bethea." According to Mississippi Confederate Grave Registration records, Richard was a Private in Co. G, 15th (or 16th) Miss. Infantry, possibly of Northern Virginia, and possibly died of wounds.
- Melborne Moore Bethea [March 16, 1863 – Nov. 30, 1863], "son of P. & M. C. Bethea."

[C-11: Leonard, Van Dorn, Vertner]
- John D. Vertner [July 24, 1807 – September 24, 1839]. John's memorial inscription reads: "By his affectionate children."
- J. E. V. [Nov. 30, 1870], "In memory of our mother." Although somewhat lacking in information, this is the stone of Jane E. *Van Dorn* Vertner, daughter of P. A. and Sophia *Caffery* Van Dorn. Her father is buried in combined plot C-15/16. Jane married John D. Vertner in 1830.
- Daniel Vertner [Jan. 12?, 1832? – Sept. 12, 1837], "son of John D. & Jane E. Vertner." This stone is rather worn. The date of birth may be suspect.
- James Douglas Vertner [died Feb. 9, 1886, in the 49th year of his age]. James' epitaph reads: "Numbered with the saints: in Glory Everlasting. Entered into the Rest of Paradise at Columbus, Miss." James married Constance Kearney in 1876.
- Baby Jane Vertner [no dates], "infant daughter of J. Douglas and Constance Vertner."
- Janie Leonard [no dates]. Janie and Baby Jane Vertner share a common grave location.

[C-12: Bethea, Foote, Holloway, Smith]
- William E. Foote [Nov. 10, 1851 – Apr. 21, 1880], a Mason and member Independent Order of Odd Fellows.
- M. C. *Bethea* Foote [Nov. 19, 1851 – Nov. 27, 1922], "wife of W. E. Foote."
- Mary E. Foote [Mar. 11, 1877 – Aug. 2, 1906]
- Willie E. *Foote* Holloway [died June 19, 1900, age 19], "wife of L. G. Holloway." These first four listed share a common obelisk.
- Jennie P. Foote [died Oct. 2, 1875]
- Jacob V. S. Smith [Dec. 28, 1849 – April 8, 1863], "son of W. & E. Smith."
- Mary [no dates]. This stone has a first name and no other information, except the letters, KOTM, indicating that Mary is a member of the sorority, Knights of the Maccabees.

[C-13: McCaleb, Morris, Watkins]
- William T. Morris [Jan. 2, 1831 – May 27, 1906], member Independent Order of Odd Fellows.
- May *McCaleb* Morris [Nov. 17, 1834 – Jan. 14, 1913], "wife of Wm. T. Morris." May married William T. Morris in 1858. Besides those listed below, they have daughters, Perla V. *Morris* Mason, buried in plot B-42, and Eugenia *Morris* Crisler, buried in plot H-42.
- Adelaide May *Morris* Watkins [July 12, 1867 – March 26, 1936], "wife of T. F. Watkins." Adelaide is the daughter of William T. and May *McCaleb* Morris. She married T. F. Watkins in 1905.
- Charles Edgar Morris [Aug. 20, 1872 – Mar. 14, 1942]. Charles is the son of William T. and May *McCaleb* Morris.
- Lucie *McCaleb* Morris [May 10, 1872 – Sept. 27, 1957], "wife of C. E. Morris." Lucie married Charles Edgar Morris in 1898.
- Elizabeth McCaleb Morris [Oct. 29, 1899 – May 19, 1972]. Elizabeth is the daughter of Charles Edgar and Lucie *McCaleb* Morris.
- Charles Edgar Morris [Nov. 6, 1900 – May 19, 1907], "son of Chas. E. & Lucy A. Morris."

- Lucy Augusta Morris [Nov. 15, 1901 – Jan. 26, 1983]. Lucy is the daughter of Charles Edgar and Lucie *McCaleb* Morris.
- Eugenia Crisler Morris [Oct. 15, 1903 – Feb. 1, 1997]. Eugenia is the daughter of Charles Edgar and Lucie *McCaleb* Morris.
- Lcdr. Perla May Morris [Aug. 22, 1905 – Oct. 28, 1982], "USNR-RET." Perla is the daughter of Charles Edgar and Lucie *McCaleb* Morris.
- Infant Daughter Morris [April 16, 1908], "infant daughter of C. E. & L. A. Morris."
- Martha Morris [June 13, 1913 – Jan. 12, 1992]. Martha is the daughter of Charles Edgar and Lucie *Mc-Caleb* Morris.

[C-14a: Beaty, Hoopes, Loury, Mason, Murphy]
- Alexander Murphy [Oct. 1803 – Sept. 1833]
- Catherine *Loury* Murphy [March 17, 1804 – Aug. 13, 1875]. Catherine married Alexander Murphy in 1827, and they share a common obelisk.
- Alexander Butler Murphy [died ae. 1 yr. 4 mo. 16 d's], "only son of Alexander & Catherine Murphy."
- Helen Maria Murphy [Aug. 26, 1831 – Dec. 16, 1899]
- Elizabeth T. *(Murphy)* Hoopes [Apr. 10, 1830 – July 10, 1913]. Elizabeth married Edward Barnes Hoopes in 1851. Edward is buried in plot B-36. Besides their daughter listed below, another daughter, Helen Kate *Hoopes* Mason, is buried in plot B-42.
- Elizabeth M. Hoopes [Apr. 3, 1852 – Apr. 17, 1913]. Elizabeth is the daughter of Edward Barnes and Elizabeth T. *Murphy* Hoopes.
- Kate Hoopes Mason [June 5, 1894 – Dec. 17, 1987]. Kate is the daughter of Charles S. and Helen Kate *Hoopes* Mason.
- William Jeremiah Beaty [died Aug't 4, 1837, aged 1 year, 4 mo.], "infant son of William & Catharine Beaty."
- Robert Emmette Beaty [died Sep. 7, 1853, aged 9 years], "son of Wm. & Catharine R. Beaty." William and Robert's parents, William and Catharine *Murphy* Beaty were married in 1834. Robert was a victim of the yellow fever epidemic.

[C-14b: Davenport, Gordon, McPherson, Middleton]
- R. F. Gordon [Feb. 17, 1832 – Oct. 25, 1894], C. S. A. stone.
- Sarah S. *(Davenport)* Gordon [Aug. 27, 1834 – Oct. 2, 1880], "wife of R. F. Gordon." Sarah's first marriage was to Jonathan Middleton in 1854. She later married Robert F. Gordon in 1860.
- Kate Gordon [May 24, 1823 – Jan. 14, 1893], "sister of R. F. Gordon."
- W. Russel (sic) Gordon [June 29, 1864 – Sept. 19, 1878], "son of R. F. & S. S. Gordon." These first four names share a common obelisk. W. Russel was a victim of the yellow fever epidemic.
- Robert F. Gordon, Jr. [May 25, 1862 – Feb. 28, 1905]. Robert is the son of Robert F. and Sarah S. *Davenport* Gordon.
- Jonathan "Sugie" Middleton [Dec. 9, 1856 – Oct. 2, 1864], "son of Jona. & S. S. Middleton."
- Laura E. McPherson [died Jan. 24, 1873]

[C-15/16: Van Dorn]. It is not clear why the two graves in this plot are facing south, while almost all other graves in the entire cemetery are pointed in the traditional easterly direction.
- Judge P. A. Van Dorn [1773 – 1837], a Mason. Peter married Sophia Caffery in 1811. Besides his son listed below, a daughter, Jane E. *Van Dorn* Vertner, is buried in plot C-11.
- Earl Van Dorn [died May 7, 1863], C. S. A. stone, "MAJ GEN, C. S. A." This is a military stone. Gen. Van Dorn also has a civilian stone with his birth year of 1820. Earl is the son of Judge P. A. and Sophia *Caffery* Van Dorn. According to Mississippi Confederate Grave Registration records, he served as Major General in the Army of Mississippi and Tennessee. His cause of death was "assassination."

- [C-17/18: Chambliss, Cobun, Elias, Gibson, Goodin, Minor, Moore]
  - Samuel Gibson [died Dec'r 19, 1817], "first settler of this place & 45 years a resident of this state."
  - Rebecca *(Cobun)* Gibson [died July 15, 1821, aged 60 years], "wife of Samuel Gibson." According to the Gibson Family Bible, Rebecca married Samuel Gibson in 1777.
  - Samuel Gibson [died January 26, 1816, aged 21 years], "son of Sam'l & Rebecca Gibson."
  - William R. Chambliss [died May 23, 1820, in the 30th year of his age], a Mason, "a native of Virginia." William married Rebecca C. Gibson in 1818.
  - John Taylor Moore [died November 30, 1807, aged 1 year 4 months and 5 days], "only son of Dr. Joseph & Esther Moore." John's stone is the oldest one found that was original to this cemetery, and as such, possibly represents the very first burial here.
  - Stephen B. Minor [died July 12, 1821, aged 33 years]
  - Ann *(Gibson)* Minor [Sept. 30, 1788 – Jan. 25, 1863]. Ann is the daughter of Samuel and Rebecca *Cobun* Gibson. She married Stephen B. Minor in 1810.
  - Stephen W. Minor [died Aug. 29, 1821, aged 1 year 2 months and 1 day], "infant son of William B. Minor."
  - Matilda Elias Goodin [died September 25, 1840, aged 2 years 1 month & 26 days], "daughter of William F. & Amanda Goodin."
  - Matilda Elias [died October 23, 1857], "daughter of Henry Elias of Philadelphia, who departed this life…while on a visit to her sister."

> "Heaven sent a rosebud from the bower of the skies.
> But death too rudely smote the flower, and here it lies.
> Rest, gentle one, e'en the brief hour of thy short stay
> Was precious, and we praise the Power that call'd thee away."
> —on stone of Matilda Elias Goodin

[C-19: Harrington, Magruder, McCray, McLean]

- T. B. Magruder [Sept. 25, 1800 – Aug. 22, 1885]
- Mrs. Elizabeth *(Harrington)* Magruder [died July 5, 1844, in the 46th year of her age], "consort of Dr. Thos. B. Magruder." Elizabeth's memorial reads: "Erected to the memory of this dear departed one, by her affectionate husband and children." Elizabeth is the first wife of Thomas B. Magruder, marrying in 1823. Besides their son listed below, another son, William Thomas Magruder, is buried in plot A-19.
- Joseph Moore Magruder [Sept. 28, 1830 – Mar. 19, 1864], C. S. A. stone. Joseph is the son of Thomas B. and Elizabeth *Harrington* Magruder. According to Mississippi Confederate Grave Registration records, he served as Corp./Captain in Co. K, 12th Miss. Infantry and Co. A, 24th Miss. Cavalry, and was killed in battle.
- Amanda Louisa *(McCray)* Magruder [March 17, 1832 – May 2, 1853], "wife of Joseph M. Magruder." Amanda married Joseph Moore Magruder in 1852.
- William Brant McLean [Sept. 26, 1846 – Apr. 19, 1901], C. S. A. stone.
- Amanda Louise *Magruder* McLean [Feb. 11, 1853 – Apr. 17, 1908], "his wife." Amanda is the daughter of Joseph Moore and Amanda Louisa *McCray* Magruder. She married William Brant McLean in 1876, and they share a common stone.
- Sarah O. Magruder [died Dec. 28, 1864, in the 45th year of her age], "wife of Dr. Thomas B. Magruder." This is Dr. Magruder's second wife.
- Mary E. Magruder [died July 7, 1858, aged 10 yrs 10 mos & 11 days], "daughter of Dr. T. B. & S. O. Magruder."

- Virginia Magruder [died Sept. 4, 1863, aged 8 yrs 10 mos & 26 days], "daughter of Dr. T. B. & S. O. Magruder."
- Charley Magruder [died Jan. 28, 1861, aged 15 mos & 3 days], "son of Dr. T. B. & S. O. Magruder."
- Rosa Magruder [April 30, 1863 – June 15, 1948]

[C-20: Bobo, Robbins]

- Sallie C. (*Robbins*) Bobo [June 9, 1849 – July 17, 1896], "wife of Wm. S. Bobo." Sallie married William S. Bobo in 1869.
- Leon R. Bobo [Mar. 29, 1873 – Aug. 23, 1878]. Sallie C. and Leon R. Bobo share a common stone.
- Elisha Robbins [Mar. 6, 1864 – Aug. 2, 1865], "son of E. & M. E. Robbins." Elisha's name is misspelled on the stone as RORBINS.

[C-21: Clarke, Weeks]

- Ann E. *Clarke* Weeks [Feb. 22, 1830 – Oct. 17, 1862], "wife of P. W. Weeks, born in Caroline Co. M. D. (sic)." Ann is the first wife of Perry W. Weeks.
- Ann Delia Weeks [died Oct. 16, 1862], "daughter of P. W. & Ann E. Weeks." Ann E. and Ann Delia Weeks share a common obelisk with the words: "Here sleeps my beloved wife with our darling babe in her arms."
- Perry W. Weeks [June 23, 1859 – April 7, 1863], "son of P. W. & Ann E. Weeks."
- Willie Weeks [Dec. 11, 1869 – June 10, 1870], "son of P. W. & Julia A. Weeks." Willie's parents, Perry W. and Julia A. *Louden* Weeks, were married in 1866.

[C-22: Green, Moore, Rowan, Watson]

- Thomas Rowan [Dec. 14, 1825 – Nov. 6, 1862]
- Clara G. Rowan [Feb. 28, 183? – Nov. 28, 1888]. Clara is the wife of Thomas Rowan. On her stone, the last number of the birth year is chipped away.
- Helen Green Rowan [Dec. 21, 1850 – June 19, 1852], "daughter of Thomas & Clara Rowan."
- Thomas B. Rowan [Nov. 25, 1848 – Sept. 10, 1880], "My Husband." Thomas married Ella Calhoun in 1876.
- Cordelia A. Rowan [Mar. 4, 1853 – Oct. 14, 1876]
- Clara Girault Rowan [Jan. 12, 1854 – Oct. 7, 1854], "third daughter of Thomas & Clara Rowan."
- Olivia *Rowan* Watson [died 1877]. Olivia married Louis Wantland Watson in 1865. Louis is buried in plot A-73.
- Charles Beaty Green [1781 – 1864]
- William Walker Moore [Sept. 10, 1885—Nov. 18, 1886], "son of W. W. & J. R. Moore." William's parents, Capt. William Walker and Julia *Rowan* Moore, are buried in plot F-16.

[C-23: Anderson, Bedon, Coleman, Galtney, McDonald, Pittman]

- Israel Coleman [died May 9, 1870, in his 74th year]
- Mrs. M. J. (*McDonald*) Coleman [Nov 11, 1807 – June 13, 1891], "Mother." Martha J. married Israel Coleman in 1823.
- H. J. Coleman [May 18, 1831 – Jan. 16, 1910]. Dr. Henry J. Coleman is the son of Israel and Martha J. *McDonald* Coleman.
- Celeste *Galtney* Coleman [Aug. 6, 1841 – Sept. 12, 1927]. Celeste married Henry J. Coleman in 1877.
- Martha Isabella Coleman [died Sept. 1, 1844, aged 5 years & 28 days], "daughter of Israel & Martha Coleman."
- Frank N. Pittman [Aug. 20, 1880 – Mar. 24, 1951]
- May *Bedon* Pittman [Oct. 17, 1876 – Nov. 22, 1967]. May is the wife of Frank N. Pittman. They have a daughter, Rosa *Pittman* Freeland, buried in combined plot A-90/164.
- Susan M. Anderson [Jan. 14, 1826 – Feb. 3, 1857], "daughter of Robert & Susan Anderson, born in Jefferson Co., Ky."

[C-24: Benton, Cameron, Crills, Gillespie, Gordon, Ingram, McKeever]
- Ann Isabelle Cameron [July 11, 1847 – May 30, 1852], "daughter of John & Sarah Cameron."
- Mary A. Cameron [died Oct. 20, 1850, aged 10 days], "daughter of John & Sarah Cameron."
- David Allen Cameron [died Aug. 29, 1853, aged 1 year & 1 month], "son of John & Sarah Cameron."
- Johnson W. Gordon [Jan. 27, 1813 – died Nov. 1, 1855], "born Washington Co., Ky., died in (unreadable location)."
- Candace *(Benton)* McKeever [died August 9, 1883]. Candace was married three times. Her first marriage was to Matthew Gillespie in 1829. They have a son, Horace William Gillespie, buried in Grand Gulf Cemetery. Candace next married Johnson W. Gordon in 1841. After his death Candace married William McKeever in 1859.
- Eloise B. Ingram [January 14, 1931]. Eloise and Candace McKeever share a common stone.
- Rose *Ingram* Crills [died May 1, 1953, age 70 years]

[C-25: Tatum, Wardlaw]
- Mary S. *(Wardlaw)* Tatum [Jan. 6, 1823 – Dec. 3, 1851], "wife of J. J. Tatum." Mary married J. J. Tatum in 1838.

[C-26: Buck, Jefferies]
- William R. Buck [Aug. 4, 1790 – Oct. 10, 1853], "born in Virginia."
- Maria Buck [Mar. 7, 1797 – Sep. 21, 1874], "Our Mother" and "wife of Wm. R. Buck." Besides those listed below, they have a daughter, Miriam *Buck* Watson, buried in plot B-52.
- W. H. Buck [Feb. 26, 1831 – June 28, 1896], C. S. A. stone. According to Mississippi Confederate Grave Registration records, Mr. Buck served as Lieutenant in Co. K, 1st Light Artillery, and may have eventually died of his wounds.
- Caroline Buck [August 2, 1833 – January 22, 1924]. Caroline is the daughter of William R. and Maria Buck.
- Dr. Charles Edward Buck [April 4, 1836 – Nov. 29, 1879], C. S. A. stone. Charles is the son of William R. and Maria Buck. According to Mississippi Confederate Grave Registration records, he was a First Lieutenant, then Captain, in Co. K, 12th Miss. Infantry and Co. C, 4th Miss. Cavalry.
- Sarah *Jefferies* Buck [Mar. 29, 1845 – Feb. 9, 1923], "wife of Dr. Chas. E. Buck." Sarah married Dr. Buck in 1864, and they share a common obelisk.
- William Henry Buck [October 14, 1868 – March 29, 1924]. William is the son of Dr. Charles Edward and Sarah *Jefferies* Buck.

According to *Port Gibson Reveille's* "Looking Back" column, dated September 27, 2012, Lt. Buck served as commander of the presidential yacht, USS Sylph (PY-5) in 1902.
- Maria Flower Buck [died Oct. 27, 1867, aged 4 weeks], "infant daughter of C. E. & S. L. Buck."

[C-27: Ely, Hall, Harlow, Rickhow, Slone]
- Alfred Harlow [died Jan'y 9, 1842, in the 28th year of his age], "a native of Bangor, Maine, died at Port Gibson."
- Mary Ann *Slone* Hall [died Aug. 5, 18?0, aged ? y, 10 m, 18 d], "wife of J. H. Hall & daughter of Wm. Slone of Tennessee." This stone is eroded making the dates unreadable.
- Isabella Rickhow [Sept. 12, 1780 – Aug. 23, 1843], "wife of Rev. Jacob Rickhow, born in Monmoth (sic) Co, New Jersey."
- Miss Sarah A. Ely [died Aug. 22, 1838, ae. 25], "daughter of Dea. Richard & Mrs. May Ely, of Lyme, Ct."

"Yes, we may weep and heaven approve the tears
For one so ripe in worth, so young in years,

For Jesus wept, & those who here pursue
The path He trod on earth, must sorrow too."
—on obelisk of Miss Sarah A. Ely

[C-28: Chevandemann, Thomas]
- Augustus Chevandemann [died December 6, 1835, aged 34 years], "born in Paris, France."
- D. Y. Thomas [died Aug. 17, 1841, in his 32nd year]. A memorial epitaph reads: "This tribute of respect is paid by friends that could appreciate his merit."

[C-29: Arnold, Bagnell, Fulkerson, Johnson, McAlpine, Stuart, Todd]
- Edward Kirby McAlpine [Jan. 18, 1865 – Aug. 30, 1919]
- Benjamin Morehead McAlpine [June 9, 1867 – Nov. 11, 1919]
- Charles Morehead McAlpine [Nov. 29, 1872 – Oct. 11, 1909]
- Mary *McAlpine* Bagnell [May 2, 1874 – April 24, 1929], member Daughters of the American Revolution. Mary and her three brothers, listed above, are children of Daniel Vertner and Julia T. *Morehead* McAlpine, buried in plot B-15. Mary was married twice, first to Albert Sidney Johnson in 1895, and then to Samuel Haring Bagnell in 1903. Samuel is buried in plot G-23.
- Julia Marie *(Johnson)* Arnold [August 20, 1896 – February 4, 1986]. Julia is the daughter of Albert Sidney and Mary *McAlpine* Johnson. She married Robert Lowry Arnold in 1920.
- W. R. McAlpine [Sept. 27, 17?? – Sept. 19, 1855]. William R. McAlpine married Melvina Harris in 1824. This stone is cracked and eroded, making some dates unreadable.
- William Boon Fulkerson [Mar. 29, 1829 – June 3, 1895], member Knights Templar order of Masons, C. S. A. stone.
- Lulee *S(tuart)*. Fulkerson [Mar. 17, 1866 – Oct. 26, 1915], "Mother." Lulee married William Boon Fulkerson in 1892.
- George H. Fulkerson [Apr. 28, 1831 – Aug. 27, 1901], a Mason, C. S. A. stone. George married Emma M. McAlpine in 1866.
- Mary E. M. Fulkerson [Oct. 14, 1868 – June 3, 1873], "daughter of G. H. & E. M. Fulkerson."
- Alexander Miller Todd [Oct. 5, 1930 – Sep. 19, 1994], "LT, US NAVY, KOREA." This is a military stone.
- Mary Ann Todd [March 27, 1929 – April 13, 2006]

[C-30: Davenport, Faulk, Granbery, Hastings]
- Orran Faulk [died July 12, 1822, aged 36 years], a Mason, "late merchant of this place."
- Eliza *Granbery* Hastings [Apr. 13, 1791 – May 17, 1883], "wife of Jonas Hastings, born in Norfolk, Va.… died in Port Gibson, Miss." Eliza married Jonas Hastings in 1810.
- Dr. John Granbery Hastings [Dec. 31, 1812 – Aug. 22, 1883], a Mason, "son of Jonas & Eliza Hastings, born in Norfolk, Va.…died in Claiborne Co., Miss." John married Rebecca Ann Chambliss in 1835. Besides those children listed below, they have a son, John G. Hastings, buried in plot A-31.
- Ann Maria *Davenport* Hastings [May 28, 1845 – Aug. 27, 1873], "wife of John Granbery Hastings, Jr." Ann married John Granbery Hastings, Jr. in 1866.
- Capt. W. H. Hastings [Feb. 21, 1838 – May 31, 1862], C. S. A. stone, "CAPT., CO. B, 12TH MISS. REGT…killed in battle…He was buried at Seven Pines, Va., where he fell." This is not a military stone, but a memorial marker.
- Julia Caroline Hastings [June 20, 1840 – Nov. 3, 1869], "wife of Robt. M. Hastings, born at Norfolk, Va." Julia is the first wife of Robert M. Hastings, buried in plot B-47.
- Infant Daughter Hastings [no dates]. This infant is buried with her mother, Julia Caroline Hastings.

An obelisk, surrounded by five individual stones, has the words: "Children of J. G. & R. A. Hastings." The individual stones belong to:

- Rebecca Ann Hastings [Mar. 25, 1836 – June 19, 1837]
- Infant Hastings [Dec. 1850]
- Ann Eliza Hastings [June 8, 1853 – Oct. 12, 1855]
- Clarissa Hastings [March 13, 1856 – Oct. 13, 1856]
- Jonas Hastings [March 17, 1858 – May 9, 1858]

[C-31: no stones]

[C-32: Clark, Hutchinson, Vanhorn]

- Pamelia E. *(Hutchinson)* Vanhorn [died July 18, 1822, in the 20th year of her age], "a native of Georgia, late consort of James Vanhorn, who departed this life…and left an infant son." Pamelia married James Vanhorn in 1819.
- Elizabeth Clark [died July 30, 1831, at the early age of eighteen], "our dear friend…eldest daughter of Martha & Joshua G. Clark of Claiborne County, Miss…loved and lamented by all."

[C-33: no stones]

[C-34: no stones]

[C-35: Dillard]

- W. Dillard [died July 17, 1839, aged 35 years]. Wiley Dillard married Eugenia Tistard in 1836.

[C-36a: Burnet, Hamilton, Quackenboss, Shaifer]

- John Burnet, Sr. [April 26, 1819 – July 15, 1899]. According to Burnet Bible records, John is the son of John and Mary *Dean* Burnet, buried in Burnet Cemetery.
- Elizabeth K. *(Shaifer)* Burnet [Jan. 24, 1828 – July 25, 1904], "wife of John Burnet." According to the book, *Threading the Generations*, by Mary Elizabeth Johnson and Carol Vickers, Elizabeth is the daughter of Abram Keller and Elizabeth *Humphreys* Shaifer. Abram Shaifer is buried in plot C-61. Elizabeth married John Burnet, Sr. in 1843. Besides those listed below, they have a daughter, Elizabeth *Burnet* Parker, buried in plot B-40.
- Amos Burnet [May 31, 1848 – Feb. 8, 1915]. Amos is the son of John and Elizabeth K. *Shaifer* Burnet. He is a Civil War veteran and, according to Mississippi Confederate Grave Registration records, was a Private in Co. C, 4th Miss. Cavalry.
- Mary *Hamilton* Burnet [Oct. 15, 1855 – Dec. 28, 1918], "wife of Amos Burnet." Mary is the daughter of Charles D. and Elizabeth *Belknap* Hamilton, buried in plot F-19, Elizabeth with last name of THRASHER. Mary married Amos Burnet in 1879.
- Sallie Barnes Burnet [Sept. 16, 1880 – Nov. 8, 1960]. Sallie is the daughter of Amos and Mary *Hamilton* Burnet.
- Carrie Lee *Burnet* Quackenboss [Feb. 5, 1882 – Dec. 16, 1975]. Carrie is the daughter of Amos and Mary *Hamilton* Burnet. She married Col. L. Wade Quackenboss in 1903.
- Abram K. Burnet [Dec. 16, 1852 – June 20, 1930]
- Sallie B. Burnet [Sept. 18, 1856 – Oct. 5, 1878], "daughter of John & Elizabeth Burnet."
- John Burnet, Jr. [Nov. 11, 1859 – May 20, 1939], "son of John and Elizabeth Burnet."
- Daniel Burnet [Dec. 28, 1861 – Oct. 8, 1862], "infant son of John & Elizabeth Burnet."
- Ruth Burnet [Aug. 1, 1870 – Feb. 8, 1876], "youngest daughter of John & Elizabeth Burnet."

[C-36b: Briscoe, Harrison, Michie, Shaifer]

- Henry F. Shaifer [Apr. 8, 1820 – Nov. 2, 1904]. Henry is the son of Abram Keller and Elizabeth *Humphreys* Shaifer. Abram Shaifer is buried in plot C-61.
- Clara J. *(Briscoe)* Shaifer [Aug. 27, 1825 – July 7, 1895]. Clara is the daughter of Parmenas and Polly Briscoe. Polly is buried in Briscoe Cemetery. Clara married Henry F. Shaifer in 1845.
- David Michie [Feb. 23, 1834 – Jan. 19, 1907]

- Mary E. *Shaifer* Michie [April 28, 1846 – Feb. 23, 1923], "wife of David Michie." Mary is the daughter of Henry F. and Clara J. *Briscoe* Shaifer.
- H. Frazer Shaifer [Dec. 3, 1848 – Jan. 25, 1899]. H. Frazer is the son of Henry F. and Clara J. *Briscoe* Shaifer.
- James P. Harrison [1852 – 1943]
- Ella N. Harrison [1864 – 1953]

[C-37: Ducket, McArthur, Pettit, Scott]
- Duncan McArthur [1835 – 1915]. After the death of Duncan's first wife, Laura, he married Emily Willis in 1876.
- Laura Ann McArthur [Feb. 3, 1842 – Sept. 29, 1874], "wife of Duncan McArthur."
- J. J. McArthur [no dates]
- Eliza A. *(Pettit)* McArthur [no dates]. According to a *Port Gibson Reveille* "Looking Back" column, Eliza married John J. McArthur in 1855, and died in 1909.
- Sarah R. McArthur [no dates]. Sarah is the daughter of John J. and Eliza *Pettit* McArthur.
- Ida *McA(rthur).* Scott [no dates]. Ida is the daughter of John J. and Eliza *Pettit* McArthur. She married L. Scott in 1879.
- Ducket [no dates]. This person has no further identification.

[C-38: Devenport, Lacy, McGinnis, Wood]. These stones are all located within a wrought iron fence.
- Maj. James Devenport [1764 – Oct. 15, 1841], "a native of Va….emigrated to Miss. A. D. 1780, died at his residence in Claiborn (sic) County…" A memorial epitaph reads: "Erected by his daughter, E. Wood." According to will records, James was married to a Nancy Devenport. Besides his daughter listed below, he has a son, Joseph Devenport, buried in Devenport Cemetery. It is interesting to note that Maj. Devenport was the first known settler here with the last name spelled as DEVENPORT. Will records show us that, through the generations, that last name has evolved into the more common spelling of DAVENPORT, and two separate and distinct lines of that name now exist.
- Mrs. Elizabeth *D(evenport).* Wood [Feb. 6, 1799 – Oct. 25, 1866], "Dear Mother." Elizabeth is the daughter of Maj. James and Nancy Devenport. She married Francis Wood in 1818.
- George W. McGinnis [no dates], C. S. A. stone. A funeral notice tells us that George died in 1914.
- Jane *Wood* McGinnis [1819 – Nov. 16, 1899], "wife of Geo. W. McGinnis." Jane married George W. McGinnis in 1866, and they share a common stone.
- James D. Wood [Jan. 23, 1821 – June 28, 1903], C. S. A. stone.
- Mary *Lacy* Wood [Oct. 2, 1834 – Jan. 12, 1917], "wife of James D. Wood." Mary married James D. Wood in 1857. They have a daughter, Sarah Jane *Wood* Pearson, buried in plot A-18a.
- Francis J. Wood [Nov. 18, 1829 – July 25, 1870]

[C-39: Millikan, Rowan]
- Alfred James Rowan, M. D. [Dec. 10, 1829 – April 21, 1866], C. S. A. stone, a Mason. After the death of Julia, listed below, Dr. Rowan married Jane Craig Ingraham in 1864.
- Julia M. Rowan [died March 29, 1863], "wife of A. J. Rowan, M. D."
- Louisa Millikan [died Sept. 29, 1861, aged 33 years], "wife of W. Millikan, a nativ (sic) of N. C."

[C-40: Briscoe, Hopkins, Jefferies, Kennard, Shelby, Walker, Young]. This lot has a cross-shaped monument bearing the names KENNARD on one side and WALKER on the other.
- J. L. K(ennard). [died Dec. 26, 1886], C. S. A. stone.
- A. B. K(ennard). [died Mar. 6, 1890]. A *Port Gibson Reveille* "Looking Back" column tells us that A. B. was married to J. L. Kennard, and that she died in her 73rd year.
- Harriet Tilghman Kennard [died Dec. 13, 1883]. Harriet is the daughter of J. L. and A. B. Kennard.
- Perry Kennard [died 1859]

- Harry Kennard [died 1861]. Harry and Perry share a common stone.
- Araminta Maude Kennard [died Feb. 23, 1930]
- Florence *Kennard* Young [died May 20, 1887], "wife of W. L. Young." Florence married W. L. Young in 1885.
- Charles Shreve Kennard [Feb. 3, 1851 – Apr. 27, 1926]
- Evana *Jefferies* Kennard [Aug. 28, 1848 – Feb. 7, 1934]. Evana married Charles Shreve Kennard in 1882. She had previously married John P. Briscoe in 1875. John Briscoe is buried in plot D-8, along with a daughter, Johnie *Briscoe* Barber.
- William Thomas Shelby [May 4, 1878 – June 21, 1950]
- Maude *Kennard* Shelby [Sept. 20, 1893 – Oct. 17, 1955]. Maude is the daughter of Charles Shreve and Evana *Jefferies* Kennard. She married William Thomas Shelby in 1909.
- N. S. Walker [1835 – 1895], C. S. A. stone, a Mason.
- Frances *Kennard* Walker [died Jan. 18, 1928]. Frances married Capt. N. S. Walker in 1867.
- Nettie *Walker* Hopkins [died Aug. 28, 1913]. Nettie is the daughter of N. S. and Frances *Kennard* Walker. She married William B. Hopkins in 1891.
- Nelson Walker [died Oct. 14, 1912]. Nelson is the son of N. S. and Frances *Kennard* Walker.
- Fannie Belle Walker [no dates]
- Florence Walker [no dates]. Florence and Fannie Belle Walker share a common stone.

"He knows the winds blow roughly here,
And often it is dark;
And little ones, like Noah's doves,
Are safest in the ark."
—on stone of Fannie Belle and Florence Walker

[C-41: Moody, Wylie]
- Harriet B. Wylie [died Jan. 21, 1855, in her 68th year], "Our Mother...wife of Rev. Wm. Wylie of Newark Ohio, formerly wife of Wm. Moody of Balt. Md."
- George V. Moody [aged fifty years], C. S. A. stone. George's biographical epitaph reads: "With uncommon personal advantages he had a great, brave, loving, generous heart, a love of right, a scorn of wrong, of coward and of knave, and of him it may truly be said that even his failings leaned to virtue's side."

[C-42: Hay?]
- Margaret Ann (last name unreadable) [died March 18, 1845?, aged 2 years & 10 days], "daughter of Thomas B. & Sarah M. Ha????." This stone is broken, with no more readable information.

[C-43: Worthington]
- Mr. Perry Worthington [died Dec. 25, 1836, in the 22 year of his age], "died at Port Gibson, Miss....youngest son of Major Worthington, of Cumberland Co., Md." A memorial epitaph reads: "This monument was erected by his brother, Thomas Worthington, Esq., of Rockwell, Md."

[C-44: Calhoun, Gordon, McClure, Moore, Rouse, Williams]
- Mrs. Christiana *Gordon* Calhoun [died Jan'y 3, 1838, in the 23rd year of her age], "wife of James E. Calhoun & youngest daughter of Adam & Aletheia Gordon." Christiana's memorial tribute reads: "This monument is erected by her husband, in whose breast her memory is consecrated," and her biographical epitaph reads: "Beneath this marble in sweet repose a fair one lies, the friend of all, called from husband beloved, a son and daughter, the hope & joy of both parents, mother to whom she was most dear, endowed with a portion of every Christian virtue. She lived beloved and respected and was deeply lamented by all in death." Christiana married James E. Calhoun in 1833.

- Rachel *(Rouse)* Williams [died October 31, 1836, in the 30th year of her age], "consort of Josiah J. Williams." Rachel married Josiah J. Williams in 1830.
- E. L. Kna (sic) McClure [died Sept. 28, 1830, aged 21 years], "a native of Clearmont (sic) Co., Ohio."
- Esther Ann Moore [died March 10, 1838, in her 24th year], "consort of Rich'd M. Moore."

"If departed worth deserves a tear,
Then gentle reader, pay that tribute here."
—on obelisk of Mrs. Christiana *Gordon* Calhoun

[C-45: Steward]
- William Steward [died Aug. 30, 1830, aged 21 years], "a native of New Lisbon, Ohio."
- Preston B. Wil??? [died Nov. 1830, aged ? years & one month]. This stone contains no more usable information.

[C-46: Campbell, Nugent]
- Capt. John Campbell [Oct. 29, 1769 – June 13, 1828], "born in Philad'a." Words of tribute read: "This stone is erected by filial gratitude."
- James Nugent [July 26, 1808 – June 30, 1831], "born…in Mourow County West Meath, Ireland, died in Port Gibson."

[C-47: Booth, Cotten, Gibbs]
- Thomas Cotten [died April 25, 1831, ae. 36 y's, 3 mo. & 19 d's], "died at Belmont."
- James Cotten [died Jan. 5, 1860, aged 60 yrs. 7 mos. & 17 ds.]. According to will records, James and Thomas Cotten are brothers. They are buried within their own wrought iron fence.
- Joseph Shewell Gibbs [Feb'y 9, 1799 – Nov'r 11, 1826], "attorney at law, son of Isaac and Ann Gibbs of Delaware." His biographical epitaph reads: "Distinguished by filial piety and fraternal affection, by native benevolence and sterling integrity, by pure morals and professional worth. He was respected in life, and lamented in death, by the wise and the good. His bereaved parents sorrowing, yet not as without hope: desiring and struggling to submit to the divine will, inscribe this stone to the memory of a beloved son."
- Joshua Booth [died July ??, ????, aged ? years], "a native of New York." Joshua married Elizabeth Rhodes in 1823. This stone is weathered and mostly unreadable.

[C-48: Carr, Clarke, Guinn, Ingles, Murdock]
- John Murdock [died August 1, 1818, in the 28th year of his age]. John's stone reads, in part: "This stone is placed by Francis Murdock over the mortal remains of his late & beloved brother John Murdock of Port Gibson." A biographical epitaph reads: "He was a native of Ireland, Monaghan County…"
- Francis Murdock [died April 21, 1838], "of Monaghan Ireland…died in Port Gibson."
- Elliott Ingles [December 22, 1790 – August 15, 1822], "… was born in Tennessee…and finished his course…in the town of Port Gibson."
- R. P. Carr [died Oct'r 4, 1819, in the 18th year of his age]. A memorial epitaph reads: "This tribute of respect is paid to his memory by his affectionate uncle, James Cage."
- Orange Clarke [died September 5, 1838, aged 40 years], "died near Port Gibson." Orange Clarke was married twice. After the death of Catharine, listed below, he married Ann Eliza White in 1838.
- Catharine *(Guinn)* Clarke [died Jan. 11, 1838, ae. 32], "consort of Orange Clarke." Catharine married Orange Clarke in 1827.

[C-49: All, Campbell, Murphy, Sadler, Strauss]
- Louisa Ann Campbell [died Sept. 6, 1831, aged 4 years, 8 months & 19 days], "eldest daughter of R. W. & H. C. Campbell."
- James Richardson Sadler [died Sept. 30, 1823, aged 2? years], "a native of Jef'n Co. Kentucky." This

stone is eroded, making some parts illegible.

- A. F. Strauss [died Sept. 29, 1823, aged 43 years], "a native of Germany (additional lines are buried)."
- Andrew W. Murphy [died Dec. 27, 1837, aged (blank) years]
- Sophia Elizabeth (*All*) Murphy [died March 12, 1845, in the 46th year of her age], "wife of Andrew W. Murphy." Sophia married Andrew W. Murphy in 1820.
- John W. Murphy [died Sept. 4, 1853, in the 31st year of his age], "eldest child of A. & S. E. Murphy." John was a victim of the yellow fever epidemic.

[C-50: Goddard, Grafton, Spencer]

- Israel Selden Spencer [died Mar. 5, 1837, ae. 74 y's 5 m's], "a native of east Haddam, Ct., who died in Port Gibson."
- Temma Spencer [died June 14, 1844, aged 81 years], "wife of I. S. Spencer, a native of Lyme, Ct."
- Maria *Spencer* Grafton [died June 24, 1840, in her 40th year], "daughter of Deacon I. S. Spencer of Connecticut." Maria is the daughter of Temma Spencer and the first wife of James F. Grafton, marrying in 1834. James Grafton is buried in plot B-35, with his second wife. Maria was previously married to a Mr. Goddard.
- Samuel S. Spencer [March 7, 1794 – Sept. 17, 1820], "died at Washington, Miss." A biographical epitaph reads: "A Christian."
- Theresa *Goddard* Spencer [died Mar. 21, 1830, ae. 26 years], "wife of Horatio N. Spencer and daughter of Rev. Samuel Goddard of Vermont." Horatio N. Spencer, Theresa's husband and father of Horatio G. and Maria Elizabeth Spencer, listed below, is buried in plot B-35. Theresa is Horatio N. Spencer's first wife.
- Horatio G. Spencer [died June 6, 1830, ae. 3 months], "infant son of H. N. Spencer." Horatio and his mother, Theresa *Goddard* Spencer, share a common stone.
- Maria Elizabeth Spencer [died Sept. 2, 1836, aged 8 years 8 months], "daughter of H. N. Spencer." Maria is the daughter of Theresa *Goddard* Spencer.
- Horatio M. Spencer [died Jan. 6, 1835, ae. 1 yr. 8 mo. 15 d's]
- Samuel M. Spencer [died Apr. 22, 1835, ae. 4 mo. 20 d's]. Horatio M. and Samuel M. Spencer share a common stone with the inscription: "Children of Horatio N. & Sarah A. Spencer."
- William Catlin Spencer [died Aug. 4, 1841, aged 3 mo. & 8 days], "son of Horatia (sic) & Sarah A. Spencer." The parents of Horatio M., Samuel M. and William Catlin Spencer are buried in plot B-35.
- Israel Selden Spencer [died August 14, 1835, ae. 1 yr. & 28 d's], "son of Israel & Mary N. Spencer." Israel's parents are buried in plot B-46.

Another raised, flat stone, badly eroded, shows the name GODDARD, with all else illegible. This stone may mark the grave of Rev. Samuel Goddard of Vermont, as determined by a previous cemetery survey.

"The Gospel was his joy and song
E'en to his latest breath,
The truth he had proclaim'd so long
Was his support in death."
—on stone of Israel Selden Spencer

[C-51: Wilson] This plot contains a lone C. S. A. stone whose owner cannot be identified.

- Arva Wilson, M. D. [died May 28, 1833, aged 56 years], "born in the State of Main (sic)." Arva's memorial epitaph reads: "This memento is erected by an affectionate wife to her departed husband, who departed with a hope of immortality, through Jesus, who is the Resurrection and the Life." He married Mrs. Sarah *Knox* Newton in 1832.

[C-52: no stones]

[C-53: Dougherty, Silver]

- James Dougherty [died November 2, 1835, aged 38 years], "a native of Londondery (sic) Ireland." James' memorial epitaph reads: "He was upright and useful as a citizen, devotedly affectionate as a husband, parent and friend. This stone is erected to commemorate the deep attachment felt for him while living and the sincerest sorrow for his death, by his beloved wife & children."
- William Harrison Silver [died Nov. 15, 1835, in the 24 year of his age], "son of James & Elizabeth Silver, born at North Bend, Ohio."

[C-54: Hamelton, Maclennan, Poor]

- R. S. Hamelton [died Dec. 24, 1836, ae. 49], "born in the Town of Cravnish, Farmanigh County, Ireland, & died at Port Gibson."
- Frederick J. Poor [July 15, ???? – May 28, 1850], "a native of ????" This stone is broken, with no more readable information.
- Ella F. Poor [died Aug. 27, 1843, aged 1 year & 10 days], "daughter of F. J. & E. J. Poor."
- Lucy B. Maclennan [died Oct. 3, 1844, aged one year & 24 days], "daughter of Jas. & L. A. Maclennan."

[C-55: Moody]

- Nathaniel P. Moody [Dec. 23, 1820 – Sept. 19, 1853], "born in Baltimore, Md….died at the post of duty in Port Gibson…of epidemic yellow fever." Nathaniel's memorial epitaph reads: "He obeyed the command to 'do justly, love mercy, and walk humbly with his God.' The whole community mourned his death. To his wife and children and to his loving brother who places this stone as a memorial, the loss of him is irreparable." Nathaniel married Ann Elizabeth Nugent in 1845.
- George Nugent Moody [April 3, 1849 – Oct. 14, 1850], "son of N. P. & A. E. Moody."
- George Edward Moody [April 22, 1843 – Jan'y 9, 1844]

[C-56: Brown, Lum, McCay, Regan, Scott, Smith]

- Catharine Tate *Scott* McCay [1803 – June 26, 1871], "Our Mother…wife of Campbell McCay, born in Kirkcudbright, Scotland."
- Agnes Jane *(McCay)* Smith [March 6, 1828 – Jan. 18, 1855], "wife of Frederick G. Smith." Agnes married Frederick G. Smith in 1849.
- Robert Cochrane McCay [Oct. 1, 1830 – July 14, 1864], "MAJOR, 38 MISS INF, CONFEDERATE STATES ARMY." This is a military stone.
- Mary E. *(Lum)* McCay Regan [Oct. 6, 1832 – Dec. 15, 1934], "Mother." Mary is the daughter of Sinai Amelia Lum, buried in Rocky Springs Cemetery. She married Robert Cochrane McCay in 1854. She later married Joseph Regan in 1873. Joseph is buried in Regan Cemetery. Besides those listed below, other offspring with her husband, Robert McCay include Laura *McCay* Lum, buried in Lum Cemetery, William L. McCay in plot H-28, Thomas Scott McCay in combined plot H-12/13, and Mary Roberta McCay in Rocky Springs Cemetery.
- Amelia Agnes McCay [Dec. 26, 1854 – July 27, 1861], "eldest dau. of R. C. & M. E. McCay."
- Kate McCay [May 27, 1856 – Aug. 26, 1869]
- Thomas White Brown [1814 – 1904]. Thomas' wife, Annie M. Brown, is buried in Henderson Cemetery.
- Robert Clinton McCay [June 15, 1860 – August 21, 1938]. Robert is the son of Robert Cochrane and Mary E. *Lum* McCay.
- Annie *Brown* McCay [June 9, 1864 – December 31, 1944]. Annie is the daughter of Thomas White and Annie M. Brown. She married Robert Clinton McCay in 1886, and they share a common stone.
- Percy Eugene Regan [Aug. 2, 1874 – May 25, 1920], a Mason. Percy is the son of Joseph and Mary E. *Lum* McCay Regan.

[C-57: Akin, Derrah, Greenwalt, Heid, Patton, Shanahan, Watkins]
- James Derrah [Sept. 4, 1801 – Oct. 19, 1849], a Mason. James married Easter Benjamin in 1837.
- Richard P. Derrah [died May 19, 1842, in his 5th year], "son of J. & E. Derrah."
- Esther Ellin Derrah [died Oct. 27, 1847, in her 3rd year], "daughter of Jas. & E. Derrah."
- James Shanahan [1846 – 1903], "Father."
- Theresa A. *(Heid)* Shanahan [1854 – 1903], "Mother." Theresa married James Shanahan in 1875, and they share a common stone.
- Joseph P. Akin [dates buried in concrete], "born in Lancaster, Ky."
- Benjamin Watkins [died Oct. 2, 1875]
- Ellenor Watkins [died Nov. 28, 1870]. Ellenor married Benjamin Watkins in 1826. She had previously been married to a Mr. James Patton. A daughter, Ann *Patton* English, is buried in plot B-24.
- Jacob Greenwalt [died Oct. 8, 1840, in the 39th year of his age]. A memorial epitaph reads: "This stone is erected by his beloved wife and son, to commemorate the deep attachment felt for him while living, and the sincerest sorrow for his death." Jacob married Elizabeth Atler in 1835.

[C-58: Denney, Jackson, Jordan, Knight, Van Rensselaer, Wright]
- Col. William H. D. Denney [Apr. 29, 1792 – Aug. 20, 1842], "a native of Virginia…died in Port Gibson, Claiborne Co., Miss." Col. Denney first married Louisa Rouse in 1826.
- Louisa A. *(Knight)* Denney [Aug. 6, 1806 – Mar. 30, 1873], "wife of Col. Wm. H. D. Denney." Louisa married H. D. Denney in 1828.
- Mrs. Virginia W. *(Denney)* Jackson [Aug. 29, 1829 – Dec. 8, 1889]. Virginia was first married to Arent Schuyler Van Rensselaer in 1853. She later married a John L. Jackson in 1869.
- Annie Aurent *(Van Rensselaer)* Wright [Feb. 2, 1856 – Feb. 10, 1918]. Annie is the daughter of Arent Schuyler and Virginia W. *Denney* Van Rensselaer. She and her mother share a common stone.
- James R. Wright [died March 29, 1841], a Mason. James married Amanda R. Phillips in 1837.
- James B. Jordan [Aug. 20, 1836 – Dec. 22, 1887], C. S. A. stone, member Independent Order of Odd Fellows, "Our Father." James first married Ellen Olivia Lee in 1861. Ellen is buried in plot B-48. James then married L. M. Van Rensselaer in 1873.

[C-59: no stones]
[C-60: no stones]
[C-61: Girault, Guice, Shaifer]. Many of these family relationships were determined through the book, *Threading the Generations*, by Mary Elizabeth Johnson and Carol Vickers.
- Abram Keller Shaifer [Oct. 9, 1774 – April 26, 1860], a Mason, "a native of Fredricktown, Md." Abram married Elizabeth Humphreys in 1817. Besides those listed below, other children include Henry F. Shaifer, buried in plot C-36b, Elizabeth K. *Shaifer* Burnet, in plot C-36a, and Margaret *Shaifer* Johnson, buried in Regan Cemetery.
- Sally A. Shaifer [died Feb. 13, 1833, aged 14 years 8 m & 10 d], "daughter of A. K. & E. H. Shaifer."
- Esther D. Shaifer [died July 2, 1831, aged 5 years 1 m & 29 days], "daughter of A. K. & E. H. Shaifer."
- A. K. Shaifer [1833 – 1921], C. S. A. stone. Abram Keller Shaifer, Jr. is the son of Abram Keller and Elizabeth *Humphreys* Shaifer. According to Mississippi Confederate Grave Registration records, he was a Private, then Sergeant, in Co. K, 1st Miss. Light Artillery, and died of old age.
- Elizabeth *Girault* Shaifer [Apr. 15, 1839 – June 16, 1864], "wife of A. K. Shaifer, Jr." Elizabeth is the daughter of Col. George R. and Henrietta *McCaleb* Girault. Col. Girault is buried in plot B-22. She married Abram Keller Shaifer, Jr. in 1857. This is A. K. Shaifer, Jr's first wife.
- Josephine G. Shaifer [1858 – 1941]
- B. H. Shaifer [1857 – 1824]. Benjamin Humphreys Shaifer is the son of Abram Keller, Jr. and Elizabeth *Girault* Shaifer.

- A. C. *(Guice)* Shaifer [1844 – 1930]. Amanda C. is the second wife of Abram Keller Shaifer, Jr., marrying in 1865. They have a son, Percy Leon Shaifer, buried in combined plot H-71/72/89/90.

[C-62: Child, Schultz]

- Hon. Joshua Child [died Mar. 1, 1834, ae. 49]. A biographical epitaph reads: "He was a native of Lincoln Massachusetts, and for many years an able lawyer and distinguished judge in this state."
- Ann Maria Schultz [Sept'r 17, 1830 – October 29, 1830], "daughter of John D. & Rebecca Schultz."
- George M. Schultz [Sept'r 1, 1829 – October 23, 1829], "their son." Ann Maria and George M. Schultz share a common stone.

"Two children sweet lie here asleep
To part us fresh in mind.
That die they must and turn to dust
And leave this world behind."
—on stone of Ann Maria and George M. Schultz

[C-63: Griffith]

- Esther Griffith [April 17, 1831 – May 30, 1831], "infant daughter of Evan and Martha Griffith."

[C-64: no stones]

[C-65: no stones]

[C-66/67/80: Adams, Davis, Foster, Frisby, Jones, Kinnison, Smith, Watkins]

- James M. Smith, Sen. [June 1, 1807 – Mar. 28, 1872], a Mason. James was married twice, first to Mrs. Nancy *Reeves* Eastly in 1832, and then to Matilda C. Kinnison in 1833.
- Emily Jane Smith [Feb. 25, 1840 – Nov. 17, 1840], "infant daughter of J. M. & M. C. Smith."
- Frank H. Foster [1852 – 1881]
- Caroline *Smith* Foster [1846 – 1928]. Caroline is the daughter of James M. and Matilda C. *Kinnison* Smith, and the wife of Frank H. Foster.
- Frank Redus Foster [July 26, 1881 – Nov. 27, 1890], "son of F. H. & C. E. Foster."
- James M. Smith, Jun. [May 30, 1849 – Feb. 2, 1874], member Independent Order of Odd Fellows. James is the son of James M. and Matilda C. *Kinnison* Smith.
- Caroline Jones [May 20, 1822 – Mar. 26, 1872]
- Jennie M. *(Jones)* Watkins [Dec. 17, 1848 – Feb. 19, 1877], "wife of Jno. C. Watkins, born in Adams Co. Miss….died in Port Gibson, Miss." Jennie married John C. Watkins in 1871. John is buried in plot G-34.
- E. J. Smith [July 26, 1835 – May 15, 1911], a Mason. E. J. Married C. Gertrude Jones in 1866. Besides Gertrude, listed below they have a son, William Myles Smith, buried in plot I-74. According to Mississippi Confederate Grave Registration records, he was a private in Co. A, 24th Miss. Batt. Miss. Cavalry and Co. C, 10th Miss. Infantry.
- Gertrude Smith [Feb. 2, 1871 – Aug. 24, 1872], "dau. of E. J. & C. G. Smith."
- Sarah J. *(Kinnison)* Adams [April 22, 1824 – Sep. 27, 1853], "wife of H. T. Adams." Sarah married Hiram T. Adams in 1842. She was a victim of the yellow fever epidemic.
- Elizabeth Ann Adams [Mar. 12, 1852 – April 8, 1853]
- Infant Child Adams [Sep. 25, 1853 – Sep. 26, 1853]. Elizabeth Ann and Infant Child Adams share a common stone with their mother, with the inscription: "Children of H. T. & S. J. Adams." This infant was a victim of the yellow fever epidemic.
- Alsey Frisby [Aug. 16, 1839 – Oct. 9, 1845], "daughter of A. J. & E. Frisby."
- Thomas Emily Davis [Apr. 13, 1845 – Oct. 8, 1848], "daughter of A. & P. A. Davis."

[C-68: Key, Marschalk, Pendleton, Smith, Wood]
- Drusilla Key [Aug. 19, 1789 – Jan. 8, 1859], "…a faithful Christian, her last words were 'Jesus Saviour.'" Drusilla married Wiley Key in 1832. She had previously been married to a Mr. Wood.
- J. Wood [Aug. 19, 1810 – Jan. 7, 1842]
- Jesse Smith [Sept. 13, 1799 – Dec. 14, 1847], a Mason and member Independent Order of Odd Fellows, "born in Chester Co. Pa." A memorial tribute reads: "A Memento by His Wife."
- Ann *(Wood)* Smith [1814 – 1889]. Will records tell us that Ann is the daughter of Drusilla Wood, now Key. Ann had married William W. Pendleton in 1830. She later married Jesse Smith in 1842.
- A. H. Marschalk [1846 – 1871], C. S. A. stone.
- Martha Ann *(Smith)* Marschalk [1846 – 1926]. Martha is the daughter of Jesse and Ann *Wood* Smith. She married A. H. Marschalk in 1866.
- W. L. Wood [Oct. 6, 1818 – April 10, 1839]
- I. S. Wood [May 2, 1828 – Dec. 22, 1855], a Mason.

[C-69: no stones]

[C-70: Haring, Zentz]
- F. P. Zentz [died April 24, 1861, aged 25 years]
- Eleazer W. Haring [1804 – 1838]. Stone reads: "To Eleazer W. Haring by Ellet Haring."

[C-71: Brown, Crow]
- Emily A. Crow [died Dec. 5, 1855, aged 4 yrs. & 11 ds.], "daughter of J. & P. Crow."
- Baldwin G. Brown [Aug. 21, 1827 – Nov. 15, 1855]
- Bassara C. Brown [Sept. 2, 1829 – Nov. 8, 1855]

[C-72: O'Conner]
- Alexander O'Conner [Apr. 4, 1842 – Apr. 15, 1854], "son of Thos. & Ann O'Conner, born in Ray Co. Mo."

[C-73: Roberts]
- Frances Elizabeth Roberts [died July 1861, in her 15th year], "daughter of John & Mahala Roberts." Calvin Roberts [died Aug. 19, 1867, in his 8th year]

[C-74: Graves, Potts]
- Joseph W. Graves [May 5, 1804 – July 10, 1837], "born in New Hampshire." A memorial epitaph reads: "This memento is place by an affectionate wife." Joseph married Sarah Patton in 1834. After the death of Joseph Graves, Sarah *Patton* Graves married Robert Potts in 1841. Margaret Frances Potts, listed below, is their daughter.
- Margaret Frances Potts [dates are buried or missing], "daughter of Robert & Sarah Potts."

[C-75: Jackson, Lynch, Smith]
- James Ishmael "Ish" Lynch [Aug. 12, 1917 – Feb. 29, 2000]
- Elizabeth "Liz" Lee *(Smith)* Lynch [June 11, 1918 – Jan. 4, 2005]. Elizabeth is the wife of James Ishmael Lynch, and they share a common stone. They have an infant daughter, Judy Marie Lynch, buried in combined plot E-7/8/9.
- Lillian B. Jackson [Feb. 11, 1925 – Dec. 2, 2007]

[C-76: Nelson] This plot contains a cross-shaped memorial stone bearing the name NELSON on one side and McCAA on the other.
- Clyde Luther Nelson, Jr. [March 29, 1931 – October 28, 2012]. Clyde is the son of Clyde L. and Josie *McCaa* Nelson, buried in combined plot I-7/8. He first married Joan Wheeless in 1955. They have a daughter, Stephanie Lynn Nelson, also buried in combined plot I-7/8. He later married Mrs. Frances Charles *Humphreys* McCaa in 1963.

[C-77: no stones]

[C-78: no stones]

[C-79: Sutton, Vernorman]

- Eliza *(Vernorman)* Sutton [Aug. 21, 18?? – April 11, 1845], "wife of James M. Sutton." Due to a crack through the stone, the year of birth is unreadable. Eliza married James M. Sutton in 1829.

[C-81: no stones]

[C-82: Loring]

- Ezekiel H. Loring [died Oct. 10, 1855, in the 20th year of his age], "died of consumption."

[C-83: Cox]

- Lizzie Cox [Dec. 24, 1851 – Sept. 6, 1853], "daughter of Gracy Cox."
- Infant Daughter Cox [died Feb. 20, 1858], "daughter of Gracy Cox."

[C-84: Bell, Martin]

- Susan Martin [died Sept. 18, 1853, aged 63 years], "wife of Samuel Martin."
- Ann Bell [died Jan. 24, 1882]

> "Alas! She has left us, her spirit has fled,
> Her body now slumbers along with the dead.
> Her Saviour hath called her, to Him she has gone,
> Be ye also ready to follow her soon."
> —on stone of Susan Martin

[C-85: Hoel]

- James Hoel [Apr. 30, 1837 – Mar. 14, 1856]

[C-86: no last name]

- Lucinda [Dec. 1849 – Aug. 1855]. No last name is given on this stone.

[C-87: no last name]

- Emily [no dates]. This stone contains no other information.

[C-88: Bradford, Byrd, Chess, Davis, Jeffers]

- Thomas D. Jeffers [died December 18, 1843, in his 42nd year], a Mason.
- Andrew Chess [died Sept. 8, 1852, aged 53 years]
- Cornelious (sic) Byrd [aged 6 weeks]
- Turner H. Byrd [aged 1 year 7 mos. 3 ds.]. Cornelious and Turner H. Byrd share a common stone with the inscription: "Children of J. N. & R. L. Byrd."
- Richard A. Byrd [Sept. 1, 1851 – May 11, 1853], "son of J. N. & R. L. Byrd."
- George E. M. Byrd [Dec. 25, 1853 – Apr. 18, 1854], "son of J. N. & R. L. Byrd."
- Virginous (sic) Byrd [died Feb. 26, 1856, aged 1 year & 5 days], "son of J. N. & R. L. Byrd."
- John Howard Byrd [July 24, 1865 – Feb. 3, 1870], "son of J. N. & R. L. Byrd." This stone's inscription reads: "Erected by his brother, Granville Byrd."
- Berry D. Bradford [died Aug. 8, 1853, aged 1 year 3 mos. & 24 ds.], "son of Nace & Margaret Bradford."
- William Davis, Esq. [July 2, 1798 – July 13, 1848], a Mason, "born…at Salisbury Md."

[C-89: Ingraham]

- Francis Ingraham [August 24, 1848], "3 ARTY., CONTINENTAL TROOPS, REV. WAR." This is a military stone. An accompanying bronze marker reads: "…placed by Pathfinder Chapter, D. A. R."

Soldier's Row

This section is dedicated to the brave soldiers, most of whom lost their lives in the Battle of Port Gibson. A large interpretive marker at this site tells of the events of that battle:

Campaign, Siege, and Defense of Vicksburg; 1863.

Battle of Port Gibson, Mississippi, May 1.

"The Union Army, under command of Maj. Gen. U. S. Grant, was composed of the 13th Corps and Logan's Division of the 17th Corps. The Confederate Army, under command of Brig. Gen. John S. Bowen, was composed of Tracy's, Cockrell's, Green's, and Baldwin's Brigades, the 6th Mississippi Infantry, the Botetourt (Virginia) Artillery, and a section of Hudson's (Mississippi) Battery. Most of the Confederate regiments made forced marches to reach the battle-field and arrived with thinned ranks. Tracy's Brigade held the right, Green's and the Sixth Mississippi the left of the Confederate line. The battle was opened at an early hour by the advance of Carr's and Hovey's Divisions on the right and Osterhaus' on the left of the Union line, Smith's Division in reserve. The Confederate left was driven back about 10 A. M. and Baldwin's Brigade, just arrived, formed a new line about one and one-half miles in rear of the first position. Two regiments, just arrived, of Cockrell's Brigade were posted on the new line; Green's Brigade and one regiment, just arrived, of Cockrell's Brigade, were ordered to the Confederate right which had retired a little from its first position. The First Brigade of Logan's Division was sent, on arrival, to the Union left, the Third reinforced the Union right and Smith's Division became engaged; the Second Brigade of Logan's Division did not arrive until near the close of the battle. The Confederate line was held until about 5:30 P. M., when both wings were driven from their positions and fell back across Bayou Pierre, the First and Fourth Missouri Infantry (consolidated) of Cockrell's Brigade arriving in time to assist in covering the retreat. Casualties: Union; killed 131, wounded 719, missing 25, total: 875, one officer killed. Confederate; killed 56, wounded 328, missing 341, total: 725, Brig. Gen. E. D. Tracy and three other officers killed."

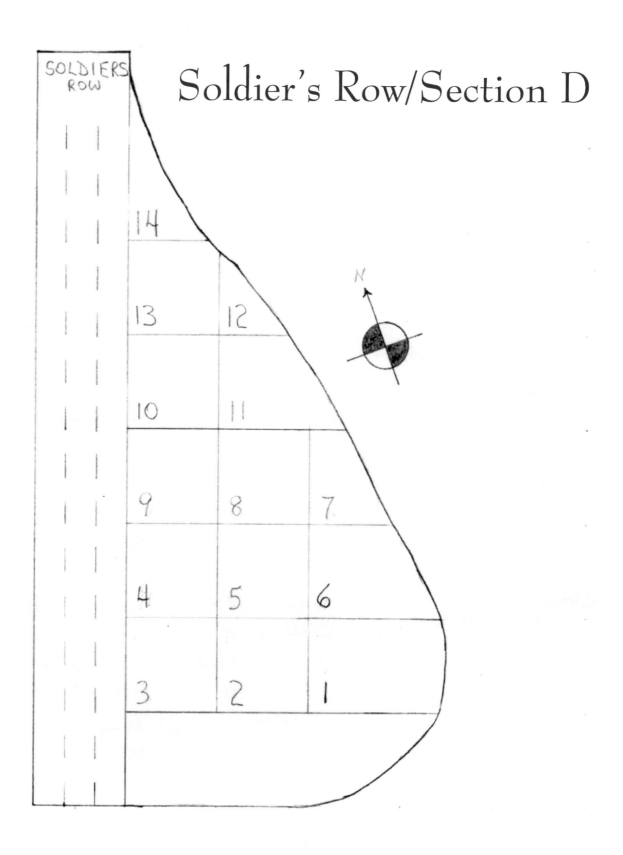

Soldier's Row/Section D

SOLDIERS ROW

N

14

13   12

10   11

9   8   7

4   5   6

3   2   1

Beginning of westernmost row, starting on south end and moving northward.

- Benjamin G. Humphreys [1808 – 1882], "BRIG GEN, 21 MISS INF, CSA." General Humphreys is actually laid to rest beside his wife in combined plot B-7/18.
- B. F. Rasberry [May 1, 1863], "CO D, 6 MISS INF, CSA"
- Samuel J. Smith [May 1, 1863], "SERG, CO I, 46 MISS INF, CSA"
- Gus Wells [May 1, 1863], "CO H, 30 ALA INF, CSA"
- Willis H. Minton [May 5, 1863], "CO F, 46 ALA INF, CSA"
- Green B. Altman [May 1, 1863], "CO I, 6 MISS INF, CSA"
- Luke R. Roberts [May 1, 1863], "CO B, 30 ALA INF, CSA"
- Joseph Cooper [May 1, 1863], "CO D, 6 MISS INF, CSA"
- J. R. Martin [May 1, 1863], "CO I, 4 MISS INF, CSA"
- J. W. Crawly [May 1, 1863], "SERG, CO H, 6 MISS INF, CSA"
- Asa Costner [May 1, 1863], "CO D, 4 MISS INF, CSA"
- W. G. Rasberry [May 1, 1863], "CO D, 6 MISS INF, CSA"
- B. F. Muckelrath [1829 – 1863], "PVT, CO 6, 6 MISS INF, CSA"
- Henry Till [May 4, 1863], "CO B, 6 MISS INF, CSA"
- Benjamin Wessendorff [May 1, 1863], "CO C, 46 MISS INF, CSA"
- Thomas Coggin [Jul. 1863], "CO H, 30 ALA INF, CSA"
- Lindsey Stinnette [May 15, 1863], "DOUTHAT'S CO, VA ARTY, CSA"
- William Whalin [May 6, 1863], "CO A, 30 ALA INF, CSA"
- J. N. Edmartan [May 1, 1863], "CO I, 30 ALA INF, CSA"
- James M. Tygret [May 1, 1863], "CO E, 30 ALA INF, CSA"
- A. M. Kelly [May 1, 1863], "CO G, 6 MISS INF, CSA"
- J. H. Harrison [May 1, 1863], "SERG, CO C, 4 MISS INF, CSA"
- James Fant [May 1, 1863], "CO I, 30 ALA INF, CSA"
- R. M. Carmichael [May 1, 1863], "CO D, 4 MISS INF, CSA"
- W. P. Stucky [May 1, 1863], "CO G, 6 MISS INF, CSA"
- George W. Dillard [May 1, 1863], CO D, 6 MISS INF, CSA"
- John Armstrong [May 3, 1863], "CO D, 30 ALA INF, CSA"
- O. E. Langley [May 1, 1863], "CO B, 30 ALA INF, CSA"
- James J. Steedman [May 1, 1863], "SERG, CO G, 20 ALA INF, CSA"
- William H. Norgrove [May 1, 1863], "2ND LIEUT, BOTETOURT VA ARTY, CSA"
- David Leips [May 1, 1863], "SERG, BOTETOURT VA ARTY, CSA"
- William T. Brewton [May 1863], "PVT, CO D, 23 ALA INF, CONFEDERATE STATES ARMY"
- James M. Douglas [1835 – 1863], "CAPT, CO A, 15 ARK INF, CSA"
- Frederick C. Noel [May 1, 1863], "PVT, BOTETOURT VA ARTY, CSA"
- William P. Douthat [May 1, 1863], "2ND LIEUT, BOTETOURT VA ARTY, CSA"
- William Couch [May 1, 1863], "PVT, BOTETOURT VA ARTY, CSA"
- James T. Greenwood [May 1, 1863], "1ST LIEUT, ADJT 5 MO INF, CSA"
- Presley Whitaker [Apr. 28, 1863], "PVT, CO A, 5 MO INF, CSA"
- Clark B. Carter [May 1, 1863], "2ND LIEUT, CO I, 15 ARK INF, CSA"
- Edward T. Woods [Apr. 1863], "SERG, WADE'S MO BTRY, CSA"
- A. B. Thomas [May 1863], "PVT, CO G, 15 ARK INF, CSA"
- William H. Seney [May 1, 1863], "PVT, CO B, 5 MO INF, CSA"
- Randolph Sharp [May 1, 1863], "PVT, CO B, 15 ARK INF, CSA"
- James A. Caldwell [May 1, 1863], "PVT, CO H, 15 ARK INF, CSA"

- Moses James [May 1, 1863], "PVT, CO B, 5 MO INF, CSA"
- Royal G. Stokely [May 1, 1863], "CAPT, CO A, 5 MO INF, CSA"
- John A. Priddy [May 1, 1863], "PVT, CO K, 5 MO INF, CSA"
- John Jacob Moman [May 1, 1863], "PVT, CO E, 5 MO INF, CSA"
- William H. Crawford [May 1, 1863], "CORP, CO H, 15 ARK INF, CSA"
- Hugh Withers [May 1, 1863], "PVT, CO D, 15 ARK INF, CSA"
- Robert L. Davis [May 1, 1863], "PVT, CO A, 5 MO INF, CSA"
- Mike Burke [1862], "PVT, CO B, 14 LA HVY ARTY, CSA"
- W. T. Maxwell [May 1, 1863], "CORP, CO G, 15 ARK INF, CSA"
- A. G. McCormack [May 1, 1863], "SERG, CO A, 5 MO INF, CSA"
- Charles Ivy [May 1, 1863], "PVT, CO E, 21 ARK INF, CSA"
- Claiborne D. Ferguson [Apr. 30, 1863], "PVT, GUIBOR'S MO BTRY, CSA"
- William B. Miller [May 1, 1863], "PVT, CO B, 5 MO INF, CSA"
- Alex B. Krider [May 1, 1863], "CAPT, CO K, 15 ARK INF, CSA"
- Thomas Holstead [May 1, 1863], "PVT, CO B, 5 MO INF, CSA"
- John C. Gideon [May 1, 1863], "PVT, CO E, 15 ARK INF, CSA"
- John N. Cargill [Apr. 20 1863], "SERG, CO G, 3 MO INF, CSA"
- William C. Fintcher [May 1, 1863], "LIEUT, CO G, 5 MO INF, CSA"
- Austin K. Etris [1863], "CAPT, CO F, 15 ARK INF, CSA"

End of westernmost row.

Beginning of middle row, starting on south end and working northward.

- John T. Mayfield [June 23, 1862], "SERG, CO C, MILES LA LEGION, CSA." John has his own civilian stone with a birth date of Jan. 5, 1838, and death date of July 5, 1862.
- William H. Hughes [Jun. 1, 1863], "CO D, MO INF, CSA"
- J. R. Glass [May 1, 1863], "CO B, 23 ARK INF, CSA"
- L. A. Hino [1862], "CONNER'S MISS BTRY, CSA"
- Leonidas Oldham [May 11, 1863], "CO G, 6 MO INF, CSA." Leonidas also has a civilian stone, indicating that he was born in Madison County, Ky. on January 1, 1808.
- Richard Lee [May 1, 1863], "1ST SERG, CO H, 5 MO INF, CSA"
- E. T. Harrell [Jul. 6, 1862], "CO E, MILES LA LEGION, CSA"
- W. C. Hathaway [Jun 25, 1862], "CO D, LA LEGION, CSA"
- Robert S. Lemons [May 1, 1863], "SERG, CO C, 6 MO INF, CSA"
- John M. Barbour [May 1, 1863], "CO K, 6 MO INF, CSA"
- J. W. Moore [May 21, 1863], "2ND LIEUT, CO E, 6 MISS INF, CSA"
- Alexander Humphreys [Jun. 23, 1862], "CO D, LA LEGION, CSA"
- Alfred Cato [May 1, 1863], "CO D, 21 ARK INF, CSA"
- J. M. Harwood [May 7, 1863], "CO D, 21 ARK INF, CSA"
- W. R. Kirkland [May 23, 1863], "CORP, CO I, 46 ALA INF, CSA"
- William Yarbrough [1863], "LANDIS MO BTRY, CSA"
- Green B. Whatley [May 16, 1863], "CO E, 31 ALA INF, CSA"
- W. L. Newberry [May 7, 1863], "CORP, CO H, 5 MO INF, CSA"
- Henry Hall [Apr. 29, 1863], "CO F, 5 MO INF, CSA"
- Jeremiah McCarty [May 1, 1863], "CO I, 6 MO INF, CSA"
- William C. Cooper [May 1, 1863], "CO K, 6 MO INF, CSA"

- Frank M. Pippins [1863], "CO C, 2 MO INF, CSA"
- William T. Smith [May 1, 1863], "CO A, 5 ARK INF, CSA"
- William P. Cranford [Jun. 22, 1863], "CO C, MILES LA LEGION, CSA"
- George W. Parks [Jun. 16, 1863], "CORP, CO G, 6 MO INF, CSA." Another stone, possibly belonging to George W. Parks reads: "…died May 23rd of wound received May 1st 1863."
- John R. Glascock [May 1, 1863], "CO B, 4 MISS INF, CSA"
- James A. Vandygriff [May 1, 1863], "CO A, 15 ARK INF, CSA"
- George W. Rogers [May 1, 1863], "CO G, 15 ARK INF, CSA"
- Marseille Wager [Jul. 1862], "CO B, MILES LA LEGION, CSA"
- John Bird [1822 – 1870], "1ST LA HV ARTY, CSA." John also has his own civilian stone with the additional information: "a native of Cambridge, Eng., died July 17, 1870, aged 48 years."
- William F. Powers [May 1, 1863], "CO I, 20 ALA INF, CSA"
- Isaac M. Lewis [May 1, 1863], "CO B, 6 MO INF, CSA." Isaac also has a civilian stone that reads: "died June 10th, of wound received May 1st, 1863, aged 22 years."
- James H. Myers [May 1, 1863], "CO B, 5 MO INF, CSA"
- James H. Ware [1863], "CO A, 3 MO INF, CSA"
- W. L. Hanks [May 1, 1863], "CO H, 15 ARK INF, CSA"
- William Buck [May 1, 1863], "CO I, 15 ARK INF, CSA"
- H. C. Conway [May 1, 1863], "CO C, 23 ALA INF, CSA"
- John Barge [1862], "CO H, MILES LA LEGION, CSA"
- Albert Alexander [May 1, 1863], "SERG, CO D, 6 MO INF, CSA"
- William M. Wyatt [May 1, 1863], "CO A, 6 MO INF, CSA"
- John Allison [July 5, 1862], "CO C, MILES LA LEGION, CSA"
- Joseph Hunter [1863], "CO I, 1 & 4 MO INF, CSA"
- Green Martin Montier [Jul 1863], "CO D, 2 MO INF, CSA"
- A. S. Pickering [May 1, 1863], "MAJ, 20 ALA INF, CSA"
- Edward B. Hachett [1863], "2ND LIEUT, 15 ARK INF, CSA"
- W. A. Savage [May 1, 1863], "CORP, CO C, 17 LA INF, CSA"
- Franklin H. Pryor [May 1, 1863], "CO G, 15 ARK INF, CSA"
- William H. Harrington [May 1, 1863], "CORP, CO G, 6 MO INF, CSA"
- J. T. Dodge [May 10, 1863], "CO B, 5 MO INF, CSA"
- Isaac Purnell [1863], "SERG, CO D, 3 MO INF, CSA"
- T. J. Walker [Jul. 1862], "CO D, MILES LA LEGION, CSA"
- F. N. Cannon [Jun. 20, 1862], "CO C, MILES LA LEGION, CSA"
- Elijah Pate [1863], "CO C, 20 ALA INF, CSA"
- John Hall [May 1, 1863], "CO C, 6 MO INF, CSA"
- Harvey St. Clair [May 1, 1863], "CO B, MO INF, CSA"
- Thomas W. Earle [May 1, 1863], "CLR SERG, CO C, 20 ALA INF, CSA"
- J. R. Moore [1862], "CONNER'S MISS B'TRY, CSA"
- Thomas G. Childers [May 1, 1863], "CO E, 5 MO INF, CSA"
- Jesse J. Dickerson [May 1, 1863], "CSA"
- C. C. McDougal [May 13, 1863], "CO C, 4 MISS INF, CSA"
- James Burras [May 1, 1863], "PVT, CO G, 5 MO INF, CSA"
- John L. Shuler [Mar. 14, 1845 – Jul. 17, 1864], "CO M, ADAMS CAV, CSA"
- Lewis B. Tackett [May 11, 1863], "PVT, CO B, 15 ARK INF, CSA"
- John L. Samuels [Nov. 1864], "SERG, CO E, 3 MO INF, CSA"

End of middle row.

Starting in the easternmost row, looking south to north, there exists no military stones, and only one civilian stone that does not have a duplicate military stone. That one stone marks the grave of:

- Thomas J. Tiernon [died Apr. 11, 1862, ae. 25], "Co. C, 10th Miss."

Completing the easternmost row, a count of grave markers with the initials, C. S. A., numbers 55. And, strangely, one marker exists with the initials, U. S. A., indicating the burial of a Union soldier.

Section D

[D-1: Coblentz, DeLuce, Englesing, Williams]. This plot has a memorial obelisk bearing the name EN-GLESING.

- Frank Clemens Englesing [Jan. 9, 1830 – Sept. 13, 1884], C. S. A. stone.
- Ellen Nora *DeLuce* Englesing [Feb. 12, 1835 – Aug. 23, 1868], "wife of F. C. Englesing."
- Henry Joseph Englesing [June 26, 1855 – Aug. 6, 1899]
- Frank Clemens Englesing [1857 – 1910]
- Sallie *Williams* Englesing [1862 – 1949]. Sallie is the daughter of Levin Powell and Lydia Margaret *Ash* Williams, buried in plot D-9. She married Frank Clemens Englesing in 1889.
- Frank Clemens Englesing [1892 – 1969]. Frank is the son of Frank Clemens and Sallie *Williams* Englesing.
- Esther *Coblentz* Englesing [1898 – 1986]. Esther married Frank Clemens Englesing in 1931.
- John Maxmillian Englesing [Feb. 26, 1860 – July 1, 1907]
- Marie Antoinette Englesing [May 25, 1862 – Feb. 17, 1875]

[D-2: Keisker]

- Infant Daughter Keisker [born & died Oct. 3, 1881], "infant daughter of A. & M. L. Keisker."

[D-3: Lischer] This plot has a lone C. S. A. stone whose owner cannot be identified.

- John E. Lischer [June 24, 1805 – Aug. 6, 1872], C. S. A. stone, "born in Dearbauch Bavaria…died in Port Gibson."

[D-4: Martin, McLaurin]

- James E. Martin [no dates], C. S. A. stone, "Lieut. Col., 48th Miss. Regt., killed in battle, Sharpsburg Md."
- William M. Martin [no dates], "Capt., Co. C, 4th Miss. Regular Cavalry, killed at Harrisburg Miss."
- William H. Martin [died Oct. 4, 1878, aged 78 years], "born in Talbot Co. Md." William was a victim of the yellow fever epidemic.
- M. E. Martin [died Sep. 23, 1878]. Will records tell us that this is Miss Mary E. Martin, daughter of William H. Martin. These first four share a common obelisk.
- Charles H. Martin [died Oct. 1, 1876], C. S. A. stone.
- Lauch McLaurin [Jan. 18, 1854 – Dec. 21, 1920]. A memorial epitaph reads: "Erected by his wife."
- Ida Stevens McLaurin [February 11, 1858 – November 2, 1935], "beloved wife of Lauch McLaurin."
- Infant Daughter McLaurin [died May 19, 1882], "daughter of L. & Ida McLaurin."

- Grace Jean McLaurin [June 29, 1883 – May 29, 1885], "daughter of Lauch & Ida McLaurin."
- Infant Son McLaurin [June 21, 1889 – June 25, 1889], "infant son of L. & Ida McLaurin."

[D-5: Drake, Harrell, Satterfield, Sturdivant, Williams]
- Milling Marion Satterfield [July 11, 1869 – July 5, 1946]
- Laura Stevenson *Drake* Satterfield [Dec. 12, 1878 – July 24, 1967], "beloved wife of Milling Marion Satterfield." Laura is the daughter of Elijah Steele and Ellen Davis *Turpin* Drake, buried in combined plot A-33/34. She married Milling Marion Satterfield in 1901.

An interesting note from *Port Gibson Reveille's* "Looking Back" column (Week of April 14, 1921): "Mrs. M. M. Satterfield was the first woman to cast a vote in Claiborne County…"
- Ellen Steele Satterfield [August 21, 1902 – June 21, 1995]. Ellen is the daughter of Milling Marion and Laura Stevenson *Drake* Satterfield. Her epitaph reads: "Gladly did she learn and gladly teach."
- Laura *Satterfield* Harrell Sturdivant [Aug. 31, 1913 – Dec. 31, 1979], "wife of E. C. Sturdivant." Laura is the daughter of Milling Marion and Laura *Drake* Satterfield. She married twice, first to W. O. Harrell in 1933.
- William Williams [died Oct. 31, 1899]
- Jane Williams [died Sept. 28, 1899]. Jane is the wife of William Williams.

[D-6: no stones]. This plot contains one C. S. A. stone whose owner cannot be identified.
[D-7: Allen, Briscoe, Marks]
- James B. Allen [1846 – 1919], C. S. A. stone, member Woodmen of the World.
- Lucie *Briscoe* Allen [1843 – 1911], "wife of James B. Allen." Lucie married James B. Allen in 1881.
- L. Briscoe Allen [1882 – 1967]. Leigh Briscoe Allen is the son of James B. and Lucie *Briscoe* Allen.
- Ethel *Marks* Allen [1881 – 1970], member Daughters of the American Revolution, "wife of L. Briscoe Allen." Ethel is the daughter of Samuel Upton and Sarah Augusta *Douglas* Marks, buried in plot G-B. She married Leigh Briscoe Allen in 1903. They have sons James Upton Allen, buried in plot G-A, and Leigh Briscoe Allen, Jr., in plot G-E.

[D-8: Barber, Briscoe]
- George A. Briscoe [April 19, 1812 – Sept. 7, 1851], "born in Kent Co. Maryland." George Briscoe, unfortunately, is dubiously noteworthy in that he was the assailant who assassinated the beloved Rev. Jeremiah Chamberlain, president of Oakland College and speaker in opposition to the institution of slavery. After Rev. Chamberlain was killed at his hands on September 5, 1851, George Briscoe, in remorse, took his own life just two days later. Besides this monument that he shares with his wife, he also has a raised vault in the Briscoe Cemetery with the same information, where he is probably actually laid to rest.
- Emily E. Briscoe [Jan. 4, 1821 – Sept.8, 1891], "born in Claiborne Co. Miss." Emily is the wife of George A. Briscoe, and they share a common obelisk with the words: "Our Father and Mother."
- John P. Briscoe [Aug. 23, 1846 – Dec. 9, 1876]. John is the son of George A. and Emily E. Briscoe. He married Evana Jefferies in 1875. Evana is buried in plot C-40, with the last name of KENNARD. John is a Civil War veteran and, according to Mississippi Confederate Grave Registration records, was a Private in Owen's Scouts/Powers Cavalry.
- Carl Elwin Barber [May 17, 1875 – Aug 16, 1916]
- Johnie *Briscoe* Barber [Nov. 6, 1876 – Oct. 13, 1933]. Johnie is the daughter of John P. and Evana *Jefferies* Briscoe. She married Carl Elwin Barber in 1901, and they share a common grave location.
- G. Leigh Briscoe [July 16, 1841 – Sep. 1, 1862], C. S. A. stone, "buried in Denmark, Tenn." G. Leigh shares a common obelisk with John P. Briscoe. According to Mississippi Confederate Grave Registration records, he served as Sergeant-Major in Garrison's Louisiana Cavalry, and was killed in battle.
- Edward P. Briscoe [Feb'y 12, 1848 – July 21, 1890], C. S. A. stone, member Independent Order of Odd Fellows. Edward is the son of George A. and Emily E. Briscoe. He married Maria Flower Watson in

1883. Maria and a daughter, Marion *Briscoe* Person, are buried in plot G-53. According to Mississippi Confederate Grave Registration records, he was a Private in Owen's Scouts/Powers Cavalry.

- Samuel M. Briscoe [Dec. 9, 1849 – Apr. 20, 1894], a Mason. Samuel is the son of George A. and Emily E. Briscoe. He married Mary C. Humphreys in 1883. Mary and a son, Ben Humphreys Briscoe, are buried in plot F-23.
- Infant Son Briscoe [no dates], "infant son of S. M. & M. H. Briscoe."

[D-9: Ash, Musgrove, Taylor, Williams]

- Levin Powell Williams [Mar. 19, 1821 – Mar. 21, 1910], "born at Tuscaloosa Ala…a resident of Port Gibson for 62 years."
- Lydia Margaret *Ash* Williams [Apr. 1, 1832 – Oct. 1, 1910], "wife of L. P. Williams, born in Nelson Co. Ky.…a resident of Port Gibson for 53 years." Levin and Lydia *Ash* Williams share a common stone. Besides those children listed below, they have a daughter, Sallie *Williams* Englesing, buried in plot D-1.
- Ella Blanche Williams [1858 – 1942]. Ella is the daughter of Levin Powell and Lydia Margaret *Ash* Williams.
- Levin Powell Williams [died November 3, 1896, aged 30 years]
- James Madison Taylor [1868 – 1943]. James is the son of John P. and V. E. Taylor, buried in plot F-27. He first married Betty Berry in 1893. Betty is buried in combined plot C-1/2.
- Maggie *Williams* Taylor [1869 – 1946], "wife of J. M. Taylor." Maggie is the daughter of Levin Powell and Lydia Margaret *Ash* Williams. She first married Robert G. Musgrove in 1891. She later married James Madison Taylor in 1938, and they share a common stone.
- Infant Daughter Musgrove [Apr. 12, 1894], "infant daughter of R. G. & M. W. Musgrove."
- John Ash Williams [May 14, 1872 – Oct. 1, 1875], "son of L. P. & L. M. Williams."

[D-10: Bethea, Smith, Watson]

- Daniel Holland Smith [March 12, 1848 – March 19, 1918], C. S. A. stone.
- Alitha *Bethea* Smith [January 28, 1854 – October 26, 1921]. Alitha married Daniel Holland Smith in 1874, and they share a common stone.
- Infant Son Smith [1876], "infant son of D. H. & A. B. Smith."
- Daniel Holland Smith, Jr. [1877 – 1938]. Daniel is the son of Daniel Holland and Alitha *Bethea* Smith.
- Malcomb Smith [December 13, 1878 – July 2, 1879]
- Roland Bethea Smith [1880 – 1946]. Roland is the son of Daniel Holland and Alitha *Bethea* Smith.
- Ralph Eugene Smith [February 19, 1889 – August 13, 1889]. Ralph is the son of Daniel Holland and Alitha *Bethea* Smith.
- Doctor John William Watson [1868 – 1939]. It is unclear why Doctor Watson has a C. S. A. stone over his grave, since he was born after the Civil War ended.

[D-11: no stones]

[D-12: no stones]

[D-13/14: Heath, McGilvary, Shannon]. This combined plot has a memorial stone bearing the name HEATH. At the stone's base is a Woodmen of the World symbol, the meaning of its presence there being unclear.

- William M. McGilvary [Aug. 5, 1830 – June 12, 1887]
- Mary F. McGilvary [March 4, 1832 – Feb. 17, 1891], "wife of Wm. M. McGilvary, born in Clark Co., Ala…died in Port Gibson." Besides a daughter listed below, they have a daughter, Mary *McGilvary* Richmond, buried in plot A-111, and John Alexander McGilvary, buried in Burnet Cemetery.
- John W. Heath [Mar. 23, 1853 – Nov. 17, 1908], member Woodmen of the World.
- Annie E. *McGilvary* Heath [Mar. 30, 1863 – Aug. 2, 1938]. Annie is the daughter of William M. and Mary F. McGilvary. She married John Wade Heath, Sr. in 1888.
- John Wade Heath, II [January 23, 1891 – January 27, 1944], "born in Port Gibson, Miss., son of Annie

Elizabeth McGilvary and John Wade Heath, Sr., married to Jane Arnold Shannon of Shelbyville, Ky., August 27, 1925. Died Fittler, Miss."

- Jane Arnold *Shannon* Heath [May 6, 1894 – April 20, 1981], "born LaGrange Ky., daughter of Lula Katherine Morlan and Robert Lee Shannon, Sr., wife of John Wade Heath, II. Died Shelbyville, Ky."
- John Wade Heath, III [June 23, 1926 – October 28, 1985], "born Vicksburg, Miss., son of Jane Arnold Shannon and John Wade Heath, II. Died Vicksburg, Miss."

Section E

[E-A: Abraham, Hastings]. This plot has a memorial stone bearing the name ABRAHAM.
- Dr. George Victor Abraham, D. D. S. [January 1, 1907 – October 1, 1988]
- Mary Alice *Hastings* Abraham [October 19, 1912 – September 20, 1970]. Mary is the daughter of Richard Granbery and Mary A. *Bagnell* Hastings, buried in plot G-23. She married Dr. George Abraham in 1946.

[E-B: Beckham, Burris, Crisler]
- Morris McCaleb Crisler [June 21, 1901 – Aug. 9, 1970]. Morris is the son of Henry Herbert and Eugenia *Morris* Crisler, buried in plot H-42.
- Hazel *Beckham* Crisler [Dec. 6, 1902 – Sept. 19, 1988]. Hazel is the wife of Morris McCaleb Crisler.
- Ruth *Crisler* Burris [Mar. 14, 1924 – Sept. 16, 1998]. Ruth is the daughter of Morris McCaleb and Hazel *Beckham* Crisler, and the three of them share a common obelisk.

[E-C/D/E/F/G/H: not used]

[E-1: Abraham, Greenlee]
- Robert Alexander Greenlee [June 6, 1911 – October 30, 1971], "Father." Robert is the son of James S. and Florence *Young* Greenlee, buried in Hermanville Cemetery.
- Maggie *Abraham* Greenlee [October 7, 1902 – October 10, 1976], "Mother." Maggie is the wife of Robert Alexander Greenlee, and they share a common grave location.
- Robert Michael Greenlee [September 10, 1964 – January 6, 1984], member Kappa Sigma Fraternity, "Our Brother-Our Son."

[E-2: Lee, Nailer]
- Goode Stallworth Lee [Mar. 15, 1907 – Aug. 20, 1973], a Gideon.
- Lucy Barrow *Nailer* Lee [January 31, 1917 – February 18, 2012]
- Howard Nailer Lee [July 12, 1954 – March 22, 1999]

[E-3: Guion, Jordan, McCollum, Robert]
- Eugene Robert [July 31, 1922 – May 27, 1972], "SFC, US ARMY, WORLD WAR II, KOREA." This is a bronze military plaque. Eugene also has a civilian stone.
- Minnie Bell Guion [November 19, 1929 – January 30, 1980]. Minnie married James Carlton McCollum in 1947, Eugene Robert in 1971, and Homer Leo Jordan in 1979. GUION is her maiden name, and JORDAN is her final married name.

[E-4: Eaton, Greer]
- Andrew Henry Eaton [July 29, 1900 – Nov. 24, 1995]
- Winnie *Greer* Eaton [Oct. 21, 1909 – Aug. 15, 1993]. Winnie is the daughter of Will G. and Martha

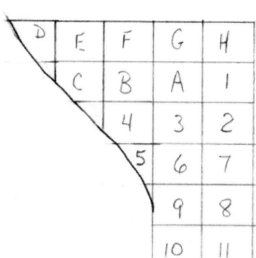

D	E	F	G	H
	C	B	A	I
		4	3	2
		5	6	7
			9	8

10	11	12
15	14	13
16	17	18
21	20	19
22	23	24
27	26	25
28	29	30
33	32	31

34	35	36	36a
39	38	37	37a
40	41	42	42a
45	44	43	

Section E

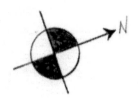

N

Mason Greer, buried in Jefferson County. She and Andrew share a common stone with the inscription: "Married Mar. 30, 1930."

[E-5: no stones]

[E-6: Andrews, Brown, Hall]

- Jesse Simms Brown [Feb. 14, 1883 – Nov. 18, 1964]. Jesse is the son of Marshall E. and Ida *Clark* Brown, buried in plot G-49.
- Victoria *Andrews* Brown [Sept. 13, 1891 – July 26, 1961]. Victoria married Jesse Simms Brown in 1911, and they share a common grave location. Besides Eleanor, listed below, they have a daughter, Bonnie Claire *Brown* Moore, buried in plot E-16, and a son, William Simms Brown, in plot K-11.
- Eleanor *Brown* Hall [Oct. 20, 1917 – Jan. 24, 1994]. Eleanor is the daughter of Jesse Simms and Victoria *Andrews* Brown.

[E-7/8/9: Cook, Lynch, Mercer, Taylor, Thomas, Trim, Way]

- Barbara Hayden Trim [Mar. 8, 1944 – Jan. 9, 1999]
- John F. Trim [January 16, 1881 – October 1, 1957]. John is the son of Walter W. and Anna J. *Russell* Trim, buried in Copiah County.
- Carrie E. *(Taylor)* Trim [February 2, 1886 – February 14, 1972]. Carrie married John F. Trim in 1905, and they share a common stone.
- Albert B. Trim [1895 – 1970], "Beloved Father."
- Mary *M(ercer)* Trim [1897 – 1973], "A Loving Mother." Mary is the wife of Albert B. Trim. Besides those listed below, other children are Cleo *Trim* Campbell, buried in plot J-58, and Sallie *Trim* Porterpan in plot J-102.
- John Paul Way [Jan. 26, 1899 – May 11, 1956]. John married Gertrude Taylor, his first wife, in 1924.
- Lillie *T(rim)* Way Thomas [Dec. 30, 1927 – May 25, 1982]. Lillie is the daughter of Albert B. and Mary *Mercer* Trim. She first was married to John Paul Way, and later married Paul James Thomas in 1957.
- Cullin Cook [Jan. 9, 1925 – Jan. 3, 1992]
- Ruth *(Trim)* Cook [Sept. 27, 1932 – Sept. 11, 1998]. Ruth is the daughter of Albert B. and Mary *Mercer* Trim. She is married to Cullin Cook, and they share a common stone.
- Mary Cathrine Cook [Oct. 20, 1969], infant.
- David Henry Trim [Nov. 21, 1967]
- Judy Marie Lynch [Oct. 16, 1962 – Oct. 21, 1962]. Judy is the daughter of James Ishmael and Elizabeth Lee *Smith* Lynch, buried in plot C-75.

[E-10: Coleman, Davenport, Drexler, Magruder, McCaa]

- Mrs. M. O. McCaa [Jan. 31, 1846 – Sept. 25, 1929]. Mary O. had first been married to a Mr. Davenport, and later married J. Oscar McCaa in 1878.
- Charles R. Drexler [April 2, 1902 – July 7, 1941]. Charles is the son of Henry Clay Drexler, buried in Owens Cemetery, and Cornelia *Regan* Drexler, buried in plot H-28, with the last name of CLARKE.
- Lottie Mae *(Coleman)* Drexler [Nov. 24, 1899 – Sept. 22, 1963]. Lottie is the wife of Charles Regan Drexler.
- Nellie F. Coleman [1901 – 1966]
- Frank Oscar Coleman [February 7, 1907 – August 8, 1977]
- Agnes *Magruder* Coleman [August 31, 1912 – May 4, 1997]. Agnes is the daughter of John Martin and Katherine *Daniell* Magruder, buried in plot G-31. She married Frank Oscar Coleman in 1936.

[E-11: James]

- Robert Loring James [Feb. 12, 1866 – May 1, 1945]
- Maude Lawson James [Nov. 6, 1878 – June 17, 1930]. Maude and Robert share a common grave location.

[E-12: Phillips, Porter]
- William Bouie Phillips [Oct. 28, 1875 – Apr. 26, 1951], member Woodmen of the World.
- Martha *Porter* Phillips [Dec. 22, 1882 – Nov. 15, 1951]. Martha is the daughter of John Sylvester and Martha *Sanders* Porter, buried in Sarepta Cemetery. She married William Bouie Phillips in 1903.

[E-13: no stones]

[E-14: Aldridge, Birdsong, Cade, Evans, Goodspeed, McCay, Montgomery, Moore, Simpson]
- Robert Buckner Evans [Oct. 28, 1867 – Dec. 21, 1935]
- Anna *Moore* Evans [June 26, 1865 – Nov. 26, 1942]. Anna is the daughter of William Walker and Ernestine *Watson* Moore, buried in plot F-16. She married Robert Buckner Evans in 1889.
- Ernestine *Evans* Simpson [April 3, 1892 – May 22, 1980], member Daughters of the American Revolution, "Mother." Ernestine is the daughter of Robert Buckner and Anna *Moore* Evans. Besides those listed below, she has a daughter, Katherine *Simpson* Middleton, buried in combined plot H-79/80.
- Annie Moore *Simpson* Cade Aldridge [August 18, 1914 – June 17, 1995]. Annie is the daughter of Ernestine *Evans* Simpson. She married Robert Solomon Cade, Jr. in 1931. Robert is buried in plot I-1.She later married Alvin David Aldridge in 1964. Alvin is buried in Hermanville Cemetery beside his first wife, Myrtie Louise *Thedford* Aldridge.
- Carolyn Louise Aldridge [September 3, 1938 – December 14, 2001]. Carolyn is the daughter of Alvin David and Myrtie Louise *Thedford* Aldridge.
- Elizabeth *S(impson)*. McCay [May 3, 1918 – Jan. 26, 1976], "Mama." Elizabeth is the daughter of Ernestine *Evans* Simpson.
- Josephine *Evans* Birdsong [June 17, 1898 – Aug. 12, 1977]. Josephine is the daughter of Robert Buckner and Anna *Moore* Evans.
- Cecile *Evans* Montgomery Goodspeed [October 15, 1901 – January 4, 1985]. Cecile is the daughter of Robert Buckner and Anna *Moore* Evans.

[E-15: Barron, Bunting, Davidson, Slay]
- Dr. Edmund D. Barron [Dec. 1, 1863 – Nov. 30, 1933]
- Nannie *S(lay)*. Barron [1886 – 1946]. Separate sources suggest that Nannie's birth year is incorrect, and should be 1866. This would confirm her to be the wife of Dr. Edmund D. Barron. Besides their son listed below, they have a daughter, Bonnibelle *Barron* Humphreys, buried in plot B-39.
- Victor E. Barron [Oct. 9, 1897 – Sept. 4, 1957], "MISSISSIPPI, SGT, 463 AIR SVC GP AAF, WORLD WAR II." This is a military stone. Victor is the son of Edmund D. and Nannie *Slay* Barron.
- Addie R. Davidson [April 26, 1856 – November 16, 1944]
- Bertha Randle Davidson [October 15, 1895 – June 18, 1980]
- William P. Bunting [February 10, 1898 – January 26, 1975], "Daddy."
- Josephine *D(avidson)*. Bunting [June 26, 1899 – June 5, 1991], "Mother." Josephine married William P. Bunting in 1917.

[E-16: Brown, Holmes, Humphreys, Moore]
- James Josiah Moore [Dec. 16, 1878 – Apr. 13, 1946], "A loving husband, a good father."
- Mary Cobun "Polly" *(Humphreys)* Moore [Feb. 12, 1882 – May 23, 1945], "A loving wife, a devoted mother, no better woman ever lived." Mary is the daughter of Baylis Earl and Elizabeth *Hamilton* Humphreys, buried in plot G-51.She married James Josiah Moore in 1903.
- William Earl Moore [May 12, 1907 – August 29, 1984]. William is the son of James Josiah and Mary Cobun *Humphreys* Moore.
- Bonnie Claire *(Brown)* Moore [October 25, 1912 – January 7, 2001]. Bonnie is the daughter of Jesse Simms and Victoria *Andrews* Brown, buried in plot E-6. She married William Earl Moore in 1933. They have a son, Earl Humphreys Moore, buried in plot K-6.

- J. Humphreys Moore [February 16, 1909 – November 21, 1990], "Beloved Husband." J. Humphreys is the son of James Josiah and Mary Cobun *Humphreys* Moore.
- Frances *H(olmes).* Moore [January 31, 1918 – February 23, 1996], "Beloved Wife." Frances is the wife of J. Humphreys Moore.
- Bettye Anne Moore [Jan. 31, 1940 – June 11, 1940], "infant daughter of F. H. & J. Humphreys Moore."

[E-17: Berry, Bitterman, Fox, Lum, McGraw, Purviance]

- Robert C. Lum [May 24, 1876 – Oct. 21, 1936]. Robert is the son of Gadi E. and Laura *McCay* Lum, buried in Lum Cemetery.
- Julia *(Fox)* Lum Bitterman [June 23, 1883 – March 15, 1940]. Julia married Robert C. Lum in 1902. She later married a Mr. Bitterman. Besides those listed below, other children include Julia *Lum* Allen, buried in plot G-A, and William Douglas Lum, buried in combined plot M-87/88.
- Robert Clinton Lum. Jr. [August 5, 1910 – February 5, 1975]. Robert is the son of Robert C. and Julia *Fox* Lum.
- Edith Lucille *Berry* Lum [January 7, 1914 – January 23, 1994]. Edith married Robert Clinton Lum. Jr. in 1934.
- Dorothy "Dot" *Lum* McGraw [June 29, 1914 – January 3, 2005]. Dorothy is the daughter of Robert C. and Julia *Fox* Lum.
- Deborah Ker *Lum* Purviance [Oct. 18, 1948 – Aug. 8, 2011]. This information is from a temporary funeral home marker. Deborah is the daughter of William Douglas and Martha *Brady* Lum, buried in combined plot M-87/88. She married Hollis Langston Purviance in 1979.
- Mary Elizabeth Purviance [Apr. 27, 1989 – Oct. 29, 2008]. Mary is the daughter of Hollis Langston and Deborah Ker *Lum* Purviance.

[E-18: Goff]

- William E. Goff [Feb. 20, 1923 – July 23, 1993]. William shares a common stone with Ruth M. Goff, whom he married in 1953. Ruth's side bears only her birth date of February 3, 1918.

[E-19: no stones]

[E-20: Daniels, Fife, Jordan, McFatter]

- Ben Jordan [1878 – 1965]
- Arissa *(McFatter)* Jordan [1883 – 1965]. Arissa is the daughter of Jeff and Kate *Williams* McFatter, buried in plot A-81. She married Ben Jordan in 1900, and they share a common stone.
- Thomas Shelby Daniels [Jan. 23, 1903 – Feb. 12, 1938]
- Joseph Frank Fife [May 24, 1909 – Aug. 8, 1985], "CPL, US ARMY, WORLD WAR II." This is a bronze military plaque. Joseph Frank is the son of William J. and Belle *Rushbrook* Fife, buried in plot I-34, Belle with the last name of BAKER.
- Marie *(Jordan)* Fife [Aug. 2, 1905 – Apr. 21, 1996]. Marie is the daughter of Ben and Arissa *McFatter* Jordan. She married Thomas Shelby Daniels, her first husband, in 1929. She later married Joseph Frank Fife in 1947, and they share a common stone.

[E-21: Farris, Ogden]

- Kyle L. Farris [June 8, 1880 – Mar. 11, 1960]. Kyle was married twice. After the death of Frances, his first wife, he married Mrs. Annie Louise *Bennett* Behr in 1944.
- Frances *Ogden* Farris [1872 – 1937]. Frances is the wife of Kyle L. Farris. They have a daughter, Katherine *Farris* Clarke, buried in Clarke Cemetery.

[E-22: Carpenter, Ogden, Terry]

- Ira W. Carpenter [1888 – 1945]
- Martha *T(erry).* Carpenter [1885 – 1980]. Martha is the wife of Ira W. Carpenter. They have a daughter, Margaret *Carpenter* Allen, buried in plot G-E.

- Lucy Clagett *Ogden* Carpenter [June 4, 1915 – September 19, 2000], "CPL, US MARINE CORPS, WORLD WAR II." This is a military stone. Lucy also has a civilian stone. She married Ira W. Carpenter, Jr., son of Ira W. and Martha *Terry* Carpenter, in 1946.

[E-23/25/26: Boling, Brown, Burks, Fortner, Foster, Sanders, Wolfe, Wood]. This plot has a memorial stone bearing the name WOLFE.

- "Pattie" E. *Fortner* Burks-Sanders [June 3, 1890 – Jan. 9, 1978], "Mother." Pattie's given name is Eugenia Gertrude Fortner. She was first married to John Robert Burks, buried in Jefferson County. After his death she married William E. Sanders, buried in Warren County. Besides Exa, listed below, other children include Barbara *Burks* Ellis, buried in plot H-18, Mary *Burks* Magee, buried in Hermanville Cemetery with the last name of CRESSMAN, and William E. Sanders, Jr., buried in Warren County.
- Willis W. Wolfe [1878 – 1946], "Father."
- Della *B(oling)*. Wolfe [1886 – 1969], "Mother." Della is the wife of Willis W. Wolfe, and they share a common grave location.
- Harold S. Wolfe [May 1, 1908 – December 30, 1976], "Father." Harold is the son of Willis W. and Della *Boling* Wolfe.
- Exa *B(urks)*. Wolfe [July 25, 1918 – June 23, 1996], "Mother." Exa is the daughter of John Robert and "Pattie" E. *Fortner* Burks. She married Harold S. Wolfe in 1943, and they share a common grave location.
- Grover Harold Wolfe [November 20, 1946 – July 26, 1967], "son of Harold S. and Exa B. Wolfe."
- Willis Waldon Wolfe, II [August 29, 1955 – November 21, 2011]. Willis is the son of Harold S. and Exa *Burks* Wolfe. He married Mildred Maury Goodwin in 1978.
- Infant Wolfe [March 9, 1986]
- Cleveland Earl Wood [January 20, 1911 – September 14, 1995], "Father."
- Helen *Wolfe* Wood [April 17, 1913 – February 5, 1997], "Mother." Helen is the daughter of Willis W. and Della *Boling* Wolfe. She married Cleveland Earl Wood in 1945, and they share a common grave location. Helen had previously been married to a Mr. Brown.
- Lois *Wolfe* Foster [April 7, 1925 – May 10, 1976], member Order of the Eastern Star. Lois is the daughter of Willis W. and Della *Boling* Wolfe. Her foundation stone inscription reads: "Husband Barney Foster" and "Daughter Lynn Della Foster."

[E-24: Manis, Preskitt]

- Joseph B. Manis [May 17, 1885 – April 7, 1969]
- Effie *P(reskitt)*. Manis [July 16, 1886 – May 22, 1940]. Effie is the daughter of W. R. Preskitt, buried in plot A-139. She is the wife of Joseph B. Manis, and they share a common stone.

[E-27: Cade]. This plot has a memorial stone bearing the name CADE.

- John Robert Cade [May 27, 1940 – July 6, 1979]. John is the son of Elvin H. and Kathleen *Wilkinson* Cade, buried in plot H-96. John married Kathleen Segrest Huff in 1968. On back of the stone are the words: "Father of John Robert Cade, Jr. and Richard Lambert Cade."

[E-28: McFatter, Porter]

- James Henry Porter [Sept. 21, 1884 – Nov. 24, 1974]. James is the son of John Sylvester and Martha *Sanders* Porter, buried in Sarepta Cemetery. He was married twice, first to Pearlie Fife in 1906. Pearlie is buried in Hedrick Cemetery.
- Maggie *McFatter* Porter [Jan. 7, 1892 – Jan. 30, 1976]. Maggie is the daughter of Dan and M. Urzilla *Dromgoole* McFatter, buried in Jefferson County. She and James Henry Porter share a common stone with the inscription: "Married Mar. 6, 1910." Another biographical statement reads: "Together almost sixty-five years…"
- H. B. "Bill" Porter [Oct. 21, 1914 – May 1, 1997]. H. B. is the son of James Henry and Maggie *McFatter*

Porter. He shares a common stone with his wife, Louise *Stovall* Porter, whose side shows only her birth date of June 21, 1919.

- Margaret Louise "Peggy" Porter [Sept. 17, 1938 – June 10, 1946]
- Bradley Puckett "Brad" Porter [June 4, 1973 – May 22, 1990]. Bradley is the grandson of H. B. and Louise *Stovall* Porter.

[E-29/30: Bobo, Goodie, Humphreys, Israel, Jones, Joyce, Lucoff, Starnes, Taylor]

- Nettie *Bobo* Taylor [Apr. 7, 1881 – Jan. 3, 1954]. Nettie is the daughter of Charles E. and Olivia Elizabeth *Guy* Bobo, buried in combined plot G-18/19. She had married three times. Her first marriage was to W. M. Israel in 1899. Her next marriage was to J. A. Humphreys in 1900. Mr. Humphreys is buried in plot A-9. Finally, she married Samuel Redus Taylor in 1911. Samuel is buried in plot F-15.
- Charlie Taylor [Mar. 19, 1896 – May 13, 1947]
- Alma *(Humphreys)* Taylor Jones [Apr. 5, 1903 – Dec. 6, 1978]. Alma is the daughter of J. A. and Nettie *Bobo* Humphreys, now TAYLOR. She married Charlie Taylor in 1920. Nettie *Bobo* Taylor, Charlie Taylor and Alma *Humphreys* Taylor Jones share a common stone. Alma later married Henry R. Jones in 1950 or 1952 (marriage records show two separate entries, with different dates). Henry R. Jones is buried in plot A-156.
- Leonard C. Bobo [Apr. 5, 1882 – Mar. 19, 1947], "Husband."
- Matilda *T(aylor)* Bobo [Nov. 9, 1891 – Oct. 7, 1969], "Wife." Matilda and her sister Gertrude, listed below, are daughters of Samuel Redus and Emma *Dixon* Taylor. Matilda married Leonard C. Bobo in 1909.
- John J. Joyce [April 3, 1899 – May 25, 1946]
- Gertrude *T(aylor)* Joyce [Mar. 27, 1898 – July 14, 1988]
- Anna B. Lucoff [July 4, 1887 – July 14, 1980]
- Milton James Starnes [April 29, 1926 – August 21, 1982]. Milton is the son of Marcus J. and Lucile *Middleton* Starnes, buried in combined plot H-79/80.
- Faye *Taylor* Starnes [November 19, 1928 – August 21, 2011]. Faye is the wife of Milton James Starnes, and they share a common grave location.
- Violet Amber Goodie [May 25, 1981]

[E-31: Dodson, Rice, Strickland]. This plot has a memorial stone bearing the name DODSON.

- James W. Dodson [March 22, 1876 – Aug. 9, 1946], "MISSOURI, PVT., 18 INF, SP. AM. WAR." This is a military stone.
- Martha *Rice* Dodson [Sept. 23, 1878 – Mar. 22, 1972]. Martha is the wife if James W. Dodson.
- James Edgar Dodson [Jan. 25, 1907 – June 18, 1985], "Father."
- Ola *Strickland* Dodson [Mar. 31, 1913 – June 3, 1993], "Mother." Ola is the daughter of Lenard S. and Maude E. *Meadows* Strickland, buried in plot A-124. She married James Edgar Dodson in 1930.
- James William Dodson [Aug. 31, 1935 – Apr. 25, 1976], "Son." James is the son of James Edgar and Ola *Strickland* Dodson, and the three of them share a common grave location. He married Ruth Elizabeth Hackler in 1958.

[E-32: Adair, Brown, Thornton]

- Washington G. Brown [Feb. 11, 1881 – Aug. 5, 1946]
- Alice M. *(Adair)* Brown [Feb. 7, 1881 – Sept. 15, 1969]. Alice is the daughter of Thomas R. and Elizabeth *Blackman* Adair, buried in Rocky Springs Cemetery. She married Washington G. Brown in 1904, and they share a common stone. They have a son, John Lowe Brown, buried in combined plot A-153/154.
- Walter Alexander Brown [June 28, 1905 – November 9, 1979]. Walter is the son of Washington G. and Alice M. *Adair* Brown.
- Sallie I. *Thornton* Brown [April 3, 1909 – May 13, 1985]. Sallie is the daughter of John A. and Martha

Flowers Thornton, buried in Flowers Cemetery. She is the wife of Walter Alexander Brown, and they share a common grave location.
- Mattie Mildred *(Brown)* Brown [Nov. 6, 1927 – Oct. 27, 1993], "Mother & Grandmother." Mattie is the daughter of Walter Alexander and Sallie I. *Thornton* Brown. She married Lyle H. Brown, Sr. in 1952. Lyle is buried in plot I-39.

[E-33: Anderson, Kirkley, Willis, Young]
- Joseph J. Anderson [Dec. 15, 1868 – Aug. 20, 1947], "Father."
- Quillie E. *(Kirkley)* Anderson [Apr. 18, 1872 – Jan. 20, 1946], "Mother." Quillie is the wife of Joseph J. Anderson, and they share a common grave location. Besides Grady, listed below, their children include: Richard H. Anderson, buried in combined plot M-44/45, Oscar H. Anderson in plot E-44, Lela Frances *Anderson* Brown in plot M-41, Olivette *Anderson* Roan in plot H-15, and Hardy Troy Anderson, buried in Hermanville Cemetery.
- Grady Anderson [Nov. 11, 1917 – Oct. 31, 2002], "Father." Grady is the son of Joseph J. and Quillie E. *Kirkley* Anderson.
- Bessie M. *(Willis)* Anderson [Jan. 17, 1921 – Sept. 24, 2014], "Mother." Bessie is the daughter of David Evan and Clara Ethel *Norwood* Willis, buried in Willis Cemetery. She married Grady Anderson in 1938, and they share a common grave location.
- James E. Young, III [Mar. 29, 1951 – Jan. 19, 2004]. James is the son of James E. and Sylvia *Disharoon* Young. Sylvia is buried in combined plot A-47/48.
- Brenda *A(nderson)*. Young [Nov. 4, 1953 – Jan. 12, 2015]. Brenda is the daughter of Grady and Bessie M. *Willis* Anderson. She is the wife of James E. Young, III, and they share a common stone.

[E-34: no stones]

[E-35: Abbott, Clark, Fleming]
- John T. Clark [Jan. 18, 1896 – Apr. 5, 1978]. John is the son of G. W. and Addie L. *Evans* Clark, buried in Sarepta Cemetery. After the death of Wilma *Abbott* Clark, listed below, he married Mrs. Marie *Abbott* St. Claire in 1950. Marie is buried in combined plot A-39/40, with last name of HUDSON.
- Wilma *A(bbott)*. Clark [Oct. 10, 1902 – Aug. 15, 1946]. Wilma married John T. Clark in 1919.
- John Thomas Clark, Jr. [Mar. 16, 1931 – Aug. 17, 1950], "MISSISSIPPI, PFC, 5 MARINES, 1 MARINE DIV, KOREA." This is a military stone. His civilian stone has the words: "Killed in action-Korea." John is the son of John T. and Wilma *Abbott* Clark, and the three of them share a common grave location.

From *Port Gibson Reveille's* "Looking Back" column (week of Sept. 22, 1951): "The body of Pfc. John Thomas Clark, Jr., who was killed in Korea on August 7 (sic), 1950, was laid to rest in his native soil on September 7th, with full military honors."
- Evan Lonnie Fleming, Jr. [December 30, 1922 – April 11, 2006], a Mason. Evan shares a common grave location with Carrie *Clark* Fleming, with the words: "Married Oct. 2, 1943." Carrie's side has only her birth date of April 16, 1924.

[E-36: no stones]

[E-36a: Deviney]
- Glen Revere Deviney [April 21, 1926 – June 1, 1998]. Glen married Audrey *Boren* Deviney in 1948, and they share a common grave location. Audrey's side has only her birth date of December 16, 1927.

[E-37a: Burlton, Ellis]
- Joseph Ellis [Nov. 20, 1922 – Oct. 16, 2000]. Joseph and his sister, Camille, are children of George and Thomenie *Oudy* Ellis, buried in combined plot G-42/43. Joseph shares a common stone with Anna *Griffith* Ellis. Anna's side has only her birth date of August 28, 1928.
- Camille Sarah *Ellis* Burlton [Jan. 15, 1926 – April 10, 2012]. Camille shares a common stone with Rogers

Christopher Burlton, M. D. Dr. Burlton's side has only his birth date of September 28, 1935.

[E-37: Baker, Martin, McCrae]. This plot appears to be divided into two parts, with Mr. McCrae in one part, and the Martins in the other.

- Peter M. McCrae [August 24, 1884 – April 3, 1952]
- Maggie *(Baker)* Martin [Nov. 19, 1892 – Nov. 23, 1967]
- John L. Martin [November 5, 1921 – July 29, 1951], "MISSISSIPPI, CPL, 5 CAVALRY, 1 CAVALRY DIV, WORLD WAR II." This is s military stone. John is the son of Maggie *Baker* Martin.

[E-38: Boren, Higgins]

- Thomas Gordon Boren, Sr. [Dec. 15, 1892 – June 29, 1968]. Thomas is the son of Davis and Ellen *Sorrels* Boren, buried in Sarepta Cemetery.
- Marie *Higgins* Boren [Nov. 24, 1899 – July 31, 1985]. Marie is the daughter of John A. and Julia Alef *Marler* Higgins, also buried in Sarepta Cemetery. She married Thomas Gordon Boren in 1920, and they share a common stone. They have a son, Edgar Allen Boren, buried in plot J-16.
- Thomas Gordon Boren, Jr. [September 1, 1923 – December 14, 1950], "MISSISSIPPI, PFC, 663 AAA, MG BTRY CAC, WORLD WAR II." This is a military stone. Thomas also has a civilian stone. He married Ida Fay Davis in 1947.
- Thomas Gordon Boren, III [Aug. 7, 1950 – Jan. 1, 2015]. This information was obtained from a temporary funeral home marker. Thomas is the son of Thomas Gordon and Ida Fay *Davis* Boren.

[E-39: Darden, Porter, Powell, Whitaker]

- Jefferson Davis Whitaker [April 1, 1893 – February 15, 1968]
- Anna *Darden* Whitaker [July 15, 1896 – December 19, 1992]. Anna is the daughter of Charles Buckner and Clara *Nesmith* Darden, buried in Darden Cemetery. She married Jefferson Davis Whitaker in 1919.
- Mary Porter [Mar. 23, 1948 – Mar. 23, 1948]
- Joe Howard "Bro. Joe" Powell [1944 – 2003]. Joe shares a common stone with Lois Jerldine "Jerri" Powell, with the words: "(married) Oct. 20, 1962." Lois' side has only her birth year of 1944.

[E-40: Harwood, Pearson, Shreve]

- William J. Pearson [1852 – 1925]. William is the son of Charles A. Pearson, buried in Pearson Cemetery in Grand Gulf Military State Park, and Clara *Warren* Pearson, buried in plot F-18.
- Agnes C. *(Harwood)* Pearson [1857 – 1886]. Agnes married William J. Pearson in 1882.
- John A. Shreve [1886 – 1951]. John is the son of John Alexander and Sue Willie *Wickliffe* Shreve, buried in plot A-30.
- Mary A. *(Pearson)* Shreve [1886 – 1964]. Mary is the daughter of William J. and Agnes C. *Harwood* Pearson. She married John A. Shreve in 1920, and they share a common stone.

[E-41: no stones]

[E-42: Baker, Qualls]

- Jesse Qualls, Sr. [Feb. 16, 1907 – Dec. 30, 1979]
- Myrtle *(Baker)* Qualls [Aug. 30, 1909 – Mar. 30, 1967]. Myrtle is the wife of Jesse Qualls, Sr. Besides those listed below, they have a son, Hester J. Qualls, Sr., buried in plot M-80.
- Tommy Qualls [August 28, 1939 – December 22, 2003]. Tommy is the son of Jesse and Myrtle *Baker* Qualls.
- Jimmy Qualls [June 2, 1943 – May 24, 2001]. Jimmy is the son of Jesse and Myrtle *Baker* Qualls.
- Wesley Qualls [Apr. 24, 1907 – Nov. 9, 1976]
- Rosie Viola *(Baker)* Qualls [August 12, 1901 – March 8, 1953]. Rosie married Wesley Qualls in 1938.

[E-42a: no stones]

[E-43: Byrd, Jordan, Monk]

- Walter Leon Jordan [December 27, 1886 – October 23, 1953], "Father."

- Sallie *Byrd* Jordan [May 11, 1888 – October 16, 1969], "Mother." Sallie married Walter Leon Jordan in 1908, and they share a common grave location.
- Elige Monk [July 30, 1879 – July 10, 1954]. Elige is the husband of Myrtle *Ainsworth* Monk, buried in plot H-61.

[E-44: Anderson, Bufkin, Heath, Pierson]

- Oscar H. Anderson [Feb. 17, 1894 – July 30, 1986] Oscar is the son of Joseph J. and Quillie E. *Kirkley* Anderson, buried in plot E-33. After the death of Lizzie, below, he married Mrs. Mary Kate *Willis* Emerson in 1958 and/or 1965. Marriage licenses were issued in both of these years.
- Lizzie *B(ufkin)*. Anderson [June 19, 1889 – June 5, 1953]. Lizzie married Oscar H. Anderson in 1915, and they share a common stone. Besides Mary, listed below, they have daughters, Maude Lee *Anderson* Willis and Ruby *Anderson* Beaube, buried in combined plot I-82/83.
- Mary *A(nderson)*. Pierson [Apr. 4, 1917 – Jan. 21, 1999]. Mary is the daughter of Oscar H. and Lizzie *Bufkin* Anderson. She married William S. Pierson in 1945.
- Leslie Diane Heath [Nov. 3, 1971 – Nov. 4, 1971], "Infant."

[E-45: Callender, Carpenter, Nelson]

- Fannie *Carpenter* Nelson [May 5, 1877 – February 28, 1966]. Fannie is the daughter of James Marcellons and Eugenia A. *Darden* Carpenter, buried in Hutchinson Cemetery. She married John Martin Nelson in 1894. John is also buried in Hutchinson Cemetery. Besides their daughter, listed below, other children are Ruth *Nelson* Guion, buried in plot H-30, and Clyde L. and Douglas E. Nelson, buried in combined plot I-7/8.
- Bertron Buie Callender [Oct. 6, 1890 – March 15, 1952]. Bertron is the son of Carrie *Buie* Callender, buried in plot H-49.
- Mildred *N(elson)*. Callender [Feb. 27, 1898 – April 19, 1959]. Mildred is the daughter of John Martin and Fannie *Carpenter* Nelson. She married Bertron Buie Callender in 1919.

Section F

[F-1: no stones]

[F-2: Ingram]

- John Saxon Ingram [Sept. 2, 1818 – Feb. 12, 1871], a Mason.

Besides the one identified stone listed above, three more stones bearing double sets of initials occupy the same plot. The initials on the stones are: H. W. I. – O. B. I., J. E. I. – C. I. and C. O. I. – C. A. I.

[F-3: Bethea, Ingram, Mandel, War]. This plot is enclosed in a wrought iron fence.

- Amaziah Ingram [Oct. 20, 1790 – April 9, 1867]
- Charlotte Ingram [Jan. 28, 1798 – July 10, 1835]
- Orran F. Ingram [Aug. 28, 1820 – Dec. 3, 1838]. A biographical epitaph reads: "He was a devoted son, an affectionate brother, with all the virtues of the good."
- Joshua Orville Ingram [Sept. 11, 1821 – Sept. 20, 1871], a Mason. His biographical epitaph reads: "He was an honest man, a devoted son, an affectionate brother, and a steadfast friend."
- Charles S. Ingram [July 11, 1823 – Jan. 4, 1869], a Mason.
- Lewis L. Mandel [May 5, 1815 – May 6, 1877], a Mason, "My Husband." Lewis married Clarinda Ingram in 1849. The Ingrams and the Mandels share a common obelisk.
- Emily I. Bethea [Sep. 20, 1850 – Oct. 27, 1852], "daughter of T. & M. A. Bethea."
- Rosa Bethea [died Aug. 1848, aged 1 week], "infant of T. and M. A. Bethea."
- James William War [died Dec. 6, 1845, aged 1 year 9 days], "son of Wm. & A. War." Rosa Bethea and James William War share a common stone.

[F-4: Beatty, Bertron, Mueller, Redus]

- Reverend Samuel Reading Bertron [Dec. 17, 1806 – Oct. 7, 1878], "born in Philadelphia…died of yellow fever near Port Gibson." Rev. Bertron was married three times. His first wife, Caroline *Christie* Bertron, is buried in Waterman Crane Cemetery. Second, he married Mrs. Catharine M. *Crane* Barnes in 1847. Catharine is buried in James Crane Cemetery. Samuel and Caroline *Christie* Bertron have a daughter, Mary *Bertron* Hughes, buried in plot A-20.
- Ottilie *Mueller* Bertron [Dec. 25, 1830 – Jan. 22, 1903], "wife of Samuel Reading Bertron, born in Freiberg, Germany…died at Port Gibson, Miss." Ottilie and Samuel share a common obelisk. Besides Mary, listed below, they have a son, Samuel Reading Bertron, buried in plot A-43.
- James C. Bertron [May 12, 1848 – June 3, 1884], C. S. A. stone. James is the son of Samuel Reading and Catharine M. *Crane* Bertron. He married his first wife, Elizabeth Fontaine Humphreys, in 1878. Eliza-

Section F

beth is buried in combined plot B-7/18. According to Mississippi Confederate Grave Registration records, James was a Private in Owen's Scouts/Powers Regt. Cavalry.

- Mary Olivia *(Beatty)* Bertron [Aug. 1, 1856 – Oct. 2, 1929], "wife of James C. Bertron."
- James C. Bertron, Jr. [Sept. 14, 1882 – Jan. 3, 1896]. James is the son of James C. and Mary Olivia *Beatty* Bertron.
- Dr. William Dickson Redus [Jan 27, 1854 – Apr. 21, 1924], "born…in Leake Co. Miss., died…in Port Gibson, Miss." Dr. Redus is the son of J. C. and H. A. Redus, buried in Copiah County.
- Mary Anna Linton *Bertron* Redus [May 5, 1859 – April 22, 1938], "wife of Dr. William Dickson Redus, born at Claremont, near Port Gibson." Mary is the daughter of Samuel Reading and Ottilie *Mueller* Bertron. She married Dr. Redus in 1880.
- Will D. Redus [Apr. 14, 1886 – Apr. 26, 1888]. Will is the son of William Dickson and Mary Anna *Bertron* Redus.
- Ottilie Bertron Redus [July 1, 1888 – January 21, 1982], member Daughters of the American Revolution, "born in Port Gibson…died at Claremont." Ottilie is the daughter of William Dickson and Mary Anna *Bertron* Redus.

[F-5: McGrady] This plot also has one C. S. A. stone whose owner cannot be identified, plus a broken C. S. A. stone.

- William McGrady [March 29, 1820 – Sept. 18, 1873]

[F-6: Anderson, Butler, Herlitz, Humphreys, Pipes, Stuart, Winston]. This plot has one C. S. A. stone whose owner cannot be identified.

- John Cobun Humphreys [June 8, 1821 – Dec. 5, 1875], C. S. A. stone. John is the son of David G. and Mary *Cobun* Humphreys, buried in plot H-10.
- Sarah *Stuart* Humphreys [Feb. 27, 1825 – Feb. 4, 1863]. Sarah married John Cobun Humphreys in 1844.
- John Cobun Humphreys, Jr. [June 5, 1850 – May 3, 1866]. John is the son of John Cobun and Mary *Stuart* Humphreys.
- James Leon Humphreys [Apr. 19, 1852 – Dec. 8, 1888], "buried in San Antonio Tex." This information is actually located on the back of John Cobun Humphreys, Jr's stone. James Leon is interred in St. Mary's Cemetery, San Antonio, Bexar County, Texas. These first four names share a common grave location.
- D. George Humphreys [1844 – 1899], C. S. A. stone. David George is the son of John Cobun and Mary *Stuart* Humphreys.
- Lord John Butler [Aug. 7, 1838 – Oct. 28, 1921], C. S. A. stone, "born Port Gibson, Miss." Lord John is the son of Rev. Zebulon and Mary Anne Butler, buried in plot B-33. According to Mississippi Confederate Grave Registration records, he served as Private, then Lieutenant, in Co. C, 4th Miss. Cavalry, TR LT Engineer, and was discharged from a New York prison in 1865.
- Kate Coburn (sic) *Humphreys* Butler [Aug. 26, 1846 – Jan. 12, 1919], "wife of Lord John Butler." Kate is the daughter of John Cobun and Mary *Stuart* Humphreys. She married Lord John Butler in 1868. Kate's middle name is misspelled and should be COBUN.
- Zebulon Butler [Nov. 5, 1869 – Dec. 4, 1869]. Zebulon and John Humphreys Butler are sons of Lord John and Kate Cobun *Humphreys* Butler, and they share a common stone.
- John Humphreys Butler [Dec. 31, 1871 – Mar. 10, 1905]
- William Anders Herlitz [August 8, 1867 – March 12, 1939], "a native of Visby, Sweden."
- Sarah *Butler* Herlitz [June 27, 1876 – August 29, 1934], "wife of William A. Herlitz." Sarah is the daughter of Lord John and Kate Cobun *Humphreys* Butler. She married William A. Herlitz in 1898. They have a daughter, Kate Humphreys *Herlitz* Guthrie, buried in combined plot G-39/40/41.
- John William Herlitz [1902 – 1959], "buried in Houston, Texas." This information is inscribed on the back of the stone of Sarah *Butler* Herlitz.

- Dr. Decatur Curran Anderson [Mar. 24, 1878 – Sep. 27, 1905]. Dr. Anderson is the son of Dr. Lomax and Nellie *Buckner* Anderson, buried in plot F-28.
- Mary Kate *Butler* Pipes [1880 – 1937], "wife of W. H. Pipes, M. D…daughter of Kate Cobun Humphreys and Lord John Butler." Mary was married twice, first to Dr. Decatur Curran Anderson in 1904. After his death she married Dr. William H. Pipes in 1915.
- William Henry Pipes [Dec. 26, 1916 – June 29, 1920], "son of William Henry and Mary Kate Butler Pipes."
- Moreau Stuart Humphreys [Oct. 17, 1848 – Feb. 2, 1903]. Moreau is the son of John Cobun and Sarah *Stuart* Humphreys.
- Anna *Winston* Humphreys [June 27, 1849 – Sept. 1, 1927]. Anna married Moreau Stuart Humphreys in 1884.
- Blount Stuart Humphreys [Nov. 5, 1855 – April 5, 1891]. Blount is the son of John Cobun and Sarah *Stuart* Humphreys.

[F-7: Bland, Magee, McCaleb, Nesmith, Rollins]

- Annie *Rollins* McCaleb [July 14, 1845 – Sept. 28, 1928]. Annie married John B. McCaleb in 1864. Besides Percy and Lucy, listed below, they have a son, Johnnie B. McCaleb, buried in plot B-34.
- Percy Rollins McCaleb [Aug. 2, 1866 – Feb. 19, 1910]. Percy is the son of John B. and Annie *Rollins* McCaleb.
- Margaret *Magee* McCaleb [Mar. 17, 1883 – Feb. 23, 1911], "wife of Percy R. McCaleb." Margaret married Percy McCaleb in 1901.
- Margaret Rollins McCaleb [Mar. 8, 1904 – Dec. 12, 1908], "daughter of Percy and Bessie McCaleb."
- Lucy Russell *McCaleb* Nesmith [Dec. 4, 1872 – Jan. 1, 1912], "wife of T. B. Nesmith." Lucy is the daughter of John B. and Annie *Rollins* McCaleb. She married Thomas B. Nesmith in 1910. Thomas is buried in Trevilion Cemetery.
- Archie Bland [Dec. 9, 1847 – March 2, 1897]

[F-8: Hackett, Krauss, Miller, Rea, Stampley]

- Thomas M. Rea [March 1, 1842 – June 26, 1919], C. S. A. stone, a Mason, "Father." According to Mississippi Confederate Grave Registration records, Thomas was a Private in Co. D, 12th Miss. Regt. Infantry. On Thomas' stone are the letters, HTWSSTKS, arranged in a circle, indicating a higher office in the Masonic organization. (Incidentally, the letters stand for "Hiram The Widow's Son, Sent To King Solomon.")
- Chestina C. (*Stampley*) Rea [Dec. 17, 1846 – Dec. 12, 1906], "Mother." Chestina married Thomas M. Rea in 1868, and they share a common grave location. Besides Nell, listed below, they have another daughter, Addie *Rea* Hackett, buried in combined plot H-64/65.
- Sidney S. Krauss [Jan. 25, 1872 – July 27, 1950]
- Nell *Rea* Krauss [Feb. 18, 1874 – Mar. 7, 1949]. Nell is the daughter of Thomas M. and Chestina *Stampley* Rea. She married Sidney S. Krauss in 1897.
- Ferdinand Thomas Krauss [Nov. 17, 1898 – May 21, 1952]. Ferdinand is the son of Sidney S. and Nell *Rea* Krauss.
- Neil Hackett Miller [Nov. 15, 1909 – Apr. 2, 1911]. Neil is the son of John Power and Rea *Hackett* Miller, buried in combined plot H-64/65.
- Infant Daughter Hackett [Sept. 6, 1917 – Sept. 7, 1917], "infant daughter of N. L. & C. H. Hackett." This infant's parents, Neil Louis and Calista *Headley* Hackett, are buried in combined plot H-64/65.

[F-9: Green, Guthrie, Hackley, Shreve]

- Charles Shreve [Nov. 25, 1813 – Aug. 31, 1878]
- Margaret B. *Hackley* Shreve [Feb. 5, 1822 – Sep. 9, 1878], "wife of Charles Shreve." Besides those listed

below, they have a son, John Alexander Shreve, buried in plot A-30.

- Charles Shreve [Feb. 12, 1857 – Sep. 11, 1878], "son of Charles & Margaret B. Shreve." These first three Shreves were victims of the yellow fever epidemic, and they share a common obelisk.
- Ruth *Shreve* Guthrie [Nov. 12, 1861 – Oct. 11, 1914], "wife of W. C. Guthrie." Ruth is the daughter of Charles and Margaret B. *Hackley* Shreve. She married Walter Craig Guthrie in 1899. Walter is buried in combined plot G-39/40/41, along with their twin children, Margaret Adeline "Gretchen" and William Shreve Guthrie.
- Infant Daughter Shreve [died Dec. 24, 1877], "infant daughter of J. A. & S. W. Shreve." This infant's parents, John Alexander and Sue Willie *Wickliffe* Shreve, are buried in plot A-30.
- Gayosa Green [Sept. 30, 1878, aged 15 years]. Gayosa and Lizzie Green were both victims of the yellow fever epidemic.
- Lizzie Green [Sept. 28, 1878, aged 17 years]

[F-10: Burch, Dick, Montgomery, Turner]

- Eliza Burch (formerly Turner) [died May 6, 1914, aged 68 years]. Eliza's maiden name is unknown. She married William H. Burch in 1872.
- Thomas Turner [died Jan'y 3, 1936, aged 69 years], "a resident of Port Gibson 1869 – 1936." Thomas is the son of Eliza Burch.
- Metella V. *Montgomery* Turner [June 23, 1870 – Apr. 30, 1939]. Metella is the wife of Thomas Turner. These three Turners share a common obelisk. Thomas and Metella also have their individual stones. Metella's maiden name is shown only on her own stone.
- Jonty M. Dick [no dates]
- Katherine *Burch* Dick [no dates]. Katherine is the daughter of William H. and Eliza Burch, and wife of Jonty M. Dick.

[F-11: no stones]

[F-12: Davenport, Ferriday, Gordon, Preston]

- Charles B. Gordon [Dec. 27, 1838 – March 8, 1880], "a native of Conn."
- Hester E. *Davenport* Gordon [Sept. 14, 1846 – Dec. 4, 1877], "wife of Charles B. Gordon." Hester married Charles B. Gordon in 1876.
- J. H. Gordon [Aug. 27, 1837 – Feb. 7, 1902]
- Joanna A. *Preston* Gordon [Aug. 5, 1839 – May 14, 1905], "wife of J. H. Gordon." These first four Gordons share a common obelisk.
- Charles A. Gordon [June 25, 1865 – April 14, 1937], "devoted husband and loyal friend." Charles is the son of John H. and Joanna A. *Preston* Gordon.
- Mary *Ferriday* Gordon [August 11, 1873 – May 22, 1950], "wife of Charles A. Gordon." Mary married Charles A. Gordon in 1893.
- W. P. Gordon [Feb. 7, 1873 – Nov. 13, 1917]. William Preston is the son of John H. and Joanna A. *Preston* Gordon. He married Josie B. Taliaferro in 1905. Josie is buried in combined plot A-75/80. They have a son, William P. Gordon, buried in plot A-141.

[F-13: Davis, Wheeless]. All names listed here share a common obelisk, with individual stones to mark their actual burial spots, with the exception of C. F. Wheeless, who has only a small stone and does not appear on the obelisk.

- G. B. Wheeless, Sr. [died July 4, 1889, aged 85 years]
- Elizabeth *(Davis)* Wheeless [died Jan. 18, 1904]. Elizabeth married Green B. Wheeless in 1843. Besides children listed below, other offspring are George W. Wheeless and Sarah Ann *Wheeless* Blomquist, buried in plot A-44, Martha C. *Wheeless* Patterson in combined plot G-13/14, Green Berry Wheeless in combined plot A-116/117, and Elizabeth *Wheeless* Shaifer in combined plot H-71/72/89/90.

- Henry Shafer Wheeless [Nov. 6, 1844 – Aug. 26, 1878], C. S. A. stone. Henry is a victim of the yellow fever epidemic.
- Mary Jane Wheeless [March 21, 1851 – Aug. 24, 1878], "daughter of G. B. & E. Wheeless." Mary Jane is a victim of the yellow fever epidemic.
- Samuel Culverson Wheeless [Oct. 12, 1861 – Sept. 1, 1875], "son of G. B. & E. Wheeless."
- John A. Wheeless [died Mar. 9, 1892, aged 19 years]
- Frank Wheeless [July 19, 1874 – Sept. 27, 1877], "son of G. B. & E. Wheeless."
- C. F. Wheeless [no dates]. C. F. is the son of Green B. and Elizabeth *Davis* Wheeless.

[F-14: Faust, Hofer, Simonson, Starker]

- Anna Christine Simonson [June 24, 1810 – Feb. 2, 1890]
- Henry Simonson [July 7, 1838 – Jan. 21, 1891], "a native of Denmark." A memorial epitaph reads: "Erected by his loving wife & children."
- Anna Maria *Starker* Simonson [Jan. 10, 1856 – Aug. 25, 1878], "wife of Hermann Simonson...died at Port Gibson." A memorial epitaph reads: "Peace to Her Ashes." Anna Maria married Hermann Simonson in 1874. She was a victim of the yellow fever epidemic.
- Charles August Hofer [Aug. 27, 1843 – Sep. 11, 1886], "born near Stockholm, Sweden...died at Memphis, Tenn." A memorial epitaph reads: "Erected by his beloved wife and children." Charles married Wilhelmina Starker in 1875.
- Conrad Faust [died Sept. 1, 1878, in his 55 year], "died of yellow fever."
- Elisabeth Faust [died Sept. 7, 1878, in her 48 year], "died of yellow fever."

[F-15: Bergquist, Fisher, Taylor]

- John Bergquist [Jan. 15, 1847 – Oct. 29, 1889], member Independent Order of Odd Fellows, "a native of Sweden." John married Mrs. Missouri *Dixon* Hicks in 1877. His last name is misspelled on the stone as BERGGUIST.
- Joseph S. Bergquist [March 9, 1889 – January 7, 1921], "MISSISSIPPI, PVT, 120 ENGINEERS, WORLD WAR I." This is a military stone.
- Sam Fisher [1875 – 1953]
- Alice B. Fisher [1882 – 1948]. Sam and Alice B. Fisher share a common stone.
- Samuel Redus Taylor [September 1860 – March 1943]. Samuel married Emma Dixon in 1884. Their daughters, Matilda *Taylor* Bobo and Gertrude *Taylor* Joyce, are buried in combined plot E-29/30. He later married Mrs. Nettie *Bobo* Humphreys in 1911. Nettie is also in combined plot E-29/30.

[F-16: Moore, Rowan, Watson]

- W. W. Moore [Jan. 14, 1841 – March 3, 1913], "CAPTAIN, 1 REGT MISS CAV, CSA." This is a bronze military plaque. His full name of William Walker Moore is shown on a separate obelisk.
- Ernestine *Watson* Moore [died May 18, 1880, aged 38 years], "born in Jefferson Co. Miss." Ernestine married William Walker Moore in 1863. Besides the children listed below, they have a daughter, Anna *Moore* Evans, buried in plot E-14.
- Louie Moore [died Mar. 26, 1879, aged 8 years], "second son of Wm. W. & Ernestine Watson Moore, born in Jefferson Co. Miss."
- Georgana Rowan [died 1876], "infant daut. of Cleveland & Ida Rowan." Georgana's mother, Ida *Maddox* Rowan, is buried in Jefferson County. Georgana, along with Ernestine *Watson* Moore and Louie Moore, share a common obelisk.
- Blanton Fleming Moore [Aug. 1873 – Sept. 1900], "son of Wm. W. & Ernestine Moore, born in Jefferson Co, Miss...died at Leland."
- Julia *Rowan* Moore [April 12, 1855 – May 3, 1927], "Mother" and "wife of William Walker Moore." Julia is the second wife of Capt. William Walker Moore, marrying in 1881. Besides Lillie Kate, listed

below, they have a son, William Walker Moore, buried in plot C-22.
- Lilly Kate Moore [died Sept. 1891, aged 3 yrs. & 11 mos.], "daughter of Wm. W. & Julia R. Moore."

[F-16a: Barnes, James]
- Dr. D. A. James [Nov. 23, 1819 – Dec. 28, 1872]
- Susan Edith *Barnes* James [Feb. 14, 1827 – Sept. 1, 1911], "wife of Dr. Daniel A. James." Susan married Dr. Daniel James in 1852.
- John B. James [Sept. 28, 1853 – Nov. 25, 1892]. John is the son of Dr. Daniel and Susan Edith *Barnes* James. He married Jennie Brooks in 1876.
- Samuel Humphreys James [Dec. 12, 1857 – May 27, 1924]

[F-17: Liebman, Martin, McCall, Myles]
- William Myles, M. D. [died June 10, 1892, aged 75 years], "a native of Ireland, a resident of Mississippi for 50 years."
- Amanda M. *McCall* Myles [March 29, 1819 – June 12, 1887], "Our Mother…wife of William Myles, born near Lexington Ky." Besides those listed below, their other children are Isabella *Myles* Person, buried in plot B-27, and Frederick F. Myles, in plot B-39.
- John Musgrave Myles [died Aug. 24, 1848, aged 14 months, ?? days], "son of W. & A. M. Myles." This stone is broken, and part of John's age is missing.
- Beverly B. Myles [August 19, 1855 – November 6, 1930]. Beverly is the son of Dr. William and Amanda *McCall* Myles.
- Jonathan McCaleb Martin [June 2, 1846 – July 13, 1924], C. S. A. stone.
- Amanda Malvina *Myles* Martin [Feb. 13, 1858 – Dec. 23, 1945], "wife of J. McC. Martin." Amanda is the daughter of Dr. William and Amanda *McCall* Myles. She married Jonathan McCaleb Martin in 1885.
- Baylissa *Myles* Liebman [October 14, 1877 – October 17, 1950]. Baylissa is the daughter of Frederick F. and Katesie Prince *Humphreys* Myles, buried in plot B-39.

[F-18: Harwood, Hastings, Linde, Pearson, Stanley, Warren]
- Clara *W(arren)* Pearson [1826 – 1909]. Clara married Charles A. Pearson in 1846. Charles is buried in Pearson Cemetery in Grand Gulf Military State Park, along with a son, Henry H. Pearson. Besides those listed below, other children include William J. Pearson, buried in plot E-40, and L. S. Pearson in plot A-18a.
- George B. Pearson [Jan. 23, 1847 – Oct. 8, 1933]. George is the son of Charles and Clara *Warren* Pearson.
- Charles Warren Pearson [Jan. 8, 1849 – Sept. 25, 1899], "born at Grand Gulf, Miss…died at Port Gibson, Miss." Charles is the son of Charles and Clara *Warren* Pearson. He also has a smaller stone with just a name and dates.
- Eleanor E. Pearson [1859 – 1918]. Eleanor is the daughter of Charles and Clara *Warren* Pearson.
- Thomas M. Harwood [1850 – 1887]
- Clara *P(earson)* Harwood [1853 – 1948]. Clara is the daughter of Charles and Clara *Warren* Pearson. She married Thomas M. Harwood in 1884.
- Herbert Stanley [July 17, 1872 – Oct. 27, 1961], "husband of Wren Pearson."
- Wren *Pearson* Stanley [November 10, 1882 – June 16, 1942]. Wren is the daughter of William J. and Agnes C. *Harwood* Pearson. She married Herbert Stanley in 1911.
- Clara Atkinson Stanley [Oct. 3, 1913 – Mar. 7, 1996]. Clara is the daughter of Herbert and Wren *Pearson* Stanley.
- Charlotte *Stanley* Hastings [Nov. 4, 1914 – June 29, 1961], "wife of Richard Granbery Hastings, Jr." Charlotte is the daughter of Herbert and Wren *Pearson* Stanley. She married Richard Granbery Hastings, Jr. in 1937.

- Charles H. G. Linde [June 29, 1883 – July 22, 1941]
- Eleanor *Pearson* Linde [Feb. 8, 1884 – Oct. 1, 1946]. Eleanor is the daughter of William J. and Agnes C. *Harwood* Pearson, and wife of Charles H. G. Linde.
- William Pearson Linde [Aug. 19, 1916 – Mar. 4, 1983], "World War II Veteran, son of Eleanor Pearson Linde and Charles H. G. Linde." This is not a military stone.
- Mary A. Linde [1913 – 1922]

[F-19: Allen, Belknap, Gannon, Glass, Hamilton, Little, Thrasher]. This plot has a memorial stone bearing the names HAMILTON and THRASHER.

- Charles D. Hamilton [Feb. 6, 1814 – March 26, 1869]
- Elizabeth *Belknap* Thrasher [Jan. 3, 1829 – Feb. 17, 1907]. Elizabeth married Charles D. Hamilton in 1853. Besides those listed below, other children are Mary *Hamilton* Burnet, buried in plot C-36a, Nannie *Hamilton* Humphreys in plot H-10, and Elizabeth *Hamilton* Humphreys in plot G-51. After Charles' death she married Stephen Thrasher in 1875. Stephen is buried in plot A-70.
- Charles M. Hamilton [Dec. 15, 1860 – Aug. 3, 1882]. Charles is the son of Charles D. and Elizabeth *Belknap* Hamilton.
- Mattie S. Hamilton [March 3, 1862 – Aug. 20, 1871]
- Robert E. Lee Hamilton [June 9, 1863 – Feb. 19, 1923]. Robert is the son of Charles D. and Elizabeth *Belknap* Hamilton.
- Nellie *A(llen)*. Hamilton [Dec. 23, 1870 – Mar. 18, 1901]. Nellie married Robert E. Lee Hamilton in 1891. This is Robert's first wife. Besides Eugenia, listed below, other children include Phoebe *Hamilton* Abraham, buried in plot A-123, and Stephen Thrasher Hamilton in plot H-34.
- Eugenia *Hamilton* Gannon [Apr. 1, 1892 – Nov. 29, 1966], Eugenia is the daughter of Robert E. Lee and Nellie *Allen* Hamilton. She married J. J. Gannon in 1913.
- Emma *Glass* Hamilton [1880 – 1921]. Emma is the second wife of Robert E. Lee Hamilton. They have a daughter, Mary Lee *Hamilton* Trimble, buried in plot I-40.
- James B. Hamilton [Jan. 18, 1867 – Nov. 20, 1898]
- Stephen E. Little [Nov. 3, 1858 – Aug. 7, 1878]

[F-20: Darden, Davenport]

- E. J. Davenport [1847 – 1911], C. S. A. stone.
- Drucilla *Darden* Davenport [1852 – 1939], "His Wife." Drucilla married E. J. Davenport in 1871, and they share a common stone. Their children, Joseph Davenport and Eva *Davenport* Seale, are buried in combined plot A-125/126.

[F-21: no stones]

[F-22: Cook, Maddox, O'Steen, Snodgrass]

- Dr. Adderton Maddox [Nov. 2, 1814 – Oct. 19, 1890], "a native of Maryland." Dr. Maddox was married twice. His first wife, Mary Jane Maddox, is buried in Jefferson County. It is interesting that the epitaphs on their stones, so far apart, are identical.
- Jennie L. *(O'Steen)* Maddox [Dec. 7, 1843 – May 5, 1927], "Mother...beloved wife of Dr. A. Maddox." Jennie married Dr. Adderton Maddox in 1863. Besides those listed below, a son, Ashby A. Maddox, is buried in plot A-20.
- Elizabeth *M(addox)*. Cook [July 7, 1866 – June 8, 1903]. Elizabeth married Thomas H. Cook in 1890.
- Mary E. Cook [April 22, 1891 – April 25, 1958]. Mary is the daughter of Thomas H. and Elizabeth *Maddox* Cook.
- Marie Maddox [June 8, 1870 – Nov. 10, 1888]
- Owens Snodgrass [1854 – 1928]
- Blanche *(Maddox)* Snodgrass [1872 – 1950], "wife of Owens." Blanche is the daughter of Dr. Adderton

and Jennie L. *O'Steen* Maddox. She and Owens share a common stone.

- Gertrude Maddox [Dec. 29, 1879 – June 4, 1907]
-

> "I leave the world without a tear,
> Save for those I hold so dear.
> I come O Lord at Thy command,
> I yield my spirit to Thy hand."
> —on stone of Dr. Adderton Maddox

[F-23: Briscoe, Brown, Humphreys, Middleton]
- Mary C. *Humphreys* Briscoe [1856 – 1939], "wife of Samuel M. Briscoe." Mary married Samuel M. Briscoe in 1883. Samuel is buried in plot D-8, along with an infant son.
- Ben Humphreys Briscoe [Dec. 15, 1888 – Oct. 11, 1949]. Ben is the son of Samuel M. and Mary C. *Humphreys* Briscoe.
- David George Humphreys [died Sep. 16, 1897]
- Edward M. Middleton [1859 – 1942]
- Bliss P. *Humphreys* Middleton [1873 – 1928], "wife of E. M. Middleton." Bliss married Edward M. Middleton in 1893.
- Katharine *Humphreys* Brown [died Aug. 25, 1881], "wife of Jos. T. Brown." Katharine married Joseph T. Brown in 1879.

[F-24: no stones]

[F-25: Davenport, Roberts, Roney]
- Alexander W. Roberts [May 7, 1837 – Oct. 3, 1891], "Father."
- Baylissa *Davenport* Roberts [March 9, 1842 – Dec. 26, 1915], "Mother." According to will records, Baylissa is the daughter of Joseph and Letitia M. *Jefferies* Devenport, buried in Devenport Cemetery. The family name changed through the years to be spelled as DAVENPORT. Baylissa married Alexander W. Roberts in 1865.
- Bernard Roney [Dec. 26, 1857 – June 14, 1926], "Father."
- Sallie *Roberts* Roney [Jan. 29, 1875 – Nov. 30, 1928], "Mother." Sallie is the wife of Bernard Roney.
- Bliss D. Roney [May 9, 1906 – Feb. 8, 1983]

[F-26: Arnold, Jefferies, Owen]
- Capt. Robert A. Owen [Apr. 18, 1833 – Apr. 21, 1921]. Robert is a Civil War veteran and, according to Mississippi Confederate Grave Registration records, he served as Sergeant and Captain in Co. K, 12th Miss, Infantry, Owen's Scouts.
- Ellen *Jefferies* Owen [Aug. 26, 1850 – July 2, 1893]. Ellen married Capt. Owen in 1876, and they share a common stone.
- Fred Osher Arnold [June 1, 1878 – Jan. 2, 1937]
- Marie *Owen* Arnold [Aug. 25, 1883 – May 18, 1985]. Marie is the daughter of Capt. Robert A. and Ellen *Jefferies* Owen. She married Fred Osher Arnold in 1908, and they share a common stone.
- Nathaniel Jefferies Owen [October 8, 1918], "MISSISSIPPI, LIEUT., 30 ENGRS." This is a military stone. Nathaniel is the son of Capt. Robert A. and Ellen *Jefferies* Owen.

From *Port Gibson Reveille's* "Looking Back" column (Week of June 2, 1921): "The remains of 1st Lt. Nathaniel Jefferies Owen, killed in France in 1918, were placed in the family square in Wintergreen Cemetery on May 19th…"

[F-26a: Metcalfe]. This plot consists of a large urn on a six-sided pedestal, located within a concrete boundary.
- Mrs. M. P. Metcalfe [no dates]

[F-27: Jarratt, Taylor]
- John P. Taylor [Dec. 1, 1847 – Sept. 11, 1893], a Mason and member Woodmen of the World, "A devoted husband, a loving father, a true friend."
- V. E. Taylor [no dates]. According to will records, V. E. is the wife of John P. Taylor, and according to a funeral notice, she died in 1897. Besides those listed below, other children include James Madison Taylor, buried in plot D-9, Cornelia *Taylor* Brashear in plot A-85, and Katherine *Taylor* Bisland in plot H-60
- H. B. Taylor [no dates]. According to a funeral notice, H. B. is the son of John P. and V. E. Taylor, and he died in 1895.
- Julia *Taylor* Jarrett (sic) [Jan. 8, 1877 – Dec. 25, 1961]. Julia is the daughter of John P. and V. E. Taylor. She married B. E. Jarratt in 1899.
- Julia Marie Jarratt [Nov. 5, 1904 – Feb. 17, 1985]. Julia is the daughter of B. E. and Julia *Taylor* Jarratt.

[F-28: Anderson, Buckner, Daugherty, Freeland, Morehead]
- Sarah *F(reeland)*. Buckner [Dec. 5, 1813 – Jan'y 19, 1892]. Sarah is the daughter of Thomas and Emily Jane *Wells* Freeland, buried Freeland Cemetery. She married Robert H. Buckner in 1830. Robert is also buried in Freeland Cemetery, along with three of their children, Robert H., Kate D. and Thomas Freeland Buckner.
- Dr. Lomax Anderson [Jan. 23, 1846 – Dec. 9, 1915]
- Nellie *Buckner* Anderson [May 1, 1846 – Mar. 20, 1919]. Nellie is the daughter of Robert H. and Sarah *Freeland* Buckner. She married Dr. Lomax Anderson in 1867. Besides Rebecca, and possibly Ruby, listed below, other children are Robert Buckner Anderson, buried in plot I-38, and Dr. Decatur Curran Anderson in plot F-6.
- Rebecca Davis Anderson [Dec. 27, 1873 – Oct. 7, 1881], "daughter of Lomax & Nellie B. Anderson."
- Ruby [no dates]. No other information exists, except that Ruby and Rebecca Davis Anderson are named on opposite sides of a common stone.
- Maria *Morehead* Anderson [June 22, 1876 – May 31, 1924], "wife of R. B. Anderson." Maria is the daughter of Benjamin H. and Mary *Sessions* Morehead, buried in plot B-15. She married Robert Buckner Anderson, buried in plot I-38, in 1899. They also have a son, Ben Morehead Anderson, buried in plot B-15.
- Lomax Anderson [Nov. 15, 1899 – Jan. 8, 1962]. Lomax is the son of Robert Buckner and Maria *Morehead* Anderson.
- Helen *Dougherty* (sic) Anderson [Aug. 18, 1905 – Mar. 12, 1980]. Helen is the daughter of Walter Eugene and Willie *Chesterman* Daugherty, buried in plot H-14. She married Lomax Anderson in 1926.

[F-29: Brown]
- William Brown, Sr. [Oct. 28, 1808 – Mar. 3, 1885], a Mason, "born in Philadelphia Pa."
- Anna W. Brown [Mar. 7, 1808 – Mar. 3, 1884], "wife of Wm. Brown, Sr., born in Philadelphia Pa."
- William Brown, Jr. [Dec. 11, 1840 – Mar. 22, 1886], C. S. A. stone, a Mason and member Independent Order of Odd Fellows, "born in Vicksburg, Miss…died…near Port Gibson Miss." William, Jr. shares a common obelisk with William Brown, Sr. and Anna W. Brown. According to Mississippi Confederate Grave Registration records, William was a Corporal, then Sergeant, in Co. K, 12th Miss. Regt. Infantry.
- William Goza Brown [Oct. 8, 1880 – Sept. 24, 1882], "little son of Annie & Wm. Brown Jr., born near Port Gibson."

[F-30: Thomas]
- Dr. Addison Edwards Thomas [July 11, 1819 – Feb. 1, 1873], "born near Waterford, Va.…died in Port Gibson, Miss."
- Angie Lee Thomas [May 29, 1829 – Sept. 22, 1886], "wife of Dr. A. E. Thomas, born in Va." Angie's and Dr. Addison Thomas' names appear on opposite sides of a common stone.

[F-31: no stones]

[F-32: Calhoun, Chamberlain, Houston, Jones]

- Archelaus Kirkland Jones [June 3, 1839 – Feb. 2, 1911]. Archelaus is the son of Joseph E. and Martha A. *Green* Jones, buried in Jones Cemetery. His obelisk features an unusual symbol with the words: "Deo Vindice," meaning "Under God, Our Vindicator," followed by the dates 1861/1865, and surrounded by the words: "Southern Cross of Honor." He is a Civil War veteran and, according to Mississippi Confederate Grave Registration records, was a Private in Co. H, 12th Miss. Infantry, and cause of death was "blood clot to brain."
- Mary *Calhoun* Jones [1842 – 1925]. Mary married Archelaus Kirkland Jones in 1867.
- John Meriwether Jones [1868 – 1941]. John is the son of A. K. and Mary *Calhoun* Jones.
- Charlotte Thomson *Chamberlain* Jones [1872 – 1927]. Charlotte is the wife of John Meriwether Jones.
- Cabell Calhoun Jones [1870 – 1902]

According to the *Port Gibson Reveille's* "Looking Back" column (this week December 20, 1902): "Mr. Cabell Calhoun Jones, 32, died after becoming ill in the Philippines where he was with the Army. He died at the Army and Navy Hospital in Washington and was buried in Arlington National Cemetery."

- Anna Amelia Jones [1871 – 1952]. Anna is the daughter of A. K. and Mary *Calhoun* Jones.
- Archelaus Kirkland Jones, Jr. [1873 – 1898]
- Virginia Hughes Jones [1881 – 1932]. Virginia is the daughter of A. K. and Mary *Calhoun* Jones.
- David Cloyd Houston [1877 – 1923]
- Mary Lou *Jones* Houston [1877 – 1970]. Mary Lou is the daughter of A. K. and Mary *Calhoun* Jones. She married David Cloyd Houston in 1912.

[F-33. Goepel, Manns]

- William John Manns [October 27, 1865 – August 2, 1936], a Shriner.
- Minnie *Goepel* Manns [May 7, 1876 – May 26, 1929], member Order of the Eastern Star. Minnie is the daughter of Herman and Sallie *Polle* Goepel, buried in plot A-50. She married William John Manns in 1897.
- Mary Eloise [Sep. 19, 1902 – Sep. 20, 1902]. No last name or further information is provided.

[F-34: Davenport, French, Hansel]

- Charles A. French [Dec. 15, 1855 – Apr. 13, 1922]
- Cyrintha *Davenport* French [Aug. 9, 1860 – July 13, 1928], "Beloved Mother." Cyrintha is the daughter of David S. and Adaline Elizabeth *Perkins* Davenport, buried in Pattona Cemetery. She married Charles A. French in 1881.
- Mollie *French* Hansel [Dec. 7, 1882 – Sept. 3, 1921]. Mollie married Charles E. Hansel in 1908.
- Charles E. Hansel, Jr. [March 17, 1909 – March 30, 1909]. Charles is the son of Charles E. and Mollie *French* Hansel.
- C. A. French, Jr. [Aug. 25, 1893 – Jan. 24, 1895]. C. A. is the son of Charles A. and Cyrintha *Davenport* French.

[F-35: no stones]

Section G

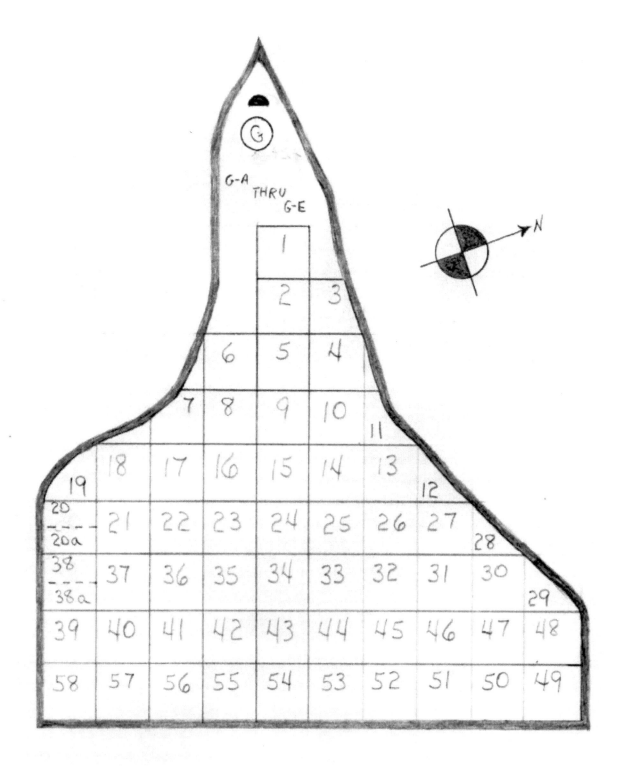

Section G

- [G: Merrifield, Peck]. Most of these names are on stones arranged in a semicircle around a large obelisk bearing duplicates of the same names. The information given below is combined from the individual stones and the obelisk. Dr. Alexander Hamilton Peck is the individual responsible for buying the land and developing the cemetery's sections and lots. The obelisk and surrounding gravestones are located very near to what was the geographic center of Wintergreen Cemetery, before additional land was bought to the east of this location.
    - Gilman M. Peck [Feb. 1, 1805 – Feb. 7, 1878], "born in Boston Mass…died in Richland Parish La."
    - Alexander Hamilton Peck, M. D. [Feb. 18, 1808 – Mar. 28, 1880], "husband of Julia Anne Peck."
    - Julia Anne *(Merrifield)* Peck [Jan. 18, 1817 – Jan. 16, 1848], "consort of A. H. Peck M. D." Julia's biographical epitaph reads: "She was a native of Vermont, of a most amiable disposition; as a wife faultless; as a mother, devoted to her children; as a Christian, of a meek and quiet spirit." Julia married Alexander H. Peck in 1836.
    - Jane Stamps Peck [Dec. 7, 1840 – Oct. 16, 1841], "dau. of A. H. & J. A. Peck."
    - Marietta (Infant Sister #1) Peck [Oct. 19, 1836 – Oct. 21, 1836], "dau. of A. H. & J. A. Peck."
    - Infant Sister #2 [unreadable date], "infant daughter of A. H. & J. A. Peck." Jane Stamps Peck and her two infant sisters share a common stone.
    - John Preston Peck [Aug. 31, 1838 – Oct. 17, 1853], "eldest son of Dr. A. H. & Julia A. Peck…died of yellow fever."
    - Clarendon Peck [April 22, 1843 – May 6, 1844], "son of Dr. Alex. H. & Julia A. Peck."
    - Sarah F. Merrifield [died Dec'r 7, 1843, aged 16 years & 9 days], "fourth daughter of Preston & Clara Merrifield of Windsor Vermont."

[G-A: Allen, Lum]
    - James Upton Allen [April 27, 1909 – September 14, 2008]. James is the son of L. Briscoe and Ethel *Marks* Allen, buried in plot D-7.
    - Julia *Lum* Allen [January 11, 1909 – October 6, 2010]. Julia is the daughter of Robert C. and Julia *Fox* Lum, buried in plot E-17, her mother with the last name of BITTERMAN. She married James Upton Allen in 1931, and they share a common stone.
    - James Bennett Allen [July 15, 1935 – June 3, 1936]. James is the son of James Upton and Julia *Lum* Allen.

[G-B: Douglas, Marks]

- Samuel Upton Marks [Oct. 8, 1832 – Aug. 25, 1908], C. S. A. stone.
- Sarah Augusta *(Douglas)* Marks [Dec. 23, 1851 – Nov. 8, 1919]. Sarah is the wife of Samuel Upton Marks. They have a daughter, Ethel *Marks* Allen, buried in plot D-7.

[G-C: Acker, Schillig]

- George Winston Acker, M. D. [April 23, 1867 – May 13, 1944]
- Freda *Schillig* Acker [August 30, 1880 – December 4, 1959]. Freda is the daughter of Stephen and Josephine *Jauch* Schillig, buried in plot G-1, Josephine with the last name of CASON. Freda married George Winston Acker in 1899.

[G-D: Remenyi, Von Ende]

- Adrienne *Remenyi* Von Ende [1873 – 1945], "daughter of Edward and Gisella de fie Remenyi."

[G-E: Allen, Carpenter]

- Leigh Briscoe Allen, Jr. [January 11, 1915 – August 8, 1971]. Leigh is the son of L. Briscoe and Ethel *Marks* Allen, buried in plot D-7.
- Margaret *Carpenter* Allen [August 23, 1917 – July 26, 2006]. Margaret is the daughter of Ira W. and Martha *Terry* Carpenter, buried in plot E-22. She married Leigh Briscoe Allen, Jr. in 1937.

[G-1: Cason, Jauch, Schillig] This plot has a memorial obelisk bearing the name SCHILLIG.

- Stephen Schillig [Dec. 8, 1844 – Dec. 16, 1895], "Altdorf, Switzerland."
- Josephine *Jauch* Schillig Cason [Oct. 25, 1852 – May 26, 1918], "Altdorf, Switzerland." Josephine is the wife of Stephen Schillig. She later married a Mr. Cason. Besides those listed below, they have a daughter, Freda *Schillig* Acker, buried in plot G-C.
- Ottilie Schillig [no dates], "daughter of Josephine and Stephen Schillig." According to *Port Gibson Reveille's* "Looking Back" column, Ottilie died in 1982, at the age of 90.
- Norine Schillig [1883 – 1968], "daughter of Josephine and Stephen Schillig."
- Bertha Schillig [Dec. 31, 1888 – June 24, 1892]. Bertha is the daughter of Stephen and Josephine *Jauch* Schillig.
- Stephen Schillig [June 11, 1893 – June 19, 1941]. Stephen is the son of Stephen and Josephine *Jauch* Schillig. Stephen married Ruth Brashear Shreve in 1921.

[G-2: Davenport, McGill]. This plot has a memorial stone bearing the name McGILL.

- James M. McGill [1820 – 1898]
- Sallie *Davenport* McGill [1830 – 1912]. According to will records, Sallie is the daughter of Joseph and Letitia M. *Jefferies* Devenport, buried in Devenport Cemetery. The family name changed through the years to be spelled as DAVENPORT. Sallie married James M. McGill in 1850.
- James D. McGill [1856 – 1888]
- Olivia L. McGill [1862 – 1945]. Olivia is the daughter of James M. and Sallie *Davenport* McGill.
- Nathaniel D. McGill [1864 – 1910]

[G-3: Davenport, Weatherly]

- Watson Weatherly [no dates]
- Lou *D(avenport)*. Weatherly [no dates]. Lou is the daughter of Dr. J. W. and Sallie A. *Russum* Davenport, buried in plot G-5. She married Scott Watson Weatherly in 1892. Her ancestors originally bore the name DEVENPORT, and the name was changed through the years.

[G-4: Benton, Newson]

- Dr. John Burnett Benton [October 11, 1869 – September 29, 1936]. John is the son of W. H. Benton, buried in plot A-24.
- Kate *Newson* Benton [August 4, 1874 – May 28, 1918]. Kate married Dr. John Burnett Benton in 1895.
- Thomas H. Benton [August 28, 1896 – September 24, 1930]
- J. B. Benton [May 5, 1901 – November 11, 1948]
- Irma Eubanks Benton [September 20, 1907 – July 30, 1974]

- Claude W. Benton [August 19, 1921 – February 20, 1932]
- John Burnett Benton III [May 16, 1935 – Feb. 22, 2001], "PO 3ʳᴰ CLASS, US NAVY…Loving husband, father & brother." This is a military stone.

[G-5: Davenport, Russum]

- Dr. J. W. Davenport [July 28 (no other dates were inscribed)], C. S. A. stone. According to will records, Joseph W. is the son of Joseph and Letitia M. *Jefferies* Devenport, buried in Devenport Cemetery. The family name changed through the years to be spelled as DAVENPORT.
- Sallie A. *(Russum)* Davenport [Feb. 16, 1847 – Nov. 3, 1898], "wife of Dr. J. W. Davenport." Sallie is the daughter of W. P. and M. D. *Watson* Russum, buried in Holly Hill Cemetery. She married Dr. Joseph W. Davenport in 1864. Besides Malcolm, listed below, other children include Lou *Davenport* Weatherly, buried in plot G-3, and Ruth *Davenport* Hayden, buried in plot G-27.
- Alexander Roberts Davenport [Feb. 23, 1874 – Sept. 22, 1913]
- Malcolm G. Davenport [Mar. 10, 1888 – Aug. 17, 1903], "son of Dr. J. W. & S. A. Davenport."

[G-6: Currie, Simmers]

- Mary Irene *Simmers* Currie [Dec. 5, 1827 – Mar. 18, 1882], "wife of Michael Morgan (Currie)."
- Stephen Morgan Currie [Aug. 22, 1869 – Aug. 8, 1879]
- Lee Robert Currie [Nov. 4, 1872 – Oct. 15, 1879]
- Mary Irene Currie [Feb. 22, 1875 – Apr. 29, 1881]
- Eugene Henry Currie [July 19, 1877 – Dec. 1, 1895]
- Maude Roberta Currie [Dec. 25, 1879 – Feb. 9, 1880]
- Tilford Kelley Currie [Mar. 26, 1881 – Oct. 20, 1954]

[G-7: no stones]

[G-8: Beard, Causey, Ogden, Van]

- W. S. Beard [Jan. 29, 1857 – Sept. 8, 1936], "Father."
- Laura Annie *(Van)* Beard [Aug. 29, 1865 – May 17, 1926], "Mother…wife of W. S. Beard."
- Martha *Beard* Ogden [June 29, 1887 – September 17, 1965], "born Port Gibson, Miss…died Biloxi, Miss…wife of James David Hill Ogden." Martha married James David Hill Ogden in 1906. *Port Gibson Reveille's* "Looking Back" column also tells of the announcement of Mrs. Mattye B. Ogden to Mr. James D. Hill Ogden on September 10, 1922.
- Marie *Beard* Causey [Nov. 29, 1893 – Apr. 27, 1969], "wife of John E. Causey." Marie is the daughter of W. S. and Laura Annie *Van* Beard.
- Dora Beard [Aug. 18, 1896 – Feb. 19, 1899]
- W. S. Beard [Jan. 18, 1903 – May 19, 1903]. Dora and W. S. Beard are children of W. S. and Laura Annie *Van* Beard, and they share a common grave location.

[G-9: Mounger, Popkins]. This plot has a memorial stone bearing the name MOUNGER.

- Henry Chamberlain Mounger [Sept. 20, 1861 – Feb. 9, 1938]. After the death of Jessie Bell *Popkins* Mounger, listed below, Henry married Julia Reynolds in 1905.
- Jessie Bell *Popkins* Mounger [Dec. 1, 1868 – May 17, 1902], "wife of H. C. Mounger."
- Edwin Henry Mounger [September 10, 1890 – January 6, 1947]
- Minerva Mounger [October 20, 1891 – July 18, 1851]
- Frank R. Mounger [January 20, 1895 – September 21, 1958]
- Harvey Mounger [Sept. 19, 1898 – June 25, 1899]
- Fred Hull Mounger [Sept. 9, 1900 – May 9, 1925]. Fred is the son of Henry Chamberlain and Jessie Bell *Popkins* Mounger.
- Infant Son [died May 7, 1902]
- James Arther Mounger [May 18, 1906 – Mar. 12, 1908]. James is the son of Henry Chamberlain and

Julia *Reynolds* Mounger.

[G-10: Ellis, Nosser, Thomas]
- George Thomas [Sept. 3, 1896 – Apr. 24, 1968]. It is possible that George's real last name is NOSSER.
- Nazera *Ellis* Thomas [April 23, 1890 – November 9, 1948]. Nazera married George Thomas Nosser in 1916.
- Paul Baloos Thomas [Oct. 27, 1916 – Jan. 20, 1982]. Paul is the son of George and Nazera *Ellis* Thomas.
- Cornelia Thomas [December 13, 1918 – February 9, 1920]
- Mary Thomas [November 25, 1919 – December 20, 1919]
- Lula Mary Thomas [November 23, 1923 – January 1, 1947]

[G-11: Griffing, Hawkins, Rollins, Smith]
- Richard Lashley Hawkins [Sept. 14, 1837 – Aug. 9, 1928], "born Southampton, England."
- Laura A. *(Smith)* Hawkins [Dec. 31, 1843 – Oct. 21, 1923], "Mother." Laura married Richard Lashley Hawkins in 1870.
- Charles Hawkins [1875 – 1948]
- Mary Lovdie *Griffing* Hawkins [Jan. 5, 1879 – Mar. 9, 1967], "wife of Charles Hawkins." Mary married Charles Hawkins in 1896. Besides those listed below, they have a son, Harry L. Hawkins, Sr., buried in plot H-84.
- Frank Lee Hawkins [Aug. 16, 1899 – July 31, 1968]. Frank is the son of Charles and Mary Lovdie *Griffing* Hawkins.
- Jessie *H(awkins)*. Rollins [Aug. 29, 1903 – Feb. 29, 1992]. Jessie is the daughter of Charles and Mary Lovdie *Griffing* Hawkins.

[G-12: Ellis]
- James Ellis [1860 – 1933], "Father."
- Nora Ellis [1865 – 1938], "Mother." Nora is the wife of James Ellis, and they share a common grave location.

[G-13/14: Cade, Patterson, Wheeless]
- Samuel Brisco Patterson [May 25, 1849 – Jan. 2, 1917], member Woodmen of the World.
- Martha C. *(Wheeless)* Patterson [Jan. 7, 1849 – Aug. 12, 1931]. Martha is the daughter of G. B. and Elizabeth *Davis* Wheeless, buried in plot F-13. She married Samuel Brisco Patterson in 1871. Besides those listed below, other children include Samuel B. Patterson, buried in plot G-58, Mary *Patterson* Lum in plot H-74, and John Patterson in plot G-37.
- Martha Stella Patterson [Jan. 22, 1887 – Dec. 1, 1948]. Martha is the daughter of Samuel Brisco and Martha C. *Wheeless* Patterson.
- Infant Daughter Patterson [Sept. 24, 1934], "infant daughter of Mr. & Mrs. Guy Patterson." This infant's parents, Guy L. and Lottye *Davis* Patterson, are buried in plot G-58.
- Louisa A. Cade [Oct. 14, 1838 – April 23, 1907], "Mother."
- Robert S. Cade [Sept. 19, 1864 – Sept. 9, 1927], "Father." A biographical epitaph reads: "He was a kind and affectionate husband, a fond father, and a friend to all."
- Lilly M. *(Patterson)* Cade [Sept. 14, 1877 – Feb. 12, 1937], "Mother." Her biographical epitaph reads: "A tender mother and a faithful friend." Lilly is the daughter of Samuel Brisco and Martha C. *Wheeless* Patterson. She married Robert S. Cade in 1907. Besides their daughter listed below, other children are Elvin H. Cade, buried in plot H-96, Mae *Cade* Crum in plot I-12, Robert Solomon Cade, Jr. in plot I-1, and James Samuel Cade in plot J-104.
- Olivia Ellis Cade [Mar. 25, 1916 – Feb. 21, 2003]. Olivia is the daughter of Robert S. and Lilly M. *Patterson* Cade.
- Charles C. Cade [Dec. 10, 1869 – Jan. 20, 1917]

[G-15: Watson]
- Scott Watson [died Dec. 11, 1914]

[G-16: Foster, Gray, Hicks]
- Mattie *Foster* Gray [July 17, 1872 – Aug. 26, 1967]. Mattie and J. W. Foster, listed below, are children of Elijah Coleman and Margaret A. *Wade* Foster, buried in plot G-20. Mattie married C. H. Gray in 1893.
- Charles P. Gray [Sept. 22, 1907 – July 30, 1954]. Charles is the son of C. H. and Mattie *Foster* Gray. He and his mother share a common grave location.
- J. W. Foster [Mar. 14, 1876 – Sept. 8, 1923], "Father."
- Luda O. *(Hicks)* Foster [June 19, 1878 – May 6, 1913], "Mother." Luda married J. Willie Foster in 1896.

[G-17: Wilson]
- Alonzo H. Wilson [Nov. 8, 1834 – Jan. 21, 1912], C. S. A. stone, "A Confederate Soldier." According to Mississippi Confederate Grave Registration records, Alonzo was a Private in Co. I, 15th Regt. Alabama Cavalry. He married Mrs. Mary *Hedrick* Elliott in 1892.

> "Their swords are rust
> Their good steeds dust,
> Their souls are with God we trust."
> —on stone of Alonzo H. Wilson

[G-18/19: Bobo, Greer, Guy, Phillips]

- Charles E. Bobo [March 22, 1845 – Dec. 23, 1927], C. S. A. stone, "Father." According to Mississippi Confederate Grave Registration records, Charles was a Private in Co. A, 24th Miss. Batt. Cavalry (Moorman's).
- Olivia Elizabeth *(Guy)* Bobo [May 11, 1850 – Jan. 11, 1921], "Mother" and "wife of C. E. Bobo." Olivia married Charles E. Bobo in 1875. Besides George, listed below, other children include Nettie *Bobo* Taylor, buried in combined plot E-29/30, and William P. Bobo, buried in plot I-23.
- Marguerite V. *(Bobo)* Greer [Nov. 23, 1883 – Sept. 24, 1944]. Marguerite married Calvin H. Phillips in 1903. Calvin is buried in plot G-32. She later married a Mr. Greer.
- Stanton Phillips [Jan. 1, 1906 – Mar. 1, 1908]
- Joseph G. Bobo [April 15, 1889 – April 4, 1927], "Brother."
- George Hoover Bobo [Feb. 19, 1894 – Feb. 7, 1908]. George is the son of Charles E. and Olivia Elizabeth *Guy* Bobo.

[G-20: Flemings, Foster, Herrmann, Wade]
- Elijah Coleman Foster [Nov. 8, 1845 – July 16, 1919], C. S. A. stone, "Father." According to Mississippi Confederate Grave Registration records, Elijah was a Private in Co. D, 24th Miss. Batt. Cavalry.
- Margaret A. *(Wade)* Foster [Jan. 12, 1846 – Oct. 21, 1929], "Mother." Margaret first married James M. Flemings in 1863. She later married Elijah Coleman Foster in 1867. Besides Bettie, listed below, other children include J. W. Foster and Mattie *Foster* Gray, buried in plot G-16, and Elijah C. Foster in plot H-35.
- Henry H. Herrmann [Dec. 16, 1863 – Feb. 16, 1947], member Woodmen of the World. Henry is the son of Samuel and Rosalee *Summer* Herrmann, buried in Port Gibson Jewish Cemetery.
- Bettie *F(oster)*. Herrmann [Jan. 19, 1869 – Aug. 23, 1951]. Bettie is the daughter of Elijah Coleman and Margaret A. *Wade* Foster. She is the wife of Henry H. Herrmann, and they share a common stone.

[G-20a: Cochran, Gradick]
- Henry C. Cochran [May 23, 1859 – April 24, 1908]
- Hattie *G(radick)*. Cochran [May 25, 1867 – Jan. 8, 1925]. Hattie married Henry C. Cochran in 1888.

They have a daughter, Johnnie *Cochran* Hartley, buried in plot H-57.

[G-21: Headley, Hunt, Massie]

- Abijah Hunt III [March 4, 1852 – April 7, 1923], "son of George Ferguson Hunt and Anna Watson, born at Huntley Plantation, Jefferson County, Mississippi…and died there."
- Marion Elizabeth *Massie* Hunt [March 13, 1870 – October 24, 1927], "wife of Abijah Hunt."
- Frank L. Headley [1892 – 1981]. Frank is the son of Shepard P. and Lenora *Vaughan* Headley, buried in plot H-3.
- Anna *Hunt* Headley [1894 – 1951]. Anna is the daughter of Abijah and Marion Elizabeth *Massie* Hunt. She is the wife of Frank L. Headley, and they share a common stone. Besides Mildred, below, they have sons Chalon S. Headley, buried in plot J-35, and Mott Roland Headley, II in Headley Cemetery.
- Frank Lewis Headley, Jr. [Jan. 29, 1917 – May 31, 1917]
- Mildred Camile Headley [April 6, 1921 – June 28, 1921]. Mildred is the daughter of Frank L. and Anna *Hunt* Headley.

[G-22: Calhoun, Martin, Young]

- William J. Martin [Sep. 11, 1835 – Feb. 14, 1890]. A biographical epitaph reads: "Diligent in business, fervent in spirit, serving the Lord."
- Florence *Calhoun* Martin [Jan. 10, 1845 – March 15, 1920], "wife of Wm. J. Martin." Florence married William J. Martin in 1872, and they share a common obelisk.
- Thomas Y. Calhoun [1866 – 1933], "Father."
- Calista *Y(oung)*. Calhoun [Nov. 29, 1873 – July 26, 1966]. Calista is the daughter of William and Lollie Corinne *Sugg* Young, buried in Pisgah Cemetery. She married Thomas Y. Calhoun in 1900.
- John C. Calhoun [May 14, 1901 – Feb. 8, 1963], "Son." John is the son of Thomas Y. and Calista *Young* Calhoun.
- Lollie C. Calhoun [June 18, 1903 – Apr. 22, 1991]. Lollie is the daughter of Thomas Y. and Calista *Young* Calhoun.
- Thomas Y. Calhoun, Jr. [Jan. 25, 1909 – Aug. 9, 1970]. Thomas is the son of Thomas Y. and Calista *Young* Calhoun.

[G-23: Bagnell, Daniell, Hastings, Powers]

- Samuel Bagnell [July 10, 1847 – Nov. 17, 1917], member Woodmen of the World. Samuel is the son of Samuel and Mary *Hynum* Bagnell, buried in Bagnell Cemetery. Samuel is a Civil War veteran and, according to Mississippi Confederate Grave Registration records, was a Private in Co. F, 24th Batt. Miss. Cavalry (Moorman's).
- Alice E. *(Powers)* Bagnell [1856 – 1946], "Mother." Alice married Samuel Bagnell in 1874.
- Samuel Haring Bagnell [1878 – 1969]. Samuel is the son of Samuel and Alice E. *Powers* Bagnell. He had previously married Mrs. Mary *McAlpine* Johnson in 1903. Mary is buried in plot C-29.
- Mary *Daniell* Bagnell [1886 – 1964], member Daughters of the American Revolution. Mary is the daughter of Smith Coffee Daniell III, buried in Freeland Cemetery, and Nannie *Hughes* Daniell, buried in plot A-20. She married Samuel Haring Bagnell in 1931, and they share a common stone.
- Richard Granbery Hastings [Oct. 21, 1875 – Nov. 15, 1931]. Richard is the son of Robert M. and Harriet Louisa *Wharton* Hastings, buried in plot B-47.
- Mary A. *Bagnell* Hastings [June 27, 1880 – Aug. 8, 1971]. Mary is the daughter of Samuel and Alice E. *Powers* Bagnell. She married Richard Granbery Hastings in 1905. They have a daughter, Mary Alice *Hastings* Abraham, buried in plot E-A.

[G-24: Barnette, Shelby, Wade]

- Battaille Harrison Wade [Sept. 14, 1856 – Aug. 11, 1926]
- Carrie Olivia *(Wade)* Wade [July 21, 1861 – March 25, 1918], "consort of Battaille Harrison Wade…a

true Christian, a devoted mother." Carrie married Battaille Harrison Wade in 1882.

- Robert Dunbar Wade [Aug. 7, 1886 – March 14, 1950], "MISSISSIPPI, PVT, 104 AMMO TN, 29 DIV, WORLD WAR I." This is a military stone.
- Willena *Shelby* Wade [November 8, 1890 – May 25, 1972]. Willena is the daughter of William L. and Mollie C. *Stone* Shelby, buried in Shelby Cemetery. She married Robert Dunbar Wade in 1918, and they share a common grave location.
- Robert D. Wade, Jr. [September 25, 1924 – July 20, 2007], "AL1, US NAVY, WORLD WAR II." This is a military stone. Robert also has a civilian stone giving years of military service. He is the son of Robert Dunbar and Willena *Shelby* Wade.
- Charlene *Barnette* Wade [February 14, 1929 – January 2, 1990]. Charlene married Robert D. Wade, Jr. in 1947, and they share a common grave location.

[G-25: Magruder, Wade]

- Thomas Magruder Wade [October 24, 1860 – January 22, 1929]
- Anna Thomas *Magruder* Wade [Feb. 24, 1862 – June 14, 1918], "wife of Thomas Magruder Wade." Anna married Thomas Magruder Wade in 1883.
- Thomas Magruder Wade, Jr. [June 16, 1889 – Sept. 16, 1971]
- Gwendolyn Webb Wade [May 14, 1910 – Aug. 26, 1972]

[G-26: Godwin, Lum, Regan]

- Joseph A. Regan [1849 – 1927]. Joseph is the son of Joseph A. and Frances A. *Lester* Regan, buried in Regan Cemetery.
- Mary E. *(Lum)* Regan [1855 – 1948]. Mary is the daughter of Edwin O. and Nancy *Barrett* Lum. Edwin is buried in Rocky Springs Cemetery. She married Joseph A. Regan in 1872, and they share a common stone.
- Leila *Regan* Godwin [April 27, 1876 – Nov. 17, 1958]. Leila is the daughter of Joseph A. and Mary E. *Lum* Regan. She married Charles E. Godwin in 1905.
- Eugene O. Regan [April 26, 1883 – May 25, 1946]. Eugene is the son of Joseph A. and Mary E. *Lum* Regan.
- George Barrett Regan [June 20, 1885 – Nov. 30, 1918], member Woodmen of the World.
- Ernest M. Regan [April 24, 1890 – August 2, 1953]. Ernest is the son of Joseph A. and Mary E. *Lum* Regan.
- Marvin Morse Regan [Aug. 31, 1892 – Nov. 2, 1952]. Marvin is the son of Joseph A. and Mary E. *Lum* Regan. He married Mary Edna Hill in 1922. Mary is buried in plot K-32.

[G-27: Davenport, Hayden]

- William Wallace Hayden [Aug. 7, 1861 – Jan. 7, 1929]
- Ruth *Davenport* Hayden [Jan. 8, 1866 – Dec. 31, 1952]. Ruth is the daughter of Dr. J. W. and Sallie A. *Russum* Davenport, buried in plot G-5. She married William Wallace Hayden in 1891. Her ancestors bore the name DEVENPORT, and the name was changed through the years.

[G-28: Gerache, Pennisi]

- Leon Pennisi [Oct. 9, 1879 – Oct. 31, 1943]
- Frances *(Gerache)* Pennisi [Nov. 1, 1885 – Feb. 20, 1945]. Frances married Leon Pennisi in 1918, and they share a common grave location.

[G-29: no stones]

[G-30: Barfield, Hynum, Ingram, Mitchell, Reinhardt]

- P. W. Hynum [Nov. 2, 1854 – Aug. 26, 1928]. P. W. married Francis Elizabeth Goza in 1884. Francis is buried in Sarepta Cemetery. Besides Murry, listed below, other children are Mamie *Hynum* Jordan, buried in plot H-78, John Mason Hynum in plot H-54, and Lura B. Hynum in Hynum Cemetery.

- Murry A. Hynum [Oct. 28, 1888 – Oct. 31, 1943], "Daddy." Murry is the son of P. W. and Francis Elizabeth *Goza* Hynum.
- Pauline *(Mitchell)* Hynum [Mar. 1, 1893 – June 16, 1967], "Mamma." Pauline married Murry A. Hynum in 1909. Besides those listed below, they have a son, James Thomas Hynum, buried in plot J-45.
- Norman Paul Hynum [Oct. 28, 1915 – Sept. 28, 1977], "CPL, US ARMY, WORLD WAR II." This is a bronze military plaque. Norman also has a civilian stone. Norman is the son of Murry A and Pauline *Mitchell* Hynum.
- Margaret *R(einhardt)*. Hynum [August 23, 1923 – December 12, 2003]. Margaret married Norman Paul Hynum in 1954, and according to records, again in 1968. She had previously been married to a Mr. Barfield.
- Lavonne *Hynum* Ingram [June 10, 1931 – April 12, 1972]. Lavonne is the daughter of Murry A. and Pauline *Mitchell* Hynum.

[G-31: Daniell, Eaton, Humphreys, Magruder, Neil]

- Robert Walter Magruder [May 14, 1850 – Feb. 6, 1926], "Father." Robert first married Carrie Sims in 1880. Carrie is buried in plot B-49.
- Annie Greenwood *Neil* Magruder [Feb. 15, 1862 – June 20, 1935], "Mother" and "wife of Robert Walter Magruder."
- John Martin Magruder [November 18, 1880 – June 5, 1951]. John is the son of Robert Walter and Carrie *Sims* Magruder.
- Katherine *Daniell* Magruder [October 7, 1882 – October 8, 1949]. Katherine is the daughter of Thomas Freeland and Catharine M. *Crane* Daniell. Thomas is buried in plot A-20. Katherine married John Martin Magruder in 1905. Their children are Katherine *Magruder* Whitfield, buried in plot M-71, Samuel B. Magruder in plot K-19b, and Agnes *Magruder* Coleman in plot E-10.
- Edgar D. Eaton [November 3, 1889 – June 13, 1958]
- Fannie *Magruder* Eaton [September 14, 1899 – February 13, 1992]. Fannie is the daughter of Robert Walter and Annie Greenwood *Neil* Magruder. She first married Charles D. Humphreys in 1919. Charles is buried in plot B-39. She later married Edgar D. Eaton.

[G-32: Phillips]

- Calvin H. Phillips [Dec. 27, 1881 – Nov. 28, 1926], member Woodmen of the World. Calvin married Marguerite V. Bobo in 1903. Marguerite is buried in combined plot G-18/19, with the name GREER.

[G-33: Blair, Farmer, Kelly, Martin, Smith, Trim]

- Nancy *Farmer* Smith Blair [1835 – 1922]. Nancy married a Mr. Smith before marrying J. B. Blair in 1886.
- W. T. Kelly [Apr. 4, 1866 – Oct. 18, 1919], member Woodmen of the World.
- Martha Anne *(Smith)* Kelly [August 22, 1869 – April 25, 1955], "Mother." Martha is the daughter of Nancy *Farmer* Smith, and wife of W. T. Kelly.
- W. Bradley Trim [Jan. 16, 1893 – Apr. 12, 1966]
- Mary *K(elly)*. Trim [June 1, 1890 – July 13, 1972]. Mary is the daughter of W. T. and Martha Anne *Smith* Kelly. She married W. Bradley Trim in 1916, and they share a common stone. Besides their son listed below, they have a son, Nick B. Trim, buried in combined plot I-75/80.
- J. N. Martin [Dec. 14, 1891 – Apr. 19, 1983]
- Maggie A. *(Kelly)* Martin [June 22, 1892 – Jan. 24, 1992]. Maggie is the daughter of W. T. and Martha Anne *Smith* Kelly. She married J. N. Martin in 1914, and they share a common stone.
- Bradley T. Trim [Oct. 17, 1918 – Nov. 21, 1958], "MISSISSIPPI, CPL, US ARMY, WORLD WAR II." This is a military stone. Bradley is the son of W. Bradley and Mary *Kelly* Trim.

[G-34: Chapman, Hall, King, Lunn, Watkins]. This plot has a memorial stone bearing the name WATKINS.

- Thomas H. Hall [Oct. 2, 1848 – May 16, 1928]. Thomas married Rhoda E. Tickell in 1895.
- John C. Watkins [Nov. 7, 1847 – Oct. 30, 1919], C. S. A. stone. According to Mississippi Confederate Grave Registration records, he was a Private in Co. G, 10th Regt. Cavalry, Frank Powers Regt. Cavalry. John had previously married Jennie M. Jones in 1871. Jennie is buried in combined plot C-66/67/80.
- Mary E. *(Hall)* Watkins [Apr. 9, 1853 – Jan. 6, 1933]. Mary married John C. Watkins in 1879.
- John Parham Watkins [Oct. 23, 1880 – Oct. 14, 1966]. John is the son of John C. and Mary E. *Hall* Watkins. After the death of his first wife, he married Mrs. Cora *Phillips* Massey in 1943. Cora is buried in combined plot I-28/29.
- Mary Jane *(Chapman)* Watkins [April 20, 1883 – April 4, 1925], "wife of John P. Watkins." Mary married John Parham Watkins in 1911. Besides their daughter listed below, they have a son, Parham M. Watkins, buried in plot K-31.
- Katherine Lucille *(Watkins)* King [Jan. 14, 1913 – June 20, 1995]. Katherine is the daughter of John Parham and Mary Jane *Chapman* Watkins. Her first marriage was to Sylvester Jack Lunn in 1940. She later married Roy E. King in 1963. Roy is buried in plot J-23.

[G-35: Baldwin, Brownlee, Smith, Walne]
- Rev. Hervey H. Brownlee [March 18, 1854 – December 4, 1948]. A biographical epitaph reads: "For 20 years pastor of Presbyterian Church, Port Gibson, Miss."
- Florence *S(mith).* Brownlee [April 4, 1860 – March 21, 1932]. Florence married Rev. Brownlee in 1879, and they share a common stone.
- Helen *Brownlee* Baldwin [March 25, 1880 – August 17, 1973]. Helen is the daughter of Rev. Hervey H. and Florence *Smith* Brownlee.
- Herschel Day Brownlee [June 17, 1884 – November 11, 1953]. Herschel is the son of Rev. Hervey H. and Florence *Smith* Brownlee.
- Flora *Walne* Brownlee [February 9, 1886 – June 9, 1970]. Flora is the daughter of Richard Eugene and Margaret *Tabor* Walne, buried in plot A-84. She is the wife of Herschel Day Brownlee, and they share a common stone.
- Mary Brownlee [died Dec. 25, 1918], "infant child of H. D. and F. W. Brownlee."
- Herschel Brownlee [Feb. 15, 1923], "infant child of H. D. and F. W. Brownlee."

[G-36: Brouillette, Ellis, Mullen]
- Pierre Laurance Brouillette, M. D. [Sept. 3, 1844 – Oct. 27, 1921]
- Ben W. Mullen [June 15, 1923 – September 30, 1993]
- Josephine *E(llis).* Mullen [September 6, 1920 – November 6, 2005]. Josephine is the daughter of George and Thomenie *Oudy* Ellis, buried in combined plot G-42/43. She is the wife of Ben W. Mullen, and they share a common grave location.

[G-37: Byrd, Davis, Hearn, McDonald, Patterson, Wright]
- Joseph G. Davis [Dec. 3, 1833 – Oct. 25, 1908], "1 LIEUT., CO. D, 6 LA. INF. C. S. A." This is a military stone.
- Mattie *McDonald* Davis [1843 – 1921]. Mattie married Joseph G. Davis in 1869. Besides their daughter listed below, other children include Mary Eliza and James Chalmers Davis, buried in plot A-103.
- Iuka Elizabeth Davis [Mar. 2, 1884 – Nov. 30, 1908]
- John Patterson [May 28, 1873 – Jan. 27, 1950]. John is the son of Samuel Brisco and Martha C. *Wheeless* Patterson, buried in combined plot G-13/14.
- Ada *Davis* Patterson [March 13, 1877 – Nov. 17, 1940]. Ada is the daughter of Joseph G. and Mattie *McDonald* Davis. She married John Patterson in 1904. She had previously been married to a Mr. Hearn.
- Stella Mae *(Hearn)* Wright [Nov. 30, 1898 – Nov. 23, 1937]. Stella married J. B. Wright in 1919.
- Ada Mae Wright [Aug. 26, 1920 – Mar. 5, 1927]

- Frances Mattie Byrd [Jan. 27, 1929 – Jan. 29, 1929]

[G-38: Davis, Dow, Dunbar, Hicks, Kelly, Tanner, Thompson, Tillman]

- Margaret J. *(Dunbar)* Hicks [Nov. 5, 1843 – Sept. 22, 1932]. Margaret was married a number of times, first to William Kelly in 1859, then to Robert J. Tillman in 1862, and finally to W. T. Hicks in 1870. W. T. and Margaret have a daughter, Dannie M. *Hicks* Ungerer, buried in plot A-114.
- C. B. Tillman [Nov. 8, 1867 – Jan. 14, 1923]. C. B. first married Lillie Hicks in 1894, and then married Mrs. Katie A. James in 1903.
- Benjamin J. Davis [July 27, 1859 – Oct. 17, 1934]
- Elizabeth *(Dow)* Davis [May 23, 1868 – Jan. 29, 1931], "wife of B. J. Davis."
- William C. Davis [June 20, 1887 – Apr. 21, 1944]. William is the son of Benjamin J. and Elizabeth *Dow* Davis.
- Maude M. *(Thompson)* Davis [May 13, 1886 – Dec. 3, 1958]. Maude first married A. W. Tanner in 1904. They have a son, Albert W. Tanner, buried in combined plot M-44/45. She later married William C. Davis in 1912, and they share a common stone.
- Robert C. Davis [1918 – 1979], "U S ARMY, WORLD WAR II." This is a bronze military plaque. Robert is the son of William C. and Maude M. *Thompson* Davis.
- Eddie Hulin Davis [April 23, 1901 – Sept. 14, 1965], "MISSISSIPPI, PFC, U S ARMY, WORLD WAR II." This is a military stone. Eddie is the son of Benjamin J. and Elizabeth *Dow* Davis.

[G-38a: Bolls, Whatley]

- Annie Laurie *(Bolls)* Whatley [Oct. 5, 1897 – Oct. 5, 1917], "wife of E. F. Whatley." Annie married Emmett Fuston Whatley in 1916.

[G-39/40/41: Brown, Gilkeson, Guthrie, Herlitz]

- S. Bettie Gilkeson [Aug. 5, 1852 – Jan. 28, 1933], "a native of Virginia."
- Emmette F. Guthrie [Oct. 29, 1849 – Dec. 13, 1940]
- Walter Craig Guthrie [September 2, 1852 – December 31, 1928]. A biographical epitaph reads: "Principal of Chamberlain-Hunt Academy 1833-1907. For more than forty years a ruling elder in the Port Gibson Presbyterian Church." Walter was married twice. He married Ruth Shreve, his second wife, in 1899. Ruth is buried in plot F-9.
- Edgar Paxton Guthrie [Feb. 8, 1896 – Jan. 5, 1963], "born in Port Gibson." Edgar is the son of Walter Craig Guthrie and his first wife.
- Margaret Adeline "Gretchen" Guthrie [Nov. 7, 1900 – Jan. 1, 1990]. Margaret Adeline and William Shreve, her twin brother, are children of Walter Craig and Ruth *Shreve* Guthrie.
- William Shreve Guthrie [Nov. 7, 1900 – June 25, 1973]
- Kate Humphreys *Herlitz* Guthrie [Dec. 27, 1900 – Mar. 17, 1980]. Kate is the daughter of William Anders and Sarah *Butler* Herlitz, buried in plot F-6. She married William Shreve Guthrie in 1923, and they share a common grave location.
- Sarah Butler Guthrie [Aug. 13, 1924 – May 1, 1986], member Daughters of the American Revolution. Sarah is the daughter of William Shreve and Kate Humphreys *Herlitz* Guthrie.
- Fred Preston Guthrie [Aug. 12, 1927 – Jan. 24, 2009]. Fred is the son of William Shreve and Kate Humphreys *Herlitz* Guthrie.
- Nancy Carol *Brown* Guthrie [July 13, 1929 – Aug. 16, 1995]. Nancy married Fred Preston Guthrie in 1951, and they share a common grave location.
- Harry Raymond Guthrie [July 6, 1868 – March 9, 1953]
- Carabelle *Gilkeson* Guthrie [Oct. 5, 1869 – Sept. 14, 1958]. Carabelle is the wife of Harry Raymond Guthrie, and they share a common stone.
- John R. Guthrie [Mar. 12, 1856 – Jan. 17, 1937]

- Frank Lyle Guthrie [February 5, 1861 – April 30, 1950]
- Carrie Tipping Guthrie [March 5, 1869 – March 11, 1949]
- Rev. David Vance Guthrie, Jr. [June 20, 1926 – July 4, 1986]
- Margaret Elizabeth *(Tirey)* Guthrie [March 31, 1927 – July 18, 2015]. This information is from a temporary funeral home marker.

[G-42/43: Assaf, Ellis, Mike, Moses, Oudy, Thomas]
- Commour *(Moses)* Ellis [Oct. 27, 1856 – Oct. 9, 1926], "Mother" and "a native of Syria."
- George Ellis [Mar. 1, 1877 – Mar. 23, 1953]. George is the son of Commour *Moses* Ellis.
- Thomenie *O(udy)*. Ellis [Aug. 5, 1886 – Oct. 16, 1975]. Thomenie is the wife of George Ellis. Besides those listed below, other children are Josephine *Ellis* Mullen, buried in plot G-36, Eli George Ellis in plot A-132, and Joseph and Camille Sarah *Ellis* Burlton in plot E-37a.
- John Ellis [Nov. 9, 1914 – Mar. 14, 1967]. John is the son of George and Thomenie *Oudy* Ellis.
- Ella May Ellis [May 3, 1917 – Mar. 26, 1975]. Ella is the daughter of George and Thomenie *Oudy* Ellis.
- Michael Ellis [Apr. 5, 1880 – Dec.18, 1968]. Michael is the son of Commour *Moses* Ellis.
- Mary *Mike* Ellis [Dec. 13, 1895 – July 5, 1962]. Mary is the wife of Michael Ellis. Besides those listed below, they have a son, Nicholas Michael Ellis, buried in combined plot I-54/55.
- Lucille Helen Ellis [Sept. 10, 1912 – Oct. 20, 1979]. Lucille is the daughter of Michael and Mary *Mike* Ellis.
- Edward George "Mike" Ellis [Dec. 1, 1918 – June 6, 1973], "MISSISSIPPI, S SGT, US ARMY, WORLD WAR II, BSM & OLC." This is a military stone. He also has a civilian stone. Edward is the son of Michael and Mary *Mike* Ellis. He married Jessie Mae McCaa in 1948. Jessie is buried in Headley Cemetery.
- James Ellis [Apr. 15, 1882 – Feb. 21, 1953]. James is the son of Commour *Moses* Ellis.
- Lula *Thomas* Ellis [Dec. 4, 1895 – July 20, 1982]. Lula married James Ellis in 1911, and they share a common grave location. Their children include Norman Nicholas Ellis and Rosalie *Ellis* Abraham, buried in plot H-18, Woodrow Wilson Ellis in plot K-44, and Mildred *Ellis* Nasif in plot M 81.
- John Ellis [Oct. 27, 1884 – June 23, 1908], "a native of Syria."
- Sam Saba Ellis [Dec. 18, 1886 – April 18, 1962], a Mason, "LOUISIANA, F3, USNRF, WORLD WAR I." This is a military stone. Sam also has a civilian stone with a slightly different birth date. He is the son of Commour *Moses* Ellis.
- Jameelie *A(ssaf)*. Ellis [Nov. 2, 1901 – Nov. 21, 1989]. Jameelie is the wife of Sam Saba Ellis, and they share a common grave location.
- Georgette Ellis [no dates]. Georgette is the daughter of Sam and Jameelie *Assaf* Ellis.

[G-44: Griffing, Hubbard, Yarborough]
- Nettye Griffing Hubbard [March 31, 1882 – August 1, 1931], "Sister."
- Vernie *G(riffing)*. Yarborough [1892 – 1976]

[G-45: Bridgers, Irwin, Jones, Price]
- Martha Irwin [Feb. 15, 1850 – July 9, 1943]
- D. I. Bridgers [Apr. 25, 1855 – Nov. 8, 1936]. D. I. is the son of Samuel James and Mary Ophelia *Barnes* Bridgers, buried in Bridgers Cemetery.
- Mary Ophelia *(Bridgers)* Bridgers [Aug. 18, 1864 – Dec. 19, 1959]. Mary is the daughter of Sampson and Nellie English Bridgers, buried in plot B-6. She married D. I. Bridgers in 1890. Besides their daughter listed below, other children are Nellie *Bridgers* Johnson, buried in plot B-6, and David Irwin Bridgers, buried in Bridgers Cemetery.
- John Jenison Jones [July 6, 1869 – July 4, 1925], a Mason.
- Orah *Bridgers* Jones [April 8, 1891 – July 12, 1947]. Orah is the daughter of D. I. and Mary Opehelia

Bridgers Bridgers. She married John Jenison Jones in 1914.

- Paul Bridgers Jones [July 15, 1915 – July 24, 1995]. Paul is the son of John Jenison and Orah *Bridgers* Jones.
- Faraba Elizabeth *Price* Jones [December 2, 1918 – December 15, 1991], member Daughters of the American Revolution. Faraba is the daughter of Stanley *Snodgrass* Price, buried in Snodgrass Cemetery. She and Paul Bridgers Jones share a common stone with words: "Married July 5, 1937."
- Nellie Travilla Bridgers [Jan. 1, 1875 – Nov. 16, 1958]

[G-46: Ikerd, Maranto, Shannon, Slayton, Watson]

- Rowan C. Slayton [Sept. 3, 1866 – May 1, 1939]. Rowan's memorial epitaph reads: "A loving husband, faithful father, and a good citizen." He is the son of Lucinda Slayton, buried in Old Colony Cemetery.
- Mary A. *(Ikerd)* Slayton [1870 – 1952], "Mother." Mary is the wife of Rowan C. Slayton. Besides the daughters listed below, other children include Luther C. Slayton, Sr., buried in combined plot M-64/65, and Lizzie *Slayton* Housley in plot A-138.
- Myrtis *Slayton* Maranto [1902 – 1972], "Your Loving Daughter." Myrtis is the daughter of Rowan C. and Mary A. *Ikerd* Slayton. She was married twice, first to Henry D. Watson in 1920, and later to Mr. Maranto.
- Eli McCullic Shannon [Oct. 15, 1886 – Sept. 18, 1948], "MISSISSIPPI, F3C, USNRF, WORLD WAR I." This is a military stone.
- Minnie Lee *Slayton* Shannon [Oct. 16, 1904 – Apr. 12, 1929], "wife of E. M. Shannon." Minnie is the daughter of Rowan C. and Mary A. *Ikerd* Slayton. She married Eli McCullic Shannon in 1924.

[G-47: Arnette, Little, Norwood, Smith]

- William Russell Smith [Feb. 4, 1852 – Dec. 12, 1934]
- Allah *Norwood* Smith [May 25, 1858 – Jan. 11, 1926]. Allah married William Russell Smith in 1874.
- Charles Clarence Little [Mar. 30, 1870 – Dec. 27, 1933]
- Laura *Smith* Little [Sept. 21, 1875 – Jan. 3, 1936]. Laura married Charles Clarence Smith in 1896.
- John Deason Arnette [Jan. 20, 1874 – Oct. 28, 1952]
- Clara *Smith* Arnette [Mar. 28, 1877 – Oct. 2, 1949]. Clara is the daughter of William Russell and Allah *Norwood* Smith. She married John Deason Arnette in 1900.
- Willie Mason Arnette [Mar. 31, 1904 – July 2, 1935]

[G-48: Hartley, Tanksley]

- Hiram H. Hartley [1875 – 1956]
- Della *T(anksley)*. Hartley [1880 – 1929]. Della is the wife of Hiram H. Hartley. Their children Colon Leon Hartley and Katie *Hartley* Preskitt, are buried in combined plot M-70/75.
- Nancy E. Hartley [1878 – 1956]. Nancy is the sister of Hiram H. Hartley.
- Mary Selena Hartley [1918 – 1921]

[G-49: Andrews, Brown, Clark]

- Marshall E. Brown [May 22, 1850 – Mar. 31, 1899], "Father."
- Ida *Clark* Brown [Mar. 17, 1856 – May 29, 1933], "Mother." Ida is the wife of Marshall E. Brown, and they share a common stone. Besides those listed below, other children are Jesse Simms Brown, buried in plot E-6, and Mamie *Brown* Clark in plot A-93.
- Louie Clark Brown [Apr. 10, 1879 – Dec. 21, 1936], a Mason. Louie is the son of Marshall E. and Ida *Clark* Brown.
- Ella Brown [Aug. 25, 1880 – Oct. 3, 1970]. Ella is the daughter of Marshall E. and Ida *Clark* Brown.
- Lilly *B(rown)*. Andrews [Sept. 21, 1881 – Aug. 15, 1974], "wife of George Dean Andrews." Lilly is the daughter of Marshall E. and Ida *Clark* Brown.
- Robert Cotton Brown [Feb. 22, 1884 – Apr. 15, 1934], a Mason. Robert is the son of Marshall E. and

Ida *Clark* Brown.

- M. V. Brown [Dec. 22, 1886 – Sept. 9, 1926], a Mason. M. V. is the son of Marshall E. and Ida *Clark* Brown.

[G-50: Coulter, Evans. Parker, Smith]

- Benjamin Franklin Parker [February 15, 1854 – April 14, 1925]
- Martha Ann Parker [Feb. 7, 1857 – Jan. 2, 1936]. Martha is the second wife of Benjamin Franklin Parker.
- Charles E. Coulter [Feb. 14, 1876 – June 24, 1945], "Father." After the death of Lena, below, he married Mrs. Marie *Lord* Campbell in 1941. Marie is buried in plot M-115a.
- Lena *(Parker)* Smith Coulter [Mar. 3, 1881 – Sept. 10, 1938], "Mother." Lena is the daughter of Benjamin Franklin Parker, by his first wife. She first married W. T. Smith in 1903. She later married Charles E. Coulter in 1920.
- Nonnie Mai Smith [Apr. 7, 1905 – Dec. 22, 1975]
- Ann Marie Evans [Oct. 18, 1907 – Oct. 10, 1962]

[G-51: Hamilton, Headley, Humphreys, Johnson, Wade]

- Baylis Earl Humphreys [Nov. 23, 1851 – Nov. 29, 1927]. Baylis is the son of George Wilson and Catharine Baylissa *Prince* Humphreys, buried in plot B-39.
- Elizabeth *Hamilton* Humphreys [Oct. 23, 1859 – Dec. 23, 1933], "wife of B. E. Humphreys." Elizabeth is the daughter of Charles D. and Elizabeth *Belknap* Hamilton, buried in plot F-19, Elizabeth with last name of THRASHER. She married Baylis Earl Humphreys in 1881. Besides their daughters listed below, they have a daughter, Mary Cobun *Humphreys* Moore, buried in plot E-16, and a son, George Wilson Humphreys in plot B-39.
- Gustavus Claude Johnson [Aug. 31, 1875 – July 11, 1930]
- Elizabeth *Humphreys* Wade [Oct. 21, 1881 – Mar. 29, 1958]. Elizabeth is the daughter of Baylis Earl and Elizabeth *Hamilton* Humphreys. She married Gustavus Claude Johnson, her first husband, in 1908. She later married a Mr. Wade.
- Infant Son Johnson [born dead Jan. 13, 1913], "infant son of G. C. & E. H. Johnson."
- Infant Son Johnson [born Mar. 26, 1914], "infant son of G. C. & B. (sic) H. Johnson."
- Arthur Mitchell Johnson [Apr. 20, 1914 – Jan. 29, 1939]
- Mott Roland Headley [Mar. 11, 1890 – Mar. 20, 1956]. Mott is the son of Shepard P. and Lenora *Vaughan* Headley, buried in plot H-3.
- Bobbie *Humphreys* Headley [Dec. 7, 1888 – Aug. 30, 1956]. Bobbie is the daughter of Baylis Earl and Elizabeth *Hamilton* Humphreys. She married Mott Roland Headley in 1914, and they share a common stone.

[G-52: Hale, Jefferies, Kirkland, Parker]

- William Terry Jefferies [May 13, 1876 – Feb. 6, 1942]. William, Nathaniel and James are sons of E. S. and Kate *Ellett* Jefferies, buried in plot B-25.
- Frances *Hale* Jefferies [Dec. 13, 1868 – Feb. 6, 1942]. Frances married William Terry Jefferies in 1904.
- Nathaniel "Uncle Nat" Jefferies [Oct. 22, 1880 – Dec. 6, 1951]
- James Earl Jefferies [June 13, 1887 – Dec. 3, 1948]
- Anna *Kirkland* Jefferies [Feb. 8, 1898 – Jan. 18, 1981]. Anna married James Earl Jefferies in 1922, and they share a common grave location. She had previously married a Mr. Parker.

[G-53: Briscoe, Montgomery, Person, Watson]. This plot has a memorial obelisk bearing the name WATSON.

- Maria Flower *Watson* Briscoe [Oct. 31, 1851 – Dec. 1, 1936], "wife of Edward P. Briscoe." Maria Flower, James Waterman and William Young Watson are children of James W. and Miriam *Buck* Watson, buried in plot B-52. Maria married Edward P. Briscoe in 1883. Edward is buried in plot D-8.
- Myles Person [June 15, 1887 – April 21, 1952]. Myles is the son of James Wells and Isabella *Myles* Person,

buried in plot B-27.

- Marion *Briscoe* Person [June 28, 1885 – May 29, 1960]. Marion is the daughter of Edward P. and Maria Flower *Watson* Briscoe. She married Myles Person in 1914.
- Maria Flower Person [Nov. 30, 1917 – July 26, 1972]. Maria is the daughter of Myles and Marion *Briscoe* Person.
- James Waterman Watson [Oct. 3, 1854 – May 11, 1920], "Major, U. S. Army, Retired." This is not a military stone.
- William Young Watson [Oct. 17, 1864 – Sept. 24, 1918], "died at Banes, Cuba." William appears to be a second son by this name, having been born after the death of the first one. The other William is buried with their parents.
- A. T. Montgomery [no dates]. This stone has only the inscription: "True Friendship Does Not Die."

[G-54/55: Ferguson, Kelley, Maldeis, Naasson]. This plot has a memorial obelisk bearing the names NAASSON on one side and KELLEY on the other.

- George William Naasson [Oct. 2, 1829 – Dec. 6, 1886], "Father."
- Margaret Rebecca *(Kelley)* Naasson [Oct. 8, 1845 – Jan. 31, 1924], "Mother." Margaret married George William Naasson in 1866.
- Mary H. Naasson [Oct. 13, 1867 – May 27, 1940]. Mary is the daughter of George William and Margaret Rebecca *Kelley* Naasson.
- George William Naasson [July 28, 1871 – Feb. 17, 1924]. George is the son of George William and Margaret Rebecca *Kelley* Naasson.
- Anna E. Naasson [Nov. 10, 1875 – June 21, 1925]. Anna is the daughter of George William and Margaret Rebecca *Kelley* Naasson.
- Fannie *Naasson* Maldeis [Feb. 9, 1878 – Nov. 6, 1942]. Fannie is the daughter of George William and Margaret Rebecca *Kelley* Naasson. She married Frederick W. Maldeis in 1918.
- Isabella James *(Kelley)* Ferguson [Oct. 27, 1853 – Apr. 19, 1930]. Isabella is the sister of Margaret Rebecca *Kelly* Naasson. She married J. H. Ferguson in 1891.

[G-56: Adair, Anderson, Girault, Rollins]

- John Anderson [Nov. 15, 1841 – Oct. 27, 1931]
- Anna *Girault* Anderson [Sept. 4, 1871 – Jan. 31, 1945]. Anna was married twice, first to Thomas R. Adair in 1891. Thomas is buried in Rocky Springs Cemetery. After his death she married John Anderson in 1896, and they share a common stone.
- Lewis G. Rollins [Dec. 23, 1893 – June 9, 1923]. Lewis is the son of John W. and Martha E. *McClure* Rollins, buried in plot H-48. He married Eula Mae Adair in 1915.

[G-57: Magruder, Neal, Scarborough]

- Isaac Dunbar Magruder [Apr. 15, 1846 – Dec. 5, 1932]. Isaac is a Civil War veteran and, according to Mississippi Confederate Grave Registration records, was a Private in Co. C, 4th Miss. Cavalry, and died of old age.
- Martha L. *Neal* Magruder [Nov. 28, 1848 – May 16, 1924], "A devoted wife and mother" and "wife of I. D. Magruder." Martha is the daughter of Joseph R. and Rebecca J. *Harmon* Neal, buried in plot B-49, Rebecca with the last name of SIMS. She married Isaac Dunbar Magruder in 1868. Besides those listed below, other children are Sarah O. Magruder and Carrie *Magruder* Dawson, also buried in plot B-49.
- Ida Magruder [July 4, 1871 – January 15, 1952]. Ida is the daughter of Isaac Dunbar and Martha L. *Neal* Magruder.
- William Sims Magruder [June 17, 1872 – Jan. 29, 1951]. William is the son of Isaac Dunbar and Martha L. *Neal* Magruder.
- Walter Scarborough [Mar. 25, 1875 – July 22, 1955], "Father."

- Rebecca *M(agruder)*. Scarborough [Sept. 17, 1877 – July 20, 1974], "Mother." Rebecca is the daughter of Isaac Dunbar and Martha L. *Neal* Magruder and wife of Walter Scarborough.
- Joseph Moore Magruder [1882 – 1924], a Mason. Joseph is the son of Isaac Dunbar and Martha L. *Neal* Magruder.
- Robert Walter Magruder [Dec. 5, 1886 – Jan. 23, 1946]. Robert is the son of Isaac Dunbar and Martha L. *Neal* Magruder.

[G-58: Davis, Lum, Patterson]. This plot has a memorial stone bearing the name PATTERSON.

- Samuel B. Patterson [October 18, 1879 – February 28, 1954]. Samuel is the son of Samuel Brisco and Martha C. *Wheeless* Patterson, buried in combined plot G-13/14.
- Lucretia *L(um)*. Patterson [January 16, 1879 – June 16, 1958]. Lucretia is the daughter of Erastus William and Emma *Powell* Lum, buried in Lum Cemetery. She married Samuel B. Patterson in 1903.
- Barton B. Patterson, Sr. [January 7, 1904 – March 2, 1979]. Barton is the son of Samuel B. and Lucretia *Lum* Patterson.
- Mattie *D(avis)*. Patterson [August 6, 1905 – June 10, 1982]. Mattie married Barton B. Patterson in 1931.
- Barton B. Patterson, Jr. [1934-2010]. This information is from a temporary funeral home marker. Barton is the son of Barton B. and Mattie *Davis* Patterson.
- Guy L. Patterson [July 30, 1908 – January 22, 1998]. Guy is the son of Samuel B. and Lucretia *Lum* Patterson.
- Lottye *D(avis)*. Patterson [September 27, 1910 – July 6, 1994] Lottye is a sister of Mattie *Davis* Patterson and wife of Guy L. Patterson. They have an infant daughter buried in combined plot G-13/14.

Section H

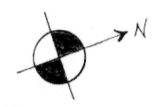

10	9	8	7	6	5	4	3	2	1
11	12	13	14	15	16	17	18	19	20
30	29	28	27	26	25	24	23	22	21
31	32	33	34	35	36	37	38	39	40
50	49	48	47	46	45	44	43	42	41
51	52	53	54	55	56	57	58	59	60
70	69	68	67	66	65	64	63	62	61
71	72	73	74	75	76	77	78	79	80
90	89	88	87	86	85	84	83	82	81
91	92	93	94	95	96	97	98	99	100

Section H

[H-1: Stampley, Watson]
- William Madison Watson [Dec. 27, 1864 – Oct. 21, 1931]
- Elizabeth *Stampley* Watson [July 20, 1872 – Dec. 30, 1951], "Mother." Elizabeth is the daughter of William and Margaret M. Stampley. Margaret is buried in plot B-19, with the last name of LIGHT. Elizabeth is the wife of William Madison Watson.
- Guilford S. Watson [Jan. 17, 1893 – Nov. 18, 1956], "Loving Brother." Guilford is the son of William Madison and Elizabeth *Stampley* Watson.

[H-2: Guice, Miller, Powers, Ragland]
- William Arthur Ragland [Sept. 1, 1856 – July 21, 1936]
- Sarah Elizabeth *(Powers)* Ragland [Feb. 11, 1860 – Aug. 27, 1929]. Sarah had previously married George W. Miller in 1876. Later in 1876 she married William Arthur Ragland, and they share a common stone. Some of their children include Emma *Ragland* Tickell, buried in plot H-45, Mary A. *Ragland* Wood and Julia *Ragland* Curtis, buried in Shiloh Cemetery, and John W. Ragland in Hermanville Cemetery.
- Eugenia *Ragland* Guice [1892 – 1949], "Mother" and "wife of Lewie G. Guice." Eugenia married Lewie G. Guice in 1909.

[H-3: Ammon, Headley, Little, Vaughan]
- Shepard P. Headley [1865 – 1958]
- Lenora *V(aughan)*. Headley [1870 – 1947]. Lenora married Shepard P. Headley in 1888, and they share a common stone. Other children include Mott Roland Headley, buried in plot G-51, Frank L. Headley, twin brother of Fred C. Headley, in plot G-21, Hal S. Headley in plot I-22, and Calista *Headley* Hackett in combined plot H-64/65.
- Fred C. Headley [Sept. 3, 1892 – May 10, 1929]. Fred is the son of Shepard P. and Lenora *Vaughan* Headley.
- Helen *L(ittle)*. Headley [Aug. 11, 1894 – Dec. 4, 1978]. Helen is the wife of Fred C. Headley.
- Fred C. Headley [July 2, 1916 – Feb. 28, 2000]. Fred is the son of Fred C. and Helen *Little* Headley.
- Evelyn *A(mmon)*. Headley [Dec. 24, 1920 – Aug. 27, 1998]. Evelyn married Fred C. Headley in 1943, and they share a common stone.
- Frank S. Headley [Apr. 12, 1918 – June 5, 1995]. Frank is the son of Fred C. and Helen *Little* Headley. He married Bessie Newlin in 1950, and they share a common stone. Bessie's side has only her birth date of August 1, 1924.

[H-4: Moore, Pahnka, Spayd]
- George F. Spayd [July 6, 1915 – Mar. 12, 2007], "MAJ, US ARMY, WORLD WAR II, BRONZE STAR MEDAL." This is a bronze military plaque.
- Bernice *Pahnka* Spayd [Sept. 10, 1920 – Jan. 24, 2013]. Bernice is the daughter of Sims D. and Ida I. *Wroten* Pahnka, buried in Jefferson County. She is the wife of George F. Spayd, and they share a common stone.
- Michael Robert Moore [November 20, 1963 – October 8, 1992]. Michael is the grandson of George F. and Bernice *Pahnka* Spayd.

[H-5: Bobo, Dungan, George, Shannon, Walters, Wroten]
- Eugene W. Wroten [May 2, 1872 – May 18, 1944]
- Misouria E. *(Walters)* Wroten [Nov. 17, 1872 – Jan. 3, 1958]. Misouria married Eugene W. Wroten in 1890, and they share a common stone. Besides those listed below, they have a son, George Warren Wroten, buried in plot A-165.
- Maude S*(hannon)*. Wroten [September 6, 1900 – April 1, 1945]. Maude is the daughter of Ammie E. *Tanksley* Shannon, buried in plot I-19. She is the first wife of George Warren Wroten.
- Ada W*(roten)*. George [January 26, 1890 – September 2, 1979]. Ada is the daughter of Eugene W. and Misouria E. *Walters* Wroten.
- Henry W. Wroten [May 14, 1898 – Dec. 1, 1927]
- James K. Wroten [June 2, 1900 – January 7, 1966]. James is the son of Eugene W. and Misouria E. *Walters* Wroten.
- Jewel *Dungan* Wroten [February 11, 1902 – September 9, 1949], "Mother." Jewel married James K. Wroten in 1921.
- Lola *Wroten* Bobo [Oct. 28, 1901 – Mar. 14, 1987], "Mother." Lola is the daughter of Eugene W. and Misouria E. *Walters* Wroten. She married Howard G. Bobo, buried in Jefferson County, in 1921. They have a son, Raymond Lavalle Bobo, buried in plot K-2.
- Robert Clark Wroten [June 18, 1914 – Aug. 3, 1957]. Robert is the son of Eugene W. and Misouria E. *Walters* Wroten.
- Inez Thomas Wroten [Aug. 28, 1913 – Oct. 25, 1938]

[H-6: Boren, May]. This plot consists of a large concrete vault, with the three stones below imbedded on top.
- James V. May [Dec. 11, 1875 – May 9, 1940], "Father."
- Hattie *Boren* May [May 1, 1878 – May 22, 1939], "Mother." Hattie married James V. May in 1904.
- James Vernon May, Jr. [Dec. 14, 1905 – March 7, 1930], "Son." James is the son of James V. and Hattie *Boren* May.

[H-7: Bailey, Barber, Haas, Sharbrough, Sorrels]
- T. Tilford Bailey, M. D. [Mar. 4, 1856 – Oct. 18, 1944]. T. Tilford first married Louise A. Ferrell in 1875.
- Helen *Sharbrough* Bailey [July 5, 1868 – Feb. 14, 1953]. Helen first married S. P. Sorrels in 1885, and later married T. Tilford Bailey.
- Harry Cramer Haas [Dec. 29, 1897 – Dec. 12, 1960], "born in Gainesville, Alabama."
- Cornelia *Bailey* Haas [Aug. 2, 1905 – Feb. 17, 1988]. Cornelia is the daughter of T. Tilford and Helen *Sharbrough* Bailey. She married Harry Cramer Haas in 1925.
- Harry Cramer Haas, Jr. [Dec. 31, 1943 – Jan. 6, 1990]. Harry is the son of Harry Cramer and Cornelia *Bailey* Haas.
- William Cornel Barber [Sept. 23, 1946 – Nov. 24, 1959]

[H-8: Lewis, McCaa, Russum, Shelton, Uptegrove]
- Matilda M. *(McCaa)* Russum [1857 – 1927]. Matilda married W. H. Russum in 1885. W. H. is buried in

Russum Cemetery. Besides those children listed below, she has a son, George McCaa Russum, buried in plot H-37.

- Minnie Lee *Russum* Lewis [Apr. 30, 1886 – Jan. 1, 1978]. Minnie is the daughter of W. H. and Matilda M. *McCaa* Russum.
- James Percy Russum [Apr. 7, 1896 – Aug. 21, 1970], "Father." James is the son of W. H. and Matilda M. *McCaa* Russum.
- Virginia *Shelton* Russum [July 11, 1910 – Jan. 14, 1984], "Mother." Virginia married James Percy Russum in 1928. Besides those listed below, other children are Gary McCaa Russum, buried in plot I-68, and Mary "Kate" *Russum* Donald in plot I-79.
- Percy Russum, Jr. [Dec. 4, 1928 – April 15, 1952]. Percy is the son of James Percy and Virginia *Shelton* Russum.
- William N. Russum [Dec. 3, 1944 – May 8, 1962]. William is the son of James Percy and Virginia *Shelton* Russum.
- William Ervin Uptegrove [Sept. 13, 1915 – Feb. 5, 1994]
- Marie Kathleen Uptegrove [Jan. 20, 1907 – July 23, 1989]

[H-9: Campbell, Hoisel, Isle, Jennings, Wolcott]. This plot has a memorial stone bearing the name WOLCOTT.

- Carrie G. Wolcott [Dec. 10, 1861 – Sept. 18, 1943], "Mother."
- Fred Swift Wolcott [May 2, 1882 – July 27, 1967], "Husband" and "Onondaga, Ingham Co., Mich." Fred is the son of Carrie G. Wolcott. Mr. Wolcott was a noted proprietor in the entertainment business as owner of The Original Rabbit's Foot Company, a traveling minstrel show utilizing black performers. For some, performing for Mr. Wolcott was a start to successful careers in the entertainment industry.
- Cathryne *Hoisel* Wolcott [June 17, 1884 – October 29, 1955], "Wife" and "Huron, South Dakota." Cathryne is the first wife of Fred Swift Wolcott.
- Jeannette *Isle* Wolcott [January 7, 1884 – December 31, 1962]. Jeannette is Fred's second wife, marrying in 1960. She had previously been married to a Mr. Jennings.
- W. S. (Bill) Campbell [May 16, 1888 – November 23, 1948], "Our Friend."

[H-10: Cobun, Hamilton, Humphreys, Moore, Wharton]

- Miss Catherine Cobun [March 3, 1794 – December 13, 1845]
- David G. Humphreys [May 17, 1794 – January 11, 1871]. David is the son of George Wilson and Sarah *Smith* Humphreys, buried in Humphreys Cemetery.
- Mary *Cobun* Humphreys [July 31, 1794 – July 19, 1874], "wife of David G. Humphreys." Their children include George Wilson Humphreys, buried in plot B-39, John Cobun Humphreys in plot F-6, Daniel Burnet Humphreys in plot A-63, and Samuel Cobun Humphreys in Humphreys Cemetery.
- David George Humphreys [1847 – 1915]. David and his brother Samuel, listed below, are sons of George Wilson and Catharine Baylissa *Prince* Humphreys, buried in plot B-39.
- Samuel Cobun Humphreys [March 4, 1849 – Oct. 31, 1895], "Our Father."
- Nannie *Hamilton* Humphreys [May 29, 1857 – May 29, 1913], "Mother" and "wife of Samuel Cobun Humphreys." Nannie is the daughter of Charles D. and Elizabeth *Belknap* Hamilton, buried in plot F-19, Elizabeth with the last name of THRASHER. Nannie married Samuel Cobun Humphreys in 1877. Besides their daughter, below, they have a son, Charles D. Humphreys, buried in plot B-39.
- Katesie *Humphreys* Moore [Feb. 20, 1882 – May 20, 1934], "wife of William Harry Moore." Katesie married William Harry Moore in 1906.
- Nannie Cobun *Humphreys* Wharton [November 5, 1887 – May 31, 1950], "wife of Paul H. Wharton." Nannie is the daughter of Samuel Cobun and Nannie *Hamilton* Humphreys. She married Paul Hopkins Wharton in 1914. Paul is buried in plot B-23.

[H-11: Allen, Farr, Hoehler, Hughes, King, Slay, Wade]

- William L. Allen [September 13, 1870 – February 16, 1934]
- Eula *Slay* Allen [May 20, 1876 – Jan. 27, 1947], "Mother." Eula married William Lafayette Allen in 1893. Besides those listed below, other children are Mildred *Allen* Robbins, buried in plot I-97, Carolyn *Allen* Bowen in plot I-11, and Hamilton Donald Allen in plot J-110.
- William Lafayette Allen, II [March 29, 1894 – December 2, 1977]. William is the son of William L. and Eula *Slay* Allen.
- Zuma *King* Allen [October 2, 1900 – May 23, 1967]. Zuma is the wife of William Lafayette Allen, II. They have a daughter, Idelle *Allen* Jones, buried in combined plot J-111/112.
- Vivian Kathryne *Allen* Farr [May 12, 1896 – September 10, 1978]. Vivian is the daughter of William L. and Eula *Slay* Allen. She married John Chambliss Hughes, buried in plot A-20, in 1913. Their children are Dolores *Hughes* Grafton, buried in plot J-110, and Florence Kathryne *Hughes* McBride in plot I-17. She later married Edwin F. Farr in 1928. She and Edwin have sons, Edwin Felix Farr, Jr. and William Allen Farr, Sr., buried in plot K-14.
- Emmie *Allen* Wade [January 5, 1877 – April 16, 1957]. Emmie is the sister of William L. Allen. She married Blount Wade in 1902. Blount is buried in Jefferson County.
- Infant Daughter Hoehler [March 1, 1943], "infant daughter of James R. & Dolores Hoehler."

[H-12/13: Anderson, Hicks, McCay, McDowell, Turnbull]. This plot has a memorial stone bearing the name McCAY.

- Thomas Scott McCay [September 28, 1861 – July 10, 1933]. Thomas is the son of Robert Cochrane and Mary E. *Lum* McCay, buried in plot C-56, Mary with the last name of REGAN.
- Leola *Hicks* McCay [July 9, 1872 – February 12, 1930]. Leola married Thomas Scott McCay in 1894.
- Robert Bernard McCay [January 24, 1896 – January 4, 1954]. Robert is the son of Thomas Scott and Leola *Hicks* McCay.
- Ida Fulton *McDowell* McCay [January 19, 1901 – October 5, 1993], "Grandmamma." Ida married Robert Bernard McCay in 1919. Besides those listed below, they have a daughter, Joyce *McCay* Disharoon, buried in combined plot A-45/46.
- Willard Jay Turnbull [March 19, 1903 – September 28, 1997]
- Mary Lea *McCay* Turnbull [May 24, 1921 – February 15, 2008]. Mary is the daughter of Robert Bernard and Ida Fulton *McDowell* McCay. She is the wife of Willard Jay Turnbull, and they share a common grave location.
- Dan Scott McCay [October 14, 1925 – April 27, 1998]. Dan is the son of Robert Bernard and Ida Fulton *McDowell* McCay. He married Bonney Ruth Butler in 1952. He shares a common grave site with Frances Joyce Broome McCay. Frances' stone has only her birth date of December 17, 1932.
- Robert Fulton McCay, Sr. [March 30, 1927 – October 9, 1999]. Robert is the son of Robert Bernard and Ida Fulton *McDowell* McCay.
- Gadi Lum McCay, Sr. [July 2, 1897 – October 4, 1961]. Gadi is the son of Thomas Scott and Leola *Hicks* McCay. He married Mattie Ellis McLemore in 1923.
- Gadi Lum McCay, Jr. [March 16, 1924 – Jan. 11, 1965], "MISSISSIPPI, 1ST LT, 860 BOMB SQ AAF, WORLD WAR II, AM & 3 OLC." This is a military stone. Gadi is the son of Gadi Lum and Mattie Ellis *McLemore* McCay. He married Mrs. Mary Louise *Scott* Snow in 1950.
- Gadi Lum McCay, III [Nov. 26, 1951 – May 16, 1976]
- William Wood "Crack" Anderson [October 29, 1954 – October 20, 2006]

[H-14: Chesterman, Daugherty, Fuller]

- Walter Eugene Daugherty [1868 – 1932]
- Willie *Chesterman* Daugherty [1873 – 1932]. Willie married Walter Eugene Daugherty in 1900. The have daughters Helen *Daugherty* Anderson, buried in plot F-28, and Ruth *Daugherty* Humphries in plot

M-40.

- Hugh Chesterman Daugherty [1903 – 1930]
- Mona Sigman Fuller [Sept. 15, 1923 – Mar. 31, 1991], "Granddaughter."

[H-15: Anderson, Greer, Roan]

- Luther Lee Roan [Oct. 23, 1903 – Aug. 8, 1978], "Father."
- Earline *Greer* Roan [Sept. 15, 1912 – Nov. 26, 1982], "Mother." Earline married Luther Lee Roan in 1929, and they share a common grave location.
- Edward W. Roan [Mar. 22, 1905 – Oct. 28, 1974], "Father."
- Olivette *A(nderson)*. Roan [June 14, 1908 – May 22, 1998], "Mother." Olivette is the daughter of Joseph J. and Quillie E. *Kirkley* Anderson, buried in plot E-33. She is the wife of Edward W. Roan, and they share a common grave location.
- E. W. Roan [Nov. 30, 1927 – Aug. 7, 1930], "Darling."
- Russell Lee Roan [Jan. 27, 1930 – Dec. 20, 1930], "Darling."
- Billy E. Roan [Mar. 5, 1933 – Nov. 18, 1938]
- Margie N. Roan [Dec. 21, 1934 – Oct. 30, 1938]

[H-16: Ammons, Cherry, McCollum, McCool]

- William T. McCollum [1868 – 1931], a Mason, "Our Father."
- Orise Ebb McCollum [March 11, 1901 – March 16, 1979]
- Martha Louise *(McCool)* McCollum [January 24, 1904 – September 6, 1972]. Martha is the wife of Orise Ebb McCollum, and they share a common grave location.
- W. T. McCollum [1923 – 1930]
- Norman Ammons [Apr. 24, 1918 – Nov. 18, 2004]
- Frances *M(cCollum)*. Ammons [Aug. 19, 1927 – Sept. 17, 2014]. Frances is the daughter of Orise Ebb and Martha Louise *McCool* McCollum. She is the wife of Norman Ammons, and they share a common grave location.
- May M. Cherry [Dec. 22, 1906 – Oct. 25, 1976]

[H-17: Byrnes, Jarratt, Jefferies, Regan]

- Percy S. Byrnes [1858 – 1935]. Percy is the son of Charles Ralston and Catharine P. *Smith* Byrnes. Charles is buried in McCaleb-Cold Springs Cemetery.
- Berry *Jefferies* Byrnes [1866 – 1947]. Berry is the daughter of E. S. and Kate *Ellett* Jefferies, buried in plot B-25. She married Percy S. Byrnes in 1891. Besides the listing below, other children are Kate *Byrnes* Regan, Nelle *Byrnes* Russum and Shelby Jefferies Byrnes, all buried in plot H-37.
- Percy S. Byrnes, Jr. [1898 – 1938]
- Annie Sue *Jarratt* Byrnes [1895 – 1940]. Julia married Percy S. Byrnes, Jr. in 1922.
- Sidney Luster Regan [June 6, 1895 – Feb. 12, 1980]
- Priscilla *Byrnes* Regan [March 11, 1903 – June 20, 1969], member Daughters of the American Revolution. Priscilla is the daughter of Percy S. and Berry *Jefferies* Byrnes. She married Sidney Luster Regan in 1922.
- Bennie S. Byrnes [1906 – 1982]. Bennie is the son of Percy S. and Berry *Jefferies* Byrnes.

[H-18: Abraham, Burks, Ellis, Shahan]

- Nader Shahan [1867 – 1931]
- Waddy Michael Abraham [Mar. 24, 1911 – Mar. 4, 2000], a Mason.
- Rosalie *Ellis* Abraham [Mar. 20, 1914 – Nov. 1, 2000], member Order of the Eastern Star. Rosalie and her brother, Norman Nicholas Ellis, listed below, are children of James and Lula *Thomas* Ellis, buried in combined plot G-42/43. Rosalie and Waddy Michael Abraham share a common grave location with words: "Married Mar. 6, 1932."
- James E. Abraham [July 7, 1933 – Feb. 8, 1992], a Mason. James is the son of Waddy Michael and Rosalie

Ellis Abraham.

- Norman Nicholas Ellis [Jun 26, 1916 – Jan 30, 1989], "US NAVY, WORLD WAR II." This is a military stone. He also has a civilian stone.
- Barbara *Burks* Ellis [March 7, 1925 – January 27, 2007]. Barbara is the daughter of John Robert Burks, buried in Jefferson County, and "Pattie" E. *Fortner* Burks, buried in combined plot E-23/25/26, Pattie with the last name of SANDERS. Barbara married Norman Nicholas Ellis in 1940, and they share a common grave location. Besides Vickie, listed below, they have a daughter, Kareemie *Ellis* Nelson, buried in combined plot I-7/8.
- Vickie Rosalie Ellis [December 6, 1950 – July 8, 1991]. Vickie is the daughter of Norman Nicholas and Barbara *Burks* Ellis.

[H-19: Hamilton, Lowe, Millsaps, Torrey, Warren]

- John C. Torrey [Oct. 24, 1854 – May 28, 1910], member Woodmen of the World.
- Leone *Warren* Torrey [Oct. 1858 – Dec. 1931]. Leone is the wife of John C. Torrey, and they share a common obelisk. Besides their son listed below, a daughter, Irene *Torrey* Foster, is buried in plot H-39.
- J. Lindsay Torrey [Oct. 21, 1880 – Jan. 12, 1957]. J. Lindsay is the son of John C. and Leone *Warren* Torrey.
- Edna *M(illsaps).* Torrey [July 15, 1881 – Oct. 9, 1960], member Daughters of the American Revolution. Edna married J. Lindsay Torrey in 1931, and they share a common stone.
- Charles M. Torrey [1902 – 1955]. Charles is the son of J. Lindsay and Edna *Millsaps* Torrey.
- Alma *L(owe).* Torrey [1906 – 1991]. Alma is the daughter of David A. and Urma *Thomas* Lowe, buried in Hermanville Cemetery. She married Charles M. Torrey in 1923. They have a son, Charles Allison Torrey, buried in plot J-106.
- Joseph L. Torrey [Aug. 27, 1914 – Jan. 5, 1935]. Joseph is the son of J. Lindsay and Edna *Millsaps* Torrey.
- George S. Torrey [December 28, 1918 – October 26, 1986]. George is the son of J. Lindsay and Edna *Millsaps* Torrey. He first married Dorothy Lee French in 1941. After the death of his second wife, he married Mrs. Mildred *Harrell* Trevilion in 1976. Mildred is buried in plot H-24.
- Martha *H(amilton).* Torrey [March 14, 1920 – May 24, 1970]. Martha married George S. Torrey in 1946.
- Infant Daughter Torrey [1951 – 1951], "infant daughter of George S. & Martha H. Torrey."

[H-20: no stones]

[H-21: Bare, Greene, McCaa, McFarland]. This plot is enclosed in a wrought iron fence.

- John Harold Bare [Dec. 28, 1899 – June 8, 1979]
- Alice *McFarland* Bare [Aug. 24, 1905 – Dec. 13, 1965]. Alice is the wife of John Harold Bare.
- John H. Bare, Jr. [Aug. 10, 1927 – July 7, 1967]. John H. is the son of John Harold and Alice *McFarland* Bare.
- Ruth *(McCaa)* Bare Greene [Dec. 31, 1928 – Feb. 17, 1986]. Ruth is the daughter of Eddie Allen and Ruth *Nelson* McCaa, now GUION, buried in plot H-30. She is the wife of John H. Bare, Jr. After his death she married a Mr. Greene.
- Geraldine McFarland [Aug. 11, 1911 – Oct. 9, 1937], "beloved sister of Alice Bare."

[H-22: Flowers, Nelson, Rundell, Shelby]

- Judith Rundell [Oct. 19, 1844 – Aug. 10, 1907]
- Goldsborough Barnes Flowers [Jan. 4, 1866 – May 26, 1942]
- Sue *Nelson* Flowers [April 17, 1869 – Nov. 10, 1948]. Sue is the wife of Goldsborough Barnes Flowers, and they share a common stone.
- Luther Love Shelby [Apr. 14, 1886 – Jan. 24, 1959]. Luther is the son of W. L. and Mollie C. *Stone* Shelby, buried in Shelby Cemetery.

- Mary Judith *(Flowers)* Shelby [Oct. 28, 1894 – Feb. 9, 1966]. Mary is the daughter of Goldsborough Barnes and Sue *Nelson* Flowers. She married Luther Love Shelby in 1917.
- John Randolph Flowers [Sept. 13, 1899 – Sept. 24, 1901], "son of G. B. & S. N. Flowers."

[H-23: Gore, Tannatt, Yancey]
- Charlie A. Tannatt [Aug. 20, 1875 – Jan. 22, 1937]
- Avrey Tannatt [Sept. 7, 1877 – June 5, 1950]
- John Harper Gore [Oct. 15, 1869 – Feb. 23, 1948], "Father."
- Johnnie *Tannatt* Gore [Nov. 4, 1878 – Sept. 13, 1937], "Mother." Johnnie is the wife of John Harper Gore. Besides their daughter listed below, they have a son, Samuel P. Gore, buried in plot I-43.
- Everett L. Yancey [Jan. 16, 1900 – July 2, 1966]
- Elwyn *Gore* Yancey [June 22, 1900 – Jan. 31, 1983]. Elwyn is the daughter of John Harper and Johnnie *Tannatt* Gore, and wife of Everett L. Yancey.

[H-24: Harrell, Torrey, Trevilion, Van]
- William Tommie Harrell [Jan. 1, 1885 – Jan. 29, 1937]
- Everlena *V(an)*. Harrell [Apr. 13, 1884 – July 11, 1973]. Everlena married William Tommie Harrell in 1908.
- Burnice Trevilion, Sr. [July 24, 1903 – Dec. 17, 1970]. Burnice is the son of John T. and Laura C. *Emrick* Trevilion, buried in plot H-29.
- Mildred *(Harrell)* Trevilion Torrey [July 21, 1917 – Jan. 1, 2002]. Mildred is the daughter of William Tommie and Everlena *Van* Harrell. She was first married to Burnice Trevilion, Sr., and later married George S. Torrey in 1976. George is buried in plot H-19.

[H-25: no stones]

[H-26: Parker, Roan]
- Walter M. Roan [June 7, 1867 – July 29, 1932], "Father."
- Mollie L. *(Parker)* Roan [July 31, 1874 – Apr. 26, 1941], "Mother." Mollie is the wife of Walter M. Roan.
- Thomas Vardaman Roan [August 28, 1914 – October 30, 1971]
- Jean Thompson Roan [December 12, 1922 – October 2, 1997], "Beloved Mother."
- Walter Wilkins Roan [June 18, 1956 – January 17, 1976]

[H-27: Campbell, Davis, Starnes]
- M. B. Starnes [July 23, 1874 – Oct. 6, 1936], a Mason.
- Lillian *Davis* Starnes [Dec. 25, 1874 – May 15, 1942], "Mother." Lillian is the wife of M. B. Starnes. Besides the son listed below, they have a daughter, Madalyn *Starnes* Spencer, buried in plot A-162.
- Davis Newton Starnes [Dec. 10, 1910 – Jan. 21, 1981]. Davis is the son of M. B. and Lillian *Davis* Starnes.
- Ruby *Campbell* Starnes [Sept. 19, 1920 – Apr. 21, 1986]. Ruby is the wife of Davis Newton Starnes, and they share a common grave location.

[H-28: Clarke, Drexler, McCay, Regan]
- William L. McCay [Jan. 3, 1859 – Dec. 20, 1942], "MISSISSIPPI, SGT, 5 U S VOL INF." This is a military stone. William is the son of Robert Cochrane and Mary E. *Lum* McCay, buried in plot C-56, Mary with the last name of REGAN.
- Nell *Regan* McCay [Dec. 30, 1876 – Mar. 2, 1962], "wife of William L. McCay." Nell and her sister Cornelia, listed below, are daughters of Charles K. and Lissa *Byrnes* Regan, buried in McCaleb-Cold Springs Cemetery.
- Cornelia *Regan* Drexler Clarke [Apr. 28, 1873 – May 24, 1962]. Cornelia married Henry Clay Drexler, buried in Owens Cemetery, in 1899. They have a son, Charles R. Drexler, buried in plot E-10. Cornelia later married Walter Addison Clarke, buried in Clarke Cemetery, in 1923.

[H-29: Barber, Emrick, Joyner, Kethley, Trevilion, Wood]

- John T. Trevilion [Dec. 23, 1869 – Sept. 9, 1936], "Father."
- Laura C. *Emrick* Trevilion [May 11, 1877 – Aug. 26, 1953], "Mother." Laura is the daughter of W. J. and Lottie *Campbell* Emrick, buried in Taylor-Emrick Cemetery. She married John T. Trevilion in 1895. Besides those listed below, other children are Thomas H. Trevilion, buried in plot A-174, Burnice Trevilion, Sr. in plot H-24, and Edith *Trevilion* Norwood in plot K-23.
- William Calvet Trevilion [Nov. 3, 1895 – July 17, 1978], "PVT, U S ARMY." This is a military stone. William is the son of John T. and Laura C. *Emrick* Trevilion. He also has a civilian stone.
- Callie Dee *Barber* Trevilion [Aug. 5, 1905 – Dec. 9, 1977], member Daughters of the American Revolution. Callie married William Calvet Trevilion in 1930, and they share a common grave location.
- Maston Lamar Trevilion [Dec. 6, 1897 – May 18, 1952]. Maston is the son of John T. and Laura C. *Emrick* Trevilion.
- Hallye *(Joyner)* Trevilion Wood [Aug. 4, 1899 – Dec. 27, 1971]. Hallye married Maston Lamar Trevilion in 1924. She later married a Mr. Wood.
- John Wesley Trevilion [August 2, 1901 – September 21, 1964]. John is the son of John T and Laura C. *Emrick* Trevilion.
- Natalie *Kethley* Trevilion [February 23, 1908 – May 28, 1991]. Natalie is the wife of John Wesley Trevilion, and they share a common grave location. They have an infant child buried in plot N-1.

[H-30: Guion, McCaa, McCown, Nelson]. This plot has a memorial stone bearing the name McCAA.
- Eddie Allen McCaa [Jan. 7, 1893 – Mar. 18, 1936]
- Ruth *(Nelson)* McCaa Guion [July 30, 1895 – June 26, 1952]. Ruth is the daughter of John Martin Nelson, buried in Hutchinson Cemetery, and Fannie *Carpenter* Nelson, buried in plot E-45. She married Eddie Allen McCaa in 1915. They have a daughter, Ruth *McCaa* Bare Greene, buried in plot H-21. After Eddie's death she married Raiford Bell Guion in 1941.
- Edgar Allen McCaa [June 19, 1916 – September 6, 1971]. Edgar is the son of Eddie Allen and Ruth *Nelson* McCaa.
- Sara *McCown* McCaa [December 13, 1919 — December 2, 2005]. Sara is the wife of Edgar Allen McCaa.
- Percy Malcolm McCaa [Jan. 3, 1925 – Dec. 7, 1960], "Father." Percy is the son of Eddie Allen and Ruth *Nelson* McCaa. He married Frances Charles Humphreys in 1947.
- Nelson Raiford McCaa [Dec. 3, 1955 – Apr. 23, 1987]. Nelson is the son of Percy Malcolm and Frances Charles *Humphreys* McCaa. Nelson first married Mary Kathryn Green in 1974. He later married Mildred Lee Abraham in 1976.

[H-31: Dubard, Greenlee, Huff, Segrest, Trim]
- Lucy *Trim* Greenlee [November 14, 1872 – November 17, 1967]
- Mert John Segrest [1892 – 1937]. Mert is the son of John D. and Nettie C. *Bridger* Segrest, buried in plot H-50.
- Willie T. *(Greenlee)* Segrest [1893 – 1979]. Willie is the daughter of Lucy *Trim* Greenlee and wife of Mert John Segrest.
- Annette *Segrest* Huff [1918 – 1961]. Annette is the daughter of Mert John and Willie T. *Greenlee* Segrest. She married Charles Lambert Huff in 1945. Charles is buried in Jefferson County.
- William Vassar Dubard, Jr. [May 23, 1914 – Jan. 8, 2004]
- Kathleen *Segrest* Dubard [Aug. 5, 1921 – Apr. 29, 2009]. Kathleen is the daughter of Mert John and Willie T. *Greenlee* Segrest, and wife of William Vassar Dubard, Jr.

[H-32: Bruce, Daniels, Hennington, Jordan]
- James Henry Hennington [July 19, 1861 – May 11, 1938], "Father." James had first married Mildred Herlong in 1884.
- Laura Amelia *(Bruce)* Hennington [July 24, 1868 – June 2, 1940], "Mother." Laura married James Henry

Hennington in 1884, and they share a common grave location.

- Henry Hennington [March 15, 1940], "MISSISSIPPI, COOK, 66 ENGRS." This is a military stone. Henry is the son of James Henry and Laura Amelia *Bruce* Hennington.
- Ola Mae Hennington [Aug. 23, 1894 – Jan. 3, 1969]. Ola married Henry Hennington in 1925. She had previously been married to a Mr. Jordan.
- Jack Ernest Daniels [May 15, 1898 – September 30, 1955]
- Shelby *Hennington* Daniels [April 27, 1900 – November 27, 1989]. Shelby is the daughter of James Henry and Laura Amelia *Bruce* Hennington. She is the wife of Jack Ernest Daniels, and they share a common grave location.

[H-33: King, McMurchy, Rogillio, Wellburn]
- Josephine Wesley McMurchy [Dec. 29, 1862 – Mar. 21, 1938], "Mother."
- Eugene Vernon Rogillio [Jan. 20, 1891 – Dec. 9, 1965], a Mason, "Father." After the death of his first wife, below, Eugene married Mrs. Emma *Stampley* Harris in 1950. Emma is buried in plot H-43.
- Mattie *McMurchy* Rogillio [Sept. 13, 1887 – Dec. 25, 1947], "Mother." Mattie married Eugene Vernon Rogillio in 1911. She had previously married Leonard H. Wellburn in 1908.
- Lillian *Rogillio* King [Oct. 28, 1913 – Apr. 24, 2010]. Lillian is the daughter of Eugene Vernon and Mattie *McMurchy* Rogillio.

[H-34: Hamilton, McCormick, Noble, Watson]
- Julia *Noble* Watson [1874 – 1938]
- Stephen Thrasher Hamilton [1895 – 1967]. Stephen is the son of Robert E. Lee and Nellie *Allen* Hamilton, buried in plot F-19. A twin sister, Phoebe *Hamilton* Abraham, is buried in plot A-123.
- Lela *Watson* Hamilton [1899 – 1980]. Lela is the daughter of Julia *Noble* Watson. She married Stephen Thrasher Hamilton in 1917, and according to marriage records, again in 1948.
- James L. McCormick [July 3, 1917 – April 25, 1986]
- Phoebe *H(amilton)*. McCormick [December 8, 1918 – September 20, 2008]. Phoebe is the daughter of Stephen Thrasher and Lela *Watson* Hamilton. She married James L. McCormick in 1940, and they share a common grave location.

[H-35: Cox, Foster, Perkins]
- Elijah C. Foster [August 15, 1883 – January 26, 1946], a Mason, "Father." Elijah is the son of Elijah Coleman and Margaret A. *Wade* Foster, buried in plot G-20.
- Clara *P(erkins)*. Foster [May 20, 1900 – October 26, 1959], "Mother." Clara is daughter of Caleb E. Perkins, buried in plot N-4. She married Elijah C. Foster in 1921. Besides those listed below, they have a daughter, Haroldene *Foster* Hudson, buried in plot M-93.
- William B. "Bill" Foster [Feb. 7, 1925 – Jan. 11, 1992]. William is the son of Elijah C. and Clara *Perkins* Foster. He married Mrs. Beverly *Buckner* Carley in 1951.
- Elijah H. "Red" Foster [Aug. 24, 1927 – Aug. 29, 1939]
- Clara Rose "Bo" *F(oster)*. Cox [Nov. 8, 1932 – Nov. 29, 1999]. Clara is the daughter of Elijah C. and Clara *Perkins* Foster.

[H-36: no stones]
[H-37: Byrnes, Parker, Regan, Russum]
- George McCaa Russum [Dec. 23, 1891 – Jan. 27, 1950]. George is the son of W. H. Russum, buried in Russum Cemetery, and Matilda M. *McCaa* Russum, buried in plot H-8.
- Nelle *Byrnes* Russum [Oct. 3, 1895 – Apr. 13, 1982], member Daughter of the American Revolution. Nelle, along with Kate *Byrnes* Regan and Shelby Jefferies Byrnes, listed below, are children of Percy S. and Berry *Jefferies* Byrnes, buried in plot H-17. She married George McCaa Russum in 1917, and they share a common stone.

- Willie Edwin Regan [February 2, 1894 – May 27, 1966]
- Kate *Byrnes* Regan [June 20, 1893 – December 1, 1980], member Daughters of the American Revolution. Kate married Willie Edwin Regan in 1915, and they share a common stone.
- Shelby Jefferies Byrnes [June 12, 1900 – Jan. 8, 1984]
- Margaret *Parker* Byrnes [Jan. 24, 1900 – Feb. 15, 1989]. Margaret married Shelby Jefferies Byrnes in 1922, and they share a common stone.

[H-38: Neal, Van]

- William Chester Neal [September 7, 1876 – November 3, 1952], "Father."
- Ophelia *Van* Neal [February 10, 1880 – August 15, 1974], "Mother." Ophelia married William Chester Neal in 1897, and they share a common stone.
- Lula Neal [August 22, 1898 – November 29, 1980]. Lula is the daughter of William Chester and Ophelia *Van* Neal. She had previously married Lewis Andrews in 1925.

[H-39: Crews, Davis, Foster, Torrey]

- Milton David Foster [March 10, 1854 – October 16, 1938], "Father."
- Lizzie *Crews* Foster [January 9, 1858 – July 4, 1954], "Mother." Lizzie is the daughter of J. W. Crews, buried in Hermanville Cemetery. She is the wife of Milton David Foster, and they share a common grave location.
- Milton Crews Foster [October 3, 1884 – January 7, 1968], "Husband." Milton is the son of Milton David and Lizzie *Crews* Foster.
- Irene *Torrey* Foster [January 3, 1882 – January 30, 1968], "Wife." Irene is the daughter of John C. and Leone *Warren* Torrey, buried in plot H-19. She married Milton Crews Foster in 1907, and they share a common grave location.
- William Lee Davis [February 12, 1883 – January 20, 1958], "Father."
- Ruby *Foster* Davis [November 20, 1895 – July 17, 1980], "Mother." Ruby is the daughter of Milton David and Lizzie *Crews* Foster. She married William Lee Davis in 1910.*
- Milton F. Davis [Nov. 18, 1921 – June 20, 1993], "SSGT, U S ARMY, WORLD WAR II." This is a military stone. Milton is the son of William Lee and Ruby *Foster* Davis. He married Betty June Hull in 1950, and later married Mrs. Sara Ann *Hodaway* Padgett in 1963.

[H-40: no stones]

[H-41: no stones]

[H-42: Crisler, Morris]. This plot has a stone monument bearing the name CRISLER.

- Henry Herbert Crisler [July 8, 1869 – Dec. 19, 1954]
- Eugenia *Morris* Crisler [July 25, 1869 – May 7, 1943], "wife of H. H. Crisler." Eugenia is the daughter of William T. and May *McCaleb* Morris, buried in plot C-13. She married Henry Herbert Crisler in 1898. Besides Eugenia, other children are Morris McCaleb Crisler, buried in plot F-B, and Edgar T. Crisler in plot A-18a.
- Eugenia Corinne Crisler [Sept. 15, 1903 – May 2, 1982]. Eugenia is the daughter of Henry Herbert and Eugenia *Morris* Crisler.

[H-43: Harris, Rhoades, Rogillio, Stampley]

- Charles Spurgeon Harris [April 17, 1896 – September 18, 1942], "TEXAS, PVT 1 CL, 360 INF, 90 DIV… A friend to his country and a believer in Christ." This is a military stone.
- Emma *S(tampley).* Harris Rogillio [Oct. 31, 1898 – Aug. 10, 1995]. Emma married Charles Spurgeon Harris in 1922. She later married Eugene Vernon Rogillio in 1950. Eugene is buried in plot H-33.
- Charles W. Rhoades [Jan. 17, 1931 – Dec. 14, 2014]
- Donnilee *H(arris).* Rhoades [Aug. 12, 1935 – Feb. 25, 2002]. Donnilee is the daughter of Charles Spurgeon and Emma *Stampley* Harris. She married Charles W. Rhoades in 1954, and they share a common grave location.

[H-44: Fontaine, Sawyer]
- Floyd Randolph Sawyer [died May 11, 1942]
- Susette *Fontaine* Sawyer [died May 5, 1947]. Susette is the wife of Floyd Randolph Sawyer, and they share a common stone. An interesting note is that Susette is the great-great-granddaughter of Patrick Henry, the noted orator of Revolutionary War fame. She is also author of the book, *The Priestess of the Hills*, set in the Civil War era and featuring local settings.
- James Floyd Sawyer [September 10, 1899 – January 26, 1968]. James is the son of Floyd Randolph and Susette *Fontaine* Sawyer. His wife, Jessie *Floyd* Jobe-Sawyer, is buried in Jobe-Floyd Cemetery.

[H-45: Griffing, Pearson, Ragland, Ransome, Tickell]
- George David Tickell [Oct. 3, 1893 – Oct. 7, 1975], "SGT, U S ARMY, WORLD WAR I." This is a military stone.
- Emma *(Ragland)* Griffing Tickell [November 5, 1896 – June 7, 1987]. Emma is the daughter of William Arthur and Sarah Elizabeth *Powers* Ragland, buried in plot H-2. She married George David Tickell in 1950. She had previously married T. A. Griffing in 1912.
- Tommie A. Griffing, Jr. [July 28, 1915 – Sept. 1, 1936]
- Myrtis Grace *Griffing* Pearson [January 30, 1920 – August 28, 2010]. Myrtis is the daughter of T. A. and Emma *Ragland* Griffing.
- Laura K. *(Ragland)* Ransome [Sept. 5, 1901 – March 18, 1962], "MISSISSIPPI, TEC 5, 49 WAC HOSP CO, WORLD WAR II." This is a military stone. Laura married Samuel Ransome in 1916.

"Shed not for her the bitter tear,
Nor give the heart to vain regret.
T'is but mere ashes that lie here,
The gem that filled it sparkles yet"
—on stone of Myrtis Grace *Griffing* Pearson

[H-46: Bruce, Dillon, Hennington, Humphreys, Phillips]
- William A. Hennington [May 25, 1866 – Sept. 17, 1940]
- Martha *Bruce* Hennington [July 8, 1870 – Oct. 29, 1952]. Martha is the daughter of William H. and Mary A. *Smith* Bruce, buried in Pisgah Cemetery. She married William A. Hennington in 1888, and they share a common stone. Besides those listed below, other children are Myrtle *Hennington* Campbell, buried in plot J-72, and Anderson Hennington, buried in Sarepta Cemetery.
- Melvin B. Hennington [July 30, 1895 – Dec. 15, 1966], "MISSISSIPPI, PVT, CO A 155 INFANTRY, WORLD WAR I." This is a military stone. He also has a civilian stone. Melvin is the son of William A. and Martha *Bruce* Hennington.
- Frances *Phillips* Hennington [Oct. 16, 1900 – Sept. 15, 1979]. Frances married Melvin B. Hennington in 1920, and they share a common stone.
- Walter Lamar Hennington [Feb. 17, 1897 – Aug. 4, 1956]. Walter is the son of William A. and Martha *Bruce* Hennington.
- Katie Mae *(Humphreys)* Hennington [March 27, 1910 – October 27, 1992]. Katie is the wife of Walter Lamar Hennington.
- Bobbie *Hennington* Dillon [July 14, 1936 – May 20, 2009], "Mother." Bobbie is the daughter of Walter Lamar and Katie Mae *Humphreys* Hennington.

[H-47: Callender, Minnis, Moore, Pixley]
- Walter A. Moore [1867 – 1939]
- Mary G. *(Pixley)* Moore [1872 – 1946]. Mary is the wife of Walter A. Moore, and they share a common

stone.

- Clarence Perry Moore [Aug. 23, 1907 – May 14, 1992]. Clarence is the son of Walter A. and Mary G. *Pixley* Moore.
- Harry O. Minnis [1891 – 1947]
- Beatrice Louise *(Callender)* Minnis [Mar. 20, 1887 – Oct. 25, 1977]. Beatrice is the daughter of J. A. and Ida W. *Herring* Callender, buried in plot A-91. She married Harry O. Minnis in 1911. Besides their daughter listed below, they have a son, Harry William Minnis, buried in plot J-13.
- Bonnie *Minnis* Moore [Apr. 10, 1916 – Jan. 28, 1984]. Bonnie is the daughter of Harry O. and Beatrice Louise *Callender* Minnis. She married Clarence Perry Moore in 1935.

[H-48: Crum, McClure, Pahnka, Rollins]
- John W. Rollins [Aug. 16, 1867 – July 3, 1939]
- Martha E. *(McClure)* Rollins [Oct. 13, 1867 – Jan. 30, 1952]. Martha married John W. Rollins in 1885, and they share a common stone. Besides their son listed below, other children are Lewis G. Rollins, buried in plot G-56, and George W. and Blanch Rollins, buried in Herlong Cemetery.
- John Dee Rollins [Aug. 30, 1898 – Jan. 23, 1967], "A Loving Father." John is the son of John W. and Martha E. *McClure* Rollins.
- William Brumfield Crum [March 19, 1914 – June 22, 1978], a Shriner, "TSGT, US ARMY, WORLD WAR II." This is a bronze military plaque. He also has a civilian stone. William's first marriage was to Idele Allen in 1939. Idelle is buried in combined plot J-111/112, with the last name of JONES.
- Leona *Pahnka* Crum [October 12, 1917 – February 19, 1996]. Leona is the daughter of Louis Allen and Della *Ahrend* Pahnka, buried in Jefferson County. She married John Dee Rollins in 1938. She later married William Brumfield Crum, and they share a common stone.
- Geraldine Rollins [Jul. 12, 1917 – Mar. 19, 1993], "CAPT, U S ARMY, WORLD WAR II." This is a military stone. Geraldine also has a civilian stone.

[H-49: Beck, Buie, Callender, Cox, Garrett]
- Thomas H. Beck [1862 – 1944]
- Sadie Cecil *(Garrett)* Beck [Jan. 25, 1875 – Oct. 3, 1941]. Sadie married Thomas H. Beck in 1894.
- Emma A. Beck [1869 – 1940]
- Mamie *G(arrett)*. Cox [Dec. 14, 1883 – Mar. 5, 1957]. Mamie has two sons, John and Robert K. Cox, buried in plot J-22.
- Carrie *Buie* Callender [Aug. 7, 1864 – June 13, 1939], "My Wife." Carrie has a son, Bertron Buie Callender, buried in plot E-45.

[H-50: Bridger, Noble, Segrest, Wailes]
- John D. Segrest [Dec. 11, 1867 – Oct. 4, 1942], a Mason.
- Nettie C. *(Bridger)* Segrest [Sept. 30, 1869 – July 27, 1940]. Nettie is the daughter of J. D. and Maria *Nesmith* Bridger, buried in Sarepta Cemetery. She married John D. Segrest in 1885, and they share a common stone. Besides those listed below, other children are Bridger D. Segrest, buried in plot A-157, and Mert John Segrest in plot H-31.
- Levin C. Wailes [Oct. 10, 1889 – Feb. 15, 1933], a Mason, "Daddy."
- Mattie *Segrest* Wailes [June 15, 1890 – Dec. 31, 1976], "Mother." Mattie is the daughter of John D. and Nettie C. *Bridger* Segrest, and wife of Levin C. Wailes.
- Lev C. Wailes [March 5, 1918 – Jan. 18, 1945], "MISSISSIPPI, STAFF SGT, 129 INF, WORLD WAR II." This is a bronze military plaque. Lev is the son of Levin C. and Mattie *Segrest* Wailes.

From *Port Gibson Reveille's* "Looking Back" column (week of February 19, 1945): "Staff Sgt. Lev C. Wailes, 26, lost his life in action in the invasion of Luzon on January 18th…"
- Shell C. Noble [February 15, 1888 – March 4, 1934], a Mason, "Daddy" and "Cpl. Miss. 162 Depot

Brig." This is not a military stone.
- Loretta *Segrest* Noble [February 4, 1895 – January 19, 1982], "Bua (sic)." Loretta is the daughter of John D. and Nettie C. *Bridger* Segrest. She married Shell C. Noble in 1919, and they share a common stone.
- Nettie Frances Noble [August 24, 1923 – July 5, 1947], "Sister."

[H-51/52: Batton, Burrell, Drake, McCarley, Person]. This combined plot has a memorial stone bearing the names DRAKE and BATTON-McCARLEY.
- Joseph Turpin Drake [August 24, 1870 – June 28, 1942]. Joseph is the son of Elijah Steele and Ellen Davis *Turpin* Drake, buried in combined plot A-33/34.
- Mary *Person* Drake [March 23, 1876 – October 7, 1956], member Daughters of the American Revolution, "wife of Joseph T. Drake." Mary is the daughter of James Wells and Isabella *Myles* Person, buried in plot B-27. She married Joseph Turpin Drake in 1914. Besides those listed below, they have an infant daughter, also buried in combined plot A-33/34.
- Joseph Turpin Drake, Jr. [February 22, 1916 – August 12, 2003]. Joseph is the son of Joseph Turpin and Mary *Person* Drake. He married Mary Rose Daniels in 1951.
- Allen Lamar Burrell [October 30, 1951 – March 17, 2006]
- Rose *Drake* Burrell [June 24, 1952 – August 7, 1993]. Rose is the daughter of Joseph Turpin and Mary Rose *Daniels* Drake. She married Allen Lamar Burrell in 1973.
- Alexander Alford Batton [December 23, 1913 – May 28, 1978]
- Isabella *Drake* Batton [September 9, 1917 – February 17, 2001]. Isabella is the daughter of Joseph Turpin and Mary *Person* Drake. She married Alexander Alford Batton in 1939. They have a son, Alexander Alford Batton, Jr., buried in plot A-135.
- Howard Allen McCarley [June 15, 1915 – August 15, 1985]
- Ellen Davis *Drake* McCarley [October 19, 1919 – January 13, 2014]. Ellen is the daughter of Joseph Turpin and Mary *Person* Drake. She married Howard Allen McCarley in 1942.
- Katherine Gordon McCarley [October 24, 1945 – November 5, 2005]. Katherine is the daughter of Howard Allen and Ellen Davis *Drake* McCarley.

[H-53: Kennedy, McCue]
- John Weir Kennedy [June 14, 1886 – August 12, 1942]
- Elizabeth *McCue* Kennedy [July 15, 1890 – July 31, 1975]. Elizabeth is the wife of John Weir Kennedy.
- John Weir Kennedy, Jr. [Dec. 20, 1919 – Sept. 15, 1942], "IN MEMORIAM…Captain U. S. Marine Corps…He gave his life in the service of his country aboard the U. S. S. Wasp (CVS 18) and was buried with his ship." John is the son of John Weir and Elizabeth *McCue* Kennedy.

[H-54: Hynum, Ikerd, Wooley]
- Charles A. Hynum [May 31, 1868 – March 24, 1940], "Father."
- Emma *Ikerd* Hynum [March 19, 1866 – Nov. 2, 1946], "Mother." Emma is the wife of Charles A. Hynum, and they share a common grave location.
- John Mason Hynum [Sept. 26, 1894 – Apr. 13, 1955]. John is the son of P. W. Hynum, buried in plot G-30, and Frances Elizabeth *Goza* Hynum, buried in Sarepta Cemetery.
- Myrtle Bell *Hynum* Hynum [May 22, 1902 – Nov. 30, 1976]. Myrtle is the daughter of Charles A. and Emma *Ikerd* Hynum. She is the wife of John Mason Hynum, and they share a common stone. They have a daughter, Vivian Lanell *Hynum* Bearden, buried in plot K-17.
- Eva L. Wooley [Sept. 30, 1888 – Jan. 7, 1940]

[H-55: Aeschliman, Byrd, Chapman, Hearn, Stephens]
- Winfield S. Byrd [Oct. 15, 1880 – Sept. 29, 1941]
- Mattie F. *(Hearn)* Byrd [Jan. 31, 1897 – Mar. 10, 1984]. Mattie married Winfield S. Byrd in 1918, and they share a common stone.

- Myrtle Byrd Chapman [May 26, 1922 – Jan. 10, 1998]
- Frances Dianne *(Aeschliman)* Stephens [Dec. 6, 1943 – May 26, 2010], "Beloved Wife and Mother." Frances shares a common stone with John Howard Stephens, whose side shows only his birth date of August 19, 1941. Their stone also bears the words: "Married June 3, 1965."
- Belinda Leigh Stephens [Mar. 1, 1973 – Aug. 22, 1973]

[H-56: Chisolm, Edgar, Fox]
- J. D. Chisolm [Dec. 13, 1889 – Oct. 3, 1942], "Daddy."
- Elizabeth Chisolm Edgar [July 2, 1895 – October 22, 1992], "Mother."
- Russell Lambert Fox [July 11, 1909 – August 24, 1973], "Daddy."
- Evelyn *Chisolm* Fox [June 7, 1915 – XXXX], "Mother." Evelyn's date of death is blank. Separate sources tell us that she died on May 16, 1990. She is the wife of Russell Lambert Fox, and they share a common stone.

[H-57: Cochran, Currie, Gradick, Hartley, Turnipseed]
- Ruth B. *(Gradick)* Currie [Mar. 4, 1865 – Oct. 3, 1956]. Ruth, along with Beulah *Gradick* Turnipseed and Irwin L. Gradick, listed below, are children of G. C. and Sallie M. *Bobo* Gradick, buried in G. C. Gradick Cemetery. Ruth married J. A. Currie, Jr. in 1886.
- Thomas B. Turnipseed [Sept. 21, 1862 – Oct. 30, 1942]
- Beulah *G(radick)* Turnipseed [Dec. 23, 1871 – Sept. 4, 1951]. Beulah married Thomas B. Turnipseed in 1897.
- Irwin L. Gradick [May 30, 1878 – Nov. 1, 1964]
- Johnnie *Cochran* Hartley [Sept. 16, 1891 – Mar. 27, 1967]. Johnnie is the daughter of Henry C. and Hattie *Gradick* Cochran, buried in plot G-20a.

[H-58: Byrnes, McCaleb, Taylor]
- James F. McCaleb, M. D. [Nov. 26, 1866 – July 25, 1943], "Father."
- Undine *Byrnes* McCaleb [July 18, 1867 – Oct. 10, 1950], "Mother" and "daughter of C. R. and Catherine Smith Byrnes." Undine's father, Charles Ralston Byrnes, is buried in McCaleb-Cold Springs Cemetery. She married Dr. James F. McCaleb in 1900, and they share a common grave location.
- William Howard McCaleb [November 23, 1903 – July 5, 1984]. William is the son of James F. and Undine *Byrnes* McCaleb.
- Pearl *Taylor* McCaleb [April 3, 1902 – April 13, 1997]. Pearl is the wife of William Howard McCaleb, and they share a common grave location.
- James Ralston McCaleb [Sept. 19, 1905 – Dec. 21, 1919], "Son." James is the son of James F. and Undine *Byrnes* McCaleb.
- Katherine McCaleb [January 8, 1908 – February 28, 2002]. Katherine is the daughter of James F. and Undine *Byrnes* McCaleb.
- Nellie Pearl McCaleb [Dec. 29, 1947 – Dec. 31, 1947], "Baby."

[H-59: Beck, Youngblood]
- Charles E. Beck [1861 – 1952]
- Madie *Y(oungblood)* Beck [1903 – 1970]. Madie married Charles E. Beck in 1931.
- James N. Beck [1864 – 1944]
- Samuel A. Beck [1874 – 1948]
- Coralie Beck [1880 – 1954]

[H-60: Bisland, Taylor]
- William Witherspoon Bisland [1878 – 1945], marker: "Daddy."
- Katherine *Taylor* Bisland [1883 – 1967], marker: "Mother." Katherine is the daughter of John P. and V. E. Taylor, buried in plot F-27. She married William Witherspoon Bisland in 1904.

[H-61: Ainsworth, Meadows, Monk]
- Columbus C. Ainsworth [1879 – 1949]
- Nancy A. *(Meadows)* Ainsworth [1881 – 1959]. Nancy is the wife of Columbus C. Ainsworth, and they share a common grave location.
- Myrtle *(Ainsworth)* Monk [Sept. 28, 1903 – Apr. 15, 1967]. Myrtle is the daughter of Columbus C. and Nancy A. *Meadows* Ainsworth. She is the wife of Elige Monk, buried in plot E-43.

[H-62: Funchess, Teasley]
- Marvin Funchess [1882 – XXXX]. The last digits of Marvin's death year were left blank. Separate sources tell us that he died in 1969.
- Mattie E. *(Teasley)* Funchess [1876 – 1957]. Mattie is the wife of Marvin Funchess, and they share a common stone.

[H-63: Adams, Haggan, Jones, Norton, Price]
- Isaac Robert Price [Mar. 25, 1877 – May 26, 1956]
- Florence G. *(Jones)* Price [July 2, 1876 – November 11, 1944]. Florence married Isaac Robert Price in 1898.
- Robert Jerome Price [Feb. 24, 1904 – Jan. 4, 1982], "Our Daddy." Robert is the son of Isaac Robert and Florence G. *Jones* Price. Robert was married twice, the first time to Otis Jones in 1924.
- Audrey *(Haggan)* Price Adams [May 25, 1925 – Aug. 13, 2003], "Our Mother." Audrey is the daughter of Garrison and Virgie Mae *Wilson* Haggan, buried in Jefferson County. She married Robert Jerome Price in 1949. She had previously married Joseph Elmo Norton in 1942, and was later married to a Mr. Adams.
- Gregory Allen Price [Sept. 8, 1963 – Dec. 8, 1964]. Gregory is the son of Robert Jerome and Audrey *Haggan* Price.

[H-64/65: Aultman, Foster, Hackett, Headley, Hightower, Miller, Rea]
- Neil L. Hackett [Jan. 28, 1866 – May 11, 1923]
- Addie *Rea* Hackett [Mar. 7, 1872 – Dec. 11, 1957]. Addie is the daughter of Thomas M. and Chestina C. *Stampley* Rea, buried in plot F-8. She married Neil L. Hackett in 1888.
- John Power Miller [July 21, 1882 – Jan. 14, 1973]
- Rea *Hackett* Miller [Nov. 18, 1889 – April 15, 1957]. Rea is the daughter of Neil L. and Addie *Rea* Hackett. She married John Power Miller in 1908. They have a son, Neil Hackett Miller, buried in plot F-8.
- Thomas Jefferson Foster [Mar. 31, 1888 – Dec. 20, 1960]
- Vernon *Hackett* Foster [Feb. 3, 1892 – Nov. 5, 1969]. Vernon is the daughter of Neil L. and Addie *Rea* Hackett. She married Thomas Jefferson Foster in 1922.
- Neil Louis Hackett, Jr. [July 19, 1894 – Mar. 3, 1961]. Neil is the son of Neil L. and Addie *Rea* Hackett.
- Calista *Headley* Hackett [Nov. 11, 1898 – Apr. 16, 1978], "Neina." Calista is the daughter of Shepard P. and Lenora *Vaughan* Headley, buried in plot H-3. She married Neil Louis Hackett, Jr. in 1916. Besides their son listed below, they have an infant daughter buried in plot F-8.
- Neil L. Hackett, III [May 27, 1921 – July 20, 1944], "Sgt., HQ Btry, 456 AAA AW Bn., Normandy, France, World War II." This is not a military stone. Neil is the son of Neil Louis and Calista *Headley* Hackett.

From *Port Gibson Reveille's* "Looking Back" column (week of August 7, 1944): "Mr. and Mrs. N. L. Hackett were notified…that their son, Neil Hackett, Jr., had been killed in action in France…"
- William Thomas Hackett [Dec. 25, 1902 – July 19, 1963]. William is the son of Neil L. and Addie *Rea* Hackett.
- Lois *Hightower* Hackett [Jan. 22, 1904 – Apr. 1, 1982]. Lois married William Thomas Hackett in 1924.

- William Thomas Hackett, Jr. [December 17, 1924 – May 17, 1993]. William is the son of William Thomas and Lois *Hightower* Hackett.
- Mary *Aultman* Hackett [May 3, 1926 – July 3, 2012]. Mary is the wife of William Thomas Hackett, Jr.

[H-66: Darden, Spencer]
- John B. Spencer [1886 – 1956]
- Katsie *D(arden).* Spencer [1886 – 1944]. Katsie married John B. Spencer in 1913, and they share a common stone.
- R. Scott Darden [1894 – 1958]. Richard is the son of William P. and Kate *Scott* Darden, buried in Jefferson County.

[H-67: Martin, Sargent]
- Wilburn P. Sargent [1890 – 1950]
- Mattie L. *(Martin)* Sargent [1901 – 1944]. Mattie married Wilburn P. Sargent in 1918.

[H-68: Callaway, Killingsworth]
- Roger T. Killingsworth [1887 – 1966]
- Nell *C(allaway).* Killingsworth [1889 – 1959]. Nell married Roger T. Killingsworth in 1920, and they share a common stone.

[H-69: Callaway, Drane, Edwards]
- Joe W. Drane [1882 – 1950]
- Fannie *C(allaway).* Drane [1885 – 1974]
- Joseph Shirley Drane [October 30, 1906 – February 1, 1982]
- Lael *Callaway* Edwards [March 30, 1894 — February 20, 1960]

[H-70: Darsey, Howard, Lofton]
- Clarence G. Howard [1874 – 1950]
- Janie *Darsey* Howard [1878 – 1974]. Janie is the wife of Clarence G. Howard, and they share a common stone.
- Denie *Darsey* Lofton [Aug. 16, 1869 – Jan. 31, 1957]. Denie is the sister of Janie *Darsey* Howard.

[H-71/72/89/90: Archer, Davidson, Fly, Montgomery, Shaifer, Washburn, Wheeless]. This four-plot section is outlined with a ground-level concrete border and has a memorial stone bearing the names SHAIFER on one side and MONTGOMERY on the other.
- Percy Leon Shaifer [October 15, 1866 – December 16, 1952]. Percy is the son of A. K. and A. C. Shaifer, buried in plot C-61.
- Elizabeth *Wheeless* Shaifer [February 27, 1866 – March 11, 1953]. Elizabeth is the daughter of G. B. and Elizabeth *Davis* Wheeless, buried in plot F-13. She married Percy Leon Shaifer in 1888, and they share a common stone.
- Edgar D. Shaifer [1889 – 1946]. Edgar is the son of Percy Leon and Elizabeth *Wheeless* Shaifer.
- Ruth *Archer* Shaifer [1893 – 1984]. Ruth married Edgar D. Shaifer in 1919.
- Laura Percy Shaifer [January 19, 1892 – April 1, 1983]. Laura is the daughter of Percy Leon and Elizabeth *Wheeless* Shaifer.
- Sylvester Malhiot Montgomery [September 22, 1899 – September 17, 1958]. Sylvester is the son of Robert Ligon and Maude Desiree Montgomery. They are buried in Hermanville Cemetery, along with his first wife, Mary *Clark* Montgomery, whom he married in 1926.
- Estelle *Shaifer* Montgomery [February 1, 1897 – May 23, 1980]. Estelle is the daughter of Percy Leon and Elizabeth *Wheeless* Shaifer. She is the second wife of Sylvester Malhiot Montgomery, marrying in 1933.
- John Malhiot Montgomery [June 14, 1934 – December 24, 1977]. John is the son of Sylvester Malhiot and Estelle *Shaifer* Montgomery.

- Sanfrid Blomquist Shaifer [September 5, 1902 – February 21, 1993]. Sanfrid is the son of Percy Leon and Elizabeth *Wheeless* Shaifer.
- Dorothy *Davidson* Shaifer [March 21, 1908 – March 15, 2005]. Dorothy married Sanfrid Blomquist Shaifer in 1930.
- Gladys *Fly* Washburn [October 24, 1901 – December 10, 1992], "granddaughter of B. H. Shaifer." Gladys is the wife of Montfort Washburn, buried in plot A-109.

[H-73: Thomas]
- Kenneth Thomas [May 10, 1944 – Nov. 9, 2012]. This information was obtained from a temporary funeral home marker.

[H-74: Dale, Lum, Patterson]. This plot has a memorial stone bearing the name LUM on one side and DALE on the other.
- Elbert L. Lum [July 7, 1877 – August 13, 1947]. Elbert is the son of Erastus William and Emma *Powell* Lum, buried in Lum Cemetery.
- Mary *Patterson* Lum [May 23, 1882 – December 14, 1966]. Mary is the daughter of Samuel Brisco and Martha C. *Wheeless* Patterson, buried in combined plot G-13/14. She married Elbert L. Lum in 1907.
- John Jarvis Dale, Sr. [May 30, 1912 – August 9, 1969]. John is the son of John J. Dale, buried in Louisiana, and Genevieve *Anderson* Dale, buried in plot A-122, with last name of BILLINGSLEA.
- Gertrude *Lum* Dale [October 27, 1915 – March 12, 2008]. Gertrude is the daughter of Elbert L. and Mary *Patterson* Lum, and wife of John Jarvis Dale, Sr.

[H-75/76: McCarstle, Miller, Moore, Scott, Styron, Thomas, Wroten]
- Wiley W. Wroten [1877 – 1947]
- Carrie I. *(Scott)* Wroten [1879 – 1956]. Carrie married Wiley W. Wroten in 1896, and they share a common stone. Besides those listed below, they have a daughter, Viola *Wroten* Slayton, buried in combined plot M-64/65.
- Everette W. Moore [July 12, 1909 – Jan. 5, 1970], "ALABAMA, CM3, USNR, WORLD WAR II." This is a military stone.
- Mildred *W(roten).* Moore [8-12-06 – 5-1-84]. Mildred is the daughter of Wiley W. and Carrie I. *Scott* Wroten. She married Everette W. Moore in 1938. She had previously been married to Howard Powell McCarstle.
- Howard Powell McCarstle, Jr. [March 29, 1924 – May 8, 1949], "MISSISSIPPI, CPL, US MARINE CORPS, WORLD WAR II." This is a military stone.
- Walter Russell Miller, Jr. [Jan. 4, 1946 – Nov. 1, 2011], "LTC, US ARMY, VIETNAM." This is a bronze military plaque. Walter also has a civilian stone bearing the word "Papaw," whose common grave location he shares with Nancy Carol *Hightower* Russell, whom he married in 1964. Nancy's side has only her birth date of August 20, 1945.
- Walter Rgussell Miller, III [May 2, 1968 – June 29, 2001]. Walter is the son of Walter Russell and Nancy Carol *Hightower* Miller. His epitaph reads: "He made us laugh."
- Percy Lee Wroten [April 1, 1911 – March 10, 1991], a Mason. Percy is the son of Wiley W. and Carrie I. *Scott* Wroten.
- Kate *Thomas* Wroten [July 22, 1920 – May 23, 2004]. Kate married Percy Lee Wroten in 1934, and apparently again in 1946, after a marriage to a Mr. Miller. They share a common grave location.
- Baby Wroten [1947]
- Lionel W. Styron [May 28, 1949 – June 1, 2010], "Father."
- Linda L. *(Wroten)* Styron [July 9, 1949 – June 25, 1986], "Mother." Linda and Lionel W. Styron share a common grave location, a vase bearing the words: "Married Aug. 23, 1968."
- Crystal Michelle Styron [August 8, 1971 – December 31, 1989]. Crystal is the daughter of Lionel W.

and Linda L. *Wroten* Styron.

[H-77: Hynum]

- Burton L. Hynum [December 23, 1913 – December 23, 1944], "MISSISSIPPI, PVT, FIELD ARTY, WORLD WAR II." This is a military stone.

From *Port Gibson Reveille's* "Looking Back" column (week of March 12, 1945): "Private Burton Lura Hynum, who was reported missing in action in Belgium since December 23rd, was killed on that day…"

- Herbert Ray Hynum [Apr. 14, 1937 – May 1, 1997], "A1C, US AIR FORCE." This is a military stone. Herbert also has a civilian stone bearing the word "Daddy," whose common grave location he shares with Lendeen Sue Hynum, with a vase bearing the words: "Wed Dec. 12, 1956." Lendeen's side has only her birth date of February 8, 1838.
- William S. (Bill) Hynum [Sept. 4, 1938 – Nov. 1, 2014]. William shares a common stone, in the form of a resting bench, with Brenda J. Hynum, with the words: "(Married) Dec. 31, 1979." Brenda's side has only her birth date of March 6, 1949.
- Ailene Barker Hynum [June 27, 1942 – December 23, 2010], "Loving Ma Ma, Ma Maw, Maw." Ailene shares a common grave location with Walter Barron Hynum, with the words: "(married) June 10, 1960." Walter's side has only his birth date of January 10, 1940.

[H-78: Hynum, Jordan, Riley]

- Anon B. Jordan Feb. 10, 1895 – Nov. 20, 1942], "Daddy." Anon is the son of James J. and Laura *Covington* Jordan, buried in Herlong Cemetery.
- Mamie *H(ynum)*. Jordan [May 16, 1897 – June 26, 1976], "Mama." Mamie is the daughter of P. W. Hynum, buried in plot G-30, and Frances Elizabeth *Goza* Hynum, buried in Sarepta Cemetery. She married Anon B. Jordan in 1917.
- Vernon Ladell Jordan [April 10, 1924 – November 30, 1944], "MISSISSIPPI, PVT, 16 INF, 1 INF DIV, WORLD WAR II." This is a military stone. Vernon is the son of Anon B. and Mamie *Hynum* Jordan.

From *Port Gibson Reveille's* "Looking Back" column (week of December 25, 1944): "Private Vernon L. Jordan lost his life in Germany, his mother, Mrs. Mamie H. Jordan…was notified on December 18th."

- Hobert Riley, Jr. [November 26, 1925 – April 26, 1994]. This is a memorial stone, indicating that he was "…buried at sea."
- Dorothy "Mama Jean" *(Jordan)* Riley [August 23, 1932 – December 5, 2002]. Dorothy is the daughter of Anon B. and Mamie *Hynum* Jordan. She married Hobert Riley, Jr. in 1948, and they share a common grave location.
- Anon Ladell "Dale" Jordan [Feb. 7, 1957 – July 24, 1986]. Anon is the son of Jeff Wade and Bertie Rose *Ebey* Jordan, buried in Herlong Cemetery.

[H-79/80: Barnett, Bowman, Middleton, Scotthorn, Simpson, Starnes, Wilson]

- James A. Middleton [June 26, 1880 – July 11, 1958], member Woodmen of the World, "Dad."
- Ella *S(cotthorn)*. Middleton [May 27, 1881 – December 4, 1959], "Mama." Ella and James share a common stone with the words: "Married March 5, 1902."
- Myra *Middleton* Barnett [January 24, 1905 – January 15, 1979]. Myra is the daughter of James A. and Ella *Scotthorn* Middleton.
- Marcus J. Starnes [July 26, 1904 – July 1, 1969], a Mason.
- Lucile *M(iddleton)*. Starnes [Aug. 5, 1907 – July 20, 1976]. Lucile is the daughter of James A. and Ella *Scotthorn* Middleton. She and Marcus J. Starnes share a common stone bearing the words: "Married May 14, 1925." They have a son, Milton James Starnes, buried in combined plot E-29/30.
- Jim Scott Middleton [November 19, 1910 – February 16, 1994], "Daddy." Jim is the son of James A. and Ella *Scotthorn* Middleton.
- Leta Lee *(Wilson)* Middleton [January 14, 1913 – January 19, 1976], "Mamma." Leta married Jim Scott

Middleton in 1931, and they share a common stone. Leta is Jim's first wife.

- Katherine *Simpson* Middleton [March 18, 1916 – January 21, 1995]. Katherine is the daughter of Ernestine *Evans* Simpson, buried in plot E-14. She is the second wife of Jim Scott Middleton, marrying in 1977.
- Jewell *Middleton* Bowman [January 11, 1915 – January 23, 1998]. Jewell is the daughter of James A. and Ella *Scotthorn* Middleton. She married Jack D. T. Bowman in 1934.

[H-81: Greer, Zadek]

- William Clyde Greer [1891 – 1947].
- Lula *Zadek* Greer [died Dec. 28, 1983]. Lula is the daughter of Isidore and Esther *Hyams* Zadek, buried in Port Gibson Jewish Cemetery. She married William Clyde Greer in 1921, and they share a common stone.

[H-82: Chisholm, McCrory, Powell, Wedgeworth]

- James A. Wedgeworth [1866 – 19XX]. The last digits of his year of death were not engraved. Separate sources tell us that he died in 1950.
- Maselete *(McCrory)* Wedgeworth [1876 – 1948]. Maselete is the wife of James A. Wedgeworth, and they share a common stone.
- Ernest S. Wedgeworth [Dec. 7, 1903 – May 28, 1950].
- Lucius H. Chisholm [Nov. 23, 1873 – Aug. 20, 1892].
- Homer C. Powell [1935 – 1950], "Our Son."

[H-83: Hand, Newlin, Norton]

- Samuel Newlin [1891 – 1948]
- Ruth *H(and)*. Newlin [1896 – 1989]. Ruth is the wife of Samuel Newlin, and they share a common stone. They have a daughter, Jane *Newlin* Spencer, buried in plot I-57.
- Gerald Norton [Apr. 21, 1916 – Oct. 16, 1994]. Gerald is the son of James David and Earnie *Taylor* Norton, buried in Jefferson County.
- Mary Ann *(Newlin)* Norton [Dec. 9, 1917 – June 23, 2007]. Mary is the daughter of Samuel and Ruth *Hand* Newlin. She married Gerald Norton in 1948, and they share a common stone.
- Roy Elden Newlin [Aug. 30, 1898 – April 15, 1968], "MISSISSIPPI, PVT, ENL-RES CORPS, WORLD WAR II." This is a military stone.

[H-84: Hawkins, Stephens]

- Harry L. Hawkins, Sr. [May 31, 1897 – April 5, 1948]. Harry is the son of Charles and Mary Lovdie *Griffing* Hawkins, buried in plot G-11.
- Annie *S(tephens)*. Hawkins [1895 – 1979]. Annie married Harry L. Hawkins, Sr. in 1917.
- Hugh Magruder Hawkins [October 3, 1918 – September 17, 1994]. Hugh is the son of Harry L. and Annie *Stephens* Hawkins.
- Charles Richard Hawkins [May 1, 1921 – January 12, 1962]. Charles is the son of Harry L. and Annie *Stephens* Hawkins.
- Harry Lashley Hawkins, Jr. [December 15, 1925 – August 10, 1997], "COX, US NAVY, WORLD WAR II." This is a bronze military plaque. Harry is the son of Harry L. and Annie *Stephens* Hawkins. He first married Marjorie Virginia Templeton in 1947. He then married Mrs. Helen Aline *Lockwood* Page in 1977. He shares a common grave location with his last wife, Vansiri *Jampanya* Hawkins. Vansiri's side has only her birth date of April 25, 1951.

[H-85: Cotton, Glodjo]

- Dwight O. Glodjo [Feb. 24, 1905 – Feb. 22, 1994].
- Myrtle *C(otton)*. Glodjo [Mar. 28, 1920 – July 4, 2000]. Myrtle is the wife of Dwight O. Glodjo.
- Lottie Lee Glodjo [Feb. 4, 1906 – Mar. 7, 1948].

- Orvell Lewis Glodjo [Nov. 11, 1948 – Feb. 22, 1958]. Orvell is the son of Dwight O. and Myrtle *Cotton* Glodjo.

[H-86: Brock, Lewis, Sandifer, Strickland]

- H. W. Brock [August 3, 1880 – June 16, 1947], "Father."
- Euna V. *(Sandifer)* Brock [October 25, 1885 – January 5, 1969], "Mother." Euna is the wife of H. W. Brock, and they share a common grave location.
- Robert Lowery Brock [April 4, 1922 – October 10, 2013], "Father." Robert is the son of H. W. and Euna V. *Sandifer* Brock.
- Martha Dale *(Strickland)* Brock [June 2, 1926 – January 9, 1990], "Mother." Martha is the daughter of Lenard S. and Gladys *Cooper* Strickland, buried in plot A-124, and wife of Robert Lowery Brock.
- Charles W. Brock [July 1, 1950 – March 20, 2009], "Dad." Charles is the son of Robert Lowery and Martha Dale *Strickland* Brock.
- D. J. Lewis, Sr. [November 10, 1907 – June 12, 1979], "Father."
- Virgie M. *(Brock)* Lewis [October 28, 1908 – April 11, 2004], "Mother." Virgie is the daughter of H. W. and Euna V. *Sandifer* Brock. She is the wife of D. J. Lewis, Sr., and they share a common grave location.

[H-87: Grant, Mengis, Shelby, Wade]

- Hiram B. Grant, Jr. [Feb. 18, 1876 – Dec. 1, 1947], member Woodmen of the World.
- Mary Evelyn (Madie) *(Shelby)* Grant [Jan. 30, 1880 – Oct. 20, 1959], member Daughters of the American Revolution and Order of the Eastern Star, "wife of Hiram Baldwyn Grant, Jr., daughter of W. L. and Mollie S. Shelby." Mary's parents, W. L. and Mollie C. *Stone* Shelby, are buried in Shelby Cemetery. She married Hiram B. Grant in 1903.
- Battaille Harrison Wade [February 5, 1903 – February 3, 1970], "LOUISIANA, LT COL, US ARMY RES, WORLD WAR II." This is a military stone.
- Geraldine *Grant* Wade [Aug. 2, 1904 – May 28, 1992]. Geraldine is the daughter of Hiram B. and Mary Evelyn *Shelby* Grant. She married Battaille Harrison Wade in 1927.
- Graves Jacques "Tiny" Grant [Nov. 30, 1908 – June 12, 1973], a Mason. Graves is the son of Hiram B. and Mary Evelyn *Shelby* Grant.
- Dorothy *Mengis* Grant [Apr. 6, 1911 – Sept. 15, 2004]. Dorothy is the wife of Graves Jacques Grant.
- Patrick S. Grant [Mar. 30, 1947 – Dec. 7, 1996], "US NAVY." This is a bronze military plaque.

[H-88: Killingsworth, Prothro, Regan, Rush, Shelton, Wallace]

- Thomas V. Rush [Mar. 24, 1883 – Mar. 26, 1959], a Mason. Thomas is the son of Sarah J. *Goza* Rush, buried in Sarepta Cemetery.
- Lissa K. *(Regan)* Rush [Mar. 23, 1884 – Apr. 3, 1919]. Lissa is the daughter of Charles K. and Lissa *Byrnes* Regan, buried in McCaleb-Cold Springs Cemetery. She married Thomas V. Rush in 1904.
- Paul Everard Rush [Nov. 12, 1911 – Dec. 30, 1991]
- Lena *Wallace* Rush [Jan. 6, 1894 – Mar. 9, 1982]. Lena and Janie, listed below, are daughters of G. G. and Sarah Jane *Landers* Wallace, buried in Wallace Cemetery. Lena is the second wife of Thomas V. Rush, marrying him in 1920.
- Janie *Wallace* Prothro [Oct. 11, 1897 – Mar. 24, 1974]. Janie married David H. Prothro in 1925.
- Helen *S(helton)*. Killingsworth [Jan. 22, 1936 – Aug. 4, 1996]

[H-91/92: Hammett, Hays, Wilmerton]. This plot has a memorial stone bearing the names HAMMETT on one side and HAYS on the other.

- Owen C. Hays [Feb. 11, 1882 – June 4, 1955]
- Edith Mae *W(ilmerton)*. Hays [Dec. 29, 1882 – Mar. 1, 1962]. Edith married Owen C. Hays in 1906.
- Oscar A. Hammett [July 25, 1894 – October 19, 1952]
- Elisabeth *Hays* Hammett [October 5, 1911 – December 5, 1988]. Elisabeth is the daughter of Owen C.

and Edith Mae *Wilmerton* Hays. She married Oscar A. Hammett in 1942.

- Owen Clyde Hays, Jr. [Jan. 28, 1914 – Dec. 20, 1979]. Owen is the son of Owen C. and Edith Mae *Wilmerton* Hays. His wife, Helen Marie *Jones* Hays, is buried in plot A-156.

[H-93: Kelly, Rush, Segrest]

- Thomas L. Rush [1862 – 1947]
- Mary Adelia *(Kelly)* Rush [1866 – 1925], "wife of Thos. L. Rush." Mary married Thomas L. Rush in 1881. Besides those listed below, other children are Ben G. Rush, Sr., buried in plot I-18, and Emma *Rush* Jones in plot A-98.
- Howard E. Rush [June 29, 1893 – July 26, 1971]. Howard is the son of Thomas L. and Mary Adelia *Kelly* Rush.
- Thomas Young Rush [Feb. 25, 1899 – Feb. 8, 1901], "son of T. L. and M. A. Rush." This is a metal "stone."
- Ella S(egrest). Rush [1879 – 1961]. Ella is the daughter of Thomas J. Segrest, buried in Segrest Cemetery, and is the second wife of Thomas L. Rush.

[H-94]. This plot consists of two separate family burials, one the local and familiar name of SHELBY, and the other, an entire burial site once known as the GREEN Cemetery, relocated to this cemetery to facilitate the routing of a new highway.

[Dudley, Shelby]

- Leslie Stone Shelby [Jan. 7, 1893 – July 31, 1972], "son of W. L. Shelby and Mary Charlotte Stone." Leslie's parents, W. L. and Mollie C. *Stone* Shelby, are buried in Shelby Cemetery.
- Grace *Dudley* Shelby [Oct. 30, 1892 – Jan. 14, 1977], member Daughters of the American Revolution, "daughter of S. E. Dudley and Erna Hughes, wife of Leslie S. Shelby." Erna *Hughes* Dudley is buried in Jones Cemetery. Grace and Leslie share a common stone.

[Carpenter, Green, Hasson]

- Horace Carpenter [May 15, 1795 – April 27, 1836], "born at Huntington, Ct...died in Port Gibson Miss. in the faith of Christ." A memorial tribute reads: "Erected by his beloved wife as the last testimonial of her affection."
- Anne *Hasson* Carpenter [September 29, 1796 – June 15, 1826], "wife of Orville Carpenter, and daughter of John & Rachel Hasson, born at Charleston, Md....died at Port Gibson." Her memorial tribute reads: "A memorial, by her only daughter, the late Mrs. Mary Hasson Green."
- Mary Hasson *Carpenter* Green [September 5, 1822 – December 11, 1844], "wife of Abram A. Green, only child of Orville & Anne Carpenter, born in Charleston, Maryland...died in Port Gibson, Miss... two children survive, Benjamin Hughes & Mary Green."
-

Dear One!
Lovely in life-lovely in death-loved forever,
in sacred urn thy ashes rest!
Far be it, O my soul, from thine expectant essence,
To be heedless, if indignity of folly desecrate these thine ashes.
Keep them safe with careful love; and let the mound be holy;
And, thou that passest by, revere the waiting dead.
—on obelisk of Mary Hasson *Carpenter* Green.

[H-95: no stones]

[H-96: Cade, Cordes, Wilkinson]

- John C. Wilkinson [1871 – 1950]

- Katie *C(ordes)*. Wilkinson [1874 – 1949]. Katie married John C. Wilkinson in 1895. Besides those listed below, they have a daughter, Cleora *Wilkinson* Cade, buried in plot J-104.
- John Cordes Wilkinson [August 31, 1898 – February 6, 1974]. John is the son of John C. and Katie *Cordes* Wilkinson.
- Lillian Mary Wilkinson [February 16, 1902 – March 26, 1966]. Lillian is the daughter of John C. and Katie *Cordes* Wilkinson.
- Herbert H. Wilkinson [1908 – 1947]. Herbert married Myrtle Gillis in 1934.
- Elvin H. Cade [1914 – 1960]. Elvin is the son of Robert S. and Lilly M. *Patterson* Cade, buried in combined plot G-13/14.
- Kathleen *Wilkinson* Cade [April 1, 1911 – May 16, 1986]. Kathleen is the daughter of John C. and Katie *Cordes* Wilkinson. She married Elvin H. Cade in 1934. They have a son, John Robert Cade, buried in plot E-27.

[H-97: Dowdell, Easley, Jett]. This plot has a memorial stone bearing the name DOWDELL.

- David Merrick Dowdell [August 12, 1896 – August 27, 1953], "MISSISSIPPI, 2ᵈ LIEUTENANT, 5 GP, MTD MG TNG CEN, WORLD WAR I." This is a military stone.
- Cornelia "Gran" *Jett* Dowdell [Mar. 9, 1900 – Feb. 4, 1985]. Cornelia is the wife of David Merrick Dowdell. They have a daughter, Jane *Dowdell* Montgomery, buried in combined plot J-48/49/64/65.
- David M. Dowdell, Jr. [May 29, 1923 – November 27, 1944], "MISSISSIPPI, 2 LIEUT, 317 INF, 80 INF DIV, WORLD WAR II." This is a military stone.

From *Port Gibson Reveille's* "Looking Back" column (week of December 18, 1944): "Second Lieutenant David M. Dowdell, Jr. was killed in battle while fighting in Germany with General Patton's army…"

- Obadiah W. Easley, Jr. [March 2, 1925 – October 8, 1955], "MISSISSIPPI, FLTO, ARMY AIR FORCES, WORLD WAR II." This is a military stone. Obadiah married Jane Dowdell in 1946.
- Scott Dowdell Easley [June 16, 1982 – June 17, 1982]
- Gregory John Easley [June 16, 1982 – June 17, 1982]. Scott Dowdell Easley and Gregory John Easley share a common stone with the words: "infant sons of David and Marilyn Easley."

[H-98: Arnold, Cotton, Davis, Eakin, Faris, Price, Sanders, Tanner]

- Joe N. Tanner [1887 – 1958]
- Olis *F(aris)*. Tanner [1888 – 1967]. Olis married Joe N. Tanner in 1905, and they share a common grave location. They have daughters, Ruby *Tanner* Hammett, buried in plot I-94, and Josie *Tanner* Rogillio in plot J-46.
- Laura Tanner Price [1916 – May 20, 1947]. This is the only information available from a temporary funeral home marker.
- Kay Eakin [March 4, 1895 – October 31, 1952]
- Esther *D(avis)*. Eakin [October 11, 1895 – May 2, 1994]. Esther is the wife of Kay Eakin.
- Hiram Butler Eakin [Aug. 22, 1915 – Aug. 6, 1980], "PFC, US ARMY, WORLD WAR II." This is a bronze military plaque. Hiram is the son of Kay and Esther *Davis* Eakin. He married Jewel Underwood in 1946.
- Baby Eakin [April 30, 1947 – April 30, 1947]
- John Bennett Arnold [Dec. 19, 1909 – July 26, 1967], "Father."
- Nora *Cotton* Arnold [Feb. 3, 1918 – Aug. 14, 2001], "Mother." Nora and John Bennett Arnold share a common grave location, with a vase bearing the words: "Married Dec. 25, 1937."
- Robert B. Sanders [Sept. 24, 1889 – May 27, 1967], "MISSISSIPPI, PVT, CO C, 46 ENGINEERS, WORLD WAR I." This is a military stone.

[H-99: Ammons, Brady, Thrailkill, Wilson]. This plot has a memorial stone bearing the names WILSON and BRADY.

- G. W. Wilson [July 2, 1906 – Apr. 5, 1947], a Mason.
- Cola *(Ammons)* W(ilson). Thrailkill [Aug. 21, 1906 – Dec. 18, 1997], member Order of the Eastern Star. Cola was first married to G. W. Wilson, and they share a common grave location. She later married a Mr. Thrailkill.
- James O. Brady [October 8, 1927 – August 24, 1985]. James is the son of Albert Neville and Henrietta A. *Wilson* Brady, buried in plot A-70.
- Dorothy *W(ilson)*. Brady [April 6, 1928 – November 6, 2010]. Dorothy is the daughter of G. W. and Cola *Ammons* Wilson. She married James O. Brady in 1950, and they share a common grave location.

[H-100: Cleveland, Jones, McFerrin]

- Samuel L. Cleveland [June 14, 1886 – July 27, 1959], "Father."
- Minnie *M(cFerrin)*. Cleveland [August 1, 1888 – March 13, 1977], "Mother." Minnie is the wife of Samuel L. Cleveland, and they share a common grave location. Besides those listed below, they have a son, David L. Cleveland, buried in plot A-138.
- Lawrence L. Cleveland [April 16, 1922 – November 16, 1969]. Lawrence is the son of Samuel L. and Minnie *McFerrin* Cleveland.
- John M. Jones [July 27, 1921 – Sept. 12, 1984], a Mason. John is the son of J. Mack and Emma *Rush* Jones, buried in plot A-98. Also buried there is his first wife, Margaret Alice *Selden* Jones, whom he married in 1943.
- Flora Lee *(Cleveland)* Jones [May 24, 1930 – Feb. 15, 2009]. Flora is the daughter of Samuel L. and Minnie *McFerrin* Cleveland. She married John M. Jones in 1953, and they share a common grave location.
- Burnice Cleveland [11-30-1923 – 04-13-2015]. This information was obtained from a temporary funeral home marker. Burnice is the son of Samuel L. and Minnie *McFerrin* Cleveland. He married Carolyn Glenn Hall in 1955.

Section I

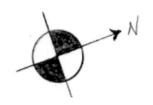

11	10	9	8	7	6	5	4	3	2	1
12	13	14	15	16	17	18	19	20	21	22
33	32	31	30	29	28	27	26	25.	24	23
34	35	36	37	38	39	40	41	42	43	44
55	54	53	52	51	50	49	48	47	46	45
56	57	58	59	60	61	62	63	64	65	66
77	76	75	74	73	72	71	70	69	68	67
78	79	80	81	82	83	84	85	86	87	88
99	98	97	96	95	94	93	92	91	90.	89

Section I

[I-1: Cade, Gayle, Jones, Taylor, Tilley]
- Dodridge Lee Jones [March 17, 1907 – October 4, 1992], "Husband."
- Laura *Gayle* Jones [June 19, 1910 – July 2, 1998], "Wife." Laura and her sister, Edna *Gayle* Cade, below, are daughters of Eugene Luther and Ida Mae *Nichols* Gayle, buried in Copiah County. Laura is the wife of Dodridge Lee Jones, and they share a common grave location.
- Harvey Maloy Taylor [March 23, 1929 – October 28, 1952], "MISSISSIPPI, CPL, CO G, 160 INF, 40 INF DIV, KOREA." This is a military stone. He also has a civilian stone with a birth date of May 23, 1929.

According to *Port Gibson Reveille's* "Looking Back" column (this week, November 22, 1952), "Corporal Harvey Maloy Taylor…was killed in action in Korea…"

- Robert Solomon Cade, Jr. [June 28, 1912 – Oct. 9, 1981]. Robert is the son of Robert S. and Lilly M. *Patterson* Cade, buried in combined plot G-13/14. His first marriage was to Annie Moore Simpson in 1931. Annie is buried in plot E-14, with the last name of ALDRIDGE.
- Edna *Gayle* Cade [Sept. 5, 1918 – Nov. 2, 2008]. Edna is the second wife of Robert Solomon Cade, Jr., marrying in 1953, and they share a common grave location. She was the widow of Harvey Maloy Taylor.
- Alvin D. Tilley [March 21, 1989 – September 21, 2010], "Beloved Son and Brother."

[I-2: Rutledge]. This plot has a memorial stone bearing the name RUTLEDGE.
- James P. Rutledge [May 6, 1874 – Feb. 27, 1953]

[I-3: Harrington, Mathews, Segrest]
- Emmie *S(egrest)*. Mathews [April 17, 1876 – May 23, 1955]. Emmie, Mary Elizabeth and Bardee are all children of Thomas J. Segrest, buried in Segrest Cemetery.
- Miller E. Harrington [1884 – 1953]
- Mary Elizabeth *Segrest* Harrington [1880 – 1970]. Mary Elizabeth married Miller E. Harrington in 1910.
- Bardee Rives Segrest [1887 – 1963]

[I-4: Furr, McFatter, Tanksley]. This plot has a memorial stone bearing the names FURR and McFATTER.
- John Adams McFatter [August 20, 1868 – April 12, 1957], "Papa." John is the son of William A. McFatter, buried in plot A-81, and Margaret J. *Hudson* McFatter, buried in Jefferson County.
- Allie *Tanksley* McFatter [February 16, 1877 – June 22, 1956], "Mama." Allie is the daughter of Cyrus and Mary *Sorrels* Tanksley, buried in Herlong Cemetery. She married John Adams McFatter in 1893,

and they share a common grave location. Besides their daughter listed below, they have a son, Louis B. McFatter, Sr., buried in plot I-20.

- Thomas LeRoy Furr [April 24, 1898 – April 17, 1966]
- Lady Lorene *McF(atter)*. Furr [December 9, 1898 – March 31, 1997]. Lady is the daughter of John Adams and Allie *Tanksley* McFatter. She married Thomas LeRoy Furr in 1921, and they share a common grave location.

[I-5/6: Dungan, Loftin, McNease, Newton, Pierce]

- Calvin L. McNease [Jan. 7, 1886 – June 7, 1967], "Father."
- Naomi *L(oftin)*. McNease [Apr. 1, 1890 – Sept. 12, 1964], "Mother." Naomi is the wife of Calvin L. Mc-Nease, and they share a common grave location.
- Jud Dungan, Jr. [Apr. 15, 1904 – June 30, 1968], "Father." Jud is the son of Jud and Effie *Clanton* Dungan, buried in Jefferson County.
- Thelma Lois *(McNease)* Dungan [Oct. 28, 1908 – Apr. 29, 1981], "Mother." Thelma is the daughter of Calvin L. and Naomi *Loftin* McNease. She married Jud Dungan, Jr. in 1933, and they share a common grave location.
- Hilda *Dungan* Newton [September 19, 1940 – March 2, 1986]. Hilda is the daughter of Jud and Thelma Lois *McNease* Dungan.
- Randle S. Pierce [Aug. 10, 1910 – Feb. 16, 1990]. Randle is the son of Hiram E. and Anner C. Pierce, buried in Jefferson County.
- Winnie *M(cNease)*. Pierce [Oct. 28, 1914 – Apr. 30, 1993]. Winnie is the daughter of Calvin L. and Naomi *Loftin* McNease. She is the wife of Randle S. Pierce, and they share a common grave location.

[I-7/8: Andress, Davis, Ellis, Lauderdale, McCaa, Nelson, Rouayheb]

- Douglas E. Nelson [Dec. 26, 1902 – Sept. 24, 1965]. Douglas and his brother, Clyde L. Nelson, listed below, are sons of John Martin Nelson, buried in Hutchinson Cemetery, and Fannie *Carpenter* Nelson, buried in plot E-45.
- Doris *Davis* Nelson [Dec. 15, 1908 – Mar. 6, 1981]. Doris married Douglas E. Nelson in 1930, and they share a common grave location.
- Calvin Russell Andress [Jan. 25, 1928 – Nov. 21, 2009]
- Dorothy *Nelson* Andress [Oct. 27, 1931 – Nov. 29, 2009]. Dorothy is the daughter of Douglas E. and Doris *Davis* Nelson. She married Calvin Russell Andress in 1953, and they share a common grave location.
- Clyde L. Nelson [1905 – 1962]
- Josie *M(cCaa)*. Nelson [1904 – 1978]. Josie is the daughter of David E. and Jessie A. *Trevilion* McCaa, buried in plot A-108. She married Clyde L. Nelson in 1929, and they share a common stone.
- James W. Lauderdale [1921 – 1987]. James shares a common stone with Marjo *Nelson* Lauderdale. Marjo's side has only her birth year of 1932.
- John Edward Nelson [November 4, 1938 – March 12, 1989]. John is the son of Clyde L. and Josie McCaa Nelson.
- Kareemie *Ellis* Nelson [October 12, 1941 – XXXX]. Kareemie's date of death is blank. Separate sources tell us that she died in 2014. Kareemie is the daughter of Norman Nicholas and Barbara *Burks* Ellis, buried in plot H-18. She is the wife of John Edward Nelson, and they share a common stone. She had previously married George Michael Rouayheb in 1960.
- John E. "Ed" Nelson, II [April 22, 1964 – March 10, 2007]. John is the son of John Edward and Kareemie *Ellis* Nelson.
- Stephanie Lynne Nelson [Nov. 14, 1956 – Dec. 22, 1956]. Stephanie is the daughter of Clyde Luther Nelson, Jr., buried in plot C-76, and Joan *Wheeless* Nelson, buried in combined plot A-116/117 with the name BEESLEY.

[I-9: Henley]

- Clark Daniel Henley [1914 – 1948]

[I-10: Brown, Hales, Tyner, Wilson]. This plot has a memorial stone bearing the names BROWN, TYNER and WILSON.

- Anse J. Brown [Sept. 27, 1903 – Dec. 25, 1960]. Anse is the son of Walter Hulon and Dora *McLendon* Brown, buried in combined plot A-128/142/143.
- Lula *H(ales)*. Brown [May 27, 1908 – Oct. 22, 1978]. Lula is the wife of Anse J. Brown.
- Andrew Jackson "Jack" Tyner [Sep. 10, 1917 – Aug. 31, 1983], "T SGT, US ARMY, WORLD WAR II, PRISONER OF WAR." This is a bronze military plaque. Andrew also has a civilian stone.
- Doris *Brown* Tyner [August 28, 1928 – March 1, 2008]. Doris is the daughter of Anse J. and Lula *Hales* Brown, and wife of Andrew Jackson Tyner. She was previously married to Marvin Ellis Wilson, Jr., buried in Hermanville Cemetery.
- James E. "Jimmy" Wilson [November 1, 1947 – September 16, 1996]. James is the son of Marvin Ellis and Doris *Brown* Wilson, now TYNER.

[I-11: Allen, Bowen]. This plot has a memorial stone bearing the name BOWEN.

- Thomas Henry Bowen [November 7, 1900 – November 23, 1952], "Father."
- Carolyn *Allen* Bowen [July 26, 1908 – January 11, 1993], "Mother." Carolyn is the daughter of William L. and Eula *Slay* Allen, buried in plot H-11. She married Thomas Henry Bowen in 1928, and they share a common grave location.

[I-12: Cade, Crum]

- Bryan C. Crum [October 18, 1906 – January 17, 1979], "Father."
- Mae *C(ade)*. Crum [May 28, 1910 – Apr. 28, 1998], "Mother." Mae is the daughter of Robert S. and Lilly M. *Patterson* Cade, buried in combined plot G-13/14. She married Bryan C. Crum in 1931, and they share a common grave location.
- Patrick "Buttons" Crum [Jan. 12, 1933 – May 6, 2002]. Patrick is the son of Bryan C. and Mae *Cade* Crum. He married Elizabeth Jane Atkins in 1952.
- Infant Son Crum [Mar. 13, 1954], "infant son of Patrick & Elizabeth Crum."
- Infant Daughter Crum [Mar. 29, 1955], "infant daughter of Patrick & Elizabeth Crum."

[I-13: Hudson, McNeil, Schooler]

- James D. Schooler [July 30, 1893 – May 11, 1956], a Mason.
- Corinne *H(udson)*. Schooler [October 29, 1893 – May 20, 1973]. Corinne is the wife of James D. Schooler.
- Sara Yvonne *(Schooler)* McNeil [September 11, 1919 – December 1, 2012[, "Beloved Mother and Daughter." Sara is the daughter of James D. and Corinne *Hudson* Schooler. She married George Lindsay Disharoon, Jr. in 1945. George Lindsay and their daughter, Elizabeth Linda Disharoon, are buried in combined plot A-45/46.

[I-14: Noble, Starnes]

- S. Clayton Noble [May 15, 1921 – Oct. 3, 1978]
- Ruth *S(tarnes)*. Noble [Apr. 23, 1921 – Sept. 24, 1988]. Ruth married S. Clayton Noble in 1943.

[I-15: Hollis]

- Elizabeth Ann Hollis [no dates], "Daughter." Separate sources tell us that Elizabeth was born and died in 1954.

[I-16: Frishman, Schwartz, Sherman, Starnes]. This plot has a memorial stone bearing the name FRISHMAN.

- Abe Frishman [April 18, 1896 – Nov. 25, 1954], "MISSISSIPPI, BN SGT MAJ, 5 GRAND DIV TC, WORLD WAR I." This is a military stone. Abe is the son of Harris and Celia Frishman, buried in Port Gibson Jewish Cemetery.

- Jean *Sherman* Frishman [Sept. 1, 1903 – Oct. 23, 1997]. Jean married Abe Frishman in 1934. She had previously married a Mr. Schwartz.
- James Sylvan "Jimmy" Starnes [July 17, 1959 – August 15, 2004], "beloved son, brother, husband, father and friend."

[I-17: Hughes, Kelly, McBride, Stone, Tubbs, Wilson]

- George L. McBride [November 2, 1889 – December 20, 1973]
- Sarah A. *(Stone)* McBride [April 10, 1902 – March 31, 1982]. Sarah is the wife of George L. McBride, and they share a common grave location.
- George K. McBride [Nov. 22, 1912 – March 19, 1969], "MISSISSIPPI, S1, USNR, WORLD WAR II." This is a military stone. George is the son of George L. McBride and a wife from a previous marriage.
- Florence Kathryne *Hughes* McBride [Feb. 4, 1915 – Feb. 12, 1955]. Florence is the daughter of John Chambliss Hughes, buried in plot A-20, and Vivian Kathryne *Allen* Hughes, buried in plot H-11 with the last name of FARR. She married George K. McBride in 1939. She had previously been married to a Mr. Wilson.
- Tony A. Kelly [May 17, 1939 – Nov. 9, 2010]. Tony shares a common grave location with Karen *McBride* Kelly, daughter of George K. and Florence Kathryne *Hughes* McBride. Karen's side has only her birth date of April 14, 1943.
- Sarah Kay *McBride* Tubbs [March 24, 1945 – July 11, 1984]. Sarah is the daughter of George K. and Florence Kathryne *Hughes* McBride.
- Charles N. McBride [April 8, 1915 – February 21, 1970]. Charles is the son of George L. McBride and a wife from a previous marriage. He married Vivian C. Hughes in 1938.

[I-18: Rush, Shields]. This plot has a memorial stone bearing the name RUSH.

- Ben G. Rush, Sr. [Dec. 11, 1887 – Apr. 30, 1970]. Ben is the son of Thomas L. and Mary Adelia *Kelly* Rush, buried in plot H-93.
- Cassye *Shields* Rush [June 21, 1893 – Mar. 23, 1973]. Cassye is the daughter of Edgar and Mollie K. *Shields* Shields, buried in Shields Cemetery. She married Ben G. Rush in 1915, and they share a common grave location.
- Edgar S. Rush [May 24, 1922 – Nov. 2, 2012], "Pop." Edgar is the son of Ben G. and Cassye *Shields* Rush. His stone has engraved on it a United States Air Force emblem.
- Mickey J. "Mickey Mama" Rush [Jan. 28, 1923 – Oct. 22, 2011]. Mickey J. and Edgar S. Rush share a common grave location.

[I-19: Adams, Schoenfield, Shannon, Tanksley]. This plot has a memorial stone bearing the names SHANNON and ADAMS.

- John O. Shannon [1887 – 1958]. John married Perla Van in 1908.
- Ammie E. *(Tanksley)* Shannon [May 19, 1875 – July 8, 1956]. Ammie is the daughter of Cyrus and Mary *Sorrels* Tanksley, buried in Herlong Cemetery. She is the second wife of B. F. Shannon, Jr., marrying in 1896. They have a daughter, Mary Olivia Shannon, also buried in Herlong Cemetery. Another daughter, Maude *Shannon* Wroten, is buried in plot H-5, and a son, Vincent Earl Shannon, is buried in Warren County.
- Ben F. Shannon [Aug. 15, 1904 – Aug. 30, 1986]. Ben is the son of Ammie E. *Tanksley* Shannon.
- Otis T. Shannon [Jan. 10, 1905 – Aug. 26, 1981]. Otis and Ben F. share a common stone.
- Ben Shannon [1930 – 1997]
- Malcolm R. Shannon [Nov. 20, 1907 – Sep. 6, 1979], "PFC, US ARMY, WORLD WAR II." This is a bronze military plaque. Malcolm is the son of Ammie E. *Tanksley* Shannon.
- Oscar E. Adams [Nov. 20, 1913 – XXXX]. Oscar's date of death is blank. Other sources tell us that he

died in 1988. His epitaph reads: "A good public servant." Oscar had previously married Flora Nstane Ratcliff in 1938.

- Florence *(Shannon)* Adams [no dates]. Florence's birth and death years are 1902-1994, per other sources. An epitaph reads: "A dear devoted wife and humanitarian." She is the daughter of Ammie E. *Tanksley* Shannon, and second wife of Oscar E. Adams, marrying him in 1939.
- Claudia *S(hannon)*. Schoenfield [no dates]. Her epitaph reads: "A Good Woman." Claudia is the daughter of Ammie E. *Tanksley* Shannon.

[I-20: Foster, McFatter]

- Louis B. McFatter, Sr. [January 2, 1903 – October 21, 1965]. Louis is the son of John Adams and Allie *Tanksley* McFatter, buried in plot I-4.
- Lillian *Foster* McFatter [February 28, 1904 – December 6, 1964]. Lillian is the daughter of John T. and Mattie M. *Smith* Foster, buried in Jefferson County, and wife of Louis B. McFatter, Sr.
- Katherine M. McFatter [Dec. 5, 1939 – Jun. 14, 2008]

[I-21: no stones]

[I-22: Headley, Hill, Horn, McCaleb, Stegall]

- James Franklin McCaleb, Jr. [August 10, 1875 – April 13, 1959]. James first married Ella Clark in 1904. Ella is buried in Hermanville Cemetery.
- Mattie *Stegall* McCaleb [March 9, 1890 – December 16, 1959]. According to Bible records, Mattie married James Franklin McCaleb, Jr. in 1914. They share a common grave location.
- Hal S. Headley [Sep. 9, 1895 – Oct. 11, 1981], "PFC, US ARMY, WORLD WAR I." This is a military stone. Hal is the son of Shepard P. and Lenora *Vaughan* Headley, buried in plot H-3.
- Katy *McCaleb* Headley [September 15, 1905 – May 8, 1986], "wife of Hal S. Headley." Katie is the daughter of James Franklin and Ella *Clark* McCaleb. She married Hal S. Headley in 1928.
- James F. McCaleb, III [Sep. 3, 1908 – Jan. 10, 1986], "US ARMY, WORLD WAR II." This is a military stone. James is the son of James Franklin and Ella *Clark* McCaleb.
- Lou Ella *Hill* McCaleb [March 23, 1910 – September 27, 1960], "wife of J. F. McCaleb, III."
- James Grover Horn, Sr. [December 12, 1917 – December 3, 2012]. James shares a common grave location with Dorothy *McCaleb* Horn, daughter of James Franklin and Ella *Clark* McCaleb. Dorothy's side has only her birth date of June 19, 1919.
- Sutie McCaleb [March 7, 1877 – December 16, 1954]. Sutie is a sister of James Franklin McCaleb, Jr.

[I-23: Bobo, Holland, Jones]. This plot has a memorial stone bearing the name JONES.

- William P. Bobo [1891 – 1962], a Mason. William is the son of Charles E. and Olivia Elizabeth *Guy* Bobo, buried in combined plot G-18/19.
- Raymond L. Jones [Feb. 17, 1913 – Nov. 19, 1995]
- Tyna *Holland* Jones [January 20, 1917 – December 23, 2010]. Tyna is the wife of Raymond L. Jones.
- Tina Marie Jones [Dec. 13, 1978 – Mar. 23, 1989]

[I-24: Carter, Stuart]. This plot as a memorial stone bearing the name CARTER.

- Hurd C. Carter [1883 – 1959]
- Bessie *S(tuart)*. Carter [1905 – 1990]. Bessie is the wife of Hurd C. Carter.

[I-25: no stones]

[I-26: Ashton, Ragland]

- Grover C. Ragland, Sr. [March 30, 1888 – February 18, 1968]. Grover married Allie Moody in 1909.
- Sarah Inez Ragland [April 24, 1898 – August 7, 1978]. Sarah and Grover share a common grave location.
- Linda Smith Ashton [Nov. 13, 1946 – Oct. 7, 1990]

[I-27: Bailey, Jordan, Linton, Masters, Rogers, Starnes]

- Wiley H. Rogers, Sr. [Mar. 8, 1872 – May 12, 1958]. Wiley is the son of William H. and Jane *Clark* Rogers, buried in Hedrick Cemetery.
- Rosa E. *Jordan* Rogers [July 23, 1879 – Jan. 7, 1971]. Rosa married Wiley H. Rogers, Sr. in 1899, and they share a common grave location. They have an infant son buried in Herlong Cemetery.
- Wiley Hugh Rogers, Jr. [Nov. 8, 1901 – Feb. 3, 1982]. Wiley is the son of Wiley H. and Rosa E. *Jordan* Rogers.
- Margaret F. *Bailey* Rogers [Jan. 11, 1908 – Dec. 22, 1972]. Margaret is the daughter of Walter Clifton and Mary *McCarthy* Bailey, buried in Jefferson County. She married Wiley Hugh Rogers, Jr. in 1924, and they share a common grave location.
- Madye Belle *Rogers* Starnes [July 29, 1906 – Feb. 14, 1958]. Madye is the daughter of Wiley H. and Rosa E. *Jordan* Rogers. She married Austin L. Starnes in 1949, and they share a common grave location. Austin's side has only his birth date of June 18, 1910. Austin is actually buried in plot K-21, beside his second wife. Madye had previously been married to a Mr. Linton.
- Harold Davis Masters [Jan. 12, 1930 – Aug. 23, 1976]. Harold married Jane Rogers in 1949, and they share a common stone. Jane's side has only her birth date of July 20, 1930.
- James Bruce Masters [Nov. 24, 1949 – Mar. 12, 1989], "US ARMY." This is a military stone. James is the son of Harold Davis and Jane *Rogers* Masters.

[I-28/29: Ammons, Massey, Phillips, Tullos, Watkins]
- Cora *(Phillips)* Massey Watkins [June 13, 1899 – October 26, 1982]. Cora is the second wife of John Parham Watkins, marrying in 1943. John is buried in plot G-34. Cora had previously been married to a Mr. Massey.
- John Howell Ammons [February 28, 1914 — January 23, 1995]
- Ethel *Massey* Ammons [February 21, 1918 – April 21, 2008]. Ethel is the daughter of Cora *Phillips* Massey. She is the wife of John Howell Ammons, and they share a common stone.
- John Charles Ammons, Sr. [July 23, 1938 – February 26, 1997]. John is the son of John Howell and Ethel *Massey* Ammons.
- Ann Helgason Ammons [January 23, 1937 – August 7, 2014]. Ann and John Charles share a common stone.
- Keith Howell Ammons [May 18, 1963 – July 5, 1987]
- Sidney F. Tullos [Mar. 4, 1912 – Feb. 17, 1974], "Father." Sidney married Earline Garrett, his second wife, in 1964. Earline is buried in plot K-24.
- Mina Maxine *(Massey)* Tullos [Sept. 28. 1915 – Sept. 19, 1957], "Mother." Mina is the daughter of Cora *Phillips* Massey. She is the first wife of Sidney F. Tullos, and they share a common grave location.

[I-30: Dow, Mason, Woods]
- Marcus N. Woods [Apr. 9, 1877 – May 26, 1957]
- Emma *Dow* Woods [Feb. 25, 1881 – July 26, 1957]. Emma is the wife of Marcus N. Woods.
- Tullie Abron Woods [May 20, 1904 – March 28, 1965]. Tullie is the son of Marcus N. and Emma *Dow* Woods.
- Gladys *Mason* Woods [February 24, 1907 – XXXX]. Gladys' death date is not filled in. Separate sources tell us that she died on June 30, 1990. Gladys is the wife of Tullie Abron Woods, and they share a common grave location.
- Marvin E. Woods [Sep. 8, 1925 – Aug. 17, 1985], "US NAVY, WORLD WAR II." This is a military stone. Marvin is the son of Tullie Abron and Gladys *Mason* Woods.

[I-31: Baker, Davis, Hannis, Lee]. This plot has a memorial stone bearing the names DAVIS on one side and HANNIS on the other.
- Auvern James Hannis [Nov. 27, 1906 – July 7, 1980], "a faithful husband & loving daddy." Auvern is the

son of W. T. Hannis, buried in plot J-19, and Mattie E. *Hennington* Hannis, buried in Sarepta Cemetery.

- Viver *Baker* Hannis [Oct. 3, 1907 – Aug. 31, 1981], "faithful wife & loving mama." Viver is the daughter of Taylor Cleveland and Angeline *McRaney* Baker, buried in plot J-12. She married Auvern James Hannis in 1930, and they share a common grave location.
- Robert Stephen Davis [Feb. 22, 1933 – March 12, 1957], "NEW JERSEY, S SGT, US AIR FORCE." This is a military stone. Robert is the first husband of Velma Louise Hannis, now LEE.
- Robert Endrew Lee [May 29, 1918 – January 28, 1997]. Robert shares a common grave location with Velma Louise *Hannis* Lee, and is her second husband. Velma's stone has only her birth date of May 19, 1931.

[I-32: Doyle, Stinson]. This plot has a memorial stone bearing the name DOYLE.

- Ellen S. Doyle [Feb. 25, 1887 – Sept. 7, 1987]
- Luther L. Doyle, Sr. [May 5, 1910 – Feb. 26, 1994]. Luther is the son of Ellen S. Doyle. After the death of Lillian, below, he married Mrs. Estelle *Fife* Giles in 1960.
- Lillian *S(tinson)*. Doyle [June 25, 1914 – Feb. 11, 1957]. Lillian is the first wife of Luther L Doyle, Sr.
- Donald R. Doyle [Apr. 12, 1938 – June 16, 1997]. Donald is the son of Luther L. and Lillian *Stinson* Doyle.
- James E. Doyle [Nov. 25, 1942 – Feb. 1, 1999], "US ARMY." This is a bronze military plaque. James is the son of Luther L. and Lillian *Stinson* Doyle.

[I-33: Ferguson, Jordan, Newman]

- Emmette McLaurin Jordan [April 2, 1892 – November 7, 1988]. Emmette is the son of Andrew Jackson and Henry Rohelia *Harrell* Jordan, buried in Herlong Cemetery.
- Bettie *F(erguson)*. Newman Jordan [February 15, 1900 – December 24, 1987]. Bettie is the wife of Emmette McLaurin Jordan, and they share a common stone. She had previously been married to a Mr. Newman.
- Walter Eugene Newman [Feb. 16, 1923 – Jan. 4, 1973], "MISSISSIPPI, S SGT, US AIR FORCE, WORLD WAR II, KOREA." This is a military stone. Walter also has a civilian stone. He is the son of Bettie *Ferguson* Newman Jordan.
- Annie Mildred Newman [August 4, 1925 – April 17, 2003]

[I-34: Baker, Fife, Rushbrook]

- William J. Fife [Aug. 27, 1888 – Aug. 26, 1921]
- William A. Baker [Jan. 13, 1879 – Sept. 2, 1964]
- Belle *(Rushbrook)* Fife Baker [Mar. 25, 1889 – Sept. 21, 1963]. Belle is the daughter of E. J. Rushbrook, buried in Hedrick Cemetery, and Emma Jane *Roan* Rushbrook, buried in Sarepta Cemetery. She married William J. Fife in 1907. Their children include Joseph Frank Fife, buried in plot E-20, James Aubrey Fife in plot J-55, and William Joseph Fife, Jr., buried in Hedrick Cemetery. After the death of her first husband, she married William A. Baker in 1924, and the three of them share a common stone.

[I-35: Arnold, Crawford, Douglas]

- Auta Lee Arnold [1910 – 1975]
- Mary *(Crawford)* Douglas Arnold [1909 – 1996]. Mary is the wife of Auta Lee Arnold, and they share a common stone. She had previously married a Mr. Douglas.

[I-36: Salter]

- John W. Salter [Oct. 20, 1906 – Nov. 24, 1976], "CCM, US NAVY, WORLD WAR II." This is a bronze military plaque. He also has a civilian stone.
- Lillian S. Salter [Sept. 9, 1914 – June 13, 1999], member Daughters of the American Revolution. Lillian is the wife of John W. Salter, and they share a common stone.

[I-37: Powers, Thaler, Ungerer]
- George W. Thaler [1883 – 1960]. George is the son of Maurice and Caroline *Wield* Thaler, buried in plot A-15.
- William C. Powers [Dec. 3, 1904 – July 4, 1974], "Father."
- Katie *U(ngerer)*. Powers [Feb. 11, 1917 – Aug. 1, 2008], "Mother." Katie is the daughter of Frederick C. and Dannie M. *Hicks* Ungerer, buried in plot A-114. She is the wife of William C. Powers, and they share a common grave location.

[I-38: Anderson, Fortenberry]. This plot has a memorial stone bearing the names ANDERSON and FORTEN-BERRY.
- Robert Buckner Anderson [Jan. 24, 1876 – Feb. 5, 1961]. Robert is the son of Dr. Lomax and Nellie *Buckner* Anderson. They and his first wife, Maria *Morehead* Anderson, are buried in plot F-28, along with a son, Lomax. Robert married Maria in 1899. He and Maria also have a son, Ben Morehead Anderson, buried in plot B-15.
- Christine Haile Anderson [Oct. 7, 1901 – Sept. 23, 1990], member Daughters of the American Revolution, "wife of R. B. Anderson." Robert Buckner and Chrisatine Haile Anderson share a common grave location.
- William Lowery Fortenberry [Sept. 20, 1927 – Apr. 21, 2005]. William shares a common grave location with Christine *Anderson* Fortenberry, daughter of Robert Buckner and Christine Haile Anderson. Christine's side shows only her birth date of October 6, 1930. Both of their markers display a bronze emblem with the words: "The Order of the First Families of Mississippi, 1699-1817."

[I-39: Brown, Carr, Felder, Russ, Storey, White, Williams]
- Ezra K. White [June 9, 1897 – Mar. 23, 1983]
- Nonnie *R(uss)*. White [Dec. 16, 1900 – Mar. 22, 2003]. Nonnie is the wife of Ezra K. White, and they share a common stone.
- Arles C. Russ [1898 – 1963], a Mason. Arles is the brother of Nonnie *Russ* White.
- Vera *W(illiams)*. Felder [August 2, 1908 – October 16, 1975]
- Robert Y. Storey [1920 – 1972]
- Gladys *C(arr)*. Storey [1921 – 1994]. Gladys is the wife of Robert Y. Storey, and they share a common grave location.
- Lyle H. Brown, Sr. [Apr. 4, 1922 – June 25, 1996]. Lyle is the husband of Mattie Mildred *Brown* Brown, buried in plot E-32. They married in 1952.

[I-40: Cornforth, Hamilton, Trimble]
- James Moore Trimble [Mar. 5, 1912 – Sept. 1, 1969]
- Mary Lee *Hamilton* Trimble [June 6, 1912 – August 21, 1989]. Mary and her sister Dorothy, below, are daughters of Robert E. Lee and Emma *Glass* Hamilton, buried in plot F-19. May is the wife of James Moore Trimble, and they share a common grave location.
- Dorothy *Hamilton* Cornforth [November 28, 1915 – July 4, 1987]

[I-41: Applin, Topping, Waller]. The first seven names listed below are found on one stone.
- John D. Applin [1896 – 1980]
- J. Mae *Waller* Applin [1900 – 1989]. Johnnie Mae is the wife of John D. Applin.
- William L. Applin [1918 – 1961]. William is the son of John D. and Johnnie Mae *Waller* Applin. He married Mrs. Elaine *Allen* Jackson in 1957.
- J. Louise *(Applin)* Topping [1921 – 2004]. J. Louise is the daughter of John D. and Johnnie Mae *Waller* Applin.
- Joyce M. Applin [1929 – 2003]. Joyce is the daughter of John D. and Johnnie Mae *Waller* Applin.
- Jimmie Lou Applin [1940 – 2005]

- Jonathan Troy Applin [1959 – 1998]
- John F. Applin [9-9-1939 – 12-6-2014]. This is represented by a funeral home marker, with no other information available.

[I-42: Bobo, Garrett, Houston, Lawrence]

- Doctor Jimmy Lawrence [April 4, 1890 – May 24, 1962]
- Martha Susan *(Houston)* Lawrence [April 24, 1893 – January 13, 1984]. Martha is the daughter of John A. and Abbie G. *Willis* Houston, buried in Sarepta Cemetery. She married Doctor Jimmy Lawrence in 1910, and they share a common grave location.
- George Henry Garrett [August 16, 1907 – September 1, 2003]
- Julia F. *Lawrence* Garrett [July 7, 1911 – December 2, 1994]. Julia is the daughter of Doctor Jimmy and Martha Susan *Houston* Lawrence. She is the wife of George Henry Garrett, and they share a common grave location.
- Thomas J. Lawrence, III [May 3, 1916 – Aug. 7, 1969], "MISSISSIPPI, S2, USNR, WORLD WAR II." This is a military stone. He also has a civilian stone. Thomas is the son of Doctor Jimmy and Martha Susan *Houston* Lawrence.
- Kenneth G. Lawrence [June 13, 1938 – Sept. 16, 2005], "SP4, US ARMY." This is a military stone. He also has a civilian stone indicating that he is a Mason. Kenneth is the son of Thomas J. Lawrence.
- William G. Lawrence [Aug. 8, 1944 – Jan. 24, 2002], "PFC, US ARMY, RDSN, US NAVY, VIETNAM." This is a military stone. He also has a civilian stone. William is the son of Thomas J. Lawrence.
- Lucille *L(awrence)*. Bobo [June 20, 1918 – May 21, 1981], "Sister." Lucille is the daughter of Doctor Jimmy and Martha Susan *Houston* Lawrence.

[I-43: Gore, Morgan]

- Samuel P. Gore [Feb. 23, 1902 – Nov. 23, 1978]. Samuel is the son of John Harper and Johnnie *Tannatt* Gore, buried in plot H-23.
- Ruth *Morgan* Gore [Sept. 28, 1907 – Mar. 1, 1983]. Ruth is the daughter of Nonie Adella *Sullivan* Morgan, buried in plot M-42a. She married Samuel P. Gore in 1924, and they share a common stone.

[I-44: Crocker, St. John]. This plot has a memorial stone bearing the name St. JOHN.

- Lewis Clifton St. John [October 15, 1903 – December 10, 1972]
- Annie Mae *(Crocker)* St. John [August 4, 1904 – March 28, 2002]. Annie is the wife of Lewis Clifton St. John.
- Robert Louis St. John [12-12-1923 – 12-30-2014]. This grave is marked by a temporary funeral home marker. Robert is the son of Lewis Clifton and Annie Mae *Crocker* St. John.
- Mrs. Jerry St. John [April 10, 1932 – June 15, 2014]. This grave is marked by a temporary funeral home marker.

[I-45: Segrest]

- Virgil Elwyn Segrest, Sr. [July 14, 1918 – June 21, 1981]. Elvin shares a common grave location with Celeste Freeman Segrest. Celeste's side has only her birth date of April 6, 1921.

[I-46: Callender, Smith]

- Hugh Marion Callender [March 17, 1909 – May 30, 1994]. Hugh is the son of J. A. and Ida W. *Herring* Callender, buried in plot A-91.
- Daisy *Smith* Callender [March 19, 1910 – April 19, 2004]. Daisy is the wife of Hugh Marion Callender.
- James Bradly Callender [January 2, 1956 – January 20, 1980]. James married Mary Cynthia Davis in 1975.
- Carole Lindsay Callender [April 26, 1977 – December 22, 1992]

[I-47: Cater, Magee]

- Henry Otis Cater [June 2, 1914 – April 13, 1964]

- Emma *Magee* Cater [July 15, 1914 – Aug. 29, 1998]. Emma is the wife of Henry Otis Cater, and they share a common grave location.

[I-48/49: Graham, Kling, McFatter, Sloan]. This plot has a memorial stone bearing the name KLING.

- John J. Kling [1888 – 1964]
- Mary *M(cFatter)*. Kling [1887 – 1984]. Mary is the daughter of Jeff and Kate *Williams* McFatter, buried in plot A-81. She is the wife of John J. Kling, and they share a common stone.
- Pete Turney Graham [1894 – 1965]
- Aline Dickinson Graham [1900 – 1974]. Pete and Aline share a common stone.
- Joseph Cecil Kling [Mar. 17, 1913 – Sep. 15, 1995], "TEC 4, US ARMY, WORLD WAR II, PURPLE HEART." This is a military stone. He also shares a civilian stone with John S. Kling, below. Joseph is the son of John J. and Mary *McFatter* Kling.
- John S. Kling [1914 – 1967]. John married Rebecca Frishman in 1949. Rebecca is buried in Port Gibson Jewish Cemetery, retaining the last name of FRISHMAN.
- Patrick Paul Kling [1919 – 1980]
- Frances Graham Kling [1923 – 2014]. Patrick and Frances share a common stone.
- Rollin Jay Sloan, Jr. [May 6, 1920 – Jan. 30, 2013]. Rollin shares a common stone with Mary Alice Kling Sloan. Mary's side has only her birth date of August 23, 1926.
- Patrick Crofton Sloan [Sept. 26, 1954 – June 26, 2011]
- Mary Sandee Sloan [Sept. 19, 1950 – Dec. 27, 1967]. Patrick Crofton and Mary Sandee Sloan share a common stone.

[I-50: Beard, Davis, Humphreys, Russum]

- Nellie *H(umphreys)*. Russum [Aug. 30, 1888 – Jan. 6, 1963]. Nellie is the third wife of Walter H. Russum, marrying in 1911. Walter H. is buried in plot A-92.
- Agnes *B(eard)*. Davis [May 16, 1902 – Aug. 20, 1986]. Agnes is the daughter of Jackson M. and Ada *Neal* Beard, buried in Jefferson County.
- William H. Russum [Dec. 19, 1906 – May 10, 1976], "PFC, US ARMY, WORLD WAR II." This is a bronze military plaque. William and his brothers Dewitt and Thomas Watson Russum, below, are sons of W. H. Russum, buried in plot A-92.
- Dewitt Russum [Sept. 19, 1907 – Oct. 8, 1967], "MISSISSIPPI, PFC, US ARMY, WORLD WAR II." This is a military stone.
- Thomas Watson Russum [August 9, 1922 – January 26, 2015]. Thomas shares a common grave location with Gertye Faye *Wroten* Russum, whom he married in 1949. Gertye's side has only her birth date of February 9, 1929.

[I-51: Killingsworth, Stephens]

- Dan H. Stephens [April 29, 1901 – October 25, 1962]
- Ellen *K(illingsworth)*. Stephens [November 29, 1905 – August 16, 1990]. Ellen is the daughter of Anapias K. and Minnie A. *Wade* Killingsworth, buried in Jefferson County. Besides those listed below, they have a daughter, Mary *Stephens* Hill, buried in plot J-86.
- Kenneth "Dan" Stephens [Nov. 26, 1926 – Jan. 5, 2013]. This information was obtained from a temporary funeral home marker. Kenneth is the son of Dan H. and Ellen *Killingsworth* Stephens. He married Cleo Kendrick in 1948.
- Edward Ray Stephens [July 26, 1928 – Nov. 9, 1984], "BM2, US NAVY, KOREA." This is a military stone. Edward is the son of Dan H. and Ellen *Killingsworth* Stephens.

[I-52: Dooley, Purser, Stringer]

- Otties W. Stringer [Jan. 26, 1916 – Dec. 23, 1980]
- Lethia C. *(Dooley)* Stringer [Mar. 19, 1917 – Nov. 7, 1985]. Lethia is the wife of Otties W. Stringer, and

they share a common grave location.

- Barbara Lynn Stringer [June 18, 1939 – July 30, 2006]. Barbara shares a common grave location with Clarence W. Stringer, son of Otties W. and Lethia *Dooley* Stringer. Clarence's side has only his birth date of February 25, 1940.
- John Clayton Stringer [Jan. 22, 1942 – Aug. 27, 1962]. John is the son of Otties W. and Lethia C. *Dooley* Stringer.
- Alice Mae Stringer Purser [12-09-1943 – 01-13-2014]. This information was obtained from a temporary funeral home marker.

[I-53: Selden, Warren]
- Hickman Warren [Mar. 25, 1920 – July 2, 1962]
- Maria *Selden* Warren [April 4, 1924 – May 29, 2007]. Maria is the daughter of Margaret *McDougall* Selden, buried in plot A-107, and wife of Hickman Warren.
- Hickman Warren [July 18, 1945 – July 27, 2010]. Hickman is the son of Hickman and Maria *Selden* Warren.

[I-54/55: Ellis, Kinnebrew]
- Nicholas Michael Ellis [July 8, 1924 – January 29, 2000]. Nicholas and his brother Louis, below, are sons of Michael and Mary *Mike* Ellis, buried in combined plot G-42/43. Nicholas shares a common grave location with Naomi *Spencer* Ellis, whom he married in 1955. Naomi's side has only her birth date of July 8, 1935.
- Louis Nader Ellis [June 2, 1915 – February 19, 2002]
- Burdeen *Kinnebrew* Ellis [January 3, 1916 – December 4, 2001]. Burdeen is the wife of Louis Nader Ellis, and they share a common stone.

[I-56: Boyte]
- Edward Denon Boyte, Jr. [Oct. 9, 1927 – Oct. 1, 2002]. Edward shares a common grave location with Reater *McFatter* Boyte. Reater's side has only her birth date of October 11, 1931.

[I-57: Garrett, Newlin, Spencer]
- Horatio Nelson Spencer, Jr. [Apr. 2, 1911 – Oct. 15, 1982]. Horatio is the son of Horatio N. and Ellie May *Hartwell* Spencer, buried in plot A-69.
- Jane *Newlin* Spencer [Sept. 7, 1915 – Dec. 17, 1984]. Jane is the daughter of Samuel and Ruth *Hand* Newlin, buried in plot H-83. She married Horatio Nelson Spencer, Jr. in 1934, and they share a common grave location.
- Vera *Spencer* Garrett [October 8, 1940 – June 13, 2006]. Vera is the daughter of Horatio Nelson and Jane *Newlin* Spencer. She married Stephen Carl Garrett in 1964.

[I-58: Hudson, Riley]
- Porter Lee Riley, Sr. [Sept. 4, 1920 – Nov. 28, 1969], a Mason.
- Sarah *Hudson* Riley [Nov. 5, 1920 – Apr. 13, 2009]. Sarah is the daughter of William Henry and Bertha *Holder* Hudson, buried in combined plot A-10/27/28. She married Porter Lee Riley, Sr. in 1941, and they share a common grave location.
- John Thomas Hudson [May 17, 1932 – July 12, 1984], "Beloved Daddy." John is the son of William Henry and Bertha *Foster* Hudson, making him half-brother to Sarah, listed above. He shares a common grave location with Corrinne *Brewer* Hudson. Corrinne's side has only her birth date of Sept. 8, 1928. John had previously married Norma Lee Gayle in 1953.

[I-59: Anglin, Bailey, Baugher, Brown, Gayle, Moore, Nauman]
- Charity Anna *(Baugher)* Moore [May 6, 1873 – April 28, 1969]. Besides her daughter, listed below, she has a daughter, Marie *Moore* Anglin, buried in plot J-88.
- George A. Nauman [July 30, 1900 – May 16, 1975]

- Elsie *(Moore)* Nauman [1908 – 1964]. Elsie is the daughter of Charity Anna *Baugher* Moore and wife of George A. Nauman.
- James A. Brown [July 31, 1917 – July 11, 1996], "Father." James is the son of Walter G. and Mamie *Kellogg* Brown, buried in Port Gibson Catholic Cemetery.
- Evelyn M. *(Anglin)* Brown [Sept. 15, 1921 – May 17, 1999], "Mother." Evelyn is the daughter of James M. and Marie *Moore* Anglin, buried in plot J-88. She married James A. Brown in 1953, and they share a common grave location. Evelyn was previously married to a Mr. Gayle.
- James V. Bailey [June 8, 1926 – Jul. 27, 1984], "PVT, US ARMY." This is a bronze military plaque. James is the son of Marie *Moore* Bailey, buried in plot J-88, and retaining her first married name of ANGLIN.

[I-60: Sullivan]
- Clinton Virgil "C. V." Sullivan [May 30, 1922 – April 18, 1991], "Father."
- Claudette Cordelia "Dee" Sullivan [July 30, 1944 – July 1, 1965], "Daughter." Claudette is the daughter of Clinton Virgil Sullivan.

[I-61: McLemore, Reed, Seemann]
- Edwin V. McLemore [May 5, 1909 – Nov. 24, 1961], "MISSISSIPPI, MR 3, USNR, WORLD WAR II." This is a military stone. He also has a civilian stone.
- Violet *Seemann* McLemore [Jan. 22, 1911 – Jan. 12, 1966]. Violet is the daughter of Walter Rubin Seemann, buried in plot I-67. She married Edwin V. McLemore in 1928, and they share a common grave location.
- Jack P. Reed [Jan. 4, 1928 – Apr. 22, 1994]
- Juanita *M(cLemore)*. Reed [May 30, 1929 – Apr. 10, 1994]. Juanita is the daughter of Edwin V. and Violet *Seemann* McLemore. She married Jack P. Reed in 1948, and they share a common grave location.

[I-62: Harmon, Parker, Sorrels]
- Willie Lee Harmon [September 13, 1898 – June 22, 1966]
- Cathleen *S(orrels)*. Harmon [June 21, 1905 – XXXX]. Cathleen's date of death is blank. A temporary funeral home marker tells us that she died on November 6, 2008. Cathleen is the daughter of Sidney and Lillian Elmore *Perkins* Sorrels, buried in Sarepta Cemetery. She married Willie Lee Harmon in 1922, and they share a common stone.
- Clifton Parker [May 27, 1921 – December 24, 1988], "Daddy."
- Ruby Louise *Harmon* Parker [July 21, 1925 – December 16, 1983], "Mama." Ruby is the daughter of Willie Lee and Cathleen *Sorrels* Harmon. She is the wife of Clifton Parker, and they share a common stone.

[I-63: Ashley, Copass, Frazier, Pickering, Thornton]
- Nannie D. *Thornton* Copass [January 8, 1897 – August 20, 1972], "Mother." Nannie is the daughter of John A. and Martha *Flowers* Thornton, buried in Flowers Cemetery. She married Loyd Frazier in 1915, and later married H. C. Copass in 1923.
- Leland K. Ashley [Aug. 6, 1913 – Jan. 31, 1989]
- Ruby *Frazier* Ashley [Sept. 11, 1916 – June 22, 2007]. Ruby is the wife of Leland K. Ashley, and they share a common grave location.
- Sheila *P(ickering)*. Ashley [Nov. 11, 1943 – Jan. 20, 2013]. Sheila shares a common stone with Gerald L. Ashley, son of Leland K. and Ruby *Frazier* Ashley, with the words: "(Married) Jan. 30, 1964." Gerald's side has only his birth date of November 5, 1941.
- Thomas Pickering Ashley [August 11, 1967 – August 26, 2014], a Mason. Thomas is the son of Gerald L. and Sheila *Pickering* Ashley.

[I-64: Fulton, Wade]
- William Albert Fulton [February 24, 1898 – March 3, 1970]

- John Rivers Fulton [March 21, 1901 – January 3, 1994]
- Adine *Wade* Fulton [August 11, 1905 – March 7, 1996]. Adine married John Rivers Fulton in 1923.
- Jerry Rivers Fulton [Dec. 8, 1939 – June 28, 1974]. Jerry is the son of John Rivers and Adine *Wade* Fulton.

[I-65: Davis, Rowan]. This plot has a memorial stone bearing the name DAVIS.
- Edwin Daniel Davis [Oct. 30, 1909 – Mar. 21, 1992], a Mason, "Father." An additional biographical stone has these words: "Mayor of Port Gibson/Member, MS State Legislature/Chairman, Grand Gulf Military Park Comm."
- Mary Elizabeth *(Rowan)* Davis [Apr. 9, 1916 – June 15, 1992], "Mother." Mary is the wife of Edwin Daniel Davis.

[I-66: Alexander, Chapman, Smith, Wells]
- Luther Lagrone Wells [Dec. 21, 1902 – Apr. 7, 1977], "Father."
- Susie Vera *(Alexander)* Wells [Aug. 12, 1912 – Dec. 6, 1990], "Mother." Susie is the wife of Luther Lagrone Wells, and they share a common grave location.
- Mattie Rene *(Wells)* Chapman [May 21, 1930 – April 28, 1968], "Mother." Mattie is the daughter of Luther Lagrone and Susie Vera *Alexander* Wells.
- Jeffrey Alan Smith [December 17, 1967 – April 11, 1986], "Son."
- Shelby Lynn Smith [Mar. 12, 1998 – Mar. 14, 1998]

[I-67: Seemann]. This plot has a memorial stone bearing the name SEEMANN. The first three listed here are brothers.
- Franklin Emerson Seemann [Jan. 19, 1881 – June 25, 1971]
- Walter Rubin Seemann [Jan. 5, 1886 – Sept. 27, 1971] Walter has daughters, Violet *Seemann* McLemore, buried in plot I-61, and Fern *Seemann* Allen in plot J-110.
- Lawrence G. Seemann [Dec. 3, 1888 – July 29, 1978]
- Lester H. Seemann [Mar. 18, 1909 – Oct. 9, 1978]. Lester is the son of Walter Rubin Seemann. He married Marie Lindley in 1928.
- Thomas Reubin Seemann [Jul. 18, 1930 – Jan. 6, 1998], "SGT, US ARMY, KOREA." This is a military stone. Thomas is the son of Lester H. and Marie *Lindley* Seemann. He married Bettye Carolyn Bollinger in 1951.

[I-68: Hudson, Russum, Scott, Stevenson]
- Bracy Percival Scott [May 18, 1911 – Jan. 8, 1971], "Father."
- Willie Ruth *(Hudson)* Scott [Aug. 19, 1918 – May 27, 1992], "Mother." Willie is the daughter of Herbert B. and Ottie *Holder* Hudson, buried in combined plot A-39/40. She married Bracy Percival Scott in 1943, and they share a common grave location.
- Gary McCaa Russum, Sr. [Jul. 3, 1934 – Apr. 7, 2010]. Gary is the son of James Percy and Virginia *Shelton* Russum, buried in plot H-8. He shares a common stone with Sybil Ruth *Scott* Russum, whom he married in 1966. Sybil's side has only her birth date of March 18, 1944.
- Celia Renee *(Russum)* Stevenson [Oct. 12, 1968 – Jan. 13, 2003]. Celia is the daughter of Gary McCaa and Sybil Ruth *Scott* Russum.

[I-69: Farr]
- Sidney Earle Farr [Feb. 3, 1893 – June 12, 1972], "NEW JERSEY, SGT, CO H, 311 INF, 78 DIV, WORLD WAR I, PH." This is a military stone.
- Verna M. Farr [Apr. 12, 1894 – Apr. 29, 1999]. Sidney and Verna share a common grave location.

[I-70: Curtis, Ensell, Fife, Godbold, Irby]
- Johnny Jeff Fife [August 17, 1902 – June 1, 1970]
- Carlin W. *(Curtis)* Fife [May 6, 1909 – August 7, 1973]. Carlin is the daughter of Carl S. and Shellie *Rushing* Curtis, buried in Jefferson County. She married Johnny Jeff Fife in 1925.

- Edward Bernard Fife [February 18, 1930 – July 3, 1997]. Edward is the son of Johnny Jeff and Carlin W. *Curtis* Fife.
- Sara Frances *(Godbold)* Fife [November 19, 1929 – April 3, 1994]. Sara is the daughter of Lauriellen *Lusk* Godbold, buried in plot A-57 with the last name of BEARDEN. She married Edward Bernard Fife in 1952.
- Dalton Boone Irby [July 23, 1930 – Jan. 17, 2004]. Dalton is the son of Daniel Boone and Bessie *Rogers* Irby, buried in Sarepta Cemetery. He married Emma Gene Fife in 1950.
- Dalton Kenneth Irby [Sep. 15, 1951 – Sep. 5, 1999], "PFC, US ARMY." This is a bronze military plaque. Dalton is the son of Dalton Boone and Emma Gene *Fife* Irby. He married Judy Carol Hynum in 1974.
- Tracy E. *Ensell* Irby [January 2, 1957 – June 23, 1979]
- Russell Hugh Irby [no dates], "Infant." Separate sources tell us that Russell and his mother, Tracy Irby, above, died in childbirth on the same date. They share a common stone.

[I-71: Hardin]
- Melissa Hardin [born and died March 25, 1970]

[I-72: Bearden, Fry, Nesmith]
- Felix H. Fry [July 20, 1902 – June 20, 1979]
- Mattie *N(esmith).* Fry [November 15, 1894 – January 25, 1979]. Mattie, along with her twin sister Fannie, below, are daughters of Thomas B. Nesmith, buried in Trevilion Cemetery, and Fannie *Funchess* Nesmith, buried in Hinds County. Mattie married Felix H. Fry in 1930, and they share a common grave location. She had previously married Richard R. Bearden in 1913. Richard is buried in plot A-57.
- Fannie Nesmith [1894 – 1969]

[I-73: Abraham, Mikell]
- Stephen T. Abraham [Mar. 30, 1918 – Sept. 11, 2003], "Father." Stephen is the son of Jacob L. and Phoebe *Hamilton* Abraham, buried in plot A-123.
- Mildred *M(ikell).* Abraham [Nov. 28, 1910 – Nov. 19, 2000], "Mother." Mildred married Stephen T. Abraham in 1945, and they share a common grave location.
- Stephen Thrasher Abraham [January 4, 1946 – April 6, 1989]. Stephen is the son of Stephen T. and Mildred *Mikell* Abraham.

[I-74: Barr, Pawlick, Ridgway, Smith]. This plot has a memorial stone bearing the name SMITH.
- William Myles Smith [1883 – 1971]. William is the son of E. J. Smith, buried in combined plot C-66/67/80.
- Agnes Elizabeth *(Pawlick)* Smith [1884 – 1972]. Agnes married William Myles Smith in 1904.
- Agnes Eloise Smith [1905 – 1969]. Agnes is the daughter of William Myles and Agnes Elizabeth *Pawlick* Smith.
- Gertrude *S(mith).* Ridgway [1909 – 1988]. Gertrude is the daughter of William Myles and Agnes Elizabeth *Pawlick* Smith. She married Dr. Huron Riley Ridgway in 1938.
- William H. Barr [1919 – 1991]. William married Maude Rita Smith, daughter of William Myles and Agnes Eloise *Pawlick* Smith, in 1944.

[I-75/80: Bryant, Cain, Rollison, Rushing, Slayton, Trim]
- William Daniel Slayton [Dec. 22, 1884 – Jan. 22, 1974], "Father."
- Sarah E. *Bryant* Slayton [July 18, 1905 – Aug. 13, 1978], "Mother." Sarah married William Daniel Slayton in 1922, and they share a common grave location.
- James Edgar Cain [September 24, 1921 – March 21, 2009], a Mason. James is the son of Cammie and Jane *Seymore* Cain, buried in Jefferson County.
- Mary Ottilie *Slayton* Cain [December 16, 1922 – October 25, 2010], member Order of the Eastern Star. Mary is the daughter of William Daniel and Sarah E. *Bryant* Slayton. She and James Edgar Cain share

a common grave location with the words: "Married Oct. 17, 1942."

- Kaitlyn Nicole Rollison [Aug. 1, 1994]
- Nick B. Trim [Dec. 25, 1922 – Aug. 18, 2008]. Nick is the son of W. Bradley and Mary *Kelly* Trim, buried in plot G-33.
- Lucille *S(layton)*. Trim [Feb. 13, 1928 – Feb. 7, 1980] Lucille is the daughter of William Daniel and Sarah E. *Bryant* Slayton. She married Nick B. Trim in 1951, and they share a common stone.
- James Brandon Rushing [June 8, 1990]

[I-76: no stones]

[I-77: no stones]

[I-78: Hurley, McFatter]

- Melvin M. McFatter [April 1, 1904 – March 21, 1999], "Daddy" and "Gramps." Melvin is the son of Dan and M. Urzilla *Dromgoole* McFatter, buried in Jefferson County.
- Lily *Hurley* McFatter [Nov. 4, 1907 – Aug. 9, 1998], "Mama" and "Granny." Lily is the daughter of Floyd R. and Carrie *Schwartz* Hurley, also buried in Jefferson County. She married Melvin M. McFatter in 1930, and they share a common grave location.

[I-79: Donald, Russum]

- Charles Edward Donald, Sr. [April 9, 1919 – January 23, 1992], "Father."
- Mary "Kate" *R(ussum)*. Donald [November 25, 1930 – June 18, 2010], "Mother." Mary is the daughter of James Percy and Virginia *Shelton* Russum, buried in plot H-8. She married Charles Edward Donald in 1956, and they share a common grave location.

[I-81: Beaube]

- William C. Beaube [Jan. 15, 1935 – Nov. 21, 2005]. William shares a common stone with Clara Ann *Willis* Beaube, whom he married in 1956. Clara's side has only her birth date of January 17, 1939.
- Richard E. Beaube [Feb. 11, 1957 – Feb. 28, 1980]. Richard is the son of William C. and Clara Ann *Willis* Beaube.
- James Allen Beaube [Nov. 30, 1967 – May 30, 1987]. James is the son of William C. and Clara Ann *Willis* Beaube.
- Melissa Ann Beaube [Oct. 31, 1984], "infant." Melissa is the daughter of James Allen Beaube.

[I-82/83: Anderson, Beaube, Foster, Willis]

- Joe Bryant Willis, Sr. [April 25, 1917 – October 16, 1993]. Joe is the son of David Evan and Clara Ethel *Norwood* Willis, buried in Willis Cemetery.
- Maude Lee *(Anderson)* Willis [June 8, 1923 – July 2, 1986] Maude and her sister, Ruby *Anderson* Beaube, below, are daughters of Oscar H. and Lizzie *Bufkin* Anderson, buried in plot E-44. Maude and Joe Bryant Willis, Sr. share a common stone with the words: "Married Jan. 2, 1938."
- Augustine Lynn Foster [Aug. 30, 1934 – Oct. 16, 1993], "A Good Man."
- Betty *Willis* Foster [Sept. 10, 1941 – XXXX]. A temporary funeral home marker tells us that Betty died on February 11, 2015. She is the daughter of Joe Bryant and Maude Lee *Anderson* Willis. Betty and Augustine Lynn Foster share a common stone with the words: "Wed 12-4-1959."
- James E. Beaube [Dec. 12, 1921 – XXXX]. A temporary funeral home marker tells us that James died on February 26, 2015. James is the son of Columbus E. and Mattie *Powers* Beaube, buried in Hinds County.
- Ruby *Anderson* Beaube [Nov. 20, 1926 – Dec. 25, 2011]. Ruby married James E. Beaube in 1946, and they share a common grave location.

[I-84: no stones]

[I-85: Stephens, Wood, Wooley]

- Henry L. Stephens [August 20, 1916 – July 19, 1980], "PVT, US ARMY, WORLD WAR II." This is a bronze military plaque. He also has a civilian stone with the words: "Husband & Father." Henry shares a common grave location with his wife Audrey *Byrd* Stephens, whom he married in 1940. Audrey's side has only her birth date of January 10, 1920.

- Arthur Clyde "Tinsy" Wood, Jr. [August 18, 1940 – July 29, 1996], "Husband & Father." Arthur is the son of Arthur Clyde and Eva *Anderson* Wood, buried in combined plot M-44/45. He shares a common grave location with Martha *Stephens* Wood, whom he married in 1966. Martha's side has only her birth date of January 27, 1944.
- Audra Claire Wooley [Feb. 20, 2000]

[I-86: Brown, Emanuel, Marx, Prisock]. This plot has a memorial stone bearing the names PRISOCK and EMANUEL.

- Barnie Elliott Prisock [June 22, 1900 – Dec. 31, 1972], "Daddy."
- Carrie *Brown* Prisock [Jan. 21, 1905 – Mar. 26, 2001], "Mama." Carrie is the daughter of S. F. "Sol" Brown, buried in Sarepta Cemetery. She and Barnie Elliott Prisock share a common stone with the words: "Married Apr. 5, 1924."
- Bennett Cammack Emanuel [Mar. 5, 1928 – Jan. 30, 1991], a Mason. Bennett is the son of Samuel E. and Clara *Cammack* Emanuel, buried in Jefferson County.
- Justine *Prisock* Emanuel [Nov. 2, 1926 – June 9, 2001]. Justine is the daughter of Barnie Elliott and Carrie *Brown* Prisock. She and Bennett Cammack Emanuel share a common stone with the words: "Married Dec. 22, 1970."
- Howard Brown "Man" Prisock [Feb. 11, 1934 – July 21, 2004]. Howard is the son of Barnie Elliott and Carrie *Brown* Prisock. He married Norma Jean Hannis in 1953 and/or 1955, the marriage records having two separate entries with the same names.
- Henry Samuel Marx [Sep. 25, 1931 – Aug. 2, 2013], "A1C, US AIR FORCE." This is a military stone. He also has a civilian stone bearing the Star of David and the words: "son of Herman and Miriam Marx." His parents are buried in Port Gibson Jewish Cemetery. He shares the common stone with his wife, Peggy *Brown* Marx, whose side has only her birth date of February 1, 1938.

[I-87: Easley, Peck]

- Obadiah Weldon Easley [Dec. 25, 1901 – Oct. 11, 1971]
- Pauline *(Peck)* Easley [Sept. 19, 1908 – Dec. 1, 1975]. Pauline is the wife of Obadiah Weldon Easley.

[I-88: Howard, Smith]

- Douglas Turner Howard [October 21, 1912 – November 2, 2005]. Douglas is the son of Jasper Douglas and Kate *Turner* Howard, buried in Howard Cemetery. He was first married to Mildred Pratt Howard, buried in plot A-74.
- Jonnel *Smith* Howard [March 3, 1911 – April 11, 1971]. Jonnel is the wife of Douglas Turner Howard.

[I-89: Barland, Rogers]

- Bernard Barland [Nov. 26, 1914 – Apr. 26, 1983]. Bernard is the son of Henry Fredrick and Emma *Perry* Barland, buried in plot N-4.
- Margaret *(Rogers)* Barland [Sept. 13, 1919 – Dec. 16, 2001]. Margaret is the wife of Bernard Barland, and they share a common grave location. They have a daughter, Katie M. *Barland* Howard, buried in plot J-50.

[I-90: Vaughan]

- Robert L. "Bobby" Vaughan [June 12, 1927 – September 9, 1993]. Robert shares a common grave location with Martha *St. John* Vaughan, whom he married in 1953. Martha's side has only her birth date of October 6, 1928.

[I-91: Buckner, Furr, Perkins]

- Colin Beverly Buckner [Feb. 21, 1902 – Apr. 13, 1985]
- Gladys *(Furr)* Perkins Buckner [July 30, 1900 – Jan. 1, 1995]. Gladys is the daughter of J. Frank and

Ella V. *Leonard* Furr, buried in Jefferson County. She is the wife of Colin Beverly Buckner, and they share a common stone. She had previously been married to a Mr. Perkins.

- Liz Perkins [1930 – 2008]. This information is from a temporary funeral home marker, and no other information is available.

[I-92/93: Corbin, Price]

- Joseph D. Price, Jr. [Mar. 12, 1927 – Oct. 31, 1986], "S1, US NAVY, WORLD WAR II." This is a bronze military plaque. Joseph also has a civilian stone that he shares with Rose *Hammett* Price. Rose's side has only her birth date of March 30, 1932.
- Lori Lee *Corbin* Price [July 23, 1960 – Sept. 19, 1994]. Lori is the wife of Steven Edward Price, son of Joseph D. and Rose *Hammett* Price, and they share a common stone. Steven's side has only his birth date of June 15, 1952.

[I-94: Coulon, Hammett, Tanner, Whaley]

- T. K. Hammett [Nov. 3, 1911 – May 10, 1982]
- Ruby *T(anner)*. Hammett [Oct. 7, 1910 – Apr. 18, 1987]. Ruby is the daughter of Joe N. and Olis *Faris* Tanner, buried in plot H-98. She married T. K. Hammett in 1929.
- Angieland Rosa *(Coulon)* Whaley [Oct. 26, 1913 – May 20, 1982]

[I-95/96: Burch, Hannis, Jordan]

- Charlie Clarence Jordan [Sep. 28, 1907 – Apr. 20, 1982], "MM1, US NAVY, WORLD WAR II." This is a bronze military plaque. He also has a civilian stone. Charlie is the son of Andrew Jackson and Henry Rohelia *Harrell* Jordan, buried in Herlong Cemetery.
- Martha Elizabeth *(Hannis)* Jordan [Aug. 5, 1909 – February 26, 1994]. Martha is the daughter of W. T. Hannis, buried in plot J-19, and Mattie E. *Hennington* Hannis in Sarepta Cemetery. She married Charlie Clarence Jordan in 1927, and they share a common grave location.
- James Decator Burch [Mar. 2, 1928 – Feb. 16, 1999], "S1, US NAVY, WORLD WAR II." This is a bronze military plaque. He also has a civilian stone.
- Tanzy *Jordan* Burch [July 7, 1931 – June 29, 2009]. Tanzy is the daughter of Charlie Clarence and Martha Elizabeth *Hannis* Jordan. She is the wife of James Decator Burch, and they share a common grave location.

[I-97: Allen, Rabbeth, Robbins]

- Mildred *A(llen)*. Robbins [Sept. 20, 1898 – Feb. 12, 1982]. Mildred is the daughter of William L. and Eula *Slay* Allen, buried in plot H-11.
- Charles R. Rabbeth [Dec. 13, 1909 – Dec. 25, 1994]

[I-98: Florence, Franklin, Puckett]

- E. Harold Puckett [Dec. 10, 1917 – Mar. 15, 1983]
- Ruth *F(ranklin)*. Puckett [Feb. 23, 1913 – June 28, 1985], "A Tender Mother and Faithful Friend." Ruth married E. Harold Puckett in 1961, and they share a common grave location. She had previously been married to a Mr. Florence.
- Edgar Harold Puckett, Jr. [Sep. 15, 1935 – Jul. 7, 1998], "1ST SGT, US ARMY." This is a military stone. He also has a civilian stone. Edgar is the son of E. Harold Puckett. He married Mrs. Mary L. *Stennett* Ross in 1978.
- Ruby F. Puckett [Jan. 20, 1936 – Aug. 15, 2013]

[I-99: no stones]

Section J

8	7	6	5	4	3	2	1
9	10	11	12	13	14	15	16
24	23	22	21	20	19	18	17
25	26	27	28	29	30	31	32
40	39	38	37	36	35	34	33
41	42	43	44	45	46	47	48
56	55	54	53	52	51	50	49
57	58	59	60	61	62	63	64
72	71	70	69	68	67	66	65
73	74	75	76	77	78	79	80
88	87	86	85	84	83	82	81
89	90	91	92	93	94	95	96
104	103	102	101	100	99	98	97
105	106	107	108	109	110	111	112.

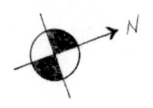

Section J

J-1: Harding, Kimbrell, Ramirez, Roan, Williams]
- Jack Eugene Harding [June 6, 1874 – March 2, 1954]
- Cora Pearl *(Kimbrell)* Harding [August 31, 1891 – February 9, 1978]. Cora is the wife of Jack Eugene Harding, and they share a common stone.
- Preston B. Williams [Feb. 26, 1893 – Nov. 17, 1953], "MISSISSIPPI, SGT, QMC, WORLD WAR I." This is a military stone. He also has a civilian stone.
- Ethel *Roan* Williams [Sept. 29, 1894 – Dec. 5, 1974]. Ethel is the daughter of John A. and Clara Anna *Porter* Roan, buried in Hedrick Cemetery. She is the wife of Preston B. Williams, and they share a common stone.
- Paullina Ramirez [April 16, 2014]
- Meylyn Paredes Ramirez [April 16, 2014]. Paullina and Meylyn share a common stone.

[J-2/15: Dungan, Lindsay, Mills, Owens]
- Evan Berry Owens [Aug. 10, 1875 – Sept. 12, 1952]. Evan married Mary Irby in 1895. Mary is buried in Sanders Cemetery, with a gravestone of identical design as that of Evan's stone. Besides those listed below, they have a daughter, Jewel *Owen* (sic) Harrison, buried in plot M-95.
- Marion Bruce Lindsay [November 18, 1886 – August 26, 1957]
- Myrtie *Owens* Lindsay [April 11, 1899 – April 30, 1977]. Myrtie is the daughter of Evan Berry and Mary *Irby* Owens. She married Marion Bruce Lindsay in 1926, and they share a common stone.
- Victor Hugo Dungan [May 28, 1905 – Apr. 29, 1970]. Victor is the son of Jud and Effie *Clanton* Dungan, buried in Jefferson County. His first marriage was to Emma Mae McBroom in 1942.
- Bess *Owens* Dungan [Feb. 11, 1909 – Aug. 11, 1999]. Bess is the daughter of Evan Berry and Mary *Irby* Owens. She is the wife of Victor Hugo Dungan, and they share a common stone.
- Harry Ogden Mills [May 1, 1912 – Dec. 7, 1974]
- Vera *Owens* Mills [Apr. 28, 1916 – July 14, 2003]. Vera is the daughter of Evan Berry and Mary *Irby* Owens. She is the wife of Harry Ogden Mills, and they share a common stone.
- Floyd Maurice Owen (sic) [August 25, 1919 – September 16, 1978]. Floyd is the son of Evan Berry and Mary *Irby* Owens.

[J-3/4: Anderson, Moore, Smith, Tatum]
- Walter Vernon Moore [June 17, 1881 – December 23, 1970]
- Mattie *Anderson* Moore [January 6, 1893 – November 23, 1973]. Mattie married Walter Vernon Moore

in 1908, and they share a common stone.

- Johnnie Carl Moore [December 3, 1912 – October 25, 1983], "TSGT, US ARMY, WORLD WAR II." This is a bronze military plaque. He also has a civilian stone. Johnnie is the son of Walter Vernon and Mattie *Anderson* Moore.
- Audrey *Smith* Moore [February 10, 1913 – March 27, 2002]. Audrey is the daughter of Marshal W. and Olivia *Case* Smith, buried in Jefferson County. She married Johnnie Carl Moore in 1952, and they share a common grave location.
- Barbara T(atum). Moore [Apr. 1, 1953 – May 14, 2009]. Barbara shares a common stone with Hal V. Moore, whom she married in 1977. Hal's side has only his birth date of December 29, 1946. Barbara was previously married to a Mr. Tatum.

[J-5: Hynum, McRaney]
- Wilford Carlos Hynum [July 4, 1899 – May 8, 1961]
- Mae *McRaney* Hynum [Dec. 9, 1898 – May 1, 1953]. Mae married Wilford Carlos Hynum in 1939, and they share a common stone.
- Billy Kent McRaney [July 29, 1930 – Jan. 28, 2007]. Billy married Mary Alice Haggan in 1954.
- Mary Lorene McRaney [Sept. 20, 1925 – Mar. 2, 2005]. Mary and Billy Kent McRaney share a common stone.

[J-6/7a: Harlan, Harrell, Loyd]
- Henry Purser Harlan [July 22, 1889 – Oct. 25, 1932], "Father."
- Iona *Harrell* Harlan [Feb. 7, 1886 – Nov. 17, 1953], "Mother." Iona married Henry Purser Harlan in 1907, and they share a common grave location.
- Lucye E. Harlan [Nov. 24, 1911 – Oct. 7, 2006]. Lucye is the daughter of Henry Purser and Iona *Harrell* Harlan.
- William Earl Loyd [Aug. 10, 1909 – Sept. 26, 1988], "Poppy." William is the son of William Abbott and Charlotte *Harrell* Loyd, buried in Hedrick Cemetery.
- Ethel *Harlan* Loyd [Apr. 4, 1914 – Nov. 9, 2000], "Mamaw." Ethel is the daughter of Henry Purser and Iona *Harrell* Harlan. She married William Earl Loyd in 1935, and they share a common grave location.
- Glen Earl Loyd [Sept. 17, 1941]. Glen's inscription reads: "The Littlest Angel."
- Henry Earle Harland (sic) [Feb. 3, 1917 – Jan. 14, 1922], "son of H. P. & I. I. Harland."
- Henry P. Harlan [May 30, 1922 – Mar. 2, 1967]. Henry is the son of Henry Purser and Iona *Harrell* Harlan.
- Mary W. Harlan [Jan. 17, 1923 – June 4, 2007]. Henry P. and Mary W. Harlan share a common grave location.
- James Sylvester Harlan [July 23, 1926 – Nov. 9, 1994]. James is the son of Henry Purser and Iona *Harrell* Harlan.

[J-7b: Alston, Burkley, May]
- Percy G. Alston [August 29, 1878 – November 29, 1945]
- Chess B(urkley). Alston [November 30, 1884 – March 12, 1978]. Chess is the daughter of Joseph Lorenzo and Maggie *Welch* Burkley, buried in Jefferson County. She is the wife of Percy G. Alston, and they share a common grave location.
- Percy A. May [October 26, 1917 – August 7, 1978]
- Arcola *A(lston)*. May [December 19, 1904 – August 16, 1983]. Arcola is the daughter of Percy G. and Chess *Burkley* Alston. She married Percy A. May in 1978, and they share a common grave location.

[J-8: no stones]
[J-9: Bell]
- Daniel Ray Bell [June 5, 1959 – Oct. 13, 2013]

[J-10: Floyd, Goodrum, Kirtfield, Lawrence, Moore]
- L. W. (John) Goodrum [Sept. 1, 1902 – Oct. 8, 1961]
- Edwin Earl Floyd [Feb. 4, 1908 – June 21, 1985]. Edwin is the son of Kenneth E. and Mahala *Jobe* Floyd, buried in Jobe-Floyd Cemetery.
- Effie Mae *Moore* Floyd [Sept. 25, 1912 – Feb. 3, 2005]. Effie and Edwin share a common grave location, a vase bearing the words: "Married Sept. 6, 1930."
- Walter Ray Moore [May 10, 1916 – Dec. 26, 1958], "Daddy." Walter is the son of Mae *Boyd* Moore, buried in Baker Cemetery.
- Louise *Lawrence* Moore [Oct. 6, 1916 – June 20, 2013], "Mother." Louise married Walter Ray Moore in 1937, and they share a common grave location.
- Mary Lynn *Moore* Kirtfield [June 21, 1945 – Dec. 9, 1999], "Loving Wife and Mother."

[J-11: Cates, Davis, Stamps, Stonaker, Young]
- Charlie M. Stamps [1875 – 1958]
- Nonnie E. *(Stonaker)* Stamps [1877 – 1962]. Nonnie married Charlie M. Stamps in 1899.
- Talmadge M. Stamps [1901 – 1972]. Talmadge is the son of Charlie M. and Nonnie E. *Stonaker* Stamps.
- Prenchel *(Stamps)* Young [1902 – 1984]. Prenchel is the daughter of Charlie M. and Nonnie E *Stonaker* Stamps. She married Eddie Davis in 1922. She later married a Mr. Young.
- M. Eugene Davis [1923 – 1975]. M. Eugene is the son of Eddie and Prenchel *Stamps* Davis.
- Mary Belle Stamps [1905 – 1986]. Mary is the daughter of Charlie M. and Nonnie E. *Stonaker* Stamps.
- Carl N. Cates [1904 – 1958]
- C. B. *(Stamps)* Cates [1908 – 1985]. C. B. is the daughter of Charlie M. and Nonnie E. *Stonaker* Stamps, and wife of Carl N. Cates.

[J-12: Baker, Greer, Horn, Jordan, McRaney]
- Taylor Cleveland Baker [Oct. 20, 1884 – Mar. 6, 1963], "Precious Daddy." Taylor was married twice, the second time to Mrs. Mary Jane *Clark* Stout in 1957.
- Angeline *McRaney* Baker [Aug. 16, 1888 – Jan. 9, 1955], "Loving Mother." Angeline is the wife of Taylor Cleveland Baker, and they share a common grave location. Besides their son listed below, other children include Viver *Baker* Hannis, buried in plot I-31, and Georgia Laudee *Baker* Williams, buried in Hermanville Cemetery.
- Charles W. Baker [July 25, 1919 – May 13, 1999], "Everloving Husband and Daddy." Charles is the son of Taylor Cleveland and Angeline *McRaney* Baker.
- Olis *Greer* Baker [July 13, 1919 – January 14, 1994], "Beloved Wife & Mother." Olis is the daughter of C. C. and Willie R. *Jones* Greer, buried in plot A-146. She married Charles W. Baker in 1938.
- Emmett P. Horn, Jr. [April 22, 1927 – April 11, 2012], "TEC 5, US ARMY, WORLD WAR II." This is a bronze military plaque. He also has a civilian stone with "Father," and giving his middle name as PERRY.
- Sarah Nell *Baker* Horn [January 24, 1924 – June 7, 2012], "Mother." Sarah is the daughter of Taylor Cleveland and Angeline *McRaney* Baker. She is the wife of Emmett P. Horn, Jr., and they share a common stone.
- Robert Clark "Butch" Jordan, Jr. [May 21, 1943 – Oct. 20, 2004]. Robert is the son of Robert Clark and Frances *Hynum* Jordan, buried in plot J-32.

[J-13: Hubbard, Minnis]
- Harry William Minnis [March 23, 1924 – June 13, 1965], "TEXAS, PVT, US MARINE CORPS RES, WORLD WAR II." This is a military stone. Harry is the son of Harry O. and Beatrice Louise *Callender* Minnis, buried in plot H-47.
- John K. Hubbard [Nov. 20, 1877 – Oct. 3, 1956]

[J-14: Huff, McKewen, Rodgers]
- Jodie S. McKewen [Mar. 17, 1891 – May 28, 1955]
- Lillian M. *Huff* McKewen Rodgers [Nov. 10, 1896 – Oct. 6, 1994]. Lillian is the wife of Jodie S. McKewen, and they share a common grave location. She later married a Mr. Rodgers.

[J-16: Abbott, Boren]
- Edgar Allen Boren [Feb. 3, 1922 – Aug. 20, 1991], "CPL, US ARMY, WORLD WAR II." This is a bronze military plaque. Edgar is the son of Thomas Gordon and Marie *Higgins* Boren, buried in plot E-38.
- Sallie *Abbott* Boren [Feb. 17, 1933 – Apr. 24, 1978]. Sallie is the daughter of Thomas Vernie and Elva *Pierce* Abbott, buried in Jefferson County. She married Edgar Allen Boren in 1950, and they share a common stone.

[J-17: Gordon, Traylor, Walsh]
- Harry Gordon [Dec. 1, 1869 – April 11, 1956]
- Ed Walsh [died Feb. 3, 1956]. Ed may have also used the last name of GENTRY.
- Percy R. Traylor [Oct. 11, 1885 – Jan. 14, 1961]. Percy is the son of A. R. and Mary Alice *Sojourner* Traylor, buried in Copiah County.

[J-18: Blake, Culley]
- Dee Lambert Culley [Mar. 13, 1886 – Mar. 22, 1956]
- Minnie *B(lake)*. Culley [Jan. 27, 1890 – June 11, 1973]. Minnie is the wife of Dee Lambert Culley, and they share a common grave location.
- L. W. Culley [Nov. 15, 1930 – Dec. 22, 2008], "Loving Husband, Father and Grandfather." L. W. is the son of Dee Lambert and Minnie *Blake* Culley.
- Maria M. Culley [Aug. 15, 1922 – Feb. 4, 2010], "Loving Wife, Mother and Grandmother." Maria is the wife of L. W. Culley, and they share a common stone.
- Lambert David Culley [Feb. 15, 1988 – June 28, 2007]

[J-19: Daniel, Hannis]
- W. T. Hannis [Jan. 4, 1868 – Mar. 27, 1964]. W. T. is the husband of Mattie E. *Hennington* Hannis, buried in Sarepta Cemetery. They have children, Auvern James Hannis, buried in plot I-31, and Martha Elizabeth *Hannis* Jordan in combined plot I-95/96.
- Willie D. Hannis [Oct. 8, 1901 – Sept. 3, 1956], "a faithful, loving husband and daddy." Willie is the son of W. T. and Mattie E. *Hennington* Hannis.
- Earline *D(aniel)*. Hannis [Apr. 23, 1906 – Feb. 3, 1993], "a faithful, loving wife and mother." Earline is the wife of Willie D. Hannis, and they share a common grave location. They have a daughter, Hazel *Hannis* Ellis, buried in plot K-40.

[J-20/21: Bufkin, Daugherty, Fuller, McIlvoy]
- Henry David Bufkin [Oct. 1, 1891 – Mar. 15, 1972]
- Mary Elizabeth *(Daugherty)* Bufkin [Nov. 21, 1901 – Feb. 23, 1982]. Mary married Henry David Bufkin in 1919, and they share a common grave location.
- Mack Fuller [Aug. 16, 1929 – Feb. 7, 1957]
- Doris *(Bufkin)* Fuller McIlvoy [June 3, 1924 – Nov. 17, 1984]. Doris is the daughter of Henry David and Mary Elizabeth *Daugherty* Bufkin, and wife of Mack Fuller. She later married Lester McIlvoy in 1964.
- Beverly J. Fuller [August 22, 1950 – June 21, 2012]. Beverly is the daughter of Mack and Doris *Bufkin* Fuller.

[J-22: Cox]
- John Cox [July 14, 1910 – July 24, 1971]. John and his brother, below, are sons of Mamie Garrett Cox, buried in plot H-49.

- Robert K. Cox [July 29, 1912 – July 19, 1974]
- Mary B. Cox [Dec. 25, 1916 – Oct. 22, 2011]
- Margaret C. Cox [Sept. 15, 1942 – Aug. 18, 2012]

[J-23: King, McCoy]
- Thomas Edgar King [1885 – 1960]
- Maude *McCoy* King [1887 – 1963]. Maude is the wife of Thomas Edgar King, and they share a common grave location.
- Roy E. King [Dec. 16, 1913 – Oct. 22, 1982]. Roy is the son of Thomas Edgar and Maude *McCoy* King. He married Mrs. Katherine Lucille *Watkins* Lunn in 1963. Katherine is buried in plot G-34.
- Thomas Leon King [Oct. 23, 1941 – April 13, 1958]. Thomas is the son of Roy E. King.

[J-24: no stones]
[J-25: no stones]
[J-26: Welch, Westrope]
- Dewitt Talmage Westrope [Jan. 26, 1887 – July 16, 1969]
- Vieta Grace *(Welch)* Westrope [Oct. 20, 1904 – Feb. 24, 1995]. Vieta is the wife of Dewitt Talmage Westrope.
- Monroe Bailey Westrope [Oct. 6, 1888 – Feb. 17, 1960], "MISSISSIPPI, PVT, 63 CO, 162 DEPOT BRIGADE, WORLD WAR I." This is a military stone. Monroe married Mattie Weathersby in 1920.
- Robert Westrope [November 3, 1909 – July 26, 1971]

[J-27: Jennings]
- Perry Jeanne Jennings [Feb. 18, 1959 – Oct. 10, 1959]

[J-28: Barland, Snellgrove]
- Johnnie Lee Barland [Dec. 24, 1897 – Sept. 17, 1959], "MISSISSIPPI, PVT, BTRY E, 62 ARTY CAC, WORLD WAR I." This is a military stone. He also has a civilian stone. Johnnie is the son of John M. Barland, buried in plot N-1.
- Iva *S(nellgrove)*. Barland [May 3, 1903 – May 29, 1989]. Iva and Johnnie Lee Barland share a common stone with the words: "Wed Dec. 26, 1922."

[J-29: Montgomery, Smith]
- Eugene Coulson Montgomery [Oct. 27, 1904 – Sept. 9, 1990]. Eugene is the son of Robert Ligon and Maude Desiree *Tenney* Montgomery, buried in Hermanville Cemetery.
- Audrey *Smith* Montgomery [Dec. 20, 1909 – Apr. 8, 1990]. Audrey is the daughter of Charles C. and Agnes *Goosey* Smith, also buried in Hermanville Cemetery. She and Eugene Coulson Montgomery share a common stone with the words: "Married June 13, 1925."
- Charles Robert Montgomery [April 26, 1926 – Jan. 16, 1959]. Charles is the son of Eugene Coulson and Audrey *Smith* Montgomery.

[J-30: Fizer, Green, Sanders]
- Clarence P. Sanders [Nov. 7, 1894 – July 19, 1970], "MISSISSIPPI, PVT, 1 DEVELOPMENT BN, WORLD WAR I." This is a military stone. He also has a civilian stone. Clarence is the son of Willie B. and Pink Ann *Westrope* Sanders, buried in Hermanville Cemetery.
- Dorothy *G(reen)*. Sanders [Oct. 19, 1901 – July 7, 1995]. Dorothy and her sister Myrtle, below, are daughters of Willie W. and Rebecca *Moody* Green, buried in Hinds County. Dorothy married Clarence P. Sanders in 1941, and they share a common grave location.
- Henry Paxton Fizer [1888 – 1958]
- Myrtle *Green* Fizer [1905 – 1970]. Myrtle is the wife of Henry Paxton Fizer. They have a daughter, Patsy *Fizer* Byrd, buried in plot K-10.

[J-31: Davenport, Sammelman, Turner]

- Pearl Shelby Turner [Sept. 2, 1902 – Aug. 27, 1958]. Pearl is the sister of Elizabeth *Turner* Davenport, below.
- Richard Joseph Davenport [March 27, 1909 – October 12, 1993]. Richard is the son of Joseph Thompson and Martha Virginia *Bryan* Davenport, buried in Pattona Cemetery.
- Elizabeth *Turner* Davenport [June 25, 1912 – January 9, 1999]. Elizabeth married Richard Joseph Davenport in 1948, and they share a common grave location. She had previously been married to a Mr. Sammelman.

[J-32: Hynum, Jordan]

- Robert Clark Jordan, Sr. [Jun. 10, 1918 – Oct. 11, 1975], "SMSGT, US AIR FORCE, WORLD WAR II, KOREA." This is a military stone. Robert is the son of Robert Benton and Eunice *Hudson* Jordan, buried in plot J-53.
- Frances *H(ynum)*. Jordan [Feb. 27, 1918 – Sept. 14, 2002], "Loving Mother & Grandmother." Frances is the wife of Robert Clark Jordan, Sr. Besides their daughter, below, they have a son, Robert Clark Jordan, Jr., buried in plot J-12.
- Pamela Ann Jordan [Nov. 6, 1957 – Apr. 25, 1958]. Pamela is the daughter of Robert Clark and Frances *Hynum* Jordan.

[J-33: Davis, Segrest]

- Carrie E. Davis [1881 – 1963]. Carrie and her brother Edward, below, are children of John W. and Julia A. *Havis* Davis, buried in combined plot A-94/95.
- Edward Davis [Sept. 10, 1886 – Dec. 8, 1959]
- Effie *S(egrest)*. Davis [Feb. 21, 1884 – Oct. 12, 1966. Effie is the daughter of Lewis Osborn and Virginia Elmer *Shelton* Segrest, buried in Copiah County. She married Edward Davis in 1908, and they share a common stone.

[J-34: Carpenter, Harmon, Holder, Roan]

- John G. Harmon [Aug. 17, 1884 – Apr. 2, 1961]
- Hattie V. *(Carpenter)* Harmon [July 5, 1891 – May 26, 1976]. Hattie is the daughter of James Marcellons and Eugenia A. *Darden* Carpenter, buried in Hutchinson Cemetery. She married John G. Harmon in 1916, and they share a common stone.
- Max Holder [February 18, 1891 – December 7, 1976]. Max is the son of William Holder, buried in Jefferson County, and Sarah *Price* Holder, buried in Herlong Cemetery.
- Nonnie *R(oan)*. Holder [November 18, 1896 – June 1, 1965]. Nonnie is the daughter of John A. and Clara Anna *Porter* Roan, buried in Hedrick Cemetery. She married Max Holder in 1921, and they share a common grave location.

[J-35: Headley]

- Chalon S. Headley [Dec. 22, 1919 – Dec. 2, 1977], "LT COL, US ARMY, WORLD WAR II, KOREA." This is a bronze military plaque. He also has a civilian stone showing his middle name as SHEPARD and the nickname, "Grandcha." Chalon is the son of Frank L. and Anna *Hunt* Headley, buried in plot G-21.
- Helen Lula "GG" Headley [Nov. 1, 1919 – June 16, 2006], "Grandmamma." Helen is the wife of Chalon S. Headley, and they share a common stone.

[J-36: Lowe, McCool]

- Robert Baker Lowe [Sept. 1, 1901 – Oct. 23, 1961]
- LaVerne *McCool* Lowe [Jan. 8, 1912 – Feb. 6, 1971]. LaVerne is the wife of Robert Baker Lowe.
- Wade Hampton Lowe, III [February 16, 1941 – December 17, 2008]. Wade is the son of Robert Baker and LaVerne *McCool* Lowe. He married Jo Anne Miller in 1962.

[J-37/38: Davis, Harrell, Snodgrass, Stewart, Trim, Westrope]

- Henry L. Trim [1875 – 1962]
- Cornelia A. *(Westrope)* Trim [1895 – 1969]. Cornelia married Henry L. Trim in 1922, and they share a common stone.
- Oscar Terry Davis [Mar. 12, 1894 – June 6, 1974], "Father."
- Johnny Bryant Davis [Aug. 18, 1923 – Dec. 9, 1961], "MISSISSIPPI, PFC, US ARMY, WORLD WAR II." This is a bronze military plaque. He also has a civilian stone with the word: "Son." Johnny is the son of Oscar Terry Davis, and they share a common grave location.
- Terry Lyle Stewart [Mar. 19, 1949 – Sept. 9, 2005], "Grandson."
- Myra "Ole Nan" *(Trim)* Snodgrass [Oct. 19, 1904 – July 18, 1978]. Myra first married George Roy Harrell in 1921. She later married a Mr. Snodgrass.

[J-39: Irby, Sanders, Westrope, Worsham]
- Joseph Miller Westrope [Sept. 30, 1898 – June 7, 1985]
- Ora Delle *Irby* Westrope [May 19, 1907 – Sept. 24, 1967]. Ora and her sister Ona, below, are daughters of William Dean and Gertrude *Baker* Irby, buried in plot A-129. Ora is the wife of Joseph Miller Westrope, and they share a common stone.
- Ona *Irby* Sanders [November 21, 1904 – March 27, 1994], "Mother." Ona married Clarence A. Sanders in 1925. Clarence is buried in Sanders Cemetery. They have a son, William Lee Sanders, buried in plot M-120.
- Robert R. Worsham [Dec. 27, 1907 – Feb. 20, 2003], "BM2, US NAVY, WORLD WAR II ..Beloved Uncle." This is a military stone. Robert is the foster-son of William Dean and Gertrude *Baker* Irby.

[J-40: Fugate, Holder, Richardson, Rogers, Starnes]
- John Rogers [April 20, 1881 – July 22, 1962]. John is the son of William H. and Jane *Clark* Rogers, buried in Hedrick Cemetery.
- Roy B. Starnes [Oct. 17, 1892 – Aug. 19, 1965]
- William Carl Holder [February 3, 1889 – October 4, 1971]. William is the son of William Holder, buried in Jefferson County, and Sarah *Price* Holder, buried in Herlong Cemetery.
- Beatrice *F(ugate)*. Richardson [April 6, 1912 – April 26, 1965], "Mother." Beatrice married Walter C. Richardson in 1959 and, according to marriage records, again in 1961. Walter is buried in plot M-92.

[J-41: Duncan, Pearson, Pettway, Rushing, Smith]
- George B. Pearson [June 16, 1898 – Apr. 18, 1988], "Beloved Husband-Father." George is the son of Lawrence S. and Sarah Jane *Wood* Pearson, buried in plot A-18a.
- Mae "Sweet" *R(ushing)*. S(mith). Pearson [Jan. 24, 1904 – Feb. 17, 1981]. Mae married George B. Pearson in 1939. She was previously married to Emmette Smith, buried in Jefferson County.
- Bobbie *Smith* Pettway [Aug. 13, 1925 – Dec. 21, 1981]. Bobbie is the daughter of Emmette and Mae *Rushing* Smith.
- Opal Lanell "Polly" *Smith* Duncan [Jan. 12, 1931 – Apr. 18, 2009], "Mother" and "loving wife of Amos C. Duncan, Jr." Opal is the daughter of Emmette and Mae *Rushing* Smith. She married Ernest Mark Smith, Jr. in 1951. She later married Mr. Duncan.

[J-42: Moss, Roddy]
- Eddy Jackson Roddy [Jan. 5, 1909 – Jan. 29, 1965]
- Tina Christine *(Moss)* Roddy [July 19, 1925 – March 25, 2007], "A loving mother and a faithful friend." Tina is the wife of Eddy Jackson Roddy.

[J-43: Chamberlain, Cogan, Fulton]
- Sidney Lee Chamberlain [Sept. 14, 1892 – May 2, 1964]. Sidney is the son of Thomas Jefferson and Johnnie Chamberlain, buried in Jefferson County.
- Cleora *(Fulton)* Chamberlain Cogan [Feb. 27, 1921 – Feb. 10, 1998]. Cleora is the daughter of David

Rivers and Cleora *Cordes* Fulton, also buried in Jefferson County. She was first married to Sydney Lee Chamberlain, and after his death, married Ernest Chilton Cogan in 1965. Ernest is buried in Jefferson County.

[J-44: Oliver, Stampley]

- Cornelius Oliver [July 9, 1894 – April 4, 1964], "MISSISSIPPI, PFC, BTRY F, 264 FIELD ARTY, WORLD WAR I." This is a military stone. He also has a civilian stone that gives his middle initial as L.
- Annie *Stampley* Oliver [April 22, 1900 – July 27, 1975]. Annie is the wife of Cornelius L. Oliver, and they share a common stone.

[J-45: Hynum, Rigdon]

- James Thomas Hynum [Sept. 22, 1923 – June 5, 1989], "CPL, US ARMY, WORLD WAR II." This is a bronze military plaque. He also has a civilian stone with the word: "Father." James is the son of Murry A. and Pauline *Mitchell* Hynum, buried in plot G-30. After the death of his first wife, he married Janie Elizabeth Way in 1966.
- Willie *Rigdon* Hynum [Aug. 16, 1927 – Aug. 18, 1963], "Mother." Willie married James Thomas Hynum in 1946, and they share a common grave location.

[J-46: Rogillio, Tanner]

- Alva H. Rogillio [1901 – 1963]. Alva is the son of Whitfield and Ella *McMurchy* Rogillio, buried in Jefferson County.
- Josie *T(anner)*. Rogillio [1917 – 2003]. Josie is the daughter of Joe N. and Olis *Faris* Tanner, buried in plot H-98. She is the wife of Alva H. Rogillio, and they share a common stone.

[J-47: Millican, Payne, Williams, Winkley]

- Dan Williams [May 1, 1895 – Mar. 2, 1963]. Dan is the son of Hugh and Lulu *Griffin* Williams, buried in Hermanville Cemetery.
- Willie *(Millican)* Williams [Oct. 25, 1898 – Oct. 17, 1976]. Willie married Dan Williams in 1936, and they share a common grave location. She was previously married to a Mr. Payne.
- Brien Robert Winkley [May 21, 1921 – October 1, 1996]. Brien shares a common stone with Mary Elizabeth Winkley. Mary's side has only her birth date of October 19, 1925.

[J-48/49/64/65: Allred, Beall, Bufkin, Carter, Dowdell, Easley, Montgomery, Roan]

- Virgie *Beall* Allred [Jan. 6, 1890 – Sept. 30, 1975]. Virgie is the sister of Alice *Beall* Carter, below.
- Curtis Carey Carter [Dec. 16, 1895 – June 19, 1966]
- Alice *Beall* Carter [Dec. 29, 1896 – Nov. 11, 1967]. Alice is the wife of Curtis Carey Carter, and they share a common grave location.
- Malcolm Montgomery [July 4, 1902 – Jan. 10, 1963]. Malcolm and his brother Everette, below, are sons of Charlie M. and Sarah M. *Pritchard* Montgomery, buried in Jefferson County.
- Myrtie *R(oan)*. Montgomery [April 22, 1902 – Sept. 27, 1989]. Myrtie and her sister Jewell, below, are daughters of John A. and Clara Anna *Porter* Roan, buried in Hedrick Cemetery. Myrtie is the wife of Malcolm Montgomery, and they share a common grave location.
- Everette Montgomery [Sept. 19, 1904 – Sept. 16, 1965]
- Jewell *R(oan)*. Montgomery [Aug. 1, 1904 – Mar. 6, 1987]. Jewell married Everette Montgomery in 1927, and they share a common grave location.
- Malcolm Montgomery, Jr. [Oct. 30, 1924 – Jan. 24, 2015], a Mason. Malcolm is the son of Malcolm and Myrtie *Roan* Montgomery.
- Jane *Dowdell* Montgomery [May 13, 1926 – May 17, 2014]. Jane is the daughter of David Merrick and Cornelia *Jett* Dowdell. They are buried in plot H-97, along with her first husband, Obadiah W. Easley, Jr., whom she married in 1946. She married Malcolm Montgomery, Jr. in 1958, and they share a common grave location.

- William Horace Bufkin [Aug. 7, 1908 – Dec. 8, 1974]. William is the son of R. Cooper and Nannie *Kendrick* Bufkin, buried in Copiah County.
- Lucille *Carter* Bufkin [Dec. 2, 1918 – Mar. 28, 1997]. Lucille is the daughter of Curtis Carey and Alice *Beall* Carter, and wife of William Horace Bufkin.
- Curtis Aubrey Carter [Nov. 18, 1927 – Aug. 13, 2004]. Curtis is the son of Curtis Carey and Alice *Beall* Carter.
- Gloria *Montgomery* Carter [April 29, 1929 – Jan. 17, 1999]. Gloria is the daughter of Everette and Jewell *Roan* Montgomery. She married Curtis Aubrey Carter in 1959, and they share a common grave location.

[J-50: Barland, Howard]
- Katie M. *(Barland)* Howard [Oct. 26, 1941 – Jan. 9, 2014], "Beloved Mother" and "Gone Fishing." Katie is the daughter of Bernard and Margaret *Rogers* Barland, buried in plot I-89. She married Joe Howard in 1958.
- Joe M. Howard, Jr. [Sept. 19, 1959 – Dec. 6, 2003]. Joe is the son of Joe and Katie M. *Barland* Howard.

[J-51: Beasley, Brooks, Hamilton, Hennington]
- Littrell A. Hamilton [July 14, 1896 – Sept. 15, 1969], "MISSISSIPPI, SGT, US ARMY, WORLD WAR I." This is a military stone.
- Hattie *B(rooks)*. Hamilton [1891 – 1965]. Hattie is the wife of Littrell A. Hamilton. She had previously married Anderson Hennington in 1914. Anderson is buried in Sarepta Cemetery.
- James Alfred Hennington [November 15, 1914 – July 7, 1967]. James is the son of Anderson and Hattie *Brooks* Hennington
- Edna *Beasley* Hennington [December 22, 1915 – April 14, 2004]. Edna is the wife of James Alfred Hennington, and they share a common grave location.

[J-52: Harrell, Richardson]
- Eugene M. Harrell [Oct. 2, 1922 – Jan. 21, 2000]
- Wilma *R(ichardson)*. Harrell [July 2, 1919 – May 1, 1997]. Wilma and Eugene share a common grave location, a vase with the words: "Married Mar. 24, 1945."

[J-53: Hudson, Jordan]
- Robert Benton Jordan [January 12, 1896 – March 21, 1966], "Father." Robert is the son of Walter A. and Rosa E. *Jones* Jordan, buried in Herlong Cemetery.
- Eunice *Hudson* Jordan [October 1, 1891 – August 14, 1974], "Mother." Eunice is the daughter of William Monroe and Emma George *Clark* Hudson, buried in Warren County. She married Robert Benton Jordan in 1916, and they share a common grave location. They have a son, Robert Clark Jordan, Sr., buried in plot J-32.
- William W. "Dub" Jordan [Sept. 8, 1929 – Apr. 8, 1998]. William is the son of Robert Benton and Eunice *Hudson* Jordan.

[J-54: Jones, Riley]
- Vernon Y. Jones [October 9, 1896 – April 20, 1966]. Vernon is the son of S. G. and Eliza Ellen *McGrew* Jones, buried in Herlong Cemetery.
- Elmo C. Jones [Feb. 26, 1925 – June 20, 1971]. Elmo is the son of Vernon Y. Jones.
- Faye *Riley* Jones [Sept. 28, 1927 – May 26, 1992]. Faye's epitaph reads: "Just Gone Fishing." Faye married Elmo C. Jones in 1946.

[J-55: Fife, Groves, Hutchins]
- Vera Mae *(Groves)* Hutchins [Mar. 22, 1897 – Sept. 15, 1980]
- James Aubrey Fife [Mar. 21, 1919 – Sep. 18, 1966], "S SGT, US ARMY, WORLD WAR II." This is a bronze military plaque. He also has a civilian stone. Aubrey is the son of William J. and Belle *Rushbrook* Fife, buried in plot I-34, Belle with the last name of BAKER.

- Helon *(Hutchins)* Fife [August 31, 1923 – November 20, 2001]. Helon is the daughter of Vera Mae *Groves* Hutchins. She is the wife of James Aubrey Fife, and they share a common grave location.

[J-56: Joyner]

- Atley Howard Joyner, Jr. [Oct. 24, 1922 – Feb. 7, 1989]. Atley shares a common stone with Hope *King* Joyner, whom he married in 1946. Hope's side has only her birth date of November 30, 1927.

[J-57: no stones]

[J-58: Campbell, Dent, Trim]

- Douglas E. Campbell [June 1, 1923 – Nov. 3, 1969], "Precious Father."
- Cleo *T(rim)*. Campbell [Mar. 12, 1930 – Oct. 2, 2008], "Loving Mother." Cleo is the daughter of Albert B. and Mary *Mercer* Trim, buried in combined plot E-7/8/9. She is the wife of Douglas E. Campbell, and they share a common grave location. They have a son, Douglas Elwood Campbell, Jr., buried in plot L-8.
- Warren B. "Pete" Dent [Jan. 4, 1930 – Feb. 10, 1999], "Husband of Cleo Campbell." Warren is the son of Warren W. and Laura *Moffett* Dent, buried in Jefferson County. He is Cleo's second husband, marrying in 1972.

[J-59: Funderburk, Smith]

- Clyde F. Smith [Sept. 26, 1908 – May 5, 1990]
- Mattie B. (Fundy) *(Funderburk)* Smith [June 22, 1907 – Sept. 12, 1979]. Mattie is the wife of Clyde F. Smith, and they share a common grave location.

[J-60: Dewitt, Newman]. This plot has a memorial stone bearing the name NEWMAN.

- Everett Cox Newman [Jan. 9, 1919 – March 12, 1968], "LCDR, USNR, WORLD WAR II." This is a military stone.
- Charles Puffer Newman [Jan. 25, 1949 – Aug. 13, 2003], "Son." Charles is the son of Everett Cox Newman. He married Mrs. Dianne *Bishop* Gillis in 1972.
- Robert I. Dewitt [May 10, 1920 – Dec. 1, 2003], "LT COL, US AIR FORCE, WORLD WAR II." This is a military stone.

[J-61: McConathy, Wheat]

- Harold Mason McConathy [Dec. 29, 1915 – Feb. 18, 1968]
- Helen *Wheat* McConathy [July 18, 1917 – July 1, 1992]. Helen is the wife of Harold Mason McConathy, and they share a common stone.

[J-62: Humphreys, Smith]

- James M. Smith [Sept. 30, 1913 – Dec. 29, 2002]
- Ethel *H(umphreys)*. Smith [Oct. 24, 1916 – Feb. 9, 1994]. Ethel is the daughter of S. W. and Janie *Ballard* Humphreys, buried in Jefferson County. She is the wife of James M. Smith, and they share a common grave location.

[J-63: Parman]

- Linnie Louise Parman [March 4, 1939 – July 3, 1980]

[J-66: Hamilton, Pullen, Wood]

- Arthur Rusk Pullen [February 29, 1908 – April 20, 1986]
- Margaret *Wood* Pullen [April 8, 1914 – June 9, 1997]. Margaret and her sister Lorraine, below, are daughters of Cleve E. and Jessie *Wright* Wood, buried in Shiloh Baptist Church Cemetery. Margaret is the wife of Arthur Rusk Pullen.
- Andrew E. Hamilton [February 9, 1919 – February 27, 1998]
- Lorraine *W(ood)*. Hamilton [November 17, 1918 – June 15, 2014]. Lorraine is the wife of Andrew E. Hamilton, and they share a common grave location.

[J-67: Ball, Pahnka]

- Benjamin F. Ball [June 13, 1915 – Mar. 8, 1970], "A Loving Husband and a Devoted Father."
- Lilly Nell (*Pahnka*) Ball [Feb. 27, 1915 – June 3, 1980]. Lilly is the daughter of Louis Allen and Della *Ahrend* Pahnka, buried in Jefferson County. She married Benjamin F. Ball in 1934, and they share a common grave location.

[J-68: Fife, Hynum]
- B. P. Hynum, Jr. [July, 1912 – June, 1970]
- Thelma Elois (*Fife*) Hynum [Apr., 1919 – Sept., 1992]. Thelma is the daughter of Wiley W. and Bina *Boren* Fife, buried in Sarepta Cemetery. She is the wife of B. P. Hynum, Jr., and they share a common grave location.
- Lewis Pierce Hynum, Sr. [Aug. 9, 1937 – June 4, 1994]. Lewis is the son of B. P. and Thelma Elois *Fife* Hynum.

[J-69: Mason]
- Lonnie Engram Mason [July 10, 1909 – Jan. 27, 1972], "Father."

[J-70: Kelly, Lutz, Storment, Taylor]
- Coral (*Lutz*) Storment [Nov. 24, 1897 – Feb. 22, 1989]. Coral and her sisters Iva and Alice, below, are daughters of Allen and Carrie *Barth* Lutz, buried in plot A-71.
- Alice (*Lutz*) Taylor [Dec. 21, 1913 – Nov. 2, 2011]. Alice and Coral share a common grave location.
- Huntley B. Kelly [July 31, 1906 – May 21, 1977]. Huntley is the son of John O'Quin and Mamie *Adair* Kelly, buried in Jefferson County.
- Iva (*Lutz*) Kelly [Aug. 6, 1906 – Feb. 18, 1999]. Iva is the wife of Huntley B. Kelly, and they share a common grave location.

[J-71: Chitty, Walter, Wilmarth]
- George W. Chitty [Oct. 5, 1891 – Dec. 3, 1974]
- Kathryn *W(ilmarth)*. Chitty [March 25, 1892 – Nov. 25, 1978]. Kathryn is the wife of George W. Chitty, and they share a common stone.
- Jack W. Chitty [1913 – 1989]. Jack is the son of George W. and Kathryn *Wilmarth* Chitty.
- Ruth *W(alter)*. Chitty [1914 – 1994]. Ruth is the wife of Jack W. Chitty, and they share a common stone.

[J-72: Campbell, Hennington]
- Lyman S. Campbell [June 22, 1891 – May 29, 1981], "Father." Lyman is the son of John G. and Mary H. *Thomas* Campbell, buried in Hermanville Cemetery.
- Myrtle *H(ennington)*. Campbell [Jan. 21, 1899 – Jan. 1, 1977], "Mother." Myrtle is the daughter of William A. and Martha *Bruce* Hennington, buried in plot H-46. She married Lyman S. Campbell in 1919, and they share a common grave location.

[J-73: Cogan, Sly]
- Shirley Arlene *Cogan* Sly [September 25, 1938 – June 30, 1978]. Shirley is the wife of Phillip William Sly, and they share a common stone. Phillip's side has only his birth date of January 25, 1938. An additional inscription reads: "Children Michele & Phillip Corey."

[J-74: no stones]
[J-75: no stones]
[J-76: no stones]
[J-77: no stones]
[J-78: no stones]
[J-79: Abney, Wood]
- Leo G. Abney [Mar. 12, 1898 – Apr. 23, 1972]
- Ruth (*Wood*) Abney [Feb. 24, 1891 – May 14, 1978]. Ruth is the daughter of John Booth and Margaret *Duval* Wood, buried in Shiloh Cemetery. She is the wife of Leo G. Abney.

[J-80: Crocker, Mercer, Sanders]
- Clyde W. Mercer [1904 – 1972]
- Grover H. Crocker [Aug. 6, 1910 – Jan. 18, 1980]
- Ruby *(Sanders)* Mercer Crocker [1921 – 1979]. Ruby is the wife of Clyde W. Mercer, her first husband, and they share a common stone. After his death she married Grover H. Crocker in 1973.

[J-81: Axley, Nesler, Sullivan, Thompson]

From *Port Gibson Reveille's* "Looking Back" column (This Week, 1979): "A single-engine plane crashed in Jefferson County in which three members of the Ron Nesler family died…"
- Joseph L. Nesler [June 19, 1914 – Oct. 13, 1972]
- Mildred *(Sullivan)* Nesler Axley [Nov. 30, 1917 – July 24, 1999]. Mildred is the wife of Joseph L. Nesler., and they share a common stone. After his death she married a Mr. Axley.
- Ronald J. Nesler [June 23, 1941 – June 5, 1979]. Ronald is the son of Joseph L. and Mildred *Sullivan* Nesler.
- Sandra *T(hompson)*. Nesler [Dec. 24, 1947 – June 5, 1979]. Sandra is the wife of Ronald J. Nesler.
- Jimmy ByRon Nesler [Oct. 7, 1974 – June 5, 1979]. Jimmy is the son of Ronald J. and Sandra *Thompson* Nesler. He was buried with his mother, and he shares a stone with both parents.

[J-82: Coleman, Sorrels]
- Samuel Perry Sorrels [November 23, 1897 – May 4, 1973]. Samuel is the son of S. P. and Beulah I. *Porter* Sorrels, buried in Sarepta Cemetery.
- Vera *Coleman* Sorrels [August 30, 1904 – October 17, 1982]. Vera is the wife of Samuel Perry Sorrels, and they share a common stone.

[J-83: Crapps, Hynum]
- Patrick W. "Pete" Hynum [Dec. 24, 1928 – Aug. 12, 2008], "Father." Patrick is the son of Lura B. and Oma Jordan Hynum, buried in Hynum Cemetery. After Ruby's death he married Mrs. Emily Jo *Windham* Walters in 1976.
- Ruby E. *(Crapps)* Hynum [April 26, 1934 – Dec. 2, 1973], "Mother." Ruby is the daughter of Paul L. and Thelma *Williams* Crapps, buried in Copiah County. Ruby married Patrick W. Hynum in 1951.

[J-84: Bunyard, Townsend]
- Austin E. Townsend [Dec. 8, 1912 – Feb. 2, 1995], "Father."
- Mary Bell *(Bunyard)* Townsend [Oct. 21, 1910 – Dec. 7, 1973], "Mother." Mary is the wife of Austin E. Townsend.
- Mary Lee Townsend [Sept. 21, 1936 – Mar. 13, 1995], "Sister." Mary is the daughter of Austin E. and Mary Bell *Bunyard* Townsend, and the three of them share a common grave location.

[J-85: Barbee, Cassell, Hanson, Smith]
- James Willie Smith [1909 – 1976]
- Cherry *Barbee* Smith [1915 – 1976]. Cherry is the wife of James Willie Smith, and they share a common stone.
- Cherry Barbee *(Smith)* Cassell [July 1, 1939 – Sept. 30, 1991]. Cherry is the daughter of James Willie and Cherry *Barbee* Smith. She married James Egbert Cassell, Sr. in 1974. She had previously married a Mr. Hanson.

[J-86: Hill, Selden, Stephens]
- Clyde A. Hill [Dec. 8, 1922 – Dec. 22, 1998]. Clyde is the son of Samuel H. and Estille *Ritter* Hill, buried in combined plot A-153/154.
- Mary *S(tephens)*. Hill [Feb. 14, 1930 – Sept. 17, 1985]. Mary is the daughter of Dan H. and Ellen *Killingsworth* Stephens, buried in plot I-51. Mary married Clyde A. Hill in 1948, and they share a common grave location.

- Lynn *Hill* Selden [Aug. 5, 1949 – Dec. 11, 2006], "Mother." Lynn is the daughter of Clyde A. and Mary *Stephens* Hill. She shares a common grave location with John Donald Selden, a vase with the words: "Married Nov. 26, 1970." John's side has only his birth date of February 26, 1950, and the word: "Father."

[J-87: Chatham, Mitchell, Rice]
- Neal Jackson Chatham [March 10, 1926 – July 16, 1979]
- Bennye *Rice* Chatham [August 18, 1929 – June 29, 1990], member Daughters of the American Revolution. Bennye is the wife of Neal Jackson Chatham, and they share a common stone.
- Gerald Britton Mitchell [November 10, 1929 – February 12, 1995]. Gerald shares a common stone with Margaret H. Mitchell. Margaret's side has only her birth date of November 28, 1931.

[J-88: Anglin, Bailey, Moore]
- James M. Anglin [June 11, 1904 – Feb. 12, 1991], "Father."
- Marie *(Moore)* Anglin [Dec. 24, 1904 – July 16, 1979], "Mother." Marie is the daughter of Charity Anna *Baugher* Moore, buried in plot I-59, and wife of James M. Anglin. She was also married to a Mr. Bailey. She and Mr. Bailey have a son, James V. Bailey, also buried in plot I-59.

[J-89: no stones]
[J-90: Rogers, Tinsley]
- Terrie Lynn *(Tinsley)* Rogers [July 8, 1958 – Oct. 1, 1994], "SSGT, US AIR FORCE." This is a military stone. She also has a civilian stone with the words, "daughter of Robert and Barbara Agee Tinsley."

[J-91: no stones]
[J-92: no stones]
[J-93: no stones]
[J-94: no stones]
[J-95: no stones]
[J-96: Barron, Dobbs, Johnson]
- Ouida *J(ohnson)*. Barron [Feb. 22, 1900 – Mar. 16, 1974]. Ouida is the sister of Ava *Johnson* Dobbs, below.
- Charlie Dobbs [Aug. 11, 1904 – Jan. 4, 1983]
- Ava *J(ohnson)*. Dobbs [Jan. 18, 1909 – Oct. 20, 1994]. Ava is the wife of Charlie Dobbs.

[J-97: no stones]
[J-98: no stones]
[J-99/100: Dennis, Roan]
- John Sylvester Roan [Feb. 9, 1899 – Mar. 15, 1984], "Daddy." John is the son of John A. and Clara Anna *Porter* Roan, buried in Hedrick Cemetery.
- Lena *Dennis* Roan [Aug. 28, 1903 – Dec. 3, 2002], "Mother." Lena is the daughter of James S. and Clara *Pritchard* Dennis, buried in Jefferson County. She married John Sylvester Roan in 1923, and they share a common grave location.
- Matthew Gray Roan [July 11, 1982]

[J-101: McFatter, Russell]
- Marline Russell [Sept. 1, 1900 – Jan. 12, 1980]
- Fannie *(McFatter)* Russell [Feb. 27, 1906 – Feb. 15, 2001]. Fannie is the daughter of Dan and M. Urzilla *Dromgoole* McFatter, buried in Jefferson County. She married Marline Russell in 1929, and they share a common grave location.

[J-102: Burch, Porterpan, Trim]
- J. W. Porterpan [June 23, 1916 – Sept. 27, 2007]
- Sallie *T(rim)*. Porterpan [Apr. 16, 1921 – Mar. 10, 1995]. Sallie is the daughter of Albert B. and Mary *Mercer* Trim, buried in combined plot E-7/8/9. She married J. W. Porterpan in 1942, and they share a common grave location. Sallie had previously married Joe E. Burch in 1937.

- John A. Porterpan [Oct. 10, 1942 – Nov. 21, 2003], "Daddy." John is the son of J. W. and Sallie *Trim* Porterpan, He shares a common stone with Etta Belle Porterpan, with the words: "Married Jan. 8, 1965." Etta's side has only her birth date of February 9, 1947, and the word: "Mama."

[J-103: no stones]

[J-104: Cade, Wilkinson]

- James Samuel Cade [Nov. 9, 1908 – Jan. 12, 1979]. James is the son of Robert S. and Lilly M. *Patterson* Cade, buried in combined G-13/14.
- Cleora *Wilkinson* Cade [Mar. 13, 1904 – Jan. 13, 1980]. Cleora is the daughter of John C. and Katie *Cordes* Wilkinson, buried in plot H-96. She is the wife of James Samuel Cade, and they share a common stone.

[J-105: no stones]

[J-106: Abraham, Brumfield, Daniel, Torrey]

- Lee H. Abraham [Sept. 18, 1923 – May 10, 1975]. Lee is the son of Jacob L. and Phoebe *Hamilton* Abraham, buried in plot A-123. He shares a common stone with Louise *Torrey* Abraham, whom he married in 1946. Louise's side has only her birth date of August 23, 1926.
- Infant Daughter Abraham [May 24, 1947], "infant dau. of Lee H. and Louise Abraham."
- Charles Allison Torrey [April 25, 1924 – January 11, 1985]. Charles is the son of Charles M. and Alma *Lowe* Torrey, buried in plot H-19. He married M(argie). Lorraine Pahnka in 1945. Margie is buried in Jefferson County.
- Cathy *Abraham* Daniel [Sept. 28, 1948 – July 18, 1998]. Cathy is the daughter of Lee H. and Louise *Torrey* Abraham. She married Charles Michael Daniel in 1969. She had previously married Elliott Murrell Brumfield in 1967.

[J-107: Smith]

- David Alan Smith [February 10, 1987 – October 3, 2010], "Beloved Son and Brother."

[J-108: Gordon, McCurley]

- Levi McCurley [Mar. 13, 1908 – Mar. 8, 1985]. Levi is the son of John R. and Virgie *Hastings* McCurley, buried in Copiah County.
- Louvia *Gordon* McCurley [Jan. 17, 1909 – Dec. 25, 1991]. Louvia is the wife of Levi McCurley, and they share a common grave location.

[J-109: Stevens, Turner]

- John Eddie Stevens [June 21, 1909 – July 22, 1978]
- Walker *Turner* Stevens [April 23, 1912 – April 17, 1993]. Walker is the wife of John Eddie Stevens.

[J-110: Allen, Grafton, Hughes, Seemann]

- Hamilton D. Allen [Oct. 20, 1910 – Jan. 10, 1997], "MM3, US NAVY, WORLD WAR II." This is a bronze military plaque. He also has a civilian stone that gives his middle name as DONALD. Hamilton is the son of William L. and Eula *Slay* Allen, buried in plot H-11.
- Fern *Seemann* Allen [December 10, 1912 – March 22, 1994]. Fern is the daughter of Walter Rubin Seemann, buried in plot I-67. She is the wife of Hamilton Donald Allen.
- Webb O. Grafton [1916 – 1994], 32nd degree Mason.
- Dolores *H(ughes)*. Grafton [1923 – 2013]. Dolores is the daughter of John Chambliss Hughes, buried in plot A-20, and Vivian Kathryne *Allen* Hughes, buried in plot H-11 with the last name of FARR. She is the wife of Webb O. Grafton, and they share a common bronze plaque.

[J-111/112: Allen, Crum, Jones]

- Oliver Albert Jones, Sr. [November 19, 1921 – April 22, 1993], "Father."
- Idelle *Allen* Jones [September 21, 1920 – May 28, 1978], "Mother" Idelle is the daughter of William Lafayette and Zuma *King* Allen, buried in plot H-11. She is the wife of Oliver Albert Jones, Sr., and they

share a common grave location. She had previously married William Brumfield Crum, buried in plot H-48, in 1939.

- Oliver Albert Jones, Jr. [Apr. 9, 1943 – Feb. 11, 2012], "US AIR FORCE, VIETNAM…Beloved Son, Brother, Husband and Father." This is a bronze military plaque. Oliver is the son of Oliver Albert and Idelle *Allen* Jones.

Section K

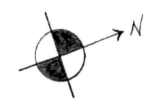

11	10	9	8	7	6	5	4	3	2	1
12	13	14	15	16	17	18	19	20	21	22
33	32	31	30	29	28	27	26	25	24	23
34	35	36	37	38	39	40	41	42	43	44
55	54	53	52	51	50	49	48	47	46	45
56	57	58	59	60	61	62	63	64	65	66
77	76	75	74	73	72	71	70	69	68	67
78	79	80	81	82	83	84	85	86	87	88
99	98	97	96	95	94	93	92	91	90	89

Section K

[K-1: Ainsworth, Irby, Priest, Sanders, Westmoreland]
- Murray H. Irby [Dec. 19, 1915 – Jan. 2, 1975], "CPL, US ARMY." This is a military stone. He also has a civilian stone, giving his middle name as HUGH.
- Ruby *W(estmoreland)*. Irby [March 18, 1920 – April 4, 1999]. Ruby was first married to a Mr. Sanders. She later married Murray Hugh Irby in 1945, and they share a common grave location. After Murray's death, she married Jerry K. Priest in 1978.
- Bobby Sanders [Apr. 28, 1943 – Sept. 3, 2009]. Bobby is the son of Ruby *Westmoreland* Sanders. He married Mrs. Patricia Ann *Jeffers* Ainsworth in 1966, and they share a common stone. Patricia's side has only her birth date of June 6, 1945.
- Robert Wayne Ainsworth [Apr. 30, 1964 – June 5, 1994]

[K-2: Bobo]
- Raymond Lavalle Bobo [Sept. 22, 1923 – Apr. 22, 1990]. Raymond is the son of Howard G. Bobo, buried in Jefferson County, and Lola *Wroten* Bobo, buried in plot H-5.
- Kelly Rene Bobo [July 2, 1964 – May 19, 1988]. Kelly is the daughter of Raymond Lavalle Bobo.

[K-3/20: Hudson]. This combined plot has a memorial stone bearing the name HUDSON.
- James E. Hudson [March 12, 1926 – Nov. 5, 2006], "LT, US NAVY, WORLD WAR II." This is a bronze military plaque. He also has a civilian stone, giving his middle name as EDWARD. James is the son of Herbert B. and Vivian G. *Abbott* Hudson, buried in combined plot A-39/40. He married Lois Lanell Berryhill in 1947.

[K-4: no stones]
[K-5: no stones]
[K-6: Moore]
- Earl Humphreys Moore [March 20, 1936 – Jan. 31, 2015]. This information was obtained from a temporary funeral home marker. Earl is the son of William Earl and Bonnie Claire *Brown* Moore, buried in plot E-16. He married Linda Wheeless in 1963.

[K-7: no stones]
[K-8: Byrnes, Heidel]
- Burton O. Byrnes [Dec. 3, 1915 – Dec. 13, 1986]. Burton is the son of Augustus McCaleb and Kathrine *Ogden* Byrnes, buried in McCaleb-Hermitage Cemetery.

- Anna M. *(Heidel)* Byrnes [Apr. 21, 1917 – Nov. 2, 1995]. Anna is the wife of Burton O. Byrnes, and they share a common grave location.

[K-9: Conn, Winborn]

- Kelly S. Conn [Sept. 12, 1917 – Dec. 9, 1999], "Father."
- Mary C. *(Winborn)* Conn [Jan. 26, 1917 – June 15, 2000], "Mother." Mary is the wife of Kelly S. Conn, and they share a common stone.

[K-10: Byrd, Doyle, Fizer]

- D. B. Byrd, Jr. [Aug. 24, 1931 – Jan. 17, 2000], "SSGT, US AIR FORCE, KOREA." This is a military stone. He also has a civilian stone giving his full name as Decatur Butler "D. B." Byrd, Jr.
- Patsy *Fizer* Byrd [Jan. 10, 1934 – July 17, 2009]. Patsy is the daughter of Henry Paxton and Myrtle *Green* Fizer, buried in plot J-30. She and Decatur Butler Byrd, Jr. share a common grave location, a vase with the words: "Married Dec. 24, 1959." Patsy had previously married Luther LaFair Doyle, Jr. in 1952.

[K-11: Barr, Brown, McBroom, Sumrall]

- Billy Ray Sumrall [November 26, 1933 – November 16, 1999]. Billy is the son of Robert G. and Florence *Buckley* Sumrall, buried in plot A-149.
- Doris *B(arr)*. Sumrall [December 22, 1934 – August 5, 2000]. Doris married Billy Ray Sumrall in 1952, and they share a common grave location.
- Charles R. McBroom [June 1, 1932 – July 22, 2011], "Beloved Husband & Father." Charles shares a common grave location with his wife, Audrey A. McBroom. Audrey's side has only her birth date of August 12, 1927.
- William Simms Brown [November 27, 1924 – December 17, 1991], "Father." William is the son of Jesse Simms and Victoria *Andrews* Brown, buried in plot E-6. He married Gloria Frances Segrest in 1953.
- Larry Simms Brown [May 7 1958 – March 28, 1988], "Son." Larry is the son of William Simms and Gloria Frances *Segrest* Brown.

[K-12: no stones]

[K-13: no stones]

[K-14: Farr]

- Edwin Felix Farr, Jr. [August 14, 1930 – August 20, 1996]. Edwin and his brother William Allen Farr, listed below, are sons of Vivian Kathryne *Allen* Farr, buried in plot H-11.
- Marguerite Gooch Farr [December 1, 1926 – February 9, 2007]. Edwin Felix and Marguerite Gooch Farr share a common grave location.
- William Allen "Pete" Farr, Sr. [Apr. 4, 1932 – Mar. 10, 2011], "MSGT, US AIR FORCE, KOREA." This is a military stone.

[K-15: Birch, Peltier]

- Edwin L. Birch [Aug. 19, 1912 – Dec. 31, 1999]
- M. Jane *(Peltier)* Birch [Nov. 3, 1913 – Dec. 8, 2006]. M. Jane is the wife of Edwin L. Birch, and they share a common stone.

[K-16: no stones]

[K-17: Bearden, Hynum]

- Vivian Lanell *Hynum* Bearden [Jan. 5, 1919 – May 14, 2008]. Vivian is the daughter of John Mason and Myrtle Bell *Hynum* Hynum, buried in plot H-54. She married Robert Mosley Bearden in 1938. Robert is buried in plot A-55.

[K-18: no stones]

[K-19a: Hudson, Prouty]

- William Francis Prouty, Jr, [Nov. 4, 1920 – July 1, 2009], "WWII Veteran-Army." This is not a military stone.

- Alice *Hudson* Prouty [December 21, 1922 – May 22, 2005]. Alice is the daughter of Edward and Marie *Abbott* Hudson, buried in combined plot A-39/40.

[K-19b: Magruder]. This plot has a memorial stone bearing the name MAGRUDER.

- Samuel B. Magruder [Mar. 15, 1917 – Dec. 19, 1990], "COL, US ARMY." This is a bronze military plaque. Samuel is the son of John Martin and Katherine *Daniell* Magruder, buried in plot G-31.

[K-21: Bostic, Crisler, Starnes]

- Austin L. Starnes [June 18, 1910 – May 2, 2002]. Austin is the son of William Austin and Ada *Thetford* Starnes, buried in Copiah County. He first married Mrs. Madye Belle *Rogers* Linton in 1949. Madye is buried in plot I-27.
- Pauline L. *(Bostic)* Starnes [Feb. 20, 1917 – Feb. 2, 2009]. Pauline is the second wife of Austin L. Starnes, and they share a common grave location.
- Edgar Theodore Crisler, Jr. [January 17, 1935 – August 10, 1997]. A biographical inscription reads: "Editor of Port Gibson Reveille." Edgar's stone displays a bronze marker with the letters S. A. R., representing Sons of the American Revolution. Edgar is the son of Edgar T. and Sarah *Pearson* Crisler, buried in plot A-18a. He shares a common stone with his wife, Emma *Flautt* Crisler. Emma's side has only her birth date of March 1, 1939.

[K-22: Ritchey, Vittitow]

- Robert Lawrence Ritchey, Sr. [October 3, 1914 – May 15, 2012]
- Mary *Vittitow* Ritchey [May 16, 1917 – January 11, 2011]. Mary is the wife of Robert Lawrence Ritchey, and they share a common stone.

[K-23: Norwood, Rosenthal, Torrey, Trevilion]

- Thomas Clinton Norwood, Sr. [December 8, 1905 – May 12, 1991]. Thomas is the son of L. T. Norwood, buried in Willis Cemetery.
- Edith *Trevilion* Norwood [July 28, 1905 – April 23, 2000]. Edith is the daughter of John T. and Laura C. *Emrick* Trevilion, buried in plot H-29. She is the wife of Thomas Clinton Norwood, Sr., and they share a common stone.
- Edith Marie Norwood [Oct. 1, 1938 – Oct. 27, 2007]. Edith is the daughter of Thomas Clinton and Edith *Trevilion* Norwood.
- Judith *Rosenthal* Torrey [April 18, 1950 – March 23, 1994]. Judith shares a common grave location with John Lindsay Torrey, II. John's side gives only his birth date of September 22, 1947.

[K-24: Garrett, Tullos]

- Earline *Garrett* Tullos [July 6, 1922 – May 27, 1991]. Earline is the second wife of Sidney F. Tullos, marrying in 1964. Sidney is buried in combined plot I-28/29. Earline shares a common grave location with her son, Sidney Franklin Tullos, Jr. Sidney's sided has only his birth date of January 19, 1965.

[K-25: Buckalew, Dunn, Harding, Murrah]

- Everett S. Dunn [Sep. 22, 1918 – Oct. 8, 1996], "TEC 4, US ARMY, WORLD WAR II." This is a bronze military plaque. He also has a civilian stone, giving his middle name as SIMPSON, and the word, "Daddy."
- Kathryn *Murrah* Dunn [Aug. 22, 1929 – June 4, 2011], "Mother." Kathryn and Everett Simpson Dunn share a common grave location, with the words: "Married Sept. 13, 1946."
- Linda Gail *(Harding)* Buckalew [Feb. 11, 1955 – Mar. 16, 1999]

[K-26a: Clyburn, Hughes]

- Edwin J. Clyburn [Nov. 4, 1930 – Dec. 9, 2009]
- Betty L. *(Hughes)* Clyburn [Jan. 1, 1926 – Jan. 27, 2000]. Betty and Edwin J. Clyburn share a common stone with the words: "(Married) 10-4-1958."
- Shaun Lee Clyburn [Nov. 14, 1985 – Nov. 22, 1999]. Shaun is the grandson of Edwin J. and Betty L. *Hughes* Clyburn.

[K-26b/27: Lum, Wylie]
- W. Gene Wylie [Nov. 15, 1931 – XXXX] W. Gene's date of death is blank. A temporary funeral home marker gives his first name as WALTER, and date of death as August 10, 2014.
- L. Jean Wylie [Aug. 24, 1932 – Nov. 22, 2003]. L. Jean and W. Gene Wylie share a common stone.
- Betty Anne *Wylie* Lum [October 27, 1935 – June 28, 2001]
- John Dekalb Wylie [June 6, 1961 – April 17, 2005]. John shares a stone memorial bench with Rose Anne Wylie. Rose's side has only her birth date of April 20, 1955.

[K-28: no stones]
[K-29: no stones]
[K-30: Goff, Richardson]
- Earnest L. Goff [Oct. 18, 1930 – June 13, 2003]
- Peggy *R(ichardson)*. Goff [Apr. 17, 1932 – Jan. 13, 2004]. Peggy and Earnest L. Goff share a common grave location, a vase with the words: "Married Nov. 15, 1947."

[K-31: Jordan, Riggs, Watkins]
- Parham M. Watkins [January 17, 1917 – November 19, 2007], "Father." Parham is the son of John Parham and Mary Jane *Chapman* Watkins, buried in plot G-34.
- Evelyn *R(iggs)*. Watkins [February 5, 1929 – August 2, 1996], "Mother." Evelyn married Parham M. Watkins in 1954.
- Earl Barron Jordan [Dec. 3, 1918 – Aug. 26, 2006], "US ARMY, WORLD WAR II." This is a military stone. He also has a civilian stone showing him as a Mason and affiliation with Order of the Eastern Star. Earl is the son of Earl and Annie Mae *Boyd* Jordan, buried in plot A-140.

[K-32: Hill, Regan]
- Mary Edna *Hill* Regan [June 12, 1900 – March 27, 1992], "wife of Marvin M. Regan." Mary is the daughter of William J. and Lou Ann *Mullinix* Hill, buried in Hill Cemetery. She married Marvin Morse Regan in 1922. Marvin is buried in plot G-26.
- Ray Lee Regan [Jul. 22, 1929 – Sep. 12, 2008], "FN, US NAVY, KOREA." This is a military stone. He also has a civilian stone. Ray and his brother Joseph Edwin, below, are sons of Marvin Morse and Mary Edna *Hill* Regan.
- Joseph Edwin Regan [Nov. 14, 1932 – June 21, 1994], "Dad."

[K-33/34: Blue, Maynard, McCaa, McIlvoy, Neese, Trim, Willis]
- Robert Lee "Pa Blue" Blue [March 11, 1923 – March 1, 2006], "Daddy."
- Vera Mae "Mammy" *(Maynard)* Blue [Jan. 25, 1933 – Feb. 1, 1994], "Mama." Vera is the wife of Robert Lee Blue. She was previously married to a Mr. McIlvoy.
- David Ernest McCaa, Jr. [1924 – 1992], "S1, US NAVY, WORLD WAR II." This is a bronze military plaque. He also has a civilian stone giving his nickname as "Buddy." David is the son of David Ernest and Myrtle *Goodrum* McCaa, buried in plot A-108. He first married Robbie K. Anderson in 1944. Robbie is buried in combined plot M-44/45, with the last name of RANER. David later married Mrs. Dorothy Mae *Purvis* Warren in 1963.
- Vernita J. *(McIlvoy)* McCaa [August 16, 1947 – March 30, 2003]. Vernita is the daughter of Vera Mae *Maynard* McIlvoy. She is the wife of David Ernest McCaa, Jr., and they share a common stone.
- Edward Willis [June 12, 1926 – Apr. 19, 1998], "Father." Edward is the son of David Evan and Clara Ethel *Norwood* Willis, buried in Willis Cemetery.
- Marietta *Neese* Willis [Nov. 18, 1928 – May 1, 1992], "Mother." Marietta and Edward Willis share a common grave location, a vase with the words: "Married Sept. 22, 1946."
- m. Nick Trim [1995]

[K-35: Mangum, Sorrels]

- Lilian *Sorrels* Mangum [August 29, 1920 – February 3, 2002]. Lilian is the daughter of Sidney and Lilian Elmore *Perkins* Sorrels, buried in Sarepta Cemetery.

[K-36: Mahoney]

- Donald F. Mahoney [Nov. 2, 1927 – Jan. 24, 2003]. Donald shares a common grave location with Jeannette J. Mahoney. Jeannette's side has only her birth date of October 2, 1929.
- Kevin R. Mahoney [Jan. 17, 1959 – May 02, 2007], member Boy Scouts of America, "Our Beloved Son and Brother."

[K-37: Bryant]

- James Charles Bryant, Sr. [July 14, 1942 – May 1, 2010]. James' rather amusing epitaph reads: "Life is not a journey to the grave with the intentions of arriving in a pretty and well preserved body, but rather to skip in sideways fully used up, totally worn out, proclaiming with a loud voice, 'Wow, What a Ride!'"

[K-38: Bryant]

- Georgia Bryant [Nov. 25, 1941 – Oct. 3, 2012]. Georgia shares a common stone with Edward Bryant, Sr. Edward's side has only his birth date of October 29, 1939.

[K-39: no stones]

[K-40: Ellis, Hannis]

- Hazel *Hannis* Ellis [Mar. 31, 1926 – May 27, 2003], "Loving Mother and Grandmother." Hazel is the daughter of Willie D. and Earline *Daniel* Hannis, buried in plot J-19.

[K-41: Dulaney, Gunn]

- Sim Clarence Dulancy [Feb. 7, 1928 – Dec. 28, 2013]
- Mary Catherine *(Gunn)* Dulaney [July 10, 1930 – June 8, 2000]. Mary is the wife of Sim Clarence Dulaney, and they share a common stone.

[K-42: no stones]

[K-43: Foster]

- Jacob Lynn "Jake" Foster [August 29, 1984 – September 17, 2011], "A Loving Daddy, Brother and Son."

[K-44: Ellis]

- Woodrow Wilson Ellis [Sept. 29, 1918 – Feb. 1, 2002]. Woodrow is the son of James and Lula *Thomas* Ellis, buried in combined plot G-42/43.
- James Ellis, II [December 22, 1945 – June 14, 2011]
- Dr. Brien Thomas Ellis [Sept. 3, 1956 – Mar. 17, 1996]

[K-45: Chambliss, Swilley]

- Thomas Earl Chambliss [May 27, 1931 – July 12, 2015], "Loving Daddy & Poppie." Thomas' date of death is from a temporary funeral home marker.
- Rachel *Swilley* Chambliss [August 31, 1937 – April 15, 1996], "Loving Mama & Grandma." Rachel is the wife of Thomas Earl Chambliss, and they share a common stone bearing the inscription: "Married May 4, 1957."
- LaVonn Ezella Chambliss [January 26, 1965 – January 29, 1965]. LaVonn is the daughter of Thomas Earl and Rachel *Swilley* Chambliss.

[K-46-48: no stones]

[K-49: Trevilion]

- Mark Absolom Trevilion [August 27, 1963 – March 31, 2012]

Section L

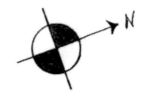

8	7	6	5	4	3	2	1
9	10	11	12	13	14	15	16
24	23	22	21	20	19	18	17
25	26	27	28	29	30	31	32
40	39	38	37	36	35	34	33
41	42	43	44	45	46	47	48
56	55	54	53	52	51	50	49
57	58	59	60	61	62	63	64
72	71	70	69	68	67	66	65
73	74	75	76	77	78	79	80
88	87	86	85	84	83	82	81
89	90	91	92	93	94	95	96
104	103	102	101	100	99	98	97
105	106	107	108	109	110	111	112

MAINTENANCE
BUILDING

Section L

This particular section appears to be the most recent to be developed, and as such, has only one plot currently occupied. That plot is:

[L-8: Campbell]

- Douglas Elwood Campbell, Jr. [January 16, 1951 – March 22, 2012]. Douglas is the son of Douglas E. and Cleo *Trim* Campbell, buried in plot J-58. He shares a common stone with Laura Ann *Valentine* Campbell. Laura's side has only her birth date of April 18, 1955.
- Bryan Douglas Campbell [Mar. 29, 1975 – Sept. 14, 2014], "Loving Father." Bryan is the son of Douglas Elwood and Laura Ann *Valentine* Campbell.

In a back corner of this particular section (which is the back corner of the entire cemetery) lies the cemetery's maintenance building. Behind this building lies a lone gravestone, whose owner is known to be buried somewhere on cemetery property, although the exact location cannot be determined for sure. The owner of this gravestone is:

[L-XX: Sanders]

- Howard Lee Sanders [July 3, 1895 – March 3, 1961], "MISSISSIPPI, PVT, 162 DEPOT BRIGADE, WORLD WAR I." This is a military stone. Howard is the son of Mary Nettie *Westrope* Sanders, buried in Sanders Cemetery. He married Bertie Thedford in 1922. Bertie is buried in Hermanville Cemetery.

Section M

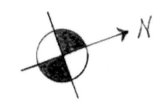

40	41	42a	42b
45	44	43	
46	47	48	
51	50	49	
52	53	54	
57	56	55	
58	59	60	
63	62	61	
64	65	66	
69	68	67	
70	71	72	
75	74	73	
76	77	78	
81	80	79	

82	83	84	
87	86	85	
88	89	90	
93	92	91	
94	95	96	
99	98	97	
100	101	102	
105	104	103	
106	107	108	
111	110	109	
112	113	114	
117	116	115a	115b
118	119	120	

Section M

[M-40: Daugherty, Humphries, Torrey]. This plot has a memorial stone bearing the names HUMPHRIES and TORREY.

- Lucien W. Torrey [1886 – 1953]
- Mattiebelle Y. Torrey [1881 – 1957]. Mattiebelle is the wife of Lucien W. Torrey. She had previously been married to a Mr. Humphries.
- Harold Y. Humphries [1902 – 1982]. Harold is the son of Mattiebelle Y. Humphries, now Torrey.
- Ruth D*(augherty)*. Humphries [1907 – 1989]. Ruth is the daughter of Walter Eugene and Willie *Chesterman* Daugherty, buried in plot H-14. She is the wife of Harold Y. Humphries.

[M-41: Anderson, Bonner, Brown]

- Clifton Brown [February 14, 1894 – February 14, 1954], "MISSISSIPPI, PVT, 2 CASUAL DET, WORLD WAR 1." This is a military stone.
- Lela Frances *Anderson* Brown [November 18, 1898 – July 17, 1986]. Lela is the daughter of Joseph J. and Quillie E. *Kirkley* Anderson, buried in plot E-33. She is the wife of Clifton Brown.
- James T. Bonner [Jan. 1, 1914 – Dec. 21, 1987]. James shares a common stone with his wife, Lennie Mae *Brown* Bonner, daughter of Clifton and Lela Frances *Anderson* Brown. Lennie's side has only her birth date of November 29, 1925.

[M-42a: Morgan, Sullivan]

- Nonie Adella *(Sullivan)* Morgan [Mar. 10, 1874 – Aug. 10, 1954]. Nonie has a daughter, Ruth *Morgan* Gore, buried in plot I-43.

[M-42b: Irby, Oldham, Templeton]

- Ella *Templeton* Irby [Oct. 13, 1876 – Jan. 15, 1962]. Ella married John F. Irby in 1895. John is buried in Jobe-Floyd Cemetery.
- William J. Oldham [July 1, 1897 – November 30, 1961]

[M-43: no stones]

[M-44/45: Alexander, Anderson, McCaa, Norwood, Raner, Stampley, Tanner, Wood]. This combined plot has a memorial stone bearing the name ANDERSON.

- Richard H. Anderson [1891 – 1954]. Richard is the son of Joseph J. and Quillie *Kirkley* Anderson, buried in plot E-33.
- Robbie K. *(Norwood)* Anderson [1892 – 1971]. Robbie is the daughter of Robert J. and Rebecca *Kirkley*

Norwood, buried in Willis Cemetery. She is the wife of Richard H. Anderson, and they share a common stone.

- Albert W. Tanner [Apr. 3, 1908 – July 12, 1981], a Mason. Albert is the son of Maude M. *Thompson* Tanner, buried in plot G-38, with the last name of DAVIS.
- Q. B. *(Anderson)* S(tampley). Tanner [May 4, 1917 – June 2, 1998], member Order of the Eastern Star. Q. B. is the daughter of Richard H. and Robbie K. *Norwood* Anderson. She is the wife of Albert W. Tanner, and they share a common grave location. She first married Walter J. Stampley in 1935. Walter is buried in plot A-184.
- Arthur Clyde Wood [Dec. 31, 1912 – Sept. 23, 1984], a Mason. Arthur is the son of Cleve E. and Jessie *Wright* Wood, buried in Shiloh Baptist Church Cemetery.
- Eva *A(nderson)*. Wood [Mar. 16, 1922 – Apr. 20, 1993], member Order of the Eastern Star. Eva is the daughter of Richard H. and Robbie K. *Norwood* Anderson. She married Arthur Clyde Wood in 1936, and they share a common grave location. They have sons Arthur Clyde Wood, Jr., buried in plot I-85, and David Jack Wood in plot M-50.
- Kenneth K. Raner [Jan. 14, 1936 – Feb. 9, 1985], "Papaw." Kenneth's first marriage was to Betty Ruth Moulder in 1957.
- Robbie K. *(Anderson)* Raner [Aug. 24, 1926 – Sept. 14, 1989], "Mamaw." Robbie is the daughter of Richard H. and Robbie K. *Norwood* Anderson. She is the wife of Kenneth K. Raner, and they share a common grave location. She had previously married David Ernest McCaa, Jr. in 1944. David is buried in combined plot K-33/34.
- Betty Diane *(Alexander)* Wood [Apr. 24, 1953 – Nov. 23, 2010]. Betty shares a common grave location with Mac Merritt Wood, Sr., son of Arthur Clyde and Eva *Anderson* Wood, whom she married in 1972. Mac's side has only his birth date of April 10, 1939.

[M-46/51: Cassell, Hammett, Harrell, Harris]

- George Thomas Harrell [Oct. 14, 1864 – Feb. 2, 1921], member Woodmen of the World.
- Allie *H(arris)*. Harrell [January 31, 1873 – October 22, 1959], "Mother." Allie married George Thomas Harrell in 1899.
- William Rollo Hammett [Nov. 23, 1896 – Oct. 16, 1974]
- Berniece *Harrell* Hammett [Sept. 3, 1904 – Aug. 20, 1975]. Berniece is the daughter of George Thomas and Allie *Harris* Harrell. She married William Rollo Hammett in 1926, and they share a common grave location.
- William Rollo Hammett, Jr. [June 18, 1927 – Mar. 24, 1986]. William is the son of William Rollo and Berniece *Harrell* Hammett.
- Mary Ola *Hammett* Cassell [June 29, 1929 – January 21, 1965], "Mother." Mary is the daughter of William Rollo and Berniece *Harrell* Hammett. She married James Egbert Cassell in 1950, and they share a common grave location. James' side has only his birth date of July 1, 1929.

[M-47: Hill, Taylor]. This plot has a memorial stone bearing the name TAYLOR.

- Claude Taylor [May 10, 1899 – Dec. 7, 1991], "Granddaddy." Claude is the son of Jasper Newton and Lucy Jane *Husband* Taylor, buried in Taylor-Emrick Cemetery.
- Annie May *(Hill)* Taylor [Apr. 4, 1898 – Apr. 9, 1994], "Gagaw." Annie is the daughter of William J. and Lou Ann *Mullinix* Hill, buried in Hill Cemetery. She married Claude Taylor in 1921.
- Charles Lee Taylor [Oct. 24, 1921 – Oct. 27, 2009], "Papaw." Charles is the son of Claude and Annie May *Hill* Taylor.
- Iva Colleen Taylor [Jan. 22, 1925 – Dec. 4, 2006], "Mamaw." Iva is the wife of Charles Lee Taylor.
- Claude Fay Taylor [Mar. 31, 1933 – Nov. 2, 1959]. Stone's inscription says: "Four Years Air Force." Claude is the son of Claude and Annie May *Hill* Taylor.

[M-48: Magruder, Williams]
- James Person Magruder [July 11, 1903 – Apr. 10, 1985]. James is the son of James Person and Katesie *Person* Magruder, buried in plot A-19.
- Blanche *Williams* Magruder [Apr. 22, 1904 – Oct. 24, 1990]. Blanche is the wife of James Person Magruder, and they share a common stone.

[M-49: no stones]

[M-50: Wood]
- David Jack Wood [Mar. 12, 1937 – Apr. 1, 2012]. David is the son of Arthur Clyde and Eva *Anderson* Wood, buried in combined plot M-44/45. He shares a common stone with Peggy *Hammett* Wood, whom he married in 1956. Peggy's side has only her birth date of January 21, 1937.

[M-52/53: Mercer, Neal]
- Robert Alton Mercer [Nov. 19, 1913 – Mar. 20, 1972]
- Lillian Ileana *(Neal)* Mercer [Oct. 27, 1920 – Feb. 27, 1998]. Lillian is the wife of Robert Alton Mercer, and they share a common grave location.

[M-54: no stones]

[M-55: no stones]

[M-56: Chamberlain, Jones, Taylor]
- David Beckwith Taylor [1911 – 1982]
- Mary *Chamberlain* Taylor [1913 – 1995]. Mary married David Beckwith Taylor in 1940.
- Elise Chamberlain Taylor [1942 – 1972]. Elise is the daughter of David Beckwith and Mary *Chamberlain* Taylor. She had married Thomas Roper Jones in 1964.

[M-57: Spencer]
- James Grafton Spencer [Aug. 22, 1904 – Jan. 27, 1998]. James is the son of Horatio N. and Ellie May *Hartwell* Spencer, buried in plot A-69.
- Prudence Hornbuckle Spencer [Jan. 11, 1905 – Apr. 30, 1972]. Prudence and James Grafton Spencer share a common grave location.

[M-58: no stones]

[M-59: no stones]

[M-60: no stones]

[M-61: Moore]
- Larson Edwin Moore, Sr. [Oct. 12, 1936 – Oct. 3, 1985], "SMSGT, US AIR FORCE, KOREA, VIETNAM." This is a military stone.

[M-62/63: Cade, Crawford]
- Walter C. Cade, Sr. [10-10-1919 – 05-04-2015]. This information was obtained from a temporary funeral home marker.
- LaRue *C(rawford)*. Cade [June 30, 1919 – November 17, 1973], "Mother." The other half of this common grave location is blank, but belongs to Walter C. Cade, Sr., her husband.
- Jeffery Barton Cade [Sept. 8, 1975 – Sept. 12, 1975]

[M-64/65: Kennedy, Slayton, Wroten]. This combined plot has a memorial stone bearing the names SLAYTON and KENNEDY.
- Luther C. Slayton, Sr. [June 20, 1890 – April 20, 1976]. Luther is the son of Rowan C. and Mary A. *Ikerd* Slayton, buried in plot G-46.
- Viola *W(roten)*. Slayton [June 30, 1897 – September 17, 1975]. Viola is the daughter of Wiley W. and Carrie I. *Scott* Wroten, buried in combined plot H-75/76. She married Luther C. Slayton in 1917.
- Marshall Wilbur Kennedy [November 29, 1903 – August 2, 1978]
- Thelma Irene *Slayton* Kennedy [June 9, 1919 – November 15, 1976]. Thelma is the daughter of Luther

C. and Viola *Wroten* Slayton, and wife of Marshell Wilbur Kennedy.

- Luther Slayton, Jr. [August 19, 1922 – April 14, 1975]. Luther is the son of Luther C. and Viola *Wroten* Slayton. He married Mrs. Wilma Lee *Graham* Palmer in 1951.

[M-66: no stones]

[M-67: no stones]

[M-68: Fox]

- Frank Creevy Fox [Sept. 14, 1906 – Apr. 5, 1975]. Frank's wife, Katherine *Calloway* Fox, is buried in Port Gibson Catholic Cemetery.
- Frank Creevy Fox, Jr. [Nov. 6, 1933 – Nov. 15, 2001], "Gramps." Frank is the son of Frank Creevy and Katherine *Calloway* Fox.

[M-69: Cox, Rena]

- Jesse T. Cox [Oct. 1, 1909 – June 17, 1974]
- Louise *R(ena)*. Cox [July 11, 1909 – Mar. 29, 1980]. Louise is the wife of Jesse T. Cox, and they share a common grave location.

[M-70/75: Hartley, Preskitt, Strickland]

- Colon Leon Hartley [Feb. 9, 1904 – Nov. 10, 1990]. Colon and his sister Katie, below, are children of Hiram H. and Della *Tanksley* Hartley, buried in plot G-48.
- Ruby *Strickland* Hartley [July 25, 1915 – May 17, 1990]. Ruby is the daughter of Lenard S. and Maud E. *Meadows* Strickland, buried in plot A-124. She is the wife of Colon Leon Hartley, and they share a common stone.
- Colon Eugene Hartley [1933 – 1979], "RM3, US NAVY, KOREA." This is a bronze military plaque. Colon is the son of Colon Leon and Ruby *Strickland* Hartley. He also has a civilian stone that he shares with Pattie *Spain* Hartley, whom he married in 1954. Pattie's side has only her birth date of June 2, 1939.
- John W. Preskitt [Sept. 2, 1899 – June 17, 1980]. John is the son of W. R. Preskitt, buried in plot A-139. He had previously married Maud L. Shannon in 1923.
- Katie *H(artley)*. Preskitt [Mar. 20, 1911 – Aug. 31, 1979]. Katie married John W. Preskitt in 1942, and they share a common stone.

[M-71: Magruder, Whitfield]

- Robert William Whitfield [October 28, 1902 – April 13, 1983]
- Katherine *Magruder* Whitfield [September 27, 1906 – February 6, 1988]. Katherine is the daughter of John Martin and Katherine *Daniell* Magruder, buried in G-31. She married Robert William Whitfield in 1933.

[M-72: no stones]

[M-73: no stones]

[M-74: no stones]

[M-76: Curle]

- Walter W. Curle [Dec. 7, 1922 – May 23, 1982]

[M-77: Barnes, Curle]

- Roy Maxwell Barnes, M. D. [August 1, 1925 – February 20, 2012]
- Rea *Curle* Barnes [October 13, 1928 – October 24, 1984]. Rea is the wife of Roy Maxwell Barnes, and they share a common stone.

[M-78: no stones]

[M-79: no stones]

[M-80: Qualls]

- Hester J. Qualls, Sr. [Oct. 7, 1930 – Aug. 25, 2010], "PFC, US ARMY, KOREA." This is a bronze military plaque. He also has a civilian stone. Hester is the son of Jesse and Myrtle *Baker* Qualls, buried in plot E-42.

- Mary L. Qualls [Nov. 18, 1928 – Aug. 25, 2010]. Hester J. and Mary L. Qualls share a common grave location.

[M-81: Ellis, Nasif]

- Murad Ameen Nasif [Nov. 24, 1914 – May 11, 1994]
- Mildred *Ellis* Nasif [May 30, 1921 – Mar. 3, 2014]. Mildred is the daughter of James and Lula *Thomas* Ellis, buried in combined plot G-42/43. She is the wife of Murad Ameen Nasif, and they share a common grave location.
- Robin Ellis Nasif [January 15, 1982 – July 13, 1984]

[M-82/83: Pickens]

- James T. Pickens [September 15, 1926 – March 24, 1995]. James is the brother of Randle Pickens, below.
- Doris F. Pickens [August 16, 1931 – April 17, 2013]. Doris is the wife of James T. Pickens, and they share a common stone.
- Randle "Ray" Pickens [Oct. 19, 1928 – Apr. 18, 2011]
- Rachel "Maxine" Pickens [Oct. 12, 1929 – March 8, 2009]. Rachel and Randle Pickens share a common stone, vases with the words: "(married) Apr. 20, 1946."

[M-84: no stones]

[M-85: no stones]

[M-86: Burton, Doerr, Guenther, Reed, Sumpter]

- William Homer Sumpter [Jan. 18, 1909 – June 23, 1999]
- Trudie *Burton* Sumpter [Mar. 30, 1914 – Mar. 3, 1996]. Trudie is the wife of William Homer Sumpter, and they share a common grave location.
- Frank Lester Reed [Sept. 2, 1922 – Apr. 16, 1999]. Frank is the son of John M. and Della *Brown* Reed, buried in Sarepta Cemetery. He had previously married Levetta Merritt in 1947, and Mrs. Rose *Slay* Wade in 1949.
- Ann *(Doerr)* Guenther Reed [June 23, 1926 – July 14, 2007]. Ann is the wife of Frank Lester Reed, and they share a common stone. She had previously been married to a Mr. Guenther.

[M-87/88: Brady, Lum]

- William Douglas Lum [Oct. 22, 1911 – Aug. 2, 1995]. William is the son of Robert C. and Julia *Fox* Lum, buried in plot E-17, Julia with the last name of BITTERMAN.
- Martha *Brady* Lum [4-29-1924 – 7-20-2014]. This information is from a temporary funeral home marker. Martha is the daughter of Albert Neville and Henrietta A. *Wilson* Brady, buried in plot A-70. She married William Douglas Lum in 1940. Besides their son listed below, they have a daughter, Deborah Ker *Lum* Purviance, also buried in plot E-17.
- Albert Brady Lum [Dec. 25, 1941 – Aug. 9, 1999]. Albert is the son of William Douglas and Martha *Brady* Lum.

[M-89: Kilpatrick, McCurley]

- Marvin Lee Kilpatrick [Nov. 30, 1906 – Mar. 1, 1984]
- Percie *McCurley* Kilpatrick [July 17, 1913 – Dec. 28, 1998]. Percie is the wife of Marvin Lee Kilpatrick, and they share a common grave location.
- Robert Lee Kilpatrick [Apr. 29, 1944 – Sept. 17, 1988]. Robert is the son of Marvin Lee and Percie *McCurley* Kilpatrick.

[M-90: no stones]

[M-91: no stones]

[M-92: Bellinger, Richardson]

- Walter C. Richardson [March 7, 1900 – March 19, 1984]. Walter was married numerous times, to Onie

Dunn, buried in Jefferson County, to Mrs. Nannie *Scott* Goza in 1951, then to Mrs. Mittie Lou *Scott* Smith in 1955, and finally to Mrs. Beatrice *Fugate* Alexander, whom marriage records tell us that he married twice, in 1959 and in 1961. Beatrice is buried in plot J-40.

- Charlie Bellinger [Sept. 24, 1913 – June 13, 1997], "Pop."
- Maggie *R(ichardson)*. Bellinger [Mar. 25, 1925 – Sept. 3, 1997], "Mama." Maggie is the daughter of Walter C. and Onie *Dunn* Richardson, and wife of Charlie Bellinger.

[M-93: Foster, Hudson]
- William Henry Hudson, Jr. [Dec. 7, 1923 – Feb. 9, 1984], a Mason, "Daddy." William is the son of William Henry and Bertha *Holder* Hudson, buried in combined plot A-10/27/28.
- Haroldene *(Foster)* Hudson [Sept. 22, 1922 – Oct. 29, 2012], member Order of the Eastern Star, "Mama." Haroldene is the daughter of Elijah C. and Clara *Perkins* Foster, buried in plot H-35. She is the wife of William Henry Hudson, Jr., and they share a common grave location.

[M-94: Jones, Robinson]
- Elizabeth Ann *(Robinson)* Jones [Aug. 1, 1941 – Dec. 5, 1992]
- Lisa Renee Jones [Oct. 13, 1965 – Oct. 13, 1984]. Lisa is the daughter of Elizabeth Ann *Robinson* Jones, and they share a common grave location.

[M-95: Harrison, Owens]
- Jewel *Owen* (sic) Harrison [Jan. 17, 1914 – Jan. 6, 1987], "Loving Daughter and Mother." Jewel is the daughter of Evan Berry Owens, buried in combined plot J-2/15, and Mary *Irby* Owens, buried in Sanders Cemetery. She married Clyde F. Harrison in 1940.

[M-96: no stones]

[M-97: no stones]

[M-98: no stones]

[M-99: Barber, Showman]
- Harold Barker Showman [October 7, 1907 – November 20, 1984]
- Katharin *Barber* Showman [October 11, 1909 – March 28, 1990]. Katharin is the daughter of John W. and Kate *Simrall* Barber, buried in combined plot A-36/37, and wife of Harold Barker Showman.
- Harold Barker Showman, Jr. [December 9, 1937 – February 15, 2015]

[M-100: no stones]

[M-101: Denley, Mullin, Simpson, Strong, Turnage]
- Lessie *M(ullin)*. Strong [April 12, 1903 – Feb. 24, 1985]. Lessie was once married to a Mr. Turnage.
- Frank Turnage [Sept. 4, 1924 – Jan. 11, 1987]. Frank is the son of Lessie *Mullin* Turnage. He first married Betty Sue Tidwell in 1953.
- Carolyn Ann *(Simpson)* Turnage [Oct. 9, 1941 – June 15, 1989]. Carolyn married Frank Turnage in 1962. She had previously married Robert Lee Denley in 1960.

[M-102: no stones]

[M-103: no stones]

[M-104: Couch]
- Chester Jay "C. J." Couch, Jr. [Feb. 24, 1985], "Our Son."

[M-105: Goff, Landrum]
- Thomas S. Goff [Jan. 8, 1927 – Dec. 12, 2001], "PFC, US ARMY, WORLD WAR II." This is a bronze military plaque. He also has a civilian stone giving his middle name as STEPHEN. Thomas had previously married Mrs. Julia Mae *Harrell* Trim in 1946.
- Mae Ethel *(Landrum)* Goff [June 3, 1932 – May 10, 2013]. Thomas Stephen and Mae Ethel *Landrum* Goff share a common stone with the words: "(Married) Jan. 3, 1948."

[M-106: no stones]

[M-107: Oswalt]
- Guy "Slim" Oswalt [July 10, 1911 – Jan. 25, 1987], "member Pipefitters Local No. 619."

[M-108 thru 114: no stones]

[M-115a: Campbell, Coulter, Lord]
- Marie *Lord* Coulter [Aug. 18, 1898 – Mar. 24, 1994]. Marie married Charles E. Coulter in 1941. Charles is buried in plot G-50. She had previously been married to a Mr. Campbell.

[M-115b: Mitchell]
- James (Buster) Mitchell [Apr. 10, 1948 – Aug. 10, 2009]

[M-116: Mascagni, Mitchell]
- Bobby Joe Mitchell [Dec. 30, 1971 – May 27, 1996]
- Emily Michel Mascagni [Mar. 24, 1969 – May 27, 1996]. Bobby Mitchell and Emily Mascagni share a common stone.

[M-117: LaBue, Qualls]
- Salvador Paul Labue [May 2, 1927 – Apr. 18, 1996], "US COAST GUARD." This is a bronze military plaque.
- Michael Lee Qualls [October 20, 1951 – June 22, 1986]
- Wesley William Qualls [February 2, 1988 – January 10, 2007]

[M-118: Eason, Ezell, Jordan]
- Harry M Jordan [Feb. 25, 1933 – Aug. 11, 1992], "US ARMY, KOREA." This is a bronze military plaque. He also has a civilian stone. Harry is the son of Earl and Annie Mae *Boyd* Jordan, buried in plot A-140.
- Pauline *E(ason)*. Jordan [July 20, 1920 – Mar. 26, 1994]. Pauline and Harry M. Jordan share a common grave location, a vase with the words: "Wed Sept. 19, 1962."
- Philip Wayne Ezell [Mar. 4, 1941 – Aug 16, 2001]. Philip as first married to Deborah Rae Fife in 1973, then to Margaret Scott in 1980.

[M-119: Bailey]
- Malcolm V. "Mickey" Bailey, Sr. [August 7, 1939 – July 25, 2005]. Malcolm shares a common stone with Nellie Marie *Jordan* Baily, with the words: "Married Dec. 24, 1962." Marie's side has only her birth date of October 8, 1938.

[M-120: Haydock, Sanders]
- William Lee Sanders [May 2, 1929 – Sept. 12, 1990]. William is the son of Clarence A. Sanders, buried in Sanders Cemetery, and Ona *Irby* Sanders, buried in plot J-39.
- Edward W. "Eddie" Haydock [Oct. 31, 1923 – Jan. 26, 1989]

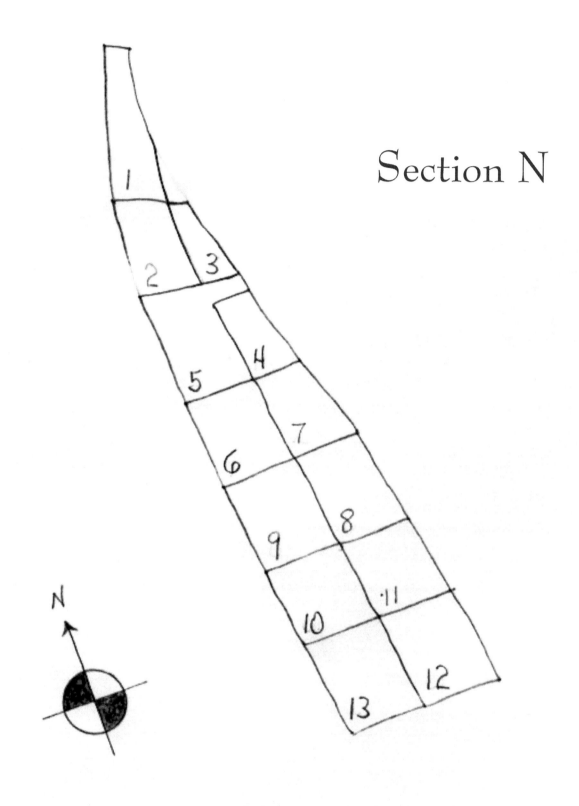

Section N

Section N

This particular section consists of a mixture of graves and names, with only a few arranged in any special order. A previous survey arranges the graves in specific groupings, so no attempt will be made here to arrange them differently.

[N-1: Barland, Hunt, Jones, Roberts, Trevilion]
- Jimmie Roberts [October 5, 1918], "MISSISSIPPI, SERGT, 71 INF, 11 DIV." This is a military stone.
- Willie F. Jones [July 2, 1938], "KENTUCKY, PVT, 6 INF, 5 DIV." This is a military stone.
- John M. Barland [1858 – 1936], "Father." John married Martha Elizabeth Russell in 1877. Besides his son listed below, another son, Johnnie Lee Barland, is buried in plot J-28.
- Lonnie A. Barland [October 25, 1918], "MISSISSIPPI, PVT, 116 INF, 29 DIV." This is a military stone. From *Port Gibson Reveille's* "Looking Back" column (week of Aug 18, 1921): "The mortal remains of Lonnie A. Barland were laid to rest in Wintergreen Cemetery on August 7th. The young hero, son of Mr. John Barland…, died in France from wounds received in battle in September, 1918."
- Samuel Martin Hunt [Sept. 5, 1897 – Sept. 30, 1922]. His stone's inscription reads: "Brief, brave and glorious was his young career."
- Infant Son Trevilion [1927], "infant son of Mr. & Mrs. J. W. Trevilion." This child's parents, John Wesley and Natalie *Kethley* Trevilion, are buried in plot H-29.

[N-1a: Clements]
- Clint Clements [Sept. 17, 1871 – May 17, 1937]

[N-2: Oudy, Pennisi, Weiss]
- Gap. John Pennisi [Sept. 19, 1824 – Dec. 15, 1898], "born in Riposto Italy…died in Port Gibson Mississippi."
- Libby Pennisi [Aug. 13, 1835 – Jan. 9, 1911], "born in Riposto, Italy…died in Port Gibson, Miss." Libby's obelisk has the words, in Italian: "*A nostra madre martire del dovere che il lielo ti accolga nel suo maestoso grenbo.*"
- Anthony Pennisi [Sept. 27, 1865 – Mar. 9, 1909], member Woodmen of the World, "To My Son" and "born in Riposto Italy…died…at Port Gibson Miss." Anthony's obelisk has the words, in Italian: "*Qui riposa A. Pennisi esempio di virtu e g arita chela terra ti sia lieve ed il cielo clemente.*"
- Frank Pennisi [Jan. 27, 1866 – Apr. 23, 1919], member Woodmen of the World, "native of Riposto,

Italy." Frank is the son of Libby Pennisi.

- Infant Pennisi [born & died Dec. 15, 1897], "infant of F. & J. Pennisi."
- John Weiss [1842 – 1927]
- Sam Oudy [1880 – 1964]
- Infant Son Oudy [died Oct. 2, 1923], "infant son of S. and L. Oudy."
- Infant Daughter Oudy [died Jan. 15, 1925], "infant daughter of S. and L. Oudy."

[N-3: no stones]

[N-4: Barland, Burch, Glodjo, Hawkins, Hensley, Perkins, Perry]

- Caleb E. Perkins [1850 – 1931]. Caleb married Mary Foster in 1868, Jane Toler in 1883, and later a third wife. His children include Clara *Perkins* Foster, buried in plot H-35, Cyrintha Irine *Perkins* Baker in Baker Cemetery, and Samuel E. Perkins in Hedrick Cemetery.
- Fannie Hawkins [November 11, 1890 – November 11, 1944]
- Joseph A. Burch [Mar. 21, 1881 – May 22, 1941], "Father."
- Dallas Glodjo [1903 – 1981]. Dallas married Ethel Louise Barnes in 1939.
- Eva Glodjo [1913 – 1935]. Dallas and Eva Glodjo share a common stone.
- Henry Fredrick Barland [Dec. 3, 1886 – Dec. 26, 1943], "Father."
- Emma *Perry* Barland [Jan. 16, 1896 – Apr. 8, 1986], "Mother." Emma is the wife of Henry Fredrick Barland, and they share a common grave location. They have a son, Bernard Barland, buried in plot I-89.
- Orville Hensley [1904 – 1932]

[N-5: Lewis]

- Nicolas Lewis [died Nov. 1895, aged about 82 yrs]
- Sara Lewis [died Mar. 29, 1889, aged about 78 yrs], "wife of Nicolas Lewis."

[N-6: Gray, Richardson]

- Adora Richardson [died Mar. 21, 1873, aged 18 y's. 1 mo. 21 d's], "wife of Thomas Richardson."
- Patsey Gray [July 4, 1854 – Feb. 19, 1874]

Index of Last Names

(the Confederate dead buried in Soldiers Row are designated by SR)

Conn K-9
Conway ....SR
Cook E-7/8/9, F-22
Cooper ....A-57, A-124, SR
Copass I-63
Corbin I-92/93
Cordes H-96
Cornforth I-40
Cossar A-90/164
Costner ....SR
Cotten C-47
Cotton B-51, H-85, H-98
Couch ....M-104, SR
Coulon I-94
Coulter G-50, M-115a
Cox............C-83, H-35, H-49, J-22, M-69
Craig A-58
Crane B-52
Cranford ....SR
Crapps J-83
Crawford ....A-98, I-35, M-62/63, SR
Crawly ....SR
Creighton A-2
Cressman A-180
Crews H-39
Crills C-24
Crisler ....A-18a, E-B, H-42, K-21
Crocker A-113, I-44, J-80
Cronin A-53
Cronly B-47
Crow C-71
Crum H-48, I-12, J-111/112
Culley J-18
Cuper A-151
Curle M-76, M-77
Currie G-6, H-57
Curtis I-70
Cutrer A-88
Dakin B-17
Dale A-122, H-74
Daniel J-19, J-106
Daniell A-19, A-20, A-112, G-23, G-31
Daniels E-20, H-32
Darden E-39, F-20, H-66
Darnall B-45
Darsey H-70

Gibson C-18
Gideon . . . . .SR
Gilkeson G-39/40/41
Gilkey B-46
Gillespie C-24
Girault B-22, C-61, G-56
Glascock . . . . .SR
Glass . . . . .F-19, SR
Glodjo H-85, N-4
Godbold A-57, I-70
Goddard C-50
Godwin G-26
Goepel A-50, F-33
Goff E-18, K-30, M-105
Goodie E-29/30
Goodin C-18
Goodrum A-108, J-10
Goodspeed E-14
Goodwin A-172/173
Gordon A-75/80, A-141, C-14b, C-24, C-44, F-12, J-17, J-108
Gore H-23, I-43
Goshorn A-127
Goslin C-2
Goza A-151
Gradick A-79, G-20a, H-57
Grafton B-35, B-47, C-50, J-110
Graham I-48/49
Granbery C-30
Grant H-87
Graves C-74
Gray B-1, G-16, N-6
Green B-7/18, C-22, F-9, H-94, J-30
Greene H-21
Greenlee E-1, H-31
Greenwalt C-57
Greenwood . . . . . .SR
Greer A-146, A-147, E-4, G-18/19, H-15, H-81, J-12
Griffing A-16, G-11, G-44, H-45
Griffith C-63
Groves A-101, J-55
Guenther M-86
Guice C-61, H-2
Guinn C-48
Guion E-3, H-30
Gunn K-41
Guthrie F-9, G-39/40/41

Lofton H-70
Long B-5
Lord M-115a
Loring B-28, C-81
Loury C-14a
Loviza A-106
Lowe H-19, J-36
Loyd J-6/7a
Lucoff E-29/30
Luebbers A-170/175
Lum . . . . .A-116/117, C-56, E-17, G-A, G-26, G-58, H-74, K-26b/27, M-87/88
Lunn G-34
Lusk A-57, A-151
Lutz A-71, J-70
Lyles B-14
Lynch B-53, C-75, E-7/8/9
Maclennan C-54
Madden A-62
Maddox A-20, F-22
Magee F-7, I-47
Magill A-67/76/77/167/178/188
Magruder A-19, A-61, A-107, B-49, C-19, E-10, G-25, G-31, G-57, K-19b, M-48, M-71
Mahoney K-36
Maldeis G-54/55
Mandel F-3
Mangel A-50
Mangum K-35
Manion B-11
Manis E-24
Mann A-65
Manns F-33
Maranto G-46
Marks . . . . .D-7, G-B
Marschalk C-68
Marshal B-35
Marshall A-8, B-35
Martin . . . . .A-38, A-133/134/137, C-84, D-4, E-37, F-17, G-22, G-33, H-67, SR
Marx I-86
Marye A-66, B-36
Mascagni M-116
Mason A-147, B-24, B-42, C-14a, I-30, J-69
Massey B-53, I-28/29
Massie A-67/76/77/167/178/188, G-21
Masters I-27
Mathews A-33/34, I-3
Maury B-7/18, B-31